Medieval Philosophy

A NEW HISTORY OF WESTERN PHILOSOPHY

VOLUME II

Medieval Philosophy

ANTHONY KENNY

CLARENDON PRESS · OXFORD

OXFORD
UNIVERSITY PRESS

Great Clarendon Street, Oxford OX2 6DP

Oxford University Press is a department of the University of Oxford.
It furthers the University's objective of excellence in research, scholarship,
and education by publishing worldwide in

Oxford New York

Auckland Cape Town Dar es Salaam Hong Kong Karachi Kuala Lumpur
Madrid Melbourne Mexico City Nairobi New Delhi Taipei Toronto
Shanghai

With offices in

Argentina Austria Brazil Chile Czech Republic France Greece
Guatemala Hungary Italy Japan South Korea Poland Portugal
Singapore Switzerland Thailand Turkey Ukraine Vietnam

Published in the United States
by Oxford University Press Inc., New York

British Library Cataloguing in Publication Data

Data available

Library of Congress Cataloging in Publication Data

Data available

ISBN 0-19-875275-X

3 5 7 9 10 8 6 4 2

Typeset by Kolam Information Services Pvt. Ltd, Pondicherry, India
Printed in Great Britain on acid-free paper by
Biddles Ltd., Kings Lynn, Norfolk

SUMMARY OF CONTENTS

CONTENTS

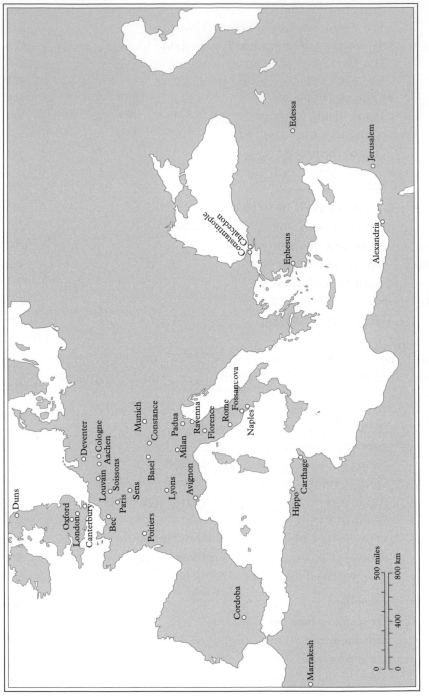

The world of medieval philosophy

INTRODUCTION

Most histories of philosophy, in this age of specialization, are the work of many hands, by specialists working in different fields and periods. In inviting me to write, single-handed, a history of philosophy from the earliest times to the present day, Oxford University Press gave expression to the belief that there is still something to be gained by presenting the development of philosophy from a single viewpoint, linking ancient, medieval, early modern, and contemporary philosophy into a single narrative concerned with connected themes. This is the second of four volumes. The first volume covered the early centuries of philosophy in classical Greece and Rome. This volume takes up the narrative from the conversion of St Augustine and continues the story up to the humanist Renaissance.

There are two quite different reasons why readers may wish to study the history of philosophy. They may be mainly interested in philosophy, or they may be mainly interested in history. We may study the great dead philosophers in order to seek illumination upon themes of present-day philosophical inquiry. Or we may wish to understand the people and societies of the past, and read their philosophy to grasp the conceptual climate in which they thought and acted. We may read the philosophers of other ages to help to resolve philosophical problems of abiding concern, or to enter more fully into the intellectual world of a bygone era.

I am by profession a philosopher, not a historian, but I believe that the history of philosophy is of great importance to the study of philosophy itself. It is an illusion to believe that the current state of philosophy represents the highest point of philosophical endeavour yet reached. These volumes are written with the purpose of showing that in many respects the philosophy of the great dead philosophers has not dated, and that one may gain philosophical illumination today by a careful reading of the great works that we have been privileged to inherit.

I attempt in these volumes to be both a philosophical historian and a historical philosopher. Multi-authored histories are sometimes structured chronologically and sometimes structured thematically. I try to combine both approaches, offering in each volume first a chronological survey, and then a thematic treatment of particular philosophical topics of abiding importance. The reader whose primary interest is historical will focus on the chronological survey, referring where necessary to the thematic sections for amplification. The reader who is more concerned with the philosophical issues will concentrate rather on the thematic sections of the volumes, referring back to the chronological surveys to place particular issues in context.

The audience at which these volumes are primarily aimed is at the level of second- or third-year undergraduate study. However, many of those interested in the history of philosophy are enrolled in courses that are not primarily philosophical. Accordingly I endeavour not to assume a familiarity with contemporary philosophical techniques or terminology. I aim also to write in a manner clear and light-hearted enough for the history to be enjoyed by those who read it not for curricular purposes but for their own enlightenment and entertainment.

Not so long ago, in many universities, courses in the history of philosophy went straight from Aristotle to Descartes, leaping over late antiquity and the Middle Ages. There was a widespread belief in academic circles that medieval philosophy was not worth studying. This belief was not usually based on any close acquaintance with the relevant texts: it was more likely to be an unexamined inheritance of religious or humanist prejudice.

There were, however, many genuine obstacles that made medieval philosophy less accessible than the philosophy of any other age. We may identify four significant barriers that have to be surmounted if one is to come to grips with the thought of the philosophers of the Middle Ages: the linguistic, the professional, the confessional, and the parochial.

Most of the philosophy of the high Middle Ages is written in Latin which even those well trained in classical Latin find very difficult to comprehend. Even Thomas Aquinas presents initial difficulties to a reader brought up on Livy and Cicero, and Aquinas is a model of simple lucidity by comparison with most of his colleagues and successors. It is only in recent years that translations into English of medieval writers have become widely available, and the task of translation is not a trivial one. Scholastic Latin is full of technical neologisms which are hard to render into other languages without cumbrous paraphrase. It is true that many of these neologisms, transliterated, survive into modern languages, and often into everyday use (e.g. 'intelligence', 'evidence', 'voluntary', 'supposition'). But the modern use is never an exact equivalent of the scholastic use, and often differs from it widely. 'Subjective' and 'objective', for instance, are two terms that have virtually reversed their meanings since medieval times.

This first, linguistic, problem is closely connected with the second problem of professionalism. The study of philosophy was more professionalized during the Middle Ages than at any other time before the present— hence the term 'scholastic'. Philosophy was largely the province of tight university communities sharing a common curriculum, a common patrimony of texts, and a common arsenal of technical terms. Most of the works that have come down to us are, in one way or another, the product of university lectures, exercises, or debates, and those who produced them could expect in their hearers or readers a familiarity with a complicated jargon and an ability to pick up erudite allusion. There was hardly any philosophy written for the general reader. Those who wrote or read it were overwhelmingly male, clerical, and celibate. An appendix to *The Cambridge History of Later Medieval Philosophy* gives brief biographies of the sixty-six most significant figures in medieval thought. None of them are women, and only two are laymen.

The third problem, again, is related to the second. Because the best-known medieval philosophers were members of the Catholic Church, their philosophy has often been regarded as a branch of theology or apologetics. This is unfair: they were all aware of the distinction between philosophical argument and dogmatic evangelism. But it is true that, since most of them concluded their academic career in the faculty of divinity, much of their best philosophical work is actually contained in their theological works, and it takes some experience to locate it.

Moreover, many of the most significant thinkers were members of religious orders, who have often been possessive of their heritage. There have been long periods when it seemed that all and only Dominicans studied St Thomas, and all and only Franciscans studied Bonaventure and Scotus. (Some scholastics were hardly studied because they belonged to no order. John Wyclif, for instance, had as his spiritual heirs only the rather small class consisting of secular clergy who had got into trouble with the Church.) After Pope Leo XIII gave Aquinas special status as a Catholic theologian, his works were studied by many who had no connection with the Dominican order. But this elevation only reinforced the view of secular philosophers that he was essentially an ecclesiastical spokesman. Moreover, within the realm of Catholic scholarship it fostered the view that only Aquinas was worth taking seriously as a philosopher. The gradual abandonment of some of his teaching in the later Middle Ages was seen as a key factor in the decline of the Church that led to the Reformation. A philosophical debate between Scotus and Ockham, from this perspective, was like a wrestling match between two men standing on the edge of a cliff from which they were both about to fall to their doom.

One effect of the professionalism and confessionalism of scholastic philosophy is that, by comparison with earlier and later writers, medieval philosophers appear as rather anonymous figures. It is not just that in some cases we have very little external information about their lives: it is that their own writings betray comparatively little of their own personalities. They produce few original monographs; most of their effort goes into commenting on, and continuing, the work of their predecessors in their order or in the Church. The whole edifice of scholasticism is like a medieval cathedral: the creation of many different craftsmen who, however individually gifted, took little pains to identify which parts of the overall structure were their own unaided work. Often it is only in the spontaneous disputations called 'quodlibets' that we feel we can come close to a living individual in action.

This generalization, of course, applies only to the high Middle Ages under the dominance of scholasticism. In the pre-scholastic period we meet philosophers who are highly colourful personalities, not constructed out of any template. Augustine, Abelard, and even Anselm are closer to the romantic paradigm of the philosopher as a solitary genius than they are to any ideal of a humble operative adding his stone to the communal cairn.

A history of Western philosophy in the Middle Ages must include a treatment of philosophers who are not 'Western' in any modern sense, because the intellectual frontiers of medieval Latin Europe were, fortunately, porous to influences from the Muslim world and the minorities living within it. Latin versions of the philosophical writings of Avicenna and Averroes had no less influence on the great scholastics than the works of their Christian predecessors. Accordingly, this volume contains some account of Muslim and Jewish philosophy, but only to the extent that these philosophies entered into the mainstream of Western thinking, not in proportion to their own intrinsic philosophical value.

My own training in philosophy began at the Gregorian University in Rome, which, in the 1950s, still aimed to teach philosophy *ad mentem Sancti Thomae* in accordance with the instructions of recent popes. I was grateful to two of my professors there, Fr. Bernard Lonergan and Fr. Frederick Copleston, for teaching me that St Thomas' own writings were much more worth reading than popular Thomists' textbooks, and that St Thomas was not the only medieval thinker who deserved attentive study.

After studying at the Gregorian I did graduate work in philosophy at Oxford in the heyday of ordinary language philosophy. I found this much more congenial than Roman scholasticism, but I was fortunate to meet Professor Peter Geach and Fr. Herbert McCabe OP, who showed me that many of the problems exercising philosophers in the analytic tradition at that time were very similar to those studied, often with no less sophistication, by medieval philosophers and logicians.

In many ways, indeed, the keen interest in the logical analysis of ordinary language which was characteristic of Oxford in the latter part of the twentieth century brought it closer to medieval methods and concerns than any other era of post-Renaissance philosophy. But this was still not widely appreciated. William Kneale, for instance, an Oxford professor of logic who wrote a well-informed and sympathetic survey of medieval logic, had this to say about the development of medieval philosophy between 1200 and 1400:

We shall not try to decide here whether the result justified the great intellectual effort that produced it. Perhaps the systems of St Thomas Aquinas and John Duns the Scot deserve only the reluctant admiration we give to the pyramids of Egypt and the palace of Versailles. And it may be that the thousands of young men who wrestled with subtle abstractions at the medieval universities would have been better employed in the literary studies which were then thought fit only for grammar schools.[1]

It was, in fact, in the area of logic that it was first appreciated that the study of medieval texts had much to offer. Medieval logicians had addressed questions that had fallen into oblivion after the Renaissance, and many of their insights had to be rediscovered during the twentieth-century rebirth of logic. *The Cambridge History of Later Medieval Philosophy* brought this to the attention of a wide public, and inaugurated a new phase in the

---

[1] *The Development of Logic* (Oxford: Oxford University Press, 1962), 226.

reception of medieval philosophy in the general, secular, academic world. The vigour of the revival can be measured by the number of excellent articles on medieval philosophy to be found in the recent *Routledge Encyclopedia of Philosophy*.

In the last decades of the twentieth century the person most responsible for the growth of interest in medieval philosophy in the English-speaking world was the principal editor of the *Cambridge History*, Norman Kretzmann. In conjunction with his fellow editor, Jan Pinborg, he brought together the work that was being done in several countries of continental Europe and introduced it to a wider audience in the United States and the United Kingdom. His own teaching in the Sage School at Cornell University bred up a brilliant group of younger scholars who in recent years have published widely and well on many topics of medieval philosophy. Paradoxically, one effect of the new medieval interest was a downgrading of Thomas Aquinas. In the *Cambridge History*, for example, his index entry is not as long as the entry for *sophismata*. Kretzmann came to realize and remedy this defect, and spent the last years of his life writing two magisterial books on St Thomas' *Summa contra Gentiles*.

Aquinas, in my view, retains the right to be classed as the greatest philosopher of the high Middle Ages. But he is an outstanding peak in a mountain range that has several other resplendent summits. Medieval philosophy is above all a continuum, and when one reads an individual philosopher, whether Abelard, Aquinas, or Ockham, one is taking a sounding of an ongoing process. And one soon learns that between every two major peaks there are minor ones that are not negligible: between Aquinas and Scotus, for instance, stands Henry of Ghent, and between Scotus and Ockham stands Henry of Harclay.

A historian of the ancient world can read, without too great exhaustion, the entire surviving corpus of philosophical writing. A comparable feat would be well beyond the powers of even the most conscientious historian of medieval philosophy. Augustine, Abelard, and the great scholastics were such copious writers that it takes decades to master the entire output of even a single one of them. Consequently, anyone who undertakes a volume such as the present must be heavily dependent on secondary sources, even if only for drawing attention to the best way to take soundings of the primary sources. I here acknowledge my own debt to the writers listed in my bibliography, from my teacher Fr. Copleston (whose history of philosophy still bears comparison with many works written since) to the most recent monographs written by colleagues and pupils of Norman Kretzmann. My debt to others is particularly heavy in the area of Islamic philosophy, since I do not know Arabic. In the course of writing this I had cause to regret deeply that it is only in Latin that I can read the work of Avicenna, whose genius, and whose influence, I have come to realize ever more.

I am particularly indebted to Dr John Marenbon and Professor Robert Pasnau, who made many helpful suggestions for the improvement of an earlier draft of this volume, and who saved me from many errors.

1

Philosophy and Faith:
Augustine to Maimonides

In the first volume of this history we traced the development of
philosophy in the ancient world up to the conversion of St Augustine
at the end of the fourth century of our era. The life of Augustine marks an
epoch in the history of ideas. In his early life he imbibed from several
sources philosophical ideas of various traditions, but especially the Platonic
tradition, whether in the sceptical version of the New Academy or in the
metaphysical version of Neoplatonism. After his conversion to Christianity
he developed, in a number of massive treatises, a synthesis of Jewish, Greek,
and Christian ideas that was to provide the backdrop for the next millennium of Western philosophical thought.

From a philosophical point of view, the most fertile period of Augustine's life was the period just before and just after his baptism as a Christian
at Easter 387. Between his conversion and his baptism he spent several
months in private preparation with friends and members of his family at
Cassiciacum, a country villa north of Milan. This period produced a
number of works that resemble verbatim transcripts of live discussions,
notably the *Contra Academicos*, which seeks to sift the true from the false in
scepticism.

Augustine also invented a new art-form to which he gave the name
'Soliloquies'. He wrote a dialogue with himself in which the two characters
are named Augustine and Reason. Reason asks Augustine what he wishes
to know. 'I want to know God and the soul,' Augustine replies. 'Nothing
more?' 'Nothing at all' (*S* 1. 2. 7).

The earliest portrait of St Augustine, from the Papal Library in the Lateran, c. 600.

Reason promises to make God appear as clearly to his mind as the sun does to his eyes. For this purpose the eyes of the soul must be cleansed of all desire for mortal things. Augustine in the dialogue renounces the pursuit of riches, honour, and sexual pleasure (this last renunciation vividly described). Reason does not yet keep the promise to display God, but it does offer Augustine a proof of the immortality of his soul. Consider the notion of truth. True things may pass away, but truth itself is everlasting. Even if the world ceased to exist, it would still be true that the world has ceased to exist. But truth has its home in the soul, so the soul, like truth, must be immortal (*S* 1. 15. 28, 2. 15. 28).

After his baptism Augustine remained in Italy for a year and a half. In this period he wrote a further brief tract on the immortality of the soul, and a more substantial work, *On the Freedom of the Will*, which we encountered in the first volume of this history. In 388 he returned to Africa and for the next few years lived the life of a private gentleman in his home town of Tagaste. In 391 he found his final vocation and was ordained priest, becoming soon after bishop of Hippo in Algeria, where he resided until his death in 430.

The great majority of his works were written during this final period of his life. He was a copious writer, and has left behind some 5 million words. Much of his output consists of sermons, Bible commentaries, and controversial tracts about theology or Church discipline. He no longer wrote philosophical pieces comparable to those of the years of his conversion. But a number of his major works contain material of high philosophical interest.

In 397 Augustine wrote a work entitled *Confessions*: a prayerful dialogue with God tracing the course of his life from childhood to conversion. It is not an autobiography of the normal kind, though it is the foundation specimen of the genre. Besides being the main source of our knowledge of Augustine's pre-episcopal life, it contains many incidental philosophical reflections and concludes with a full-fledged monograph on the nature of time.[1] Its enchanting style has always made it the most popular of Augustine's works.

Between 400 and 417 Augustine worked on another masterpiece, fifteen books entitled *On the Trinity*. The earlier books of the treatise are largely

---

[1] See Ch. 5 below.

concerned with the analysis of biblical and ecclesiastical texts concerning the mystery of three persons in one God. Philosophers find matter of much greater interest in the subtle portrayal of human psychology employed in the later books in the course of a search for an analogy of the heavenly Trinity in the hearts and minds of men and women.[2]

Augustine on History

The most massive and most laborious of Augustine's works was *The City of God*, on which he worked from 413 to 426. Written at a time when the Roman Empire was under threat from successive barbarian invasions, it was the first great synthesis of classical and Christian thought. This is implicit in the very title of the work. The Christian gospels have much to say about the Kingdom of God; but for Greece and Rome the paradigm political institution was not the kingdom but the city. Even emperors liked to think of themselves as the first citizens of a city; and the philosophical emperor Marcus Aurelius thought the city we should love above all was the city of Zeus. *The City of God* sets Jesus, the crucified King of the Jews, at the apex of the idealized city-state of pagan philosophy.

Like Aristotle in his *Metaphysics*. Augustine surveys the history of philosophy from the distant days of Thales, showing how earlier philosophers approximated to, but fell short of, the truth that he now presents. But whereas Aristotle was mainly interested in the physical theories of his predecessors, Augustine is concerned above all with their philosophical theology—their 'natural' theology, as he called it, giving currency to an expression with a long history ahead of it (*DCD* VIII. 1–9). Throughout the work Augustine sets Christian teaching side by side with the best of ancient philosophy, and especially with the writing of his favourites, the Neoplatonists, whom he regarded as almost-Christians (*DCD* VIII. 8–9). An engaging instance is the following:

Plotinus uses the beauty of flowers and leaves to show that the providence of God—whose beauty is beyond words and visible only to the mind—extends even to lowly and earthly things. These castaways, he argues, doomed to swift decay, could not display such delicate patterns if they did not draw their shapes from a

---

[2] See Ch. 7 below.

realm in which a mental and unchangeable form holds them all together in a unity. And this is what the Lord Jesus tells us when he says 'Consider the lilies of the field, how they grow; they toil not, neither do they spin: and yet I say unto you that even Solomon in all his glory was not arrayed like one of these. Wherefore, if God so clothe the grass of the field, which today is, and tomorrow is cast into the oven, shall he not much more clothe you, o ye of little faith?' (*DCD* X. 14; cf. Plotinus, *Enneads* 3. 2. 13; Matt. 6: 28–9).

But while Augustine is prepared to read Platonism into the Sermon on the Mount, he has little sympathy with attempts to give philosophical and allegorical interpretations of traditional Roman religion. The original impetus for the composition of *The City of God*—which took thirteen years to complete—came from the sack of Rome by Gothic invaders. Pagans blamed this disaster on the Christians' abolition of the worship of the city's gods, who had therefore abandoned it in its hour of need. Augustine devoted the first books of his treatise to showing that the gods of classical Rome were vicious and impotent and that their worship was disgusting and depraving.

The Romans had long identified their senior gods—Jupiter, Juno, Venus, and the like—with the characters of the Homeric pantheon, such as Zeus, Hera, and Aphrodite. Augustine follows Plato and Cicero in denouncing as blasphemous the myths that represent such deities as engaged in arbitrary, cruel, and indecent behaviour. He mocks too at the proliferation of lesser gods in popular Roman superstition: is heaven so bureaucratized, he asks, so that while to look after a house a single human porter suffices, we need no less than three gods: Forculus to guard the doors, Cardea for the hinges, and Limentinus for the threshold? (*DCD* IV. 18). The identification and individuation of these minor divinities raise a number of philosophical problems, which Augustine illustrates. More often he uses against late Roman paganism the weapon of erudite sarcasm that Gibbon, thirteen centuries later, was to deploy so teasingly against historic Christianity.

A brief, eloquent, survey of the history of the Roman Republic suffices to show that the worship of the ancient Gods does not guarantee security from disasters. The eventual unparalleled greatness of the Roman Empire, Augustine says, was the reward given by the one true God to the virtues of the best among the citizens. 'They placed no value on their own wealth in comparison with the commonwealth and the public purse; they shunned avarice and gave freely of themselves to the fatherland; they were guilty of no breach of law or licentious conduct. Thus by a sure way they strove towards honour, power, and glory' (*DCD* V. 15). The reward which they sought has come to them: they were able to impose their law on many nations and they are renowned in the annals of many people. But they have no part in the heavenly city, for they did not worship the one true God, and they aimed only at self-glorification.

A large part of Augustine's attack on Roman religion focuses on the degrading nature of the public spectacles held in honour of the gods. No doubt many a modern liberal would be no less disgusted than Augustine at much of what went on in Roman theatres and amphitheatres. She would probably be more shocked by the cruelty of Roman entertainment than by its indecency; with Augustine it appears to have been the other way round.

Augustine does not regard the gods of pagan myth as complete fictions. On the contrary, he thinks that they are wicked spirits who take advantage of human superstition to divert to themselves worship that is due only to the one true God (*DCD* VII. 33). Several Platonists had spoken of a threefold classification of rational beings: gods, men, and *daimones* (demons). Gods dwelt in heaven, men on earth, and demons in the air between. Demons were like gods in being immortal, but like men in being subject to passions. Many demons are bad, but some are good, such as the *daimon* who was the familiar of Socrates.[3] Good demons, these Platonists thought, could be of service as intermediaries between men and gods (*DCD* VIII. 14, IX. 8, X. 9).

Augustine does not reject the idea that the air is full of demons, but he does not accept that any of them are good, still less that they can mediate between God and man. In many ways they are inferior to human beings. 'They are utterly malevolent spirits, totally indifferent to justice, swollen with pride, green with envy, cunning in deception. They do indeed live in the air, suitably imprisoned there after having been cast down from the heights of the upper heaven because of their irreparable crime' (*DCD* VIII. 22). In other words, Augustine identifies the Platonic *daimones* with the fallen angels whom most English readers first encounter in Milton's *Paradise Lost*. It was indeed Augustine who fastened onto the imagination of Christianity the story that before creating human beings of flesh and blood God created

[3] See vol. i, p. 43.

orders of wholly spiritual beings, some of whom took part in a pre-cosmic rebellion that led to their eternal damnation.

Augustine admits that the Bible is uninformative about the early history of angels. Genesis does not mention them in the seven days of creation, and we have to turn to Psalms or Job to learn that angels are indeed God's creatures. If we are to fit them into the Genesis story, we should conclude that they were created on the first day: on that day God created light and the angels as the first partakers of divine illumination (*DCD* XI. 9). On the same day, the Bible tells us, God divided the light from the darkness: and here Augustine sees divine foresight at work. 'Only He could foresee, before it happened, that some angels would fall and be deprived of the light of truth and left for ever in the darkness of their pride' (*DCD* XI. 19). 'There are two societies of angels, contrasted and opposed: one good by nature and upright of will, one good by nature, but perverted of will. These are shown by more explicit testimonies elsewhere but indicated here in Genesis by the words "Light" and "Darkness" ' (*DCD* XI. 34). These two cohorts of angels are the origin of the two cities that are the ostensible theme of the entire work, even though their history is not taken up in detail until the twelfth book. There are good and bad angels, and good and bad humans: but we do not have to think that there are four cities; men and angels can unite in the same communities.

Between the creation of angels and the creation of humans, Augustine tells us, came the creation of animals. All animals, whether solitary like wolves or gregarious like deer, were created by God in multiple specimens simultaneously. But the human race was created in a single individual, Adam: from him came Eve, and from this first pair came all other humans. This unique creation did not imply that man was an unsocial animal; just the contrary. 'The point was to emphasize the unity of human society, and to stress the bonds of human concord, if human beings were bound together not merely by similarity of nature but also by the affection of kinship' (*DCD* XII. 22). The human race, Augustine says, is, by nature, more sociable than any other species. But—he goes on to add—it is also, through ill will, more quarrelsome than any other (*DCD* XII. 28).

Human beings stand in the middle between angels and dumb animals: they share intellect with angels, but they have bodies as the beasts do. However, in the original divine plan they would have had a greater kinship with the angels, because they would have been immortal. After a life of obedience to God they would have passed into fellowship with the angels without death intervening. It was because of Adam's sin in Paradise that humans became mortal, subject to the bodily death that had always been natural for beasts. After the Fall death would be the common lot of all humans; but after death some, by God's grace, would be rewarded by admission to the company of the good angels, while others would be punished by damnation alongside the evil angels—a second death more grievous than the first (*DCD* XIII. 12, XIV. 1).

When Plato described the origin of the cosmos in the *Timaeus*, he attributed the creation of humans not to the supreme being who fashioned the world, but to lesser gods, creatures of his, who were his agents (*Tim.* 41c). Augustine does not deny the existence of such august divine servants: he simply treats Plato's word 'gods' as a misnomer for angels. But he is resolutely opposed to the idea that such superior executives can be called creators. Bringing things into existence out of nothing is a prerogative of the one true God, and whatever service an angel may render to God in the development of lesser creatures, he is no more a creator than is a gardener or a farmer who produces a crop (*DCD* XII. 26).

The contrast between the biblical and the Platonic conception of the human creature comes into sharp relief if we ask the question: Is death—the separation of soul and body—a good thing or a bad thing? For Genesis, death is an evil: it is a punishment for sin. In a world of innocence body and soul would remain forever united (*DCD* XIII. 6). For many Platonists, however, and for Plato himself in some of his writings, the soul is only happy when stripped of the body and naked before God (*DCD* XIII. 16 and 19; cf. *Phaedo* 108c; *Phaedr.* 248c). Again, it is a common Platonic theme that souls after death may be forced to return into bodies (other human bodies, perhaps, or even animal bodies) as a punishment for sins in their previous life. According to the prophets of the Old and New Testament, however, the souls of the virtuous will in the end return to their own bodies, and this reunion of body and soul will be a source of everlasting happiness (*DCD* XIII. 17 and 22, XXII. 19).

Augustine does not deny—indeed he emphasizes—that bodily desires and passions can impede spiritual progress; he quotes the book of Wisdom: 'the corruptible body weighs down the soul'. But this is true only of the body of fallen humans in their mortal life. The human body in Paradise had no disturbing emotions and no unruly desires. Adam and Eve lived without pain or fear, for they enjoyed perfect health and were never in physical danger; their bodies were incapable of injury, and childbirth, but for the Fall, would have been painless. They ate only what was necessary for the preservation of their bodies, and their sexual organs were under the entire control of cool reason, to be used only for procreation (*DCD* XIII. 23, XIV. 26). But though they lived without passion, they were not without love. 'The couple, living in true and loyal partnership, shared an untroubled love for God and for each other. This was a source of immense joy, since the beloved one was always present for enjoyment' (*DCD* XIV. 10).

Augustine's Two Cities

Augustine traces the history of the human race from its origins in Adam and Eve, fitting it into the template of his master narrative, the two cities. 'Though there are many great nations throughout the world living under different systems of religion and ethics, and diversified by language, arms, and dress, nonetheless it has come to pass that there are only two principal divisions of human society, which scripture allows us to call two cities' (*DCD* XIV. 1). One city lives according to the flesh, another according to the spirit; one is created by self-love, the other by the love of God; one glories in itself, the other is given glory by God (*DCD* XIV. 280). One is predestined to join the Devil in final punishment which will destroy it as a city; the other is predestined to reign with God for ever and ever (*DCD* XV. 1 and 4).

The division between the two cities begins with the children of the primal pair. 'Cain was the first son born to the two parents of the human race, and he belonged to the city of man; Abel, their younger son, belonged to the city of God' (*DCD* XV. 2). The enmity of the two cities is first expressed in Cain's slaughter of Abel; and Cain's fratricidal example was followed by Romulus, the founder of Rome, who slew his brother Remus (*DCD* XV. 5).

In the fifteenth and sixteenth books of *The City of God* Augustine traces the early history of the City of God, following the narrative of Genesis and seeing the City as incarnate in the Hebrew Patriarchs, through Noah, Abraham, Isaac, Jacob, Joseph, and Moses. The seventeenth book seeks illumination about the City of God from the writings of the prophets and psalmists. The prophecies that exalt the kingdom of David and the Jewish priesthood and promise them everlasting duration must have their true fulfilment elsewhere since the institutions of Israel no longer exist (*DCD* XVII. 7).

We return to secular history with the eighteenth book, which narrates the rise and fall of a series of pagan empires: Assyria, Egypt, Argos, and Rome. Augustine is anxious to reconcile biblical and secular chronologies, assigning the Mosaic exodus to the time of the mythical king Cecrops of Athens and placing the fall of Troy in the period of the judges in Israel. He treats as simultaneous the foundation of Rome, the beginnings of philosophy in Ionia, and the deportation of Israel. The destruction of the temple in Jerusalem, he tells us, happened in the reign of Tarquinius Priscus in Rome; the Babylonian captivity of the Jews ended at the same time as the expulsion of the kings and the foundation of the Roman Republic. One of the purposes of his rather dizzying chronology is to emphasize that the teaching of the Hebrew prophets antedated the researches of the Greek philosophers (XVIII. 37).

In Augustine's narrative Jerusalem becomes the emblem of the City of God and Babylon becomes the emblem of the city of the world. Babylon was the city of confusion, where God had shattered the original unity of human language in order to frustrate the building of the tower of Babel (Gen. 11: 1–9). In the city of the world philosophers speak with as many different tongues as the builders of Babel. Some say there is only one world; some say there are many; some say this world is everlasting, others say that it will perish. Some say it is controlled by a divine mind, others that it is the plaything of chance. Some say the soul is immortal, others that it perishes with the body. Some place the supreme good in the soul, others in the body, others in external goods. Some say the senses are to be trusted, others that they are to be treated with contempt. In the secular city there is no authority to decide between these conflicting views: Babylon embraces all alike, without discrimination and without adjudication (*DCD* XVIII. 42). How different in the City of God, where all accept the authority of canonical Scripture!

The most important disputations among philosophers are those that concern the ultimate good and the ultimate evil. The ultimate good is that for which other things are desirable, while it is itself desirable for its own sake. Philosophers have sought to place the ultimate good in the present life: some hold that it is pleasure, some that it is virtue, some that it is tranquillity, others that it is in the enjoyment of the basic goods with which nature has endowed us. Many sects regard the ultimate good as constituted by one or other combination of these. But the City of God knows that eternal life is the supreme good, and eternal death the supreme evil, and that it is only by faith and grace that the supreme good can be achieved and the supreme evil avoided (*DCD* XIX. 1–4).

It is clear from Augustine's description of the two cities that one cannot simply identify Babylon with the pagan empire and Jerusalem with the Christian empire. The city of God was already a community long before the birth of Christ, and longer before the conversion of Constantine. The Christian empire contains sinners as well as saints, as Augustine illustrates with the example of the emperor Theodosius, whom St Ambrose forced to do penance for the brutality with which he suppressed a rebellion at Thessalonica in 391 (*DCD* V. 26). Nor is the City of God to be identified with the Church on earth, even though in later ages Augustine's book was sometimes taken to be a guide to relations between Church and State. The nature of the two cities is not fully understood until we consider their final state, which Augustine does in the last three books of *The City of God*.

Augustine combs the sayings of the prophets, the sermons of Jesus, the epistles of the Apostles, and the book of Revelation, for information about the future of the world. Between the resurrection of Jesus and the end of history there is a period of a thousand years as described in the book of Revelation (*DCD* XX. 1–6). During this period the saints are reigning with Christ. Their thousand-year reign evolves in two stages: during their lives on earth the saints are the dominant members of a Church that includes sinners, and after their death they are still in some mysterious way in communion with the Church that is the kingdom of God (*DCD* XX. 9). Augustine is contemptuous of any interpretation of Revelation that looks forward to a thousand-year orgy of wassail for the saints after the end of history. Whether we interpret John's millennium literally, or take the number 1,000 as a symbol of perfection, we are already in the middle of the saints' reign (*DCD* XX. 7).

Augustine tells us that the final drama, after the numbered years have passed, will play itself out in seven acts. First the prophet Elijah will come and convert the Jewish people to Christ (XX. 29). Secondly, Satan will be unloosed and for three and a half years Antichrist will persecute the

The *Massa Damnata*. This MS of the *City of God* shows Adam and Eve meeting death after expulsion from Eden, and the human race going on its way to Hell while the elect are saved by divine grace.

faithful, using as his agents the nations of Gog and Magog. The saints will endure their sufferings until the onslaughts of Gog and Magog have burnt themselves out (*DCD* XX. 11–12. 19). Thirdly, Jesus will return to earth to judge the living and the dead. Fourthly, in order to be judged, the souls of the dead will return from their resting place and be reunited with their bodies. Fifthly, the judgement will separate the virtuous from the vicious, with the saints assigned to eternal bliss and the wicked to eternal damnation (*DCD* XX. 22. 27). Sixthly, the present world will be destroyed in a cosmic conflagration, and a new heaven and a new earth will be created

(*DCD* XX. 16–18). Seventhly, the blessed and the damned will take up the everlasting abode that has been assigned to them in heaven and in hell (*DCD* XX. 30). The heavenly Jerusalem above and the unquenchable fires below are the consummation of the two cities of Augustine's narrative.

Augustine realizes that his predictions are not easy to accept, and he singles out as the most difficult of all the idea that the wicked will suffer eternal bodily punishment. Bodies are surely consumed by fire, it is objected, and whatever can suffer pain must sooner or later suffer death. Augustine replies that salamanders thrive in fire, and Etna burns for ever. Souls no less than bodies can suffer pain, and yet philosophers agree that souls are immortal. There are many wonders in the natural world— Augustine gives a long list, including the properties of lime, of diamonds, of magnets, and of Dead Sea fruit—that make it entirely credible that an omnipotent creator can keep alive for ever a human body in appalling pain (*DCD* XXI. 3–7).

Most people are concerned less about the physical mechanism than about the moral justification for eternal damnation. How can any crime in a brief life deserve a punishment that lasts for ever? Even in human jurisprudence, Augustine responds, there is no necessary temporal proportion between crime and punishment. A man may be flogged for hours to punish a brief adulterous kiss; a slave may spend years in prison for a momentary insult to his master (*DCD* XXI. 11). It is false sentimentality to believe, out of compassion, that the pains of hell will ever have an end. If you are tempted by that thought, you may end up believing, like the heretic Origen, that one day even the Devil will be converted (*DCD* XXI. 17)!

Step by step Augustine seeks to show not only that eternal punishment is possible and justified, but that it is extremely difficult to avoid it. A virtuous life is not enough, for the virtues of pagans without the true faith are only splendid vices. Being baptized is not enough, for the baptized may fall into heresy. Orthodox belief is not enough, for even the most staunch Catholics may fall into sin. Devotion to the sacraments is not enough: no one knows whether he is receiving them in such a spirit as to qualify for Jesus' promises of eternal life (*DCD* XXI. 19–25). Philanthropy is not enough: Augustine devotes pages to explaining away the passage in St Matthew's Gospel in which the Son of Man separates the sheep from the goats on the basis of their performance or neglect of works of mercy to their fellow men (Matt. 25: 31–46; *DCD* XXI. 27).

13

And so at last, in the twenty-second book of *The City of God*, we come to the everlasting bliss of the saints in the New Jerusalem. To those who doubt whether earthly bodies could ever dwell in heaven, Augustine offers the following highly Platonic reply:

Suppose we were purely souls, spirits without any bodies, and lived in heaven without any contact with terrestrial animals. If someone said to us that we were destined to be joined to bodies by some mysterious link in order to give life to them, would we not refuse to believe it, arguing that nature does not allow an incorporeal entity to be bound by a corporeal tie? Why then cannot a terrestrial body be raised to a heavenly body by the will of God who made the human animal? (*DCD* XXII. 4)

No Christian can refuse to believe in the possibility of a celestial human body, since all accept that Jesus rose from the dead and ascended into heaven. The life everlasting promised to the blessed is no more incredible than the story of Christ's resurrection.

It is incredible that Christ rose in the flesh and went up into heaven with his flesh. It is incredible that the world believed so incredible a story, and it is incredible that a few men without birth or position or experience should have been able to persuade so effectively the world and the learned world. Our adversaries refuse to believe the first of these three incredible things, but they cannot ignore the second, and they cannot account for it unless they accept the third. (*DCD* XXII. 5)

To show that all these incredible things are in fact credible, Augustine appeals to divine omnipotence, as exhibited in a series of miracles that have been observed by himself or eyewitnesses among his friends. But he accepts that he has to answer difficulties raised by philosophical adversaries against the whole concept of a bodily resurrection.

How can human bodies, made of heavy elements, exist in the ethereal sublimity of heaven? No more problem, says Augustine, than birds flying in air or fire breaking out on earth. Will resurrected bodies all be male? No: women will keep their sex, though their organs will no longer serve for intercourse and childbirth, since in heaven there will no longer be marriage. Will resurrected bodies all have the same size and shape? No: everyone will be given the stature they had at maturity (if they died in old age) or the stature they would have had at maturity (if they died young). What of those who died as infants? They will reach maturity instantaneously on rising.

All resurrected bodies will be perfect and beautiful: the resurrection will involve cosmetic surgery on a cosmic scale. Deformities and blemishes will be removed; amputated limbs will be restored to amputees. Shorn hair and nail clippings will return to form part of the body of their original owners, though not in the form of hair and nails. 'Fat people and thin people need not fear that in that world they will be the kind of people that they would have preferred not to be while in this world' (*DCD* XXII 19).

Augustine raises a problem that continued to trouble believers in every century in which belief in a final resurrection was taken seriously. Suppose that a starving man relieves his hunger by cannibalism: to whose body, at the resurrection, will the digested human flesh belong? Augustine gives a carefully thought-out answer. Before A gets so hungry that he eats the body of B, A must have lost a lot of weight—bits of his body must have been exhaled into the air. At the resurrection this material will be transformed back into flesh, to give A the appropriate avoirdupois, and the digested flesh will be restored to B. The whole transaction should be looked on as parallel to the borrowing of a sum of money, to be returned in due time (*DCD* XXII. 30).

But what will the blessed *do* with these splendid risen bodies? Augustine confesses, 'to tell the truth, I do not know what will be the nature of their activity—or rather of their rest and leisure'. The Bible tells us that they will see God: and this sets Augustine another problem. If the blessed cannot open and shut their eyes at will, they are worse off than we are. But how could anyone shut their eyes upon God? His reply is subtle. In that blessed state God will indeed be visible, to the eyes of the body and not just to the eyes of the mind; but he will not be an extra object of vision. Rather we will see God by observing his governance of the bodies that make up the material scheme of things around us, just as we see the life of our fellow men by observing their behaviour. Life is not an extra body that we see, and yet when we see the motions of living beings we do not just believe they are alive, we *see* they are alive. So in the City of God we will observe the work of God bringing harmony and beauty everywhere (*DCD* XXII. 30).

Though it is dependent on the Bible on almost every page, *The City of God* deserves a significant place in the history of philosophy, for two reasons. In the first place, Augustine constantly strives to place his religious worldview into the philosophical tradition of Greece and Rome: where possible he tries to harmonize the Bible with Plato and Cicero; where this is not possible he feels obliged to recite and refute philosophical anti-Christian arguments. Secondly, the narrative Augustine constructed out of biblical and classical elements provided the framework for philosophical discussion in the Latin world up to and beyond the Renaissance and the Reformation.

Augustine was one of the most interesting human beings ever to have written philosophy. He had a keen and lively analytic mind and at his best he wrote vividly, wittily, and movingly. Unlike the philosophers of the high Middle Ages, he takes pains to illustrate his philosophical points with concrete imagery, and the examples he gives are never stale and ossified as they too often are in the texts of the great scholastics. In the service of philosophy he can employ anecdote, epigram, and paradox, and he can detect deep philosophical problems beneath the smooth surface of language. He falls short of the very greatest rank in philosophy because he remains too much a rhetorician: to the end of his life he could never really tell the difference between genuine logical analysis and mere linguistic pirouette. But then once he was a bishop his aims were never purely philosophical: both rhetoric and logic were merely instruments for the spreading of Christ's gospel.

The Consolations of Boethius

In the fifth century the Roman Empire experienced an age of foreign invasion (principally in the West) and of theological disputation (principally in the East). Augustine's *City of God* had been occasioned by the sack of Rome by the Visigoths in 410; in 430, when he died in Hippo, the Vandals were at the gates of the city. Augustine's death prevented him from accepting an invitation to attend a Church council in Ephesus. The Council had been called by the emperor Theodosius II because the patriarchates of Constantinople and Alexandria disagreed violently about how to formulate the doctrine of the divine sonship of the man Jesus Christ.

In the course of the century the Goths and the Vandals were succeeded by an even more fearsome group of invaders, the Huns, under their king Attila. Attila conquered vast areas from China to the Rhine before being fought to a standstill in Gaul in 451 by a Roman general in alliance with a Gothic king. In the following year he invaded Italy, and Rome was saved from occupation only by the efforts of Pope Leo the Great, using a mixture of eloquence and bribery.

The Council of Ephesus in 431 condemned Nestorius, the bishop of Constantinople, because he taught that Mary, the mother of Jesus, was not the mother of God. How could he hold this, the Alexandrian bishop Cyril argued, if he really believed that Jesus was God? The right way to formulate the doctrine of the Incarnation, the Council decided, was to say that Christ, a single person, had two distinct natures, one divine and one human. But the Council did not go far enough for some Alexandrians, who believed that the incarnate Son of God possessed only a single nature. These extremists arranged a second council at Ephesus, which proclaimed the doctrine of the single nature ('monophysitism'). Pope Leo, who had submitted written evidence in favour of the dual nature, denounced the Council as a den of robbers.

Heartened by the support of Rome, Constantinople struck back at Alexandria, and at a council at Chalcedon in 451 the doctrine of the dual nature was affirmed. Christ was perfect God and perfect man, with a human body and a human soul, sharing divinity with his Father and sharing humanity with us. The decisions of Chalcedon and first Ephesus henceforth provided the test of orthodoxy for the great majority of Christians, though in eastern parts of the empire substantial communities of Nestorian and monophysite Christians remained, some of which have survived to this day. In the history of thought the importance of these fifth-century councils is that they hammered out technical meanings for terms such as 'nature' and 'person' in a manner that influenced philosophy for centuries to come.

After the repulse of Attila the western Roman Empire survived a further quarter of a century, though power in Italy had largely passed to barbarian army commanders. One of these, Odoacer, in 476, decided to become ruler in name and not just in fact. He sent off the last fainéant emperor, Romulus Augustulus, to exile near Naples. For the next half-century Italy became a Gothic province. Its kings, though Christians, took little interest in the recent Christological debates: they subscribed to a form of Christianity, namely Arianism, that had been condemned as long ago as the time of Constantine I. Arianism took various forms, all of which denied that Jesus, the Son of God, shared the same essence or substance with God the Father. The most vigorous of the Gothic kings, Theodoric (reigned 493–526), established a tolerant regime in which Arians, Jews, and Orthodox Catholics lived together in tranquillity and in which art and culture thrived.

Boethius with his father-in-law Symmachus, from a ninth century manuscript of his treatise on arithmetic.

One of Theodoric's ministers was Manlius Severinus Boethius, a member of a powerful Roman senatorian family. Born shortly after the end of the Western Empire, he lost his father in childhood and was adopted into the family of the consul Symmachus, whose daughter he later married. He himself became consul in 510 and saw his two sons become consuls in 522. In that year Boethius moved from Rome to Theodoric's capital at Ravenna, to become 'master of offices', a very senior administrative post which he held with integrity and distinction.

As a young man Boethius had written handbooks on music and mathematics, drawn from Greek sources, and he had projected, but never completed, a translation into Latin of the entire works of Plato and Aristotle. He wrote commentaries on some of Aristotle's logical works, showing some acquaintance with Stoic logic. He wrote four theological tractates dealing with the doctrines of the Trinity and the Incarnation, showing the influence both of Augustine and of the fifth-century Christological debates. His career appeared to be a model for those who wished to combine the contemplative and active lives. Gibbon, who could rarely bring himself to praise a philosopher, wrote of him, 'Prosperous in his fame and fortunes, in his public honours and private alliances, in the cultivation of science and the consciousness of virtue, Boethius might have been styled happy, if that precarious epithet could be safely applied before the last term of the life of man' (*Decline and Fall*, ch. 19).

Boethius, however, did not hold his honourable office for long, because he fell under suspicion of being implicated, as a Catholic, in treasonable correspondence urging the emperor Justin at Constantinople to invade Italy and end Arian rule. He was imprisoned in a tower in Pavia and condemned to death by the senate in Rome. It was while he was in prison, under sentence of death, that he wrote the work for which he is most remembered, *On the Consolation of Philosophy*. The work has been admired for its literary beauty as well as for its philosophical acumen; it has been translated many times into many languages, notably by King Alfred and by Chaucer. It contains a subtle discussion of the problems of relating human freedom to divine foreknowledge; but it is not quite the kind of work that might be expected from a devout Catholic facing possible martyrdom. It dwells on the comfort offered by pagan philosophy, but there is no reference to the consolations held out by the Christian religion.

At the beginning of the work Boethius describes how he was visited in prison by a tall woman, elderly in years but fair in complexion, clothed in an exquisitely woven but sadly tattered garment: this was the Lady Philosophy. On her dress was woven a ladder, with the Greek letter P at its foot and the Greek letter TH at its head: these meant the Practical and Theoretical divisions of Philosophy and the ladder represented the steps between the two. The lady's first act was to eject the muses of poetry, represented by Boethius' bedside books; but she was herself willing to provide verses to console the afflicted prisoner. The five books of the *Consolation* consist of alternating passages of prose and poetry. The poems vary between sublimity and doggerel; it often takes a considerable effort to detect their relevance to the developing prose narrative.

In the first book Boethius defends himself against the charges that have been brought against him. His troubles have all come upon him because he entered public office in obedience to Plato's injunction to philosophers to involve themselves in political affairs. Lady Philosophy reminds him that he is not the first philosopher to suffer: Socrates suffered in Athens and Seneca in Rome. She herself has been subject to outrage: her dress is tattered because Epicureans and Stoics tried to kidnap her and tore her clothes, carrying off the torn-off shreds. She urges Boethius to remember that even if the wicked prosper, the world is subject not to random chance but to the governance of divine reason. The book ends with a poem that looks rather like a shred torn off by a Stoic, urging rejection of the passions.

> Joy you must banish
> Banish too fear
> All grief must vanish
> And hope bring no cheer.

The second book, too, develops a Stoic theme: matters within the province of fortune are insignificant by comparison with values within oneself. The gifts of fortune that we enjoy do not really belong to us: riches may be lost, and are most valuable when we are giving them away. A splendid household is a blessing to me only if my servants are honest, and their virtue belongs to them not me. Political power may end in murder or slavery; and even while it is possessed it is trivial. The inhabited world is only a quarter of our globe; our globe is minute in comparison with the celestial sphere; for a man to boast of his power is like a mouse crowing over other mice. The greatest of fame lasts only a few years that add up to zero in comparison with never-ending eternity. I cannot find happiness in wealth, power, or fame, but only in my most precious possession, myself. Boethius has no real ground of complaint against fortune: she has given him many good things and he must accept also the evil which she sends. Indeed, ill fortune is better for men than good fortune. Good fortune is deceitful, constant only in her inconstancy; bad fortune brings men self-knowledge and teaches them who are their true friends, the most precious of all kinds of riches.

The message that true happiness is not to be found in external goods is reinforced in the third book, developing material from Plato and Aristotle:

happiness (*beatitudo*) is the good which, once achieved, leaves nothing further to be desired. It is the highest of all goods, containing all goods with itself; if any good was lacking to it, it could not be the highest good since there would be something left over to be desired. So happiness is a state which is made perfect by the accumulation of all the goods there are. (*DCP* 3. 2)

Wealth, honour, power, glory do not fulfil these conditions, nor do the pleasures of the body. Some bodies are very beautiful, but if we had X-ray eyes we would find them disgusting. Marriage and its pleasures may be a fine thing, but children are little tormentors. We must cease to look to the things of this world for happiness. God, Lady Philosophy argues, is the best and most perfect of all good things; but the perfect good is true happiness; therefore, true happiness is to be found only in God. All the values that are sought separately by humans in their pursuit of mistaken forms of happiness—self-sufficiency, power, respect, pleasure—are found united in the single goodness of God. God's perfection is extolled in the ninth poem of the third book, *O qui perpetua*: a hymn often admired by Christians, though almost all its thoughts are taken from Plato's *Timaeus* and a Neoplatonic commentary thereon.[4] Because all goodness resides in God, humans can only become happy if, in some way, they become gods. 'Every happy man is a god. Though by nature God is one only; but nothing prevents his divinity from being shared by many' (*DCP* 3. 10).

[4] In Chaucer's (prose) translation it commences: 'O thou father, creator of heaven and of earth, that governest this world by perdurable reason, that commandest the times to go from since that age had its beginning: thou that dwellest thyself aye steadfast and stable, and givest all other things to be moved . . .'.

In the fourth book Boethius asks Lady Philosophy to answer the question 'Why do the wicked prosper?' The universe, he agrees, is governed by an ideal ruler, God; but it looks like a house in which the worthless vessels are well looked after while the precious ones are left to grow filthy. Philosophy draws arguments from Plato's *Gorgias* to show that the prosperity of the wicked is only apparent. The will to do evil is itself a misfortune, and success in doing so is a worse disaster. Worse still is to go unpunished for one's misdeeds. While a good man can aspire to divinity, a bad man turns into a beast: avarice makes you a wolf, quarrelsomeness makes you a dog, cheating a fox, anger a lion, fear a deer, sloth an ass, and lust a pig.

All things are ruled by God's providence: does this mean that everything happens by fate? Lady Philosophy makes a distinction. Providence is the divine reason that binds all things together, while fate is what organizes the motions of things scattered in place and time; the complicated arrangements of fate proceed from the simplicity of providence. We can see only the apparent disorder of the operation of fate; if we could see the overall scheme as designed by providence, we would realize that whatever happens happens justly, and whatever is, is right.

Throughout the first four books Lady Philosophy has had much to say about Lady Luck. The fifth book addresses the question 'In a world governed by divine providence, can there be any such thing as luck or chance?' There cannot be purely random chance, if philosophy is to be believed; but human choice is something different from chance. Free choice, however, even if not random, is difficult to reconcile with the existence of a God who foresees everything that is to happen. 'If God foresees all and cannot in any way be mistaken, then that must necessarily happen which in his providence he foresees will be.' The reply offered is that God is outside time, and so it is a mistake to speak of providence as involving *fore*knowledge at all. This subtle but mysterious answer was to be much studied and developed in later ages.[5]

It is to be hoped that Boethius found consolation in his philosophical writing, because he was brutally tortured, a cord being fastened round his head and tightened until his eyes started from their sockets. He was finally executed by being beaten with clubs. Many Christians regarded him as a martyr, and some churches venerated him as St Severinus. The humanist

---

[5] Boethius' argument is analysed in detail in Ch. 9 below.

Lorenzo Valla in the fifteenth century called him 'the last of the Romans, the first of the scholastics', and Gibbon says that he was 'the last of the Romans whom Cato or Tully could have acknowledged for their country-man'.

Boethius was not only the last philosopher of the old Latin philosophical tradition: his *Consolation* can be read as an anthology of all that he valued in classical Greek philosophy. It was perhaps as a compliment to the pagan thinkers from whom he had learnt that he eliminated from his philosophical testament any Christian element. Even the treatment of the relation between divine foreknowledge and human freedom, so influential during the Christian centuries, is couched within the framework of the Stoic discussion of the relation between providence and fate.

The Greek Philosophy of Late Antiquity

Pagan Greek philosophy, however, had not quite come to an end at the time when Boethius met his death: the schools of Athens and Alexandria were still active. The head of the Athens school in the previous century had been the industrious and erudite Proclus, who was said to have been capable of producing, each working day, five lectures and 700 lines of philosophical prose. Proclus wrote commentaries on several of Plato's dialogues and an encyclopedic work on Plotinus' *Enneads*. His *Elements of Theology* has served, even in modern times, as a convenient compendium of Neoplatonism.

Proclus' system is based on Plotinus' trinity of One, Mind, and Soul, but he develops Plotinus' ideas by a multiplication of triads, and a general theory of their operation (*ET* 25–39). Within each triad there is a develop-mental process. From the originating element of the triad there emerges a new element which shares its nature but which yet differs from it. This new element both resides in its origin, proceeds beyond it, and returns back towards it. This law of development governs a massive proliferation of triads. From the initial One there proceed a number of divine Units (henads) (*ET* 113–65). The Henads, collectively, beget the world of Mind, which is divided into the spheres of Being, Life, and Thought. In the next, lower, world, that of Soul, Proclus provides a habitation for the traditional gods of the pagan pantheon. The visible world we live in is the work of these divine souls, which guide it providentially.

The pagan philosopher Hypatia, beset by a Christian mob, takes refuge at an altar, in this Victorian painting by C. W. Mitchell.

Human beings, for Proclus, straddle the three worlds of Soul, Mind, and One (*ET* 190–7). As united to our animal body, the human soul expresses itself in Eros, focused on earthly beauty. But it has also an imperishable, ethereal body made out of light. Thus it passes beyond love of beauty in search of Truth, a pursuit that brings it into contact with the ideal realities of the world of Mind. But it has a faculty higher than that of thought, and that brings it, by mystical ecstasy, into union with the One.

The theory of triads bears some resemblance to the Christian doctrine of the Trinity, but in fact Proclus, though a devotee of many superstitions, was bitterly hostile to Christianity. He was, indeed, reputed to have written eighteen separate refutations of the Christian doctrine of creation. Nonetheless, many of his ideas entered the mainstream of Christian thought by indirect routes. Boethius himself made frequent, if unacknowledged, use of his work. A contemporary Christian Neoplatonist wrote a series of treatises inspired by Proclus, passing them off as the work of Dionysius the Areopagite, who was an associate of St Paul in Athens (Acts 17). Another channel by which Proclus' ideas flowed into medieval philosophy was a book known as the *Liber de Causis*, which circulated under the name of Aristotle. Even Thomas Aquinas, who was aware that the book was not authentic, treated it with great respect.

In fifth-century Alexandria, where there was a powerful Christian patriarch, it was more difficult than in Athens for pagan philosophy to flourish. Hypatia, a female Neoplatonist mathematician and astronomer, stands out in a man's world of philosophy in the same way as Sappho stands out in a man's world of poetry. While Augustine was writing *The City of God* in Hippo, Hypatia was torn to pieces in Alexandria by a fanatical Christian mob (AD 415).[6] The most important philosopher of the school of Alexandria in its last days was Ammonius, an elder contemporary of Boethius. He was more effective as a teacher than a writer, and owes his fame to the distinction of his two most famous pupils, Simplicius and Philoponus.

Both these philosophers lived in the reign of the emperor Justinian, who succeeded to the purple in 527, two or three years after the execution of Boethius. Justinian was the most celebrated of the Byzantine emperors, renowned both as a conqueror and as a legislator. His generals conquered

---

[6] Sadly, very little is known of Hypatia. Charles Kingsley made the most of what there is in his novel *Hypatia* (1853).

large portions of the former Western Empire and united them for a while under the rule of Constantinople. His jurists collected and rationalized into a single code all the extant imperial edicts and statutes, and appended a digest of legal commentaries. The Code of Civil Law that was handed down in the course of his reign influenced most European countries until modern times.

Justinian's reign was not, however, as favourable to philosophy as it was to jurisprudence. The school of Athens continued the anti-Christian Neoplatonic tradition of Proclus, which brought it into imperial disfavour. Simplicius was one of the last group of scholars to adorn the school. He devoted great effort and erudition to the writing of commentaries on Aristotle, whose teachings he was anxious to reconcile with the thought of Plato as interpreted in late antiquity. Scholars of later generations are in his debt because in the course of this enterprise he quoted extensively from his predecessors as far back as the Presocratics, and is our source for many of their surviving fragments. Simplicius was still working there when, in the year 529, Justinian closed down the school because of its anti-Christian tendency. His edict, in the words of Gibbon, 'imposed a perpetual silence on the schools of Athens and excited the grief and indignation of the few remaining votaries of Grecian science and superstition' (*Decline and Fall*, ch. 40).

Philoponus, too, suffered under Justinian, but for different reasons. While Simplicius was a pagan philosopher based in Athens, Philoponus was a Christian philosopher based in Alexandria. While Simplicius was the most ardent admirer of Aristotle in antiquity, Philoponus was his severest critic. Whereas previous philosophers had either ignored Aristotle (like the Epicureans and Stoics) or interpreted him irenically (like the Neoplatonists), Philoponus knew him very well and attacked him head-on.

As a Christian, Philoponus rejected the doctrine of the eternity of the world, and demolished the arguments of Aristotle and Proclus to the effect that the world had no beginning. He carried his attack throughout the whole of Aristotle's physics, rejecting the theories of natural motion and natural place, and denying that the heavenly bodies were governed by physical principles different from those obtaining here below.[7] It was

---

[7] Philoponus' physics is discussed in detail in Ch. 5 below.

congenial to his Christian piety to demolish the notion that the world of the sun and moon and stars was something supernatural, standing in a relation to God different from that of the earth on which his human creatures live.

Philoponus wrote treatises on Christian doctrine as well as commentaries on Aristotle. They were not well received by the orthodox, who thought his treatment of the doctrine of the Trinity laid him open to the charge of believing in three Gods. Surprisingly, he accepted the Platonic belief in the existence of human souls prior to conception; even more surprisingly, this belief of his does not seem to have troubled his Christian brethren. But like many previous Alexandrian Christians, he was a monophysite, believing that in the incarnate Christ there was only a single nature, not, as defined by the Council of Chalcedon, two natures,

This mosaic from S. Vitale in Ravenna shows the Emperor Justinian and his court.

human and divine. He was summoned to Constantinople by the emperor to defend his views on the Incarnation, but failed to answer the summons. Philoponus outlived Justinian by a few years, but was condemned after his death for his heretical teaching about the Trinity. He was the last significant philosopher of the ancient world, and after his death philosophy went into hibernation for two centuries.

Between 600 and 800 the former Roman Empire shrank to little more than Greece, the Balkans, and part of Asia Minor. Intellectual talent was expended mainly on theological disputation. The monophysite church to which John Philoponus belonged had been excluded from communion by the orthodox, who believed that Christ had not just one, but two, natures, human and divine. During the seventh century attempts were made by emperors and patriarchs to reunite the Christian communions by agreeing that even if Christ had two natures, nonetheless he had only one will; or that even if he had two wills, one human and one divine, these two were united in a single activity of willing, a single actuality, or *energeia*. Any concession of this kind was strongly resisted by a retired imperial officer called Maximus, who wrote copiously against 'monothelitism', the doctrine of the single will.

Maximus (known as 'the Confessor') succeeded in having the doctrines of the single will and the single actuality condemned at a council in Rome in 649, later endorsed in Constantinople in 681. Christ's human will and the divine will were always in perfect agreement, but they were two separate entities. In persuading the guardians of orthodoxy of this teaching, Maximus was obliged to investigate in detail the concepts of *will* and *actuality*. The English word 'will' and its equivalents and their cognates in Greek (*thelesis/thelema*) and Latin (*voluntas*) can refer to a faculty (as in 'Human beings have free will, animals do not'), a disposition of the will (e.g. a willingness to be martyred), an act (e.g. 'I will' in a marriage ceremony), or an object willed (as in 'Thy will be done'). Maximus analysed these concepts carefully and with a degree of originality: but he was not so original as to deserve to be credited, as some have done, with being the inventor of the concept of the will *tout court* (PG 90).[8]

---

[8] The great theological debate of the succeeding century concerned the worship of images or icons. It might have been expected that the iconoclastic controversy would have thrown up interesting contributions to semiotics, the philosophical theory of signs. But this hope appears, from a brief survey of the literature, to be vain.

Philosophy in the Carolingian Empire

Outside the Roman Empire the world was transformed beyond recognition. The life of the prophet Muhammad came to an end in 633, and within ten years of his death the religion of Islam had spread by conquest from its native Arabia throughout the neighbouring Persian Empire and the Roman provinces of Syria, Palestine, and Egypt. In 698 the Muslims captured Carthage, and ten years later they were masters of all North Africa. In 711 they crossed the Straits of Gibraltar, easily defeated the Gothic Christians, and flooded through Spain. Their advance into northern Europe was halted only in 732, when they were defeated at Poitiers by the Frankish leader Charles Martel.

Charles Martel's grandson Charlemagne, who became king of the Franks in 768, drove the Muslims back to the Pyrenees, but did no more than nibble at their Spanish dominions. To the east, however, he conquered Lombardy, Bavaria, and Saxony, and had his son proclaimed king of Italy. When Pope Leo III was driven out of Rome by a revolution, Charlemagne restored him to his see. In gratitude the Pope crowned him as Roman emperor in St Peter's on Christmas Day 800—a date which, if not the most memorable in history, is at least the easiest to remember. Thus began the Holy Roman Empire, which at Charlemagne's death in 814 included almost all the Christian inhabitants of continental western Europe.

Charlemagne was anxious to improve standards of education and culture in his dominions, and he collected scholars from various parts of Europe to form a 'Palatine School' at his capital, Aachen. One of the most distinguished of these was Alcuin of York, who took a keen interest in Aristotle's *Categories*. The logic textbook which he wrote, *Dialectica*, takes the form of a dialogue in which the pupil Charlemagne asks questions and the teacher Alcuin gives answers. Alcuin retired in the last years of his life to run a small school in the abbey of St Martin of Tours, of which he later became abbot. He spent his time, he told the emperor, dispensing to this pupils the honey of Scripture, the wine of classical literature, and the apples of grammar. To a privileged few he displayed the treasures of astronomy—Charlemagne's favourite hobby.

When philosophy revived between the ninth and eleventh centuries, it did so not within the old Roman Empire of Byzantium, but in the Frankish

Empire of Charlemagne's successors and in the Abbasid court of Muslim Baghdad. The leading philosophers of the revival were, in the West, John the Scot, and in the East, Ibn Sina (Avicenna).

John was born in Ireland in the first decades of the ninth century. He is not to be mistaken for the more famous John Duns Scotus, who flourished in the fourteenth century. It is undoubtedly confusing that there are two medieval philosophers with the name John the Scot. What makes it doubly confusing is that one of them was an Irishman, and the other was for all practical purposes an Englishman. The ninth-century philosopher, for the avoidance of doubt, gave himself the surname Eriugena, which means Son of Erin.

By 851 Eriugena had migrated from Ireland to the court of Charles the Bald, the grandson of Charlemagne. This was probably at Compiègne, which Charles thought of renaming Carlopolis, on the model of Constantinople. Charles was a lover of things Greek, and the astonishingly learned Eriugena, who had mastered Greek (no one knows where), won his favour and wrote him flattering poems in that language. He taught liberal arts at the court for a while, but his interests began to turn towards philosophy. Once, commenting on a text on the borderline between grammar and logic, he wrote 'no one enters heaven except through philosophy'.[9]

Eriugena first engaged in philosophy in 851 when invited by Hincmar, the archbishop of Reims, to write a refutation of the ideas of a learned and pessimistic monk, Gottschalk. Gottschalk had taken up the problem of predestination where Augustine had left off. He was reported to have deduced from the texts of Augustine something that was generally there left implicit, namely that predestination affected sinners as well as saints. It was, he taught, not only the blessed in heaven whose ultimate fate had been predestined, the damned also had been predestined to hell before they were ever conceived. This doctrine of double predestination seemed to Archbishop Hincmar to be heretical. At the very least, like the monks of Augustine's time, he regarded it as a doctrine inimical to good monastic discipline: sinners might conclude that, since their fate had been sealed long ago, there was no point in giving up sinning. Hence his invitation to Eriugena to put Gottschalk down (PL 125. 84–5).

Whether or not Gottschalk had been accurately reported, Eriugena's refutation of his alleged heresy was, from Hincmar's point of view, worse

---

[9] See J. J. O'Meara, *Eriugena* (Oxford: Clarendon Press, 1988), chs. 1 and 2.

than the disease. Eriugena's arguments were weak, and in attacking the predestination of the damned, he emasculated the predestination of the blessed. There could not be a double predestination, he said, because God was simple and undivided; and there was no such thing as *pre*destination because God was eternal. The first argument is unconvincing because if a double predestination threatens God's simplicity, so too does the distinction between predestination and foreknowledge, which was the favoured solution of Gottschalk's opponents. The second argument does not provide the desired incentive to the sinner to repent, because whatever temporal qualification we give to the divine determining of our fate, it is certainly, on the Augustinian view, independent of any choice of ours (CCCM 50. 12).

The Frankish kingdom was torn by doctrinal strife, and both Gottschalk and Eriugena found themselves condemned by Church councils. The Council of Quierzy in 853—the third of a series—defined, against Gottschalk, that while God predestined the blessed to heaven, he did not predestine others to sin: he merely left them in the human mass of perdition and predestined only their punishment, not their guilt. The condemnation of Eriugena, at Valence in 855, affirmed that there was indeed a predestination of the impious to death no less than a predestination of the elect to life. The difference was this: that in the election of those to be saved the mercy of God preceded all merit, whereas in the damnation of those who were to perish evil desert preceded just judgement. The Council fathers were not above vulgar abuse, saying that Eriugena had defiled the purity of the faith with nauseating Irish porridge.

Despite his condemnation, Eriugena remained in favour with Charles the Bald and was commissioned by him in 858 to translate into Latin three treatises of Dionysius the Areopagite: the *Divine Names*, the *Celestial Hierarchy*, and the *Ecclesiastical Hierarchy*. He found the Neoplatonic ideas of Dionysius congenial and went on to construct his own system on somewhat similar lines, in a work of five volumes called *On Nature*—or, to give it its Greek title, *Periphyseon*.

There are, according to Eriugena, four great divisions of nature: nature creating and uncreated, nature created and creating, nature created and uncreating, and nature uncreating and uncreated (1. 1). The first such nature is God. The second is the intellectual world of Platonic ideas, which creates the third nature, the world of material objects. The fourth is God again, conceived not as creator but as the end to which things return.

Eriugena tells us that the most important distinction within nature is that between the things that are and the things that are not. It is disconcerting to be told that God is among the things that are not; however, Eriugena does not mean that there is no God, but rather that God does not fit into any of Aristotle's ten categories of being (2. 15). God is above being, and what he is doing is something better than existing. One name that we can give to the ineffable and incomprehensible brilliance of the divine goodness is 'Nothing'.[10]

Eriugena's third division, the material world, is the easiest to comprehend (3. 3). Like Philoponus, he believes that heaven and earth are made out of the same elements; there is no special quintessence for the heavenly bodies. The cosmos, he tells us, consists of three spheres: the earth in the centre, next to it the sphere of the sun (which is roughly 45,000 miles away), and outermost the sphere of the moon and the stars (roughly 90,000 miles away). While Eriugena thinks that the sun revolves around the world, he takes some steps towards a heliocentric system: Jupiter, Mars, Venus, and Mercury, he believed, were planets of the sun, revolving around it.

Where do human beings fit into Eriugena's fourfold scheme? They seem to straddle the second and third division. As animals, we belong in the third division, and yet we transcend the other animals. We can say with equal propriety that man is an animal and that he is not an animal. He shares reason, mind, and interior sense with the celestial essences, but he shares his flesh, his outward self, with other animals. Man was created twice over: once from the earth, with the animals, but once with the intellectual creatures of the second division of nature. Does this mean that we have two souls? No, each of us has a single, undivided, soul: wholly life, wholly mind, wholly reason, wholly memory. This soul creates the body, acting as the agent of God, who does not himself create anything mortal. Even when soul and body are separated at death, the soul continues to govern the body scattered throughout the elements (4. 8).

As the creator of the body, the soul belongs to that division of nature which is both created and creative. This second division consists of what

---

[10] Eriugena's theology is discussed at greater length in Ch. 9 below.

Eriugena calls 'the primordial causes of things', which he identifies with the Platonic Ideas (2. 2). These were pre-formed by God the Father in his eternal Word. The Idea of Man is that in accordance with which man is made in the image of God. But that image is deformed in fallen humans. Had God not foreseen that Adam would fall, humans would not have been divided into male and female; they would have propagated as angels do. Their bodies would have been celestial and would have lacked metabolism. After the resurrection, our bodies will resume their sexless and ethereal form. When the world finally ends, place and time will disappear, and all creatures will find salvation in the nature that is uncreated and uncreating.

Eriugena was one of the most original and imaginative thinkers of the Middle Ages and built the ideas of his Greek sources into a system that was uniquely his own. Reading him is not easy, but his text can cast a fascinating spell on the reader. He has a fanatical love of paradox: whenever he writes a sentence he can hardly bear not to follow it with its contradictory. He often displays great subtlety and ingenuity in showing that the two apparent contradictions can be interpreted in such a way as to reconcile them. But sometimes his wayward intellect leads him into sheer nonsense, as when he writes 'In unity itself all numbers are at once together, and no number precedes or follows another, since all are one' (3. 66).

Though Eriugena constantly quotes the Bible, his system is closer to pagan Neoplatonism than to traditional Christian thought, and it is unsurprising that *On Nature* was eventually condemned by ecclesiastical authority. In 1225 Pope Honorius III ordered all surviving copies of the work to be sent to Rome to be burned. But legend was kind to his memory. The story was often told of Charles the Bald asking him, over dinner, what separates a Scot from a sot, and being given the answer 'only this table'. And at one time the University of Oxford implausibly venerated him as its founder.[11]

Muslim and Jewish Philosophers

The Christian Eriugena was a much less important precursor of Western medieval philosophy than a series of Muslim thinkers in the countries that are now Iraq and Iran. Besides being significant philosophers in their own

[11] See O'Meara, *Eriugena*, 214–16.

The patron saint of Latin philosophy was St Catherine of Alexandria, who according to legend defeated fifty pagan philosophers in disputation before the Emperor Maxentius. Pintoricchio, in this fresco in the Borgia apartments of the Vatican, shows her defeating, for good measure, a pair of Islamic philosophers too.

right, these Muslims provided the roundabout route through which much Greek learning was eventually made available to the Latin West.

In the fourth century there was, at Edessa in Mesopotamia, a school of Syrian Christians who made a serious study of Greek philosophy and medicine. These Christians did not accept the condemnation of Nestorius at the Council of Ephesus in 431, and they were not reconciled by the Council of Chalcedon in 451. Accordingly, their school was closed by the emperor Zeno in 489. The scholars migrated to Persia, where they continued the work they had begun at Edessa of translating the logical works of Aristotle from Greek into Syriac.

After the Muslim conquest of Persia and Syria, scholars from this school were invited to the court of Baghdad in the era of the enlightened caliphs of the *Arabian Nights*. Between 750 and 900 these Syrians translated into Arabic much of the Aristotelian corpus, as well as Plato's *Republic* and *Laws*. They also made available to the Muslim world the scientific and medical works of Euclid, Archimedes, Hippocrates, and Galen. At the same time mathematical and astronomical works were translated from Indian sources. The

'arabic' numerals that we use today, which were enormously more convenient for arithmetical purposes than the Roman and Byzantine numerals that
they superseded, were imported from India in the same period.

The introduction of Greek, and especially Aristotelian, philosophy had a
very significant effect on Muslim thought. Islamic theology (*kalam*) had
already developed a rudimentary philosophical vocabulary and was initially—and subsequently—hostile to this foreign system of ideas (*falsafa*).
For instance, the thinkers of *kulam* (known as Mutakallimun) deployed a
series of proofs to show that the world had had a beginning in time; the
new philosophers produced Aristotelian arguments to prove that it had
always existed.[12] Whereas for Western thinkers like Augustine the vulgar
Latin of Bible translations had made Christianity initially distasteful,
for the *kalam* scholars of the Quran it was the broken Arabic of the
Aristotelian translations that proved a stumbling block to the acceptance
of philosophy. For a while they resisted the idea that logic had universal
validity, treating it rather as an obscure branch of Greek grammar.

The person traditionally regarded as the father of Muslim philosophy is
al-Kindi (*c*.801–66), a contemporary of Eriugena, who occupied a middle
ground between *kalam* and *falsafa*. He wrote a treatise called *The Art of
Dispelling Sorrows*, which bears a resemblance to Boethius' *Consolation*. More
important is his treatise on First Philosophy, which develops in a highly
formal way the *kalam* argument for the finitude of the world in time.[13] He is
also remembered for his writings on human understanding, in one of
which he suggests that our intellect is brought into operation by a single
cosmic intelligence, perhaps to be identified with the Mind, which occupies
second place in the Neoplatonic trinity of One, Mind, and Soul. This idea
was taken up by a later philosopher, al-Farabi, a member of the school of
Baghdad who died in 950. He used it to explain the baffling passage in
Aristotle's *De Anima* which speaks of two minds, a mind to make things, and
a mind to become things.[14]

Al-Farabi made a clear distinction between grammar and logic, which he
regarded as a preparatory tool for philosophy. Philosophy proper, for him,
had three divisions: physics, metaphysics, and ethics. Psychology was a part

[12] See William Lane Craig, *The Kalam Cosmological Argument* (London: Macmillan, 1979).
[13] This is set out in detail in Ch. 5 below.
[14] See vol. i, p. 246.

of physics, and theology was a quite separate discipline that studied the attributes of God as rewarder and punisher. One could, however, use philosophical arguments to prove the existence of God as first mover and necessary being. Al-Farabi was a member of the mystical sect of the Sufis and stressed that the task of humans was to seek enlightenment from God and return to him from whom we originally emanated.

A contemporary of al-Farabi was Saadiah Gaon (882–942), the first Jewish philosopher of the Middle Ages, who was born in Egypt and moved to Babylon, where he became head of the school of biblical studies. He translated the Bible into Arabic and wrote widely on Jewish liturgy and tradition. He was anxious to reconcile biblical doctrine with rational philosophy, which he conceived as being two twigs from the same branch. In this task he drew on Neoplatonic sources and on material taken from the *kalam*. His most influential book was entitled *The Book of Doctrines and Beliefs*.

Human certainties, Saadiah says, arise from three sources: sense, reason, and tradition. Reason is of two kinds: rational intuition, which provides the truths of logic and knowledge of good and evil, and rational inference, which derives truths by argument from the premises provided by sense and intuition. It is by rational inference that we know that humans possess a soul and that the universe has a cause. The tradition of the Jewish people, of which the most important element is the Bible, is a further source of knowledge, whose validity is certified by the prophets' performance of miracles. This is an independent source, but it has to be interpreted judiciously in the light of information obtained from other sources.

The senses, Saadiah says, cannot tell us whether the world had a beginning or has existed for ever, so we must look to reason. He offers four proofs that the world was created in time: (1) everything in the universe is finite in size, so the force that holds it together must be finite and cannot have existed for ever; (2) the elements of the cosmos are complex but fit each other admirably, so they must be the work of a skilful creator; (3) all substances in the natural world are contingent, and need a necessary creator; (4) an infinite series cannot be grasped or traversed, so time must be finite. Some of these arguments go back as far as Philoponus, and some of them had a long future ahead of them (*PMA* 344–50).

Avicenna and his Successors

The greatest of all Muslim philosophers was Ibn Sina, known in the West as Avicenna (980–1037). He was a Persian, born near Bokhara (in present-day Uzbekistan), who was educated in Arabic and wrote most of his works in that language. He is reputed to have mastered logic, mathematics, physics, and medicine in his teens. He began to practise as a doctor when he was 16. In his autobiography, edited by his pupil Juzjani, he describes how he then took up philosophy:

> For a year and a half, I devoted myself to study. I resumed the study of logic and all parts of philosophy. During this time I never slept the whole night through and did nothing but study all day long. Whenever I was puzzled by a problem . . . I would go to the mosque, pray, and beg the Creator of All to reveal to me that which was hidden from me and to make easy for me that which was difficult. Then at night I would return home, put a lamp in front of me, and set to work reading and writing.[15]

Thus, he tells us, he had mastered all the sciences by the time he was 18. At the age of 20 he published an encyclopedia—the first of five in the course of his life, four in Arabic and one in Persian.

Avicenna's medical skill was much in demand; he was summoned to treat the sultan of Bokhara and made full use of his splendid library. Between 1015 and 1022 he was both court physician and vizier to the ruler of Hamadan. Later he occupied a similar position in the court of Isfahan. He left behind about 200 works, of which more than 100 have survived. His *Canon of Medicine* summarizes much classical clinical material and adds observations of his own; it was used by practitioners in Europe until the seventeenth century.

Avicenna's main philosophical encyclopedia was called in Arabic *Kitab-al-Shifa*, or 'Book of Healing'. It is divided into four parts, of which the first three treat of logic, physics, and mathematics respectively. The second part includes a development of Aristotle's *De Anima*. The fourth part, whose Arabic name means 'Of Divine Things', was known in the medieval West as his *Metaphysics*. When translated into Latin in Toledo around 1150 it had an enormous influence on the Latin philosophy of the Middle Ages.

---

[15] Quoted in J. L. Esposito, *Islam: The Straight Path* (New York: Oxford University Press, 1991), 57.

Avicenna said that he had read Aristotle's metaphysics forty times and had learnt it by heart without understanding it—only when he came across a commentary by al-Farabi did he understand what was meant by the theory of being *qua* being.[16] His own *Metaphysics* is much more than a commentary on Aristotle; it is a thoroughly thought-out original system. The book, in ten treatises, falls into two parts: the first five books treat of ontology, the science of being in general; the remaining books are devoted principally to natural theology. In the early books Avicenna deals with the notions of substance, matter and form, potentiality and actuality, and the problem of universals. In the later books he examines the nature of the first cause and the concept of necessary being, and the way in which creatures, human beings in particular, derive their being and nature from God.

As an illustration of the way in which Avicenna modifies Aristotelian concepts we may take the doctrine of matter and form. Any bodily entity, he maintains, consists of matter under a substantial form, a form of corporeality, which made it a body. All bodily creatures belong to particular species, but any such creature, e.g. a dog, has not just one but many substantial forms: as well as corporeality, it has the forms of animality and caninity. Since souls, for an Aristotelian, are forms, human beings, on this theory, have three souls: a vegetative soul (responsible for nutrition, growth, and reproduction), an animal soul (responsible for movement and perception), and a rational soul (responsible for intellectual thought). None of the souls exist prior to the body, but while the two inferior souls are mortal, the superior one is immortal and survives death in a condition either of bliss or of frustration, in accordance with the merits of the life it has led. Avicenna followed al-Farabi's interpretation of Aristotle on the intellect, and accepted, in addition to the receptive human mind that absorbs information routed through the senses, a single superhuman active intellect that gives humans the ability to grasp universal concepts and principles.[17]

In describing the unique nature of God, Avicenna introduced a novel idea that occupied a central role in all succeeding metaphysics: the distinc-

---

[16] Avicenna, *The Life of Ibn Sina*, trans. W. E. Gohlman (Albany: State University of New York Press, 1974).

[17] The philosophy of mind of al-Farabi and of Avicenna is discussed in detail in Ch. 7 below.

tion between essence and existence.[18] In all creatures essence and existence are distinct: not even the fullest investigation into *what kind* of thing a particular species is will show *that* any individuals of that species exist. But God is quite different: in his case, and only in his case, essence entails existence. God is the only necessary being, and all others are contingent. Since God's existence depends only in his essence, his existence is eternal; and so too, Avicenna concluded, is the world that emanates from him.[19]

Though he was irregular and unobservant in practice, Avicenna was a sincere Muslim, and took care to reconcile his philosophical scheme with the Prophet's teaching and commands, which he regarded as a unique enlightenment from the Active Intellect. But his systematic treatment of religion in the second part of his *Metaphysics* makes no special appeal to the authority of the Quran. It gives rationalistic justifications for Islamic ritual and social practices (including polygamy and the subordination of women), but it is based on religious principles of a general and philosophical kind. It was this that made it possible for his writing to be influential among the Catholic philosophers of the Latin West; but it also brought his work under suspicion among conservative Muslims. Owing to the favour of princes, however, he escaped serious persecution. He met his end in Hamadan in 1037 during a campaign against that city led by the ruler of Isfahan. He took a poison, we are told, misprescribed as a medication for an ailment brought on by his dissolute life.

A younger contemporary of Avicenna, Solomon Ibn Gabirol (c.1021–1058), made a distinctive contribution to metaphysics. Though a devout Jew and a liturgical poet, Ibn Gabirol wrote a philosophical work, *The Fountain of Life*, which betrays no trace of its Jewish origin—so much so that when it was translated into Latin in the mid-twelfth century, it was thought to be the work of a Muslim, to whom Westerners gave the name Avicebron.

Ibn Gabirol's system is fundamentally Neoplatonic, but it contains one neo-Aristotelian element. All created substances, he maintained, whether corporeal or spiritual, whether earthly or heavenly, are composed of

---

[18] Some writers have claimed that the distinction goes back to Aristotle, but this is doubtful (see vol. i, p. 224).
[19] Avicenna's metaphysics is discussed in detail in Ch. 6 below.

matter and form. There is spiritual matter as well as corporeal matter: the universe is a pyramid with the immaterial godhead at the summit and formless prime matter at the base. Since one can no longer equate 'material' with 'bodily' in his system, Ibn Gabirol has to introduce, like Avicenna, a form of corporeality to make bodies bodies. Ibn Gabirol's universal hylomorphism was to have a considerable influence on thirteenth-century Latin Aristotelianism (*PMA* 359–67).

Meanwhile, both in Christianity and in Islam, the eleventh century saw a reaction against philosophy on the part of conservative theologians. St Peter Damiani (1007–72), angered by philosophical criticisms of Catholic beliefs about the Eucharist, trumpeted that God had not chosen to save his people by means of dialectic. He did, however, himself make use of philosophical reasoning when discussing divine attributes, and it led him to some strange conclusions. If these fell foul of the principle of contradiction, so be it: logic was not the mistress, but the maidservant, of theology.[20]

Towards the end of the century the Persian philosopher and mystic al-Ghazali (1058–1111) wrote a work, *Tahafut al-falasifa* ('The Incoherence of the Philosophers'), in which he sought to show not only that Muslim philosophers, in particular Avicenna, were heretical to Islam, but also that they were fallible and incoherent by their own philosophical lights. His criticisms of Avicenna's arguments for the existence of God and for the immortality of the soul were often well taken. But he is now best remembered because his *Incoherence* provoked a reply from a twelfth-century philosopher of greater weight, Averroes.

Anselm of Canterbury

Despite these clashes between dialecticians and conservatives, the eleventh century produced one thinker who was both an original philosopher in his own right and a theologian sufficiently orthodox to be canonized: St Anselm of Canterbury (1033–1109). Born in Aosta he became, at the age of 27, a monk at the abbey of Bec. There he studied the works of Augustine under its abbot Lanfranc, himself a highly competent scholar, who later became the first archbishop of Canterbury after the Norman conquest of

---

[20] Damiani's unusual views on omnipotence are discussed below in Ch. 9.

England. As a monk, prior, and finally abbot of Bec, Anselm wrote a series of brief philosophical and meditative works.

The *Monologion*, dedicated to Lanfranc, has as its purpose to teach students how to meditate upon the nature of God. The greater part of it (sections 29–80) is concerned with the Christian doctrine of the Trinity, but the initial sections present arguments for the existence of God—from the degrees of perfection to be found in creatures, and from dependent versus independent being. It is in a slightly later work, the *Proslogion*, that he puts forward his celebrated argument for the existence of God as that than which nothing greater can be conceived. It is on this argument (commonly called the 'ontological argument') that his philosophical fame principally rests.[21] The *Proslogion*, a brief address to God in the style of Augustine's *Confessions*, shares with that work an engaging literary charm that has made it an enduring classic of philosophical literature.

Anselm, as said earlier, was distinguished both as a philosopher and as a theologian, and in his writing he does not make a sharp distinction between the two disciplines. When treating of God he does not make a systematic distinction, as later scholastics were to do, between natural theology (what can be discovered of God by unaided reason) and dogmatic theology (what can be learnt only from revelation). He sums up his own attitude in a passage at the beginning of the *Proslogion* (c. 1).

I do not aim, Lord, to penetrate your profundity, because I know my intellect is no kind of match for it; but I want to understand in some small measure that truth of yours that my heart believes and loves. For I do not seek to understand that I may believe; but I believe that I may understand. For I believe this too, that unless I believe, I shall not understand. (Isa. 7: 9)

So he treats both the existence of God and the mystery of the Trinity in the same manner, as truths that he believes from the outset, but which he wishes to understand more fully. If, in the course of this, he discovers philosophical arguments that may be used to influence also the unbeliever, that is a bonus rather than the purpose of his inquiry.

Several treatises thus straddle philosophy and theology. *On Truth* analyses different applications of the word 'true'—to sentences, to thoughts, to sense-perceptions, to actions, and to things. It concludes that there is only a single truth in all things, which is identical with justice. *On Free Will* explores

---

[21] Anselm's arguments for the existence of God are analysed in Ch. 9 below.

Anselm's Tower in Canterbury Cathedral. He is buried under a simple slab in a chapel at its foot.

to what extent human beings are capable of avoiding sin. *On the Fall of the Devil* deals with one of the most excruciating versions of the problem of evil: how could initially good angels, supremely intelligent and with no carnal temptations, turn away from God, the only true source of happiness?

While at Bec, Anselm did write one purely philosophical work. *On the Grammarian* reflects on the interface between grammar and logic, and on the relation between signifiers and signified. Against the background of Aristotle's categories Anselm analysed the contrasts between nouns and adjectives, concrete and abstract terms, substances and qualities; and he related these contrasts to each other.

In 1093 Anselm succeeded Lanfranc as archbishop of Canterbury, an office which he held until his death. His last years were much occupied with disputes over jurisdiction between the king (William II) and the Pope (Urban II). But he found time to write an original justification for the Christian doctrine of the Incarnation under the title *Why did God Become Man?* Justice demands, he says, that where there is an offence, there must be satisfaction: the offender must offer a recompense that is equal and opposite to the offence. In feudal style, he argues that the magnitude of an offence is judged by the importance of the person offended, while the magnitude of a recompense is judged by the importance of the person making it. Human sin is infinite offence, since it is offence against God; human recompense is only finite, since it is made by a creature. Unaided, therefore, the human race is incapable of making satisfaction for the sins of Adam and his heirs. Satisfaction can only be adequate if it is made by one who is human (and therefore an heir of Adam) and also divine (and therefore capable of making infinite recompense). Hence the necessity of the Incarnation. In the history of philosophy this treatise of Anselm's is important because of its concept of satisfaction, which, along with deterrence and retribution, long figured in philosophical justifications of punishment in the political as well as the theological context.

Just before becoming archbishop, Anselm had become embroiled in a dispute with a pugnacious theologian, Roscelin of Compiègne (c.1050–1120). Roscelin is famous for his place in a quarrel that had a long history ahead of it: the debate over the nature of universals. In a sentence such as 'Peter is human' what does the universal term 'human' stand for? Philosophers down the ages came to be divided into realists, who thought that such a predicate stood for some extra-mental reality, and nominalists, who thought that no entity corresponded to such a word in the way that the man Peter corresponds to the name 'Peter'. Roscelin is often treated in the history of philosophy as the founder of 'nominalism', but his views were in fact more extreme than those of most nominalists. He claimed not just that universal predicates were mere names, but that they were mere puffs of breath. If this theory is applied to the doctrine of the Trinity, it raises a problem. Father, Son, and Holy Ghost are each God. But if the predicate 'God' is a mere word, then the three persons of the Trinity have nothing in common. Anselm had Roscelin condemned at a council in 1092 on a charge of tritheism, the heresy that there are three separate Gods.

Abelard

No logical work survives that can be confidently ascribed to Roscelin. All that we can be sure came from his pen is a letter to his most famous pupil, Abelard. Abelard was born into a knightly family in Brittany in 1079 and came to study under Roscelin shortly after he had been condemned. About 1100 he moved to Paris and joined the school attached to the Cathedral of Notre Dame. The teacher there was William of Champeaux, who espoused a realist theory of universals at the opposite extreme from Roscelin's nominalism. The universal nature of man, he maintained, is wholly present in each individual at one and the same time. Abelard found William's doctrine no more congenial than that of his former master, and left Paris to set up a school at Melun. He wrote the earliest of his surviving works, word-by-word commentaries on logical works of Aristotle, Porphyry, and Boethius.

Later he returned to Paris and founded a school in competition to William, whom in 1113 he succeeded as master of the Notre Dame school. While teaching there he lodged with one of the canons of the cathedral, Fulbert, and became tutor to his 16-year-old niece Héloïse. He became her lover, probably in 1116, and when she became pregnant married her secretly. Héloïse had been reluctant to marry, lest she interfere with Abelard's career, and she retired to a convent shortly after the wedding and the birth of her son. Her outraged uncle Fulbert sent to her husband's room by night a pair of thugs who castrated him. Abelard became a monk at St Denis, while Héloïse took the veil at the convent of Argenteuil.

Abelard supported Héloïse out of his tutorial earnings and the pair renewed their relationship by means of edifying correspondence. One of Abelard's longest letters, written some years later, is called *History of my Calamities*. It is the main source of our knowledge of his life up to this point, and is the liveliest piece of autobiography between Augustine's *Confessions* and the diary of Samuel Pepys.

While at St Denis, Abelard continued to teach, and began to write theological treatises. The first one, *Theology of the Highest Good*, addressed the problem that set Anselm and Roscelin at odds: the nature of the distinction between the three divine persons in the Trinity, and the relationship in the Godhead between the triad 'power, wisdom, goodness' and the triad 'Father, Son, and Spirit'. Like Roscelin, Abelard got into trouble with the Church; his work was condemned as unsound by a synod at Soissons in 1121. He had to burn the treatise with his own hand and he was briefly imprisoned in a correctional monastery.

On his return to St Denis, Abelard was soon in trouble again for denying that the abbey's patron had ever been bishop of Athens. He was forced to leave, and set up a country school in an oratory that he built in Champagne and dedicated to the Paraclete (the Holy Spirit). From 1125 to 1132 or thereabouts he was abbot of St Gildas, a corrupt and boisterous abbey in Brittany, where his attempts at reform were met with threats of murder. Héloïse meanwhile had become prioress of Argenteuil. When she and her nuns were made homeless in 1129, Abelard installed them in the Paraclete oratory.

Some time early in the 1130s Abelard returned to Paris, teaching again on the Mont Ste Geneviève. He spent most of the rest of his working life there, lecturing on logic and theology and writing copiously. He wrote a commentary on the Epistle to the Romans, and an ethical treatise with the Socratic title *Know Thyself*. He continued to assemble a collection of authoritative texts on important theological topics, grouping them in contradictory pairs under the title *Sic et Non* ('Yes and No'). He developed the ideas of his *Theology of the Supreme Good* in several succeeding versions, of which the definitive one was *The Theology of the Scholars*, which was finished in the mid-1130s.

This book brought him into conflict with St Bernard, abbot of Clairvaux and second founder of the Cistercian order, later to be the preacher of the Second Crusade. Bernard took out of the book (sometimes fairly, sometimes unfairly) a list of nineteen heresies, and had them condemned at a council at Sens in 1140. Among the condemned propositions were some that were quite inflammatory, for example, 'God should not and cannot prevent evil' and 'The power of binding and losing was given only to the Apostles and not to their successors' (DB 375, 379). Abelard appealed to Rome against the condemnation, but the only result was that the Pope condemned him to perpetual silence. He had by now retired to the abbey of Cluny, where he died two years later; his peaceful death was described by the abbot, Peter the Venerable, in a letter to Héloïse.

Of all medieval thinkers, Abelard is undoubtedly one of the most famous; but to the world at large he is more famous as a tragic lover than as an original philosopher. Nonetheless, he has an important place in the history of philosophy, for two reasons especially: for his contribution to logic and for his influence upon scholastic method.

Three logical treatises survive. The first two are both called 'Logic' and are distinguished from each other by reference to the first words of their

Heloise and Abelard, united in death, in a tomb in the Paris cemetery of Pere Lachaise.

Latin text: one is the *Logica Ingredientibus* and the other the *Logica Nostrorum Petitioni*. The third is entitled *Dialectica*. It used to be the common opinion of scholars that the third treatise was the definitive one, dating from the last years of Abelard's life. Some recent scholars have suggested, on the other hand, that it dates from a much earlier period, partly on the uncompelling ground that examples like 'May my girlfriend kiss me' and 'Peter loves his girl' are unlikely to have been included in a textbook written after the affair with Héloïse.[22] When Abelard wrote, very few of Aristotle's logical works were available in Latin, and to that extent he was at a disadvantage compared with later writers in succeeding centuries. It is, therefore, all the more to the credit of his own insight and originality that he contributed to the subject in a way that marks him out as one of the greatest of medieval logicians.

One of Abelard's works that had the greatest subsequent influence was his *Sic et Non*, which places in opposition to each other texts on the same topic by different scriptural or patristic authorities. This collection was not made with sceptical intent, in order to cast doubt on the authority of the sacred and ecclesiastical writers; rather, the paired texts were set out in a systematic pattern in order to stimulate his own, and others', reflection on the points at issue.

Later, in the heyday of medieval universities, a favourite teaching method was the academic disputation. A teacher would put up one of his pupils, a senior student, plus one or more juniors, to dispute an issue. The senior pupil would have the duty to defend some particular thesis— for instance, that the world was created in time; or, for that matter, that the world was not created in time. This thesis would be attacked, and the opposite thesis would be presented, by other pupils. The instructor would then settle the dispute, trying to bring out what was true in what had been said by the one and what was sound in the criticisms made by the others. Many of the most famous masterpieces of medieval philosophy—the great majority of the writings of Thomas Aquinas, for example—observe, on the written page, the pattern of these oral disputations.

Abelard's *Sic et Non* is the ancestor of these medieval disputations. The main textbook of medieval theology, Peter Lombard's *Sentences*, bore a

---

[22] On the dating of Abelard's logical works, see John Marenbon, *The Philosophy of Peter Abelard* (Cambridge: Cambridge University Press, 1997), 36–53.

structure similar to Abelard's work, and promoted the kind of debate standard in the schools. Thus it can be argued that it was ultimately due to Abelard that the structure of philosophical discussion took a form that was adversarial rather than inquisitorial, with pupils in the role of advocates and the teacher in the role of a judge. Though never himself more than a schoolmaster, Abelard imposed a style of thought on academic professors right up to the Renaissance.

Averroes

Several of Abelard's Christian contemporaries made contributions to philosophy. Most of them belonged to schools in or around Paris. At Chartres a group of scholars promoted a revival of interest in Plato: William of Conches commented on the *Timaeus* and Gilbert of Poitiers sponsored a moderate version of realism. The Abbey of St Victor produced two notable thinkers: a German, Hugh, and a Scotsman, Richard, both of whom combined a taste for mysticism with energetic attempts to discover a rational proof of God's existence. In the capital itself Peter Lombard, the bishop of Paris, wrote a work on the model of Abelard's *Sic et Non*, called the *Sentences*. This was a compilation of authoritative passages drawn from the Old and New Testaments, Church councils, and Church Fathers, grouped topic by topic, for and against particular theological theses. This became a standard university textbook.

However, the only twelfth-century philosophers to approach Abelard in philosophical talent came from outside Christendom. Both were born in Cordoba, within a decade of each other, the Muslim Averroes (whose real name was Ibn Rushd) and the Jew Maimonides (whose real name was Moses ben Maimon). Cordoba was the foremost centre of artistic and literary culture in the whole of Europe, and Muslim Spain, until it was overrun by the fanatical Almohads, provided a tolerant environment in which Christians and Jews lived peaceably with Arabs.

Averroes (1126–98) was a judge, and the son and grandson of judges. He was also learned in medicine, and wrote a compendium for physicians called *Kulliyat* 'General Principles'. He entered the court of the sultan at Marrakesh; while there he caught sight of a star not visible in Spain, and this convinced him of the truth of Aristotle's claim that the world was round. Back in Spain he was commissioned in 1168 by the caliph, Abu Yakub, to provide a summary of Aristotle's works. In 1182 he was appointed court physician in addition to his judgeship, and he combined these offices with his Aristotelian scholarship until, in 1195, he fell into disfavour with the caliph al-Mansur. He was briefly placed under house arrest, and his books were burnt. He returned to Morocco and died at Marrakesh in 1198.

Throughout his life Averroes had to defend philosophy against attacks from conservative Muslims. In response to al-Ghazali's *Incoherence of the Philosophers* he wrote a book called *The Incoherence of the Incoherence*, defending the right of human reason to investigate matters of theology. He also wrote a treatise, *The Harmony of Philosophy and Religion*. Is the study of philosophy, he asks, allowed or prohibited by Islamic law? His answer is that it is prohibited to the simple faithful, but for those with the appropriate intellectual powers, it is positively obligatory, provided they keep it to themselves and do not communicate it to others (*HPR* 65).

Averroes' teaching in the *Incoherence* was misinterpreted by some of his followers and critics as a doctrine of double truth: the doctrine that something can be true in philosophy which is not true in religion, and vice versa. But his intention was merely to distinguish between different levels of access to a single truth, levels appropriate to different degrees of talent and training.

Al-Ghazali's diatribe had been directed especially against the philosophy of Avicenna. In his response to al-Ghazali, Averroes is not an uncritical defender of Avicenna; his own position is often somewhere between that of the two opponents. Like Avicenna, he believes in the eternity of the world: he argues that this belief is not incompatible with belief in creation, and he seeks to refute the arguments derived from Philoponus to show that eternal motion is impossible. On the other hand, Averroes gradually abandoned Avicenna's scheme of the emanation from God of a series of celestial intelligences, and he rejected the dichotomy of essence and existence which Avicenna had put forward as the key distinction between creatures and creator. He came to deny also Avicenna's thesis that the agent intellect produced the natural forms of the visible world. Against al-Ghazali, Averroes insisted that there is genuine causation in the created cosmos: natural causes produce their own effects, and are not mere triggers for the exercise of divine omnipotence. But in the case of human intelligence he reduced the role of natural causation further even than Avicenna had done: he maintained that the passive intellect, no less than the active, was a single, superhuman, incorporeal substance (*PMA* 324–34).[23]

Averroes' most important contribution to the development of philosophy was the series of commentaries—thirty-eight in all—that he wrote on the works of Aristotle. These come in three sizes: short, intermediate, and long. For some of Aristotle's works (e.g. *De Anima* and *Metaphysics*) all three commentaries are extant, for some two, and for some only one. Some of the commentaries survive in the original Arabic, some only in translations into Hebrew or Latin. The short commentaries, or 'epitomes', are essentially summaries or digests of the arguments of Aristotle and his successors. The long commentaries are dense works, quoting Aristotle in full and commenting on every sentence; the intermediate ones may be intended as more popular versions of these highly professional texts.

Averroes knew the work of Plato, but he did not have the same admiration for him as he had for Aristotle, whose genius he regarded as the supreme expression of the human intellect. He did write a paraphrase of Plato's *Republic*—perhaps as a *faute de mieux* for Aristotle's *Politics*, which was then unavailable in Spain. He omitted some of the principal passages about Platonic Ideas, and he tweaked the book to make it closer to the *Nicomachean Ethics*. In general, he saw it as one of his tasks as a commentator to free Aristotle from Neoplatonic overlay, even though in fact he preserved more Platonic elements than he realized.

Averroes made little mark on his fellow Muslims, among whom his type of philosophy rapidly fell into disfavour. But his encyclopedic work was to prove the vehicle through which the interpretation of Aristotle was mediated to the Latin Middle Ages, and he set the agenda for some of the major thinkers of the thirteenth century. Dante gave him an honoured place in Limbo, and placed his Christian follower Siger of Brabant in heaven flanking St Thomas Aquinas. For Thomas himself, and for generations of Aristotelian scholars, Averroes was *the* Commentator.

Maimonides

Many features of Averroes' life are repeated in those of Maimonides (1138–1204). Both were born in Cordoba as sons of religious judges, both were

---

[23] Averroes' teaching on the intellect is described in detail in Ch. 7 below.

learned in law and medicine, and both lived a wandering life, dependent on the favour of princes and the vagaries of toleration. Driven from Cordoba by the fundamentalist Almohads when he was 13, Maimonides migrated with his parents to Fez and then to Acre, and finally settled in Cairo. There he was for five years president of the Jewish community, and from 1185 he was a court physician to the vizier of Saladin.

In his lifetime his fame was due principally to his rabbinic studies: he wrote a digest of the Torah, and drew up a definitive list of divine commandments (totalling not ten, but 613). But his lasting influence worldwide has been due to a book he wrote in Arabic late in life, the *Guide of the Perplexed*. This was designed to reconcile the apparent contradictions between philosophy and religion, which troubled educated believers. Biblical teaching and philosophical learning complement each other, he maintained; true knowledge of philosophy is necessary if one is to have full understanding of the Bible. Where the two appear to contradict each other, difficulties can be resolved by an allegorical interpretation of the sacred text.

Maimonides was candid in avowing his debt to Muslim and pagan philosophers. His interest in philosophy awoke early, and at the age of 16 he compiled a logical vocabulary under the influence of al-Farabi. Avicenna, too, he read, but found him less impressive. His greatest debt was to Aristotle, whose genius he regarded as the summit of purely human intelligence. But it was impossible to understand Aristotle, he wrote, without the help of the series of commentaries culminating in those of Averroes.

Maimonides' project for reconciling philosophy and religion depends on his heavily agnostic view of the nature of theology. We cannot say anything positive about God, since he has nothing in common with people like us: lacking matter and totally actual, immune from change and devoid of qualities, God is infinitely distant from creatures. He is a simple unity, and does not have distinct attributes such as justice and wisdom. When we attach predicates to the divine name, as when we say 'God is wise', we are really saying what God is *not*: we mean that God is not foolish. To seek to praise God by attaching laudatory human epithets to his name is like praising for his silver collection a monarch whose treasury is all gold.

The meaning of 'knowledge', the meaning of 'purpose' and the meaning of 'providence', when ascribed to us, are different from the meanings of these terms when ascribed to Him. When the two providences or knowledges or purposes are taken to have one and the same meaning, difficulties and doubts arise. When, on the other hand, it is known that everything that is ascribed to us is different from everything that is ascribed to him, truth becomes manifest. (*Guide*, 3. 20)[24]

We have no way of describing God, Maimonides maintained, except through negation. If we are not to fall into idolatry, we must explain as metaphor or allegory every anthropomorphic text in the Bible.

If religion and Aristotelianism are to be reconciled, concessions have to be made on both sides. To illustrate the way in which Maimonides carries out his reconciling project we may consider two instances: the doctrine of creation and the doctrine of providence. In the case of creation, it is Aristotle's cosmology that has to give way; in the case of providence, traditional piety must be taught sobriety.

As a believer in the Jewish doctrine that the world was created in time, Maimonides rejected Aristotle's conception of an eternal universe, and offered criticisms of philosophical arguments to show that time could have no beginning. But he did not believe that unaided reason could establish the truth of creation. Human beings cannot deduce the origin of the world from the world as it now is, any more than a man who had never met a female could work out how humans come into existence. Maimonides rejected Aristotle's view that the world consisted of fixed and necessary species. It is disgraceful to think, he says, that God could not lengthen the wing of a fly.

On the other hand, we should not think that God's governance of the universe is concerned with every individual event in the world: his providence concerns human beings individually, but it concerns other creatures only in general.

Divine providence watches only over the individuals belonging to the human species, and in this species alone all the circumstances of the individuals and the good and evil that befall them are consequent upon their deserts. But regarding all the other animals and, all the more, the plants and other things, my opinion is that of Aristotle. For I do not at all believe that this particular leaf has fallen because of a providence watching over it; nor that this spider has devoured this fly because God has now decreed and willed something concerning individuals.... For all this is in my opinion due to pure chance, just as Aristotle holds. (*Guide*, 3. 17)

[24] Trans. S. Pines, 2 vols. (Chicago: Chicago University Press, 1963).

Nonetheless, Maimonides' intention was orthodox and indeed devout. The aim of life, he insists, is to know, love, and imitate God. The prophet can learn more swiftly than the philosopher what little there is to be known about God. Knowledge should lead to love—a love that is expressed in the passionless imitation of divine action to be found in the lives of biblical prophets and lawgivers. Those who are neither prophets nor philosophers must be cajoled into well doing by stories that are less than true, such as that God answers prayers and is angered by sin.

Like Averroes, Maimonides fell foul of conservative believers who thought his interpretation of sacred texts blasphemous. Indeed some Jews in France tried to enlist the support of the Inquisition in trying to stamp out his heresies. But unlike Averroes, Maimonides after his death retained the interest and respect of his co-religionists as well as that of Latin Christians.

2

The Schoolmen:
From the Twelfth Century to the
Renaissance

In the twelfth century a series of devoted translators made a contribution to philosophy no less significant than that of the century's original thinkers. At the beginning of the century the only works of Aristotle known in Latin were the *Categories* and *De Interpretatione* in the translations of Boethius. Some twenty years later Boethius' translations of Aristotle's other logical works were recovered from virtual oblivion, and James of Venice translated the *Posterior Analytics* to complete the Latin *Organon*. By the middle of the century James had translated also the *Physics*, *De Anima*, and the early books of the *Metaphysics*, the rest of which was translated, with the exception of book 11, by an anonymous scholar. Only a portion of the *Nicomachean Ethics*, books 2 and 3 (the 'old Ethics'), was translated in the twelfth century.

In the second half of the century important philosophical texts were translated from the Arabic: works of al-Kindi, al-Farabi, al-Ghazali, and Ibn Gabirol, and substantial portions of Avicenna's great *Kitab-al-Shifa*. A number of other treatises also circulated in translation, often Neoplatonic works, under the name of Aristotle. Most important for the future history of Latin Aristotelianism was the translation of the major commentaries of Averroes into Latin, a gigantic task undertaken by Michael Scot from about 1220.

Early in the thirteenth century, therefore, philosophers had available to them a very substantial corpus of Aristotelian text and commentary. Many of these early translations were superseded by the work of later translators, particularly William of Moerbeke, who worked between 1260 and 1280 and whose versions were given canonical status through their use by Thomas Aquinas and other great scholastics. But already from the earliest decades of the century the influence of Aristotle was the dominant stimulus to the development of philosophy.

The thirteenth century was a time of uncommon intellectual energy and excitement. The context for this ferment of ideas was created by two innovations that occurred early in the century: the new universities and the new religious orders.

Bologna and Salerno have claims to be the oldest universities in Europe. Bologna celebrated its nine-hundredth anniversary in 1988 and Salerno was a flourishing institution in the mid-twelfth century. But Bologna had no permanent university buildings until 1565 and Salerno's academic glory quickly faded; moreover, both were specialized schools, concentrating on law and medicine respectively. It was at Paris and Oxford that the institution really took root, Paris receiving its charter in 1215 and Oxford having its status confirmed by a papal legate one year earlier.

The university is, in essentials, a thirteenth-century innovation, if by 'university' we mean a corporation of people engaged professionally, full-time, in the teaching and expansion of a corpus of knowledge in various subjects, handing it on to their pupils, with an agreed syllabus, agreed methods of teaching, and agreed professional standards. Universities and parliaments came into existence at roughly the same time, and have proved themselves the most long-lived of all medieval inventions.

A typical medieval university consisted of four faculties: the universal undergraduate faculty of arts, and the three higher faculties, linked to professions, of theology, law, and medicine. Students in the faculties learnt both by listening to lectures from their seniors and, as they progressed, by giving lectures to their juniors. A teacher licensed in one university could teach in any university, and graduates migrated freely in an age when all academics used Latin as a common language.

The teaching programme in the faculties was organized around set texts. It took some time to settle the canon in the arts faculty: in 1210 an edict at the University of Paris forbade any lectures on Aristotle's natural philosophy and ordered his texts to be burnt. But though reinforced by papal bulls, the condemnation seems to have quickly become a dead letter, and by 1255 not only Aristotle's physics, but his metaphysics and ethics, and indeed all his known works, became compulsory parts of the syllabus. In theology the text on which lectures were based, in addition to the Bible, was the *Sentences* of Peter Lombard. The lawyers took as their core text Justinian's codification of Roman law or Gratian's *Decretals*. In the medical faculties the set texts varied from university to university. The boundaries between the faculties are not necessarily what someone familiar with modern universities would expect. Material which we would nowadays consider philosophical is as likely to be found in the writings of medieval theologians as in the lectures that survive from the arts faculty.

For the intellectual life of the age, the foundation of the religious orders of mendicant friars, the Franciscans and the Dominicans, was no less important than the creation of the universities. St Francis of Assisi secured papal approval in 1210 for the rule he had laid down for his small community of poor, wandering preachers. St Dominic, a tireless fighter for orthodoxy, founded convents of nuns to pray and friars to preach against heresy: his order was approved by the Pope in 1216. Like the Franciscans ('Friars Minor', 'Grey Friars'), the Dominicans ('Friars Preachers', 'Black Friars') were to live on alms, but at the outset their ethos was less romantic and more scholarly than that of the Franciscans. However, after the first generation of wholly other-worldly friars, the Franciscans became just as successful academically as the Dominicans. By 1219 both orders were established in the University of Paris. The Black Friars arrived in Oxford in 1221 and the Grey Friars in 1224. By 1230 each order had founded a school there.

The roll-call of the great philosophers in the high Middle Ages is largely drawn from these two orders. Five of the most distinguished thinkers are St Albert, St Thomas Aquinas, St Bonaventure, John Duns Scotus, and William Ockham. Of these the first two are Dominicans and the last three Franciscans. Only in the fourteenth century, with John Wyclif, do we meet a philosopher of comparable talent who was a member of the secular (parish) clergy rather than a friar. Wyclif's eventual lapse from orthodoxy made him, in the minds of ecclesiastical historians of philosophy, a doubtful exception to the rule that it was thinkers of the religious orders who enjoyed pre-eminence.

This fresco from the upper church of St Francis in Assisi shows Pope Innocent III
approving the rule of the Fransciscan Order.

Robert Grosseteste and Albert the Great

The three innovating impulses of the thirteenth century—the reception of
Aristotle, the development of the universities, and the influence of the
mendicant orders—can all be seen at work in the career of a remarkable
Englishman, Robert Grosseteste, (1170?–1253), who became bishop of Lin-
coln in 1235. He studied at Oxford and was one of the first chancellors of
that university. From 1225 to 1230 he taught in the Oxford schools. In 1230
he moved to the newly founded Franciscan house and was lecturer there
for five years before his appointment to the episcopate. Besides writing a
number of original philosophical and scientific works, he composed the
first commentary on the Latin version of Aristotle's *Posterior Analytics*, and
comparatively late in life he learnt Greek and made his own translation of
the *Nicomachean Ethics*.

Grosseteste belonged to a generation earlier than the great thirteenth-century scholastics, and in the opinion of many scholars he holds a more important place in the history of science than in the history of philosophy. In working on the *Analytics* he became aware of difficulties with the Aristotelian concept of science as a corpus of demonstrated necessary truths. Among Aristotle's favourite topics are eclipses of the moon. How can there be necessary truths about them, since they are comparatively rare events? Grosseteste replies that the necessary truths are of a conditional form—if the sun and the earth are in such-and-such positions, then there will be an eclipse. More importantly, he suggests that some of these conditional truths are established by experiment, not by deduction. You observe that eating the root of a certain type of convolvulus is followed by the passing of red bile. To establish with certainty that this plant really is a purgative, you have to feed it repeatedly to patients while screening out other possible purgatives (*CPA* 214–15, 252–71).

On the basis of this and other passages, Grosseteste has been hailed as the father of experimental science in western Europe. Undoubtedly he had considerable scientific curiosity, which he displays in discussing phenomena that occur in Aristotle's text only as examples—the falling of autumn leaves, the twinkling of the stars, the cause of thunder, the flooding of the Nile. He also wrote independent treatises on astronomy and meteorology (*The Sphere, On Comets*), and in his theological commentary on Genesis (*Hexaemeron*) he takes many opportunities to display knowledge of natural history. Medieval legend, indeed, credited him with magical powers, such as making a robot that could answer difficult questions, and riding a horse to Rome in a single night. Both the medieval gossip and the modern plaudits seem exaggerated. In his overall view of the nature of human scientific endeavour, as laid out in his commentary on the *Analytics*, Grosseteste was closer to Augustine than to either Paracelsus or Francis Bacon.

There are, he says, five types of universal with which human knowledge is concerned. The first are eternal reasons in the mind of God. (Plato called these 'Ideas', but the notion that they are separate substances is a misbegotten error.) Secondly, there are forms that God impresses on the minds of angels: these, like Platonic Ideas, serve as paradigms, or examples, for creaturely activity. Thirdly, objects on earth have *rationes causales* in the heavenly spheres: stellar and planetary forms operate in causal fashion to bring about sublunar effects. Fourthly, there are the forms that belong to earthly substances, collocating them in their species and genera. Fifthly, there are the accidental forms of objects, which provide information about the substances in which they inhere (*CPA* 224, 142–8).

The close interweaving of science and metaphysics is displayed clearly in one of Grosseteste's most original contributions, his theory of light, expounded in the *Hexaemeron* and also in a separate treatise, *On Light*. Light, he maintained, was the first corporeal form to be created: it unites with prime matter to form a simple dimensionless substance. In the first moment of time this simple substance spread instantaneously to the furthest bounds of the universe, creating tridimensionality. From the outermost sphere, the firmament, it returned inward, creating one after the other nine celestial spheres, of which the ninth is the sphere of the moon. From this sphere light travelled earthward, and produced four terrestrial spheres of fire, air, water, and earth as it moved to our world, where it produced the four familiar elements.

So far we have a physical theory; but Grosseteste at once moves into theology. Light is the natural essence that most closely imitates the divine nature: like God it can create, unaided, from within itself; like God it can fill the universe from a single point (*Hex.* 8. 4. 7). Of all creatures it is the closest to being pure form and pure act (*Hex.* 11. 2. 4). Indeed God himself is eternal light, and the angels are incorporeal lights; God is a universal form of everything, not by uniting with matter, but as the exemplar of all forms. It is only by the light of God, the supreme Truth, that the human intellect can attain to truth of any kind.

Metaphysics and science are intermingled also in the work of Albert the Great, the first German philosopher. In his work, however, science occupies a more substantial proportion. Born in Swabia in the first years of the thirteenth century, Albert studied arts in Padua and became a Dominican in 1223. He taught theology at Paris from 1245 to 1248, having among his pupils the young Thomas Aquinas, whom he took with him to Cologne in 1248 to establish a new house of studies. Thenceforth Cologne was his principal base until his death in 1280, though he moved around as provincial of the German Dominicans (1254–7), bishop of Ratisbon (1260–2), and preacher of St Louis IX's crusade.

Albert was the first of the scholastics to give a wholehearted welcome to the newly translated works of Aristotle. After commenting, as a theologian, on Lombard's *Sentences*, he wrote commentaries on Aristotle's *Ethics*,

De Anima, and *Metaphysics*—lengthy paraphrases in the manner of Avicenna, rather than line-by-line exegesis in the style of Averroes. He was the author of the first Latin commentary on Aristotle's *Politics*. Albert was a copious writer and the critical edition of his works is still in progress; the previous complete edition extended to thirty-eight volumes. He read widely in Greek, Arabic, and Jewish authors, and acquired an encyclopedic know-ledge of previous learning. His mind was capacious rather than precise, and—despite the warnings of his pupil Aquinas—he accepted as genuine several pseudo-Aristotelian works, such as the *Liber de Causis*, which meant that his Aristotelianism retained a Neoplatonic tinge.

Unlike later medieval Aristotelians, Albert shared Aristotle's own inter-est in the empirical and experimental observation of nature. He wrote treatises on vegetables, plants, and animals, and a geographical text entitled *On the Nature of Places*. His enthusiasm for scientific inquiry, uncommon among his peers, led to his acquiring—like Grosseteste—a posthumous reputation as an alchemist and magician. A number of spurious and curious works were attributed to him, such as *The Secrets of Women* and *The Secrets of the Egyptians*.

St Bonaventure

Just as the Franciscan order had initially been more mystical and less scholastic than the Dominican order, so the first great Franciscan philoso-pher was more Augustinian and less Aristotelian than the Dominican Albert. John of Fidanza, the son of an Italian physician, was born near Viterbo in 1221. As a young child he fell ill, and when he recovered his cure was attributed by his family to St Francis. His name was changed to Bonaventure and he joined the Franciscans around 1240.

In 1243 Bonaventure went to Paris, and studied under Alexander of Hales, an English secular priest who had joined the Franciscans while already a professor. Alexander became the first head of the Franciscan school, and it was he who first introduced the *Sentences* of Peter Lombard as the standard theological textbook. He composed himself, with considerable assistance from his pupils, a vast *Summa Halesiana*, a theological synthesis that exhibits knowledge of the whole Aristotelian corpus; it was itself often used as a textbook by later Franciscans after his death in 1245.

Bonaventure received his licence to teach in 1248 and wrote his own commentary on the *Sentences*; he became head of the Paris Franciscans in 1253, though troubles in the university made it difficult for him to exercise his office. During this period he wrote a textbook of theology called *Breviloquium*. Four years later he was made minister-general of the whole order, and was faced with the delicate task of reconciling the different factions who, since St Francis' death, claimed to be the true perpetuators of the Franciscan spirit. He reunited and reorganized the order and wrote two lives of St Francis, one of which he imposed as the sole official biography, ordering all others to be destroyed. Not every Franciscan, of course, welcomed his reforms: 'Paris, you destroy Assisi', objected one dissident. But it would be quite wrong to see Bonaventure as primarily an academic and an administrator. In the middle of his troubles as minister-general he wrote a devout mystical treatise, *The Journey of the Mind to God*, the book by which he is nowadays best known. It presents itself as an interpretation of the vision of St Francis on Monte Alvernia, where he received the stigmata, the impression of the wounds of Christ.

Bonaventure's administrative gifts were widely admired, and in 1265 he was chosen by the Pope to be archbishop of York. He begged to be excused, thus depriving that see of its chance to compete in the history of philosophy with Canterbury's St Anselm. He was unable, however, to decline appointment in 1273 as cardinal bishop of Albano. In that year he wrote his last work, *Collationes in Hexameron*, dealing with the biblical account of creation. A year later he died at the Council of Lyons, having preached there the sermon that marked the (short-lived) reunion of the Churches of East and West.

In his writings Bonaventure, unusually for the Latin Middle Ages, presents himself explicitly as a Platonist. Aristotle's criticisms of Plato's Theory of Ideas, he believes, are quite easily refuted. From the initial error of rejecting the Ideas there follow all the other erroneous theses of Aristotelianism: that there is no providence, that the world is eternal, that there is only a single intellect, that there is no personal immortality, and therefore no heaven and no hell (*CH*, vision III. 7). Bonaventure did not, however, believe that Ideas existed outside the divine mind; they were 'eternal reasons', exemplars on which creaturely existence was patterned. These, and not the material objects in the natural world, are the primary objects of human knowledge.

In Bonaventure's writing, as in Grosseteste's, the notion of light plays a central role. There are four different lights that illumine the soul. The first, inferior, light consists in mechanical skill. This appears to be 'light' only in metaphor. Next, there is the light of sense-perception: and here we go beyond metaphor. Each sense is a recipient of light at a different degree of intensity: sight takes it in pure, hearing takes it in mixed with air, taste takes it in mixed with fluid, and so on. Thirdly, there is the light that guides us in the search of intellectual truth: this light illumines the three domains of philosophy: logic, physics, and ethics. Finally, the supreme light enables the mind to understand saving truth: this is the light of Scripture. Like Augustine, Bonaventure is fond of number symbolism, and he points out that if one counts each branch of philosophy as a separate light, then the number of these lights adds up to six, which corresponds to the six days of creation. 'There are in this life six illuminations, and each has its twilight, for all science will be destroyed: for that reason too there follows a seventh day of rest, a day which knows no evening, the illumination of glory' (PMA 461–7).

Only in another life, when the blessed see God face to face, will the human mind be directly acquainted with the eternal reasons, the Ideas in the mind of God. But in the present life we acquire knowledge of necessary and eternal truths through their reflected light, just as our eyes see everything by the light of the sun though they cannot look on the sun itself. We do acquire knowledge of a kind through the senses and experience, but the created light of the human intellect is not sufficient to reach any certainty about things. To attain the real truth about anything whatever we need in addition a special divine illumination (II Sent. 30. 1; Sermo IV. 10. V). Knowledge and faith can reside alongside each other in the same person.[1]

Bonaventure is familiar with the work of Aristotle, but he engages with him principally in order to refute his errors. It was impossible, he thought, to accept both that the world was created and that it had existed from all eternity: accordingly, he proposed a series of arguments, similar to those used by Philoponus and the Kalam theologians, to prove that the world had a beginning in time (II Sent. 1. 1. 1. 2. 1–3). Bonaventure accepted Aristotle's distinction between the agent and the receptive intellect but

---

[1] Bonaventure's teaching on the relation between faith and reason is described in more detail below in Ch. 4.

maintained that each of these were faculties of the individual human being. The tasks which Aristotle's Arabic commentators had assigned to the unique separate agent intellect are performed, in Bonaventure's system, by God's direct illumination. Since each human person has an individual intellectual capacity, each of us is personally immortal and will be held responsible after our death for our deeds in this life.

Bonaventure accepted Aristotelian hylomorphism and accepted that the human soul was the form of the human body. He uses this as an argument against Arabic monopsychism: 'since human bodies are distinct, the rational souls that inform those bodies will also be distinct' (*Brev.* 2. 9). Unlike Aristotle, however, and like Ibn Gabirol, he applies the structure of hylomorphism to the soul itself. Everything other than God, he maintained, is composed of matter and form; even angelic spirits who lack bodies contain 'spiritual matter'. Because Bonaventure accepted that the soul contained matter, he was able to reconcile the survival of individual disembodied souls with the commonly accepted thesis that matter was the principle of individuation. He thus avoided a difficulty that faced those, like Aquinas, who maintained that a disembodied soul was wholly immaterial; on the other hand, it is clear that the notion of 'spiritual matter' needs very careful explanation if it is not to be a plain contradiction in terms.

Thomas Aquinas

Thomas Aquinas was born into the feudal nobility of Italy at Roccasecca, probably in 1225. As a 5-year-old he was sent by his father to be brought up by the Benedictine monks of the great abbey of Monte Cassino. The abbey was on the borders between the Papal States and the Neapolitan kingdom of the emperor Frederick II, and Thomas' elementary studies came to an end in 1239 when its premises were occupied by troops in the course of a quarrel between Pope and emperor. After a period at home he studied the liberal arts at the newly founded University of Naples. Here he was introduced to Aristotelian logic and physics, studying under one Peter of Ireland.[2]

---

[2] My account of Aquinas' life depends heavily on J. Weisheipl, *Friar Thomas d'Aquino* (Oxford: Blackwell, 1974) and on J. P. Torrell, *Saint Thomas Aquinas*, i (Washington: Catholic University of America Press, 1996).

Aquinas the Dominican. In this fresco by Filippo Lippi in the Dominican church of Sta Maria sopra Minerva in Rome he is shown presenting a Dominican cardinal to the Virgin Mary.

In 1244 Thomas became a Dominican friar, to the irritation of his family, who had hoped he would follow the more socially acceptable vocation of a Benedictine monk. He hoped to escape from family pressure by migrating to Paris, but was kidnapped on the way and kept under house arrest for more than a year in one or other family castle. He employed his time in prison composing two brief logical treatises, a handbook on fallacies, and a fragment on modal propositions

The Aquino family failed to dent his resolve to be a friar. An attempt to seduce him by placing a prostitute in his cell only reinforced his determination to live a life of chastity: henceforth, his biographer tells us, he avoided women as a man avoids snakes. At length he was released, and he continued his journey to Paris. There he became a student of Albert the Great. The family made one more attempt to set him on a career path of their choice: they procured an offer from the Pope to allow him to be abbot of Monte Cassino while remaining a Dominican. Thomas refused and followed Albert to Cologne, where he listened to his lectures on Aristotle. As a student his taciturnity and corpulence earned him the nickname 'the dumb ox'. Albert quickly appreciated his astonishing talents, and predicted that the dumb ox would fill the whole world with his bellowing.

In 1252 Aquinas moved to Paris and began studying for the mastership in theology. As a bachelor he lectured on the Bible and on the *Sentences* of Peter Lombard. His commentary on the *Sentences* is the first of his major surviving works, and already displays his original genius. In the same period he wrote a pamphlet on Aristotelian metaphysics, much influenced by Avicenna, with the title *De Ente et Essentia* ('On Being and Essence'), which was to have an influence quite out of proportion to its size. He proceeded as master in theology in the year 1256.

The Dominican order controlled two of the twelve chairs of theology in Paris. Friars were unpopular with the traditional clergy, and the university had tried to suppress one of their chairs in 1252. In the ensuing controversy many professors went on strike, and Aquinas' first lectures as bachelor were given as a blackleg. But the chair survived, and Aquinas was appointed to it shortly after becoming master. At the time of his inaugural lecture anti-Dominican feeling was so high that the priory needed a permanent guard of royal troops. St Bonaventure and his Franciscans suffered similarly during the same period.

Aquinas remained in Paris for three years, lecturing on the book of Isaiah and the Gospel of St Matthew. As a professor it was his duty to oversee the formal disputations of the bachelors, and we possess the text of the disputations over which he presided, called, after the topic of the first of them, *Quaestiones Disputatae* ('Disputed Questions on Truth'). In fact they range over many different topics: truth and the knowledge of truth in God, angels, and men; providence and predestination; grace and justification; reason, conscience, and free will; emotion, trances, prophecy, education, and many other topics. The collection consists of 253 individual disputations, called 'articles' in the editions, and grouped by themes into twenty-nine 'questions'. The text of the series amounts to over half a million words.

In addition to these structured disputations the medieval curriculum imposed on masters the duty of undertaking a number of 'quodlibetical' disputations. These were impromptu discussions in which any member of the audience could raise a question on any topic. They were held in Advent and Lent: no doubt they were a penitential experience for the master. Of the quodlibets that survive from Aquinas' Paris period, some concern topical issues related to the controversy over the mendicant orders: for instance, the question 'Are friars obliged to perform manual labour?' Others are of less immediate impact, such as 'Are there real worms in hell?' A final legacy of this time is an unfinished commentary on Boethius' *On the Trinity*, which discusses the relationship between natural science, mathematics, and metaphysics, ranging these disciplines in a hierarchy of increasing abstraction from matter.

In 1259 Aquinas gave up his Paris professorship and spent some time in Italy. When Urban IV became pope in 1261, the papal court moved to Orvieto, and St Thomas went there too. During the early 1260s he was to be found teaching at Orvieto, Rome, and Viterbo, and mingling with the scholars, diplomats, and missionaries in attendance on the Pope. At the court of Urban IV he met William of Moerbeke, the most accurate of the translators of Aristotle, and began a fruitful association which was to result in a magnificent series of commentaries on the philosopher's major works. The saint was also employed by Pope Urban as a writer of prayers and hymns, especially for the liturgy of the new feast of Corpus Christi. This was instituted in 1264 in honour of the sacrament of the Eucharist, in which, according to Catholic belief, bread and wine were changed into the body and blood of Christ. The hymns which St Thomas wrote for the office remain popular among Catholics, and the sequence of the Mass, *Lauda Sion*, renders the doctrine of transubstantiation into surprisingly lively and singable verse.

The most important achievement of this middle period of St Thomas' life was the *Summa contra Gentiles*, begun just before the departure from Paris, and completed at Orvieto in 1265. Its title, literally translated, means 'Summary, or Synopsis, against Unbelievers'; its most frequently used English translation bears the title *On the Truth of the Catholic Faith*. According to a fourteenth-century tradition, now often discounted by scholars, the book was a missionary manual, written at the request of the Spanish Dominican Raymond of Penafort, who was evangelizing non-Christians in Spain and North Africa.

Whatever the truth of this story, the book differs from St Thomas' other major treatises in taking its initial stand (throughout the first three of its four books) not on Christian doctrine, but on philosophical premises that could be accepted by Jewish and Muslim thinkers versed in Aristotelian philosophy. Thomas explains his method thus:

Muslims and pagans do not agree with us in accepting the authority of any Scripture we might use in refuting them, in the way in which we can dispute against Jews by appeal to the Old Testament and against heretics by appeal to the New. These people accept neither. Hence we must have recourse to natural reason, to which all men are forced to assent. (*ScG* 1. 2)

Thus, the text is not a work of revealed theology, but of natural theology, which is a branch of philosophy.

The *Summa contra Gentiles* is a treatise, not a record of disputations; it is in four books of a hundred or so chapters each, amounting in total to some 300,000 words. The first book is about the nature of God, in so far as this is held to be knowable by reason unaided by revelation. The second concerns the created world and its production by God. The third expounds the way in which rational creatures are to find their happiness in God, and thus ranges widely over ethical matters. The fourth is devoted to specifically Christian doctrines such as the Trinity, the Incarnation, the sacraments, and the final resurrection of the saints through the power of Christ. In the first three books Aquinas is scrupulous to use biblical or ecclesiastical texts only as illustrations, never as premises from which the arguments start.

After the completion of the *Summa contra Gentiles* Aquinas went to Rome to establish a Dominican institute attached to the Church of Sta Sabina on the Aventine. While acting as regent master there it was once again his duty to preside over disputations. There are three groups of these, ten entitled *On the Power of God* (1265–6), and shorter series, *On Evil* (1266–7) and *On Spiritual Creatures*. These questions are in general less profound in content than the earlier ones entitled *On Truth*: this presumably reflects the fact that the students at a small house in Rome were not as sharp as those at the University of Paris. But the third of the questions on power, consisting of nineteen articles on the topic of creation, contains material of the highest interest. During the same period Thomas started, but never finished, a compendium of theology structured around the virtues of faith, hope, and charity.

It was in Rome that Aquinas began his magisterial series of commentaries on the works of Aristotle. The first was on the *De Anima*; after many further centuries of Aristotelian scholarship it is still regarded by experts as worth consulting. This was followed, at an uncertain date, by a commentary on the *Physics*. But the most important development of the Roman regency, which probably grew out of teaching experience there, was the commencement of Aquinas' masterpiece, the *Summa Theologiae*.

The *Summa Theologiae* is an immense work, of over 2 million words, divided into three parts; most of the first was probably written at Sta Sabina. In style, it falls between the *Summa contra Gentiles* and the *Disputed Questions*: it is not a record of live scholastic disputation, but it is, like a disputation, divided into questions and articles, not into chapters. However, the multiple arguments for and against a particular thesis that introduce a genuine disputation are replaced by an introductory set (usually a triad) of difficulties against the position that Aquinas intends to take up in the body of the article. This initial section is the *Videtur quod non* ('It seems not'). These objections are followed by a single consideration on the other side—usually the citation of an authoritative text—beginning with the words 'Sed contra' ('On the other hand'). After this, in the main body of the article, Aquinas sets out his own position with the reasons that support it. Each article then concludes with the solution of the difficulties set out in the introductory objections.

The method, while initially puzzling to a modern reader, provides a powerful intellectual discipline to prevent a philosopher from taking things for granted. By adopting it, St Thomas imposed on himself the question 'Whom have I got to convince of what, and what are the strongest things that can be said on the other side?'

To illustrate the structure of the *Summa* I quote one of its shortest articles, the tenth article of question nineteen of the First Part, which poses the question 'Does God have free will?'

It seems that God does not have free will.

1. St Jerome says, in his homily on the Prodigal Son, 'God is the only one who is not, and cannot be, involved in sin; all other things, since they have free will, can turn either way.'

2. Moreover, free will is the power of reason and will by which good and evil are chosen. But God, as has been said, never wills evil. Therefore, there is no free will in God.

But on the other hand, St Ambrose, in his book on Faith, says this: 'The Holy Spirit makes his gifts to individuals as he wills, in accordance with the choice of his free will, and not in observance of any necessity.'

I reply that it must be said that we have free will in regard to those things which we do not will by necessity or natural instinct. Our willing to be happy, for instance, is not a matter of free will but of natural instinct. For this reason, other animals, which are driven in certain directions by natural instinct, are not said to be directed by free will. Now God, as has been shown above, wills his own goodness of necessity, but other things not of necessity; hence, with regard to those things which he does not will of necessity, he enjoys free will.

To the first objection it must be said that St Jerome wants to exclude from God not free will altogether, but only the freedom which includes falling into sin.

To the second objection it must be said that since, as has been shown, moral evil is defined in terms of aversion from the divine goodness in respect of which God wills everything, it is clear that it is impossible for him to will moral evil. Nonetheless, he has an option between opposites, in so far as he can will something to be or not to be, just as we, without sinning, can decide to sit down or decide not to sit down. (*ST* 1. 19. 10)

In its own fashion, the *Summa Theologiae* is a masterpiece of philosophical writing. Once one has become accustomed to the syntax of medieval Latin and the technicalities of scholastic jargon one finds the style smooth, lucid, civil, and judicious. The work is almost entirely free from rhetoric, and Thomas never lets his own ego obtrude.

The First Part of the *Summa Theologiae* covers much of the same ground as the first two books of the *Summa contra Gentiles*. The first forty-three questions are concerned with the existence and nature of God. Since Thomas is writing for Catholic theology students rather than for a possibly infidel philosophical audience, he can present the doctrine of the Trinity immediately after listing the divine attributes, without having to segregate it in a special book on the mysteries of faith. But he remains careful to distinguish between truths discoverable by reason and truths available only through revelation. Five dense questions follow, dealing with the metaphysics of creation, and these are followed by fifteen questions on the nature of angels. The section on human nature (qq. 75–102) is, for a modern reader, the most rewarding part of the book.[3] It is fuller and more systematic than the corresponding section in the second book of the earlier work, and it is less heavily loaded with criticisms of Arabian exegesis of Aristotle's psychology.

While writing the First Part of the *Summa* St Thomas began a political treatise, *On Kingship*, laying down principles for the guidance of secular governments in a way that leaves no doubt that kings are subject to priests and that the pope enjoys a secular as well as a spiritual supremacy. Unfinished when Aquinas died, it was completed by the historian Tolomeo of Lucca.

In 1268, having declined an invitation to become archbishop of Naples, Aquinas was called back to Paris, where the mendicant orders were again an object of hostility. More importantly, Aristotelian ideas were being brought into disrepute by a group of arts professors, the 'Latin Averroists', who followed Arabic commentators to conclusions incompatible with Catholic orthodoxy. Aquinas wrote two polemical pamphlets, *On the Single Intellect:—Against the Averroists*, and *On the Eternity of the World:—Against the Grumblers*. He restated his long-held positions that both the agent and the receptive intellect are faculties of the individual person, and that the beginning of the world in time can be neither established nor refuted by philosophical argument. In this last treatise he was fighting on two fronts: both against the Averroists, who thought that creation in time could be disproved, and against Franciscan theologians, who thought it could be proved.

The controversies convinced Thomas that the best antidote to heterodox Aristotelianism was a thorough knowledge of the entire Aristotelian

---

[3] Aquinas' account of the human mind is described in detail in Ch. 6.

system, so he continued with his task of providing commentaries. Probably during this period he wrote line-by-line commentaries on two of Aristotle's logical works, on the entire *Nicomachean Ethics*, and on twelve books of the *Metaphysics*. Though based on an imperfect translation of defective manuscripts, these commentaries are still found valuable by modern interpreters of Aristotle.

But the most important of Aquinas' works during this second Paris regency was the Second Part of the *Summa Theologiae*. This, much the longest of the three parts, is always further divided in editions: the first part of the Second Part (*Prima Secundae*, cited as 1a 2ae) and the second part of the Second Part (*Secunda Secundae*, cited as 2a 2ae). This corresponds in subject matter to the third book of the *Summa contra Gentiles*, but it is very much fuller and owes much more to Aristotle's *Nicomachean Ethics*, on which Aquinas was simultaneously writing his commentary.[4]

The *Prima Secundae* begins, like Aristotle's treatise, by considering the ultimate end or goal of human life. Like Aristotle, Aquinas identifies the ultimate end with happiness, and like him he thinks that happiness cannot be equated with pleasure, riches, honour, or any bodily good, but must consist in activity in accordance with virtue, especially intellectual virtue. The intellectual activity that satisfies the Aristotelian requirements for happiness is to be found perfectly only in contemplation of the essence of God; happiness in the ordinary conditions of the present life must remain imperfect. True happiness, then, even in Aristotle's terms, is to be found only in the souls of the blessed in heaven. The saints will in due course receive a bonus of happiness, undreamt of by Aristotle, in the resurrection of the body in glory.

Virtue, according to Aristotle, was a psychic disposition that found expression in both action and emotion. Aquinas, accordingly, prefaces his account of virtue with a treatise on human action (qq. 6–21) and human emotion (qq. 22–48). He also offers a general study of the concept of disposition (*habitus*): an original philosophical investigation of a topic whose importance was lost sight of when philosophy became impoverished at the Renaissance. The account of the nature of virtue itself, of the distinction between moral and intellectual virtues, and of the relation between virtue and emotion, is modelled closely on Aristotle. But Aquinas

---

[4] Aquinas' ethical teaching is described in detail in Ch. 8.

adds to Aristotle's list of virtues some Christian virtues—the 'theological' virtues of faith, hope, and charity, listed as a trio in a famous passage of St Paul. Aquinas links Aristotelian virtues with the gifts of character prized by Christians, and connects Aristotelian vices with biblical concepts of sin.

The two final sections of the *Prima Secundae* concern law and grace. Questions 90–108 constitute a treatise on jurisprudence: the nature of law; the distinction between natural and positive law; the source and extent of the powers of human legislators; the contrast between the laws of the Old and New Testament. In questions 109–14 Aquinas treats of the relation between nature and grace, and the justification and salvation of sinners: topics that were to be the focus of much controversy at the time of the Reformation. The position he adopts on these issues stands somewhere between those later taken up by Catholic and Protestant controversialists.

The *Prima Secundae* is the General Part of Aquinas' ethics, while the *Secunda Secundae* contains his detailed teaching on individual moral topics. Each virtue is analysed in turn, and the sins listed that conflict with it. First come the theological virtues: thus faith is contrasted with the sins of unbelief, heresy, and apostasy. It is in the course of this section that Aquinas sets out his views on the persecution of heretics. The virtue of charity is contrasted with the sins of hatred, envy, discord, and sedition; in treating of these sins Aquinas sets out the conditions under which he believes the making of war is justified.

The other virtues are treated within the overarching framework of the four 'cardinal' virtues, prudence, justice, fortitude, and temperance, a quartet dating back to the early dialogues of Plato. The treatise on justice covers the topics that would nowadays appear in a textbook of criminal law; but one of the special branches of justice is piety, the virtue of giving God his due. Here Aquinas ranges widely over many topics, from tithe-paying to necromancy. The discussion of fortitude provides an opportunity to treat of martyrdom, magnanimity, and magnificence. The final cardinal virtue is temperance, the heading under which Aquinas treats of moral questions concerned with food, drink, and sex.

Aquinas' list of virtues does not altogether tally with Aristotle's, though he works hard to Christianize some of the more pagan characters who figure in the *Ethics*. Aristotle's ideal man is great-souled, that is to say, he is a highly superior being who is very conscious of his own superiority to others. How can this be reconciled with the Christian virtue of humility, according to which each should esteem others better than himself? By a remarkable piece of intellectual legerdemain, Aquinas makes magnanimity not only compatible with humility but part of the very same virtue. There is a virtue, he says, that is the moderation of ambition, a virtue based on a just appreciation of one's own gifts and defects. Humility is the aspect that ensures that one's ambitions are based on a just assessment of one's defects, magnanimity is the aspect that ensures that they are based on a just assessment of one's gifts.

The *Secunda Secundae* concludes, as did the *Nicomachean Ethics*, with a comparison between the active and the contemplative life, to the advantage of the latter. But the whole is, of course, transposed into a Christian key, and when Aquinas comes to discuss the religious orders he gives the Aristotelian theme a special Dominican twist. Whereas the purely contemplative life is to be preferred to the purely active life, the best life of all for a religious is a life of contemplation that includes teaching and preaching. 'Just as it is better to light up others than to shine alone, it is better to share the fruits of one's contemplation with others than to contemplate in solitude.'

Aquinas' second Paris regency was a period of amazing productivity. The Second Part and the Commentary on the *Metaphysics* are each nearly a million words in length. When one reviews the sheer bulk of Aquinas' output between 1269 and 1272 one can believe the testimony of his chief secretary that it was his habit to dictate, like a grand master at a chess tournament, to three or four secretaries simultaneously. The learned world can be grateful that the pressure of business forced him to compose by dictation, because his own autographs are quite illegible to any but the most highly trained specialists.

In 1272 Thomas left Paris for the last time. The Dominican order assigned him the task of setting up a new house of studies in Italy; he chose to attach it to the Priory of San Domenico in Naples. His lectures there were sponsored by the king of Naples, Charles of Anjou, whose brother St Louis IX had taken the measure of his genius in Paris. He continued to work on his Aristotle commentaries and began the Third Part of the *Summa*. This concerns strictly theological topics: the Incarnation, the Virgin Mary, the life of Christ, the sacraments of baptism, confirmation, Eucharist, and penance. But reflection on these topics gave Aquinas opportunity to discuss many philosophical issues, such as personal identity and individuation and the logic of predication. The treatise on the Eucharist, in particular, called for discussion of the doctrine of transubstantiation and thus for a final presentation of Aquinas' thought on the nature of material substance and substantial change.

The *Summa* was never completed. Though not yet 50, Aquinas became subject to ever more serious fits of abstraction, and in December 1273, while saying Mass, he had a mysterious experience—perhaps a mental breakdown, or, as he himself believed, a supernatural vision—which put an end to his academic activity. He could not continue to write or dictate, and when his secretary Reginald of Piperno urged him to continue with the *Summa*, he replied, 'I cannot, because all that I have written now seems like straw.' Reginald and his colleagues, after Aquinas' death, completed the *Summa* with a supplement, drawn from earlier writings, covering the topics left untreated: the remaining sacraments and the 'four last things', death, judgement, heaven, and hell.

In 1274 Pope Gregory X called a council of the Church at Lyons, hoping to reunite the Greek and Latin Churches. St Thomas was invited to attend, and in spite of his poor condition he set out northwards, but his health deteriorated further and he was forced to stop at his niece's castle near Fossanova. After some weeks he was carried into the nearby Cistercian monastery, where he died on 7 March 1274.

The Afterlife of Aquinas

In the centuries since his death Aquinas' reputation has fluctuated spectacularly. A few years after he died several of his opinions were condemned by the universities of Paris and Oxford. An English friar who travelled to Rome to appeal against the sentence was condemned to perpetual silence. It was some fifty years before Aquinas' writings were generally regarded as theologically sound.

In 1316, however, Pope John XXII began a process of canonization. It was hard to find suitable accounts of miracles. The best that could be found concerned a deathbed scene. At Fossanova the sick man, long unable to eat, expressed a wish for herrings. These were not to be found in the Mediterranean: but surprisingly, in the next consignment of sardines, a batch of fish turned up which Thomas was happy to accept as delicious herrings. The Pope's judges did not find this a sufficiently impressive miracle. But the canonization went ahead. 'There are as many miracles as there are articles

Charles of Anjou, who sponsored Aquinas in his last academic post, at the University of Naples. According to a legend, believed by Dante, he found the Saint politically unreliable and had him poisoned.

of the *Summa*,' the Pope is reported to have said; and he declared Thomas a saint in 1323.

Paris, rather belatedly, revoked the condemnation of his works in 1325. Oxford, however, seems to have taken no academic notice of the canonization, and throughout the Middle Ages Aquinas did not enjoy, outside his own order, the special prestige among Catholic theologians that he was to enjoy in the twentieth century. True, the *Summa* was set in a place of honour, beside the Bible, during the deliberations of the Council of Trent; but it was not until the encyclical letter *Aeterni Patris* of Pope Leo XIII in 1879 that he was made, as it were, the official theologian of the whole Roman Catholic Church.

All those who study Aquinas are indebted to Pope Leo for the stimulus which his encyclical gave to the production of scholarly editions of the *Summa* and of other works. But the promotion of the saint as the official philosopher of the Church had also a negative effect. It closed off the philosophical study of St Thomas by non-Catholic philosophers, who were repelled by someone whom they came to think of as simply the spokesman of a particular ecclesiastical system. The problem was aggravated when in 1914 Pius X singled out twenty-four theses of Thomist philosophy to be taught in Catholic institutions.

The secular reaction to the canonization of St Thomas' philosophy was summed up by Bertrand Russell in his *History of Western Philosophy*. 'There was little of the true philosophical spirit in Aquinas: he could not, like Socrates, follow an argument wherever it might lead, since he knew the truth in advance, all declared in the Catholic faith. The finding of arguments for a conclusion given in advance is not philosophy but special pleading.'

It is not in fact a serious charge against a philosopher to say that he is looking for good reasons for what he already believes in. Descartes, sitting beside his fire, wearing his dressing gown, sought reasons for judging that that was what he was doing, and took a long time to find them. Russell himself spent much energy seeking proofs of what he already believed: *Principia Mathematica* takes hundreds of pages to prove that 1 and 1 make 2.

We judge a philosopher by whether his reasonings are sound or unsound, not by where he first lighted on his premises or how he first came to believe his conclusions. Hostility to Aquinas on the basis of his official position in Catholicism is thus unjustified, however understandable, even for secular philosophers. But there were more serious ways in which the actions of Leo XIII and Pius X did a disservice to Thomas' philosophical reputation in non-Catholic circles.

The official respect accorded to Aquinas by the Church meant that his insights and arguments were frequently presented in crude ways by admirers who failed to appreciate his philosophical sophistication. Even in seminaries and universities the Thomism introduced by Leo XIII often took the form of textbooks and epitomes *ad mentem Thomae* rather than a study of the text of the saint himself.

Since the Second Vatican Council, St Thomas seems to have lost the pre-eminent favour he enjoyed in ecclesiastical circles, and to have been superseded, in the reading lists of ordinands, by lesser, more recent authors. This state of affairs is deplored by Pope John Paul in *Fides et Ratio*, the most recent papal encyclical devoted to Aquinas. On the other hand, the devaluation of St Thomas within the bounds of Catholicism has been accompanied by a re-evaluation of the saint in secular universities in various parts of the world. In the first years of the twenty-first century it is not too much to speak of a renaissance of Thomism—not a confessional Thomism, but a study of Thomas that transcends the limits not only of the Catholic Church but of Christianity itself.

The new interest in Aquinas is both more varied and more critical than the earlier, denominational reception of his work. The possibility of very divergent interpretations is inherent in the nature of Aquinas' *Nachlass*. The saint's output was vast—well over 8 million words—so that any modern study of his work is bound to concentrate only on a small portion of the surviving corpus. Even if one concentrates—as scholars commonly do— on one or other of the great *Summae*, the interpretation of any portion of these works will depend in part on which of many parallel passages in other works one chooses to cast light on the text under study. Especially now that the whole corpus is searchable by computer, there is great scope for selectivity here.

Secondly, though Aquinas' Latin is in itself marvellously lucid, the translation of it into English is not a trivial or uncontroversial matter. Aquinas' Latin terms have English equivalents that are common terms in contemporary philosophy; but the meanings of the Latin terms and their English equivalents are often very different.[5] Not only have the English

---

[5] This is a point well emphasized by Eleonore Stump in her *Aquinas* (London: Routledge, 2003), 35.

words come to us after centuries of independent history, they entered the language from Latin at a date when their philosophical usage had been influenced by theories opposed to Aquinas' own. We must be wary of assuming, for instance, that 'actus' means 'act' or that 'objectum' means 'object', or that 'habitus' means 'habit'.

Thirdly, in the case of a writer such as Plato or Aristotle, it is often possible for an interpreter to clear up ambiguities in discussion by concentrating on the concrete examples offered to illustrate the philosophical point. But Aquinas—in common with other great medieval scholastics—is very sparing with illustrative examples, and when he does offer them they are often second-hand or worn out. A commentator, therefore, in order to render the text intelligible to a modern reader, has to provide her own examples, and the choice of examples involves a substantial degree of interpretation.

Finally, any admirer of Aquinas' genius wishes to present his work to a modern audience in the best possible light. But what it is for an interpreter to do his best for Aquinas depends upon what he himself regards as particularly valuable in philosophy. In particular, there is a fundamental ambiguity in Aquinas' thinking that lies at the root of the philosophical disagreements among his commentators. Aquinas is best known as the man who reconciled Christianity with Aristotelianism; but, as we shall see in later chapters, there are considerable elements of Platonism to be found in his writings. Many modern commentators take Aquinas' Aristotelianism seriously and disown the Platonic residues, but there are those who side with the Platonic Thomas against the Aristotelian Thomas. The motive for this may be theological: such an approach makes it easier to accept the doctrines that the soul survives the death of the body, that angels are pure forms, and that God is pure actuality. Aquinas himself, in fact, was an Aristotelian on earth, but a Platonist in heaven.

For those who are more interested in philosophy than in history, the variety of interpretations of Aquinas on offer is something to be welcomed. His own approach to the writings of his predecessors was in general extremely irenic: rather than attack a proposition that on the face of it was quite erroneous, he sought to tease out of it—by 'benign interpretation' often beyond the bounds of historical probability—a thesis that was true or a sentiment that was correct. His capacious welcome to a motley of Greek, Jewish, and Muslim texts both opens to his successors the possibility of widely divergent interpretations of his work, and encourages them to follow his example in valuing the ecumenical pursuit of philosophical truth higher than utter fidelity to critical plausibility.

Siger of Brabant and Roger Bacon

In the decades immediately after his death, Aquinas had few faithful followers. Late in life he had devoted much energy in combating a radical form of Aristotelianism in the arts faculty at Paris. These philosophers maintained that the world had always existed and that there was only a single intellect in all human beings. The former was undoubtedly a fundamental part of the cosmology of Aristotle; the latter was the interpretation of his psychology favoured by his most authoritative commentator, Averroes. For this reason the school has often been called 'Latin Averroism': its leading spokesman was Siger of Brabant (1235–82). The characteristic teachings of these Parisian scholastics were difficult to reconcile with the Christian doctrines of a creation at a date in time and a future life for individual human souls. Some claimed merely to be reporting, without commitment, the teaching of Aristotle; Siger himself seems to have taught at one time that some propositions of Aristotle and Averroes are provable in philosophy, though faith teaches the opposite.

In 1270 the archbishop of Paris condemned a list of thirteen doctrines beginning with the proposition 'the intellect of all men is one and numerically the same' and 'there never was a first man'. The condemnation may have been the result partly of the two monographs that Aquinas had written against Siger's characteristic doctrines. But despite this dispute between them, the two thinkers were often grouped together in the minds of their younger contemporaries. On the one hand, sets of propositions were condemned in Paris and Oxford in 1277 that included theses drawn from both Siger and Aquinas. On the other hand, Dante places the two of them side by side in Paradise and makes St Thomas praise Siger for the eternal light that is cast by the profundity of his thought. This compliment has puzzled commentators; but perhaps Dante thought of Siger as a representative of the contribution made by pagan and Muslim thinkers to the Thomist synthesis, a Christian thinker standing in for the unbelieving philosophers who were barred from Paradise.

Dante himself, though professionally untrained, was well versed in philosophy, and the *Divina Commedia* often renders scholastic doctrines into exquisite verse. For instance, the account of the gradual development of the human soul in *Purgatorio* 25 is extremely close to the account given in Aquinas' *Summa Theologiae*. Dante's own most substantive contribution to philosophy is his book *On Monarchy*. This argues that human intellectual development can only take place in conditions of peace, which, in a world of national rivalries, can only be achieved under a supranational authority. This, he argues, should not be the pope, but the Holy Roman emperor.

An older contemporary of Dante was Roger Bacon, who outlived Siger by some ten years. Born in Ilchester about 1210, he studied and taught in the Oxford arts faculty until about 1247. He then migrated to Paris, and in the next decade joined the Franciscan order. He disliked Paris and compared the Parisian doctors Alexander of Hales and Albert the Great unfavourably with his Oxford teacher Robert Grosseteste. The only Parisian doctor he admired was one Peter of Maricourt, who taught him the importance of experiment in scientific research, and led him to believe that mathematics was 'the door and key' to certainty in philosophy. For reasons unknown, in 1257 he was forbidden by his Franciscan superiors to teach; but he was allowed to continue to write and in 1266 the Pope, no less, asked him to send him his writings. Sadly, this pope, Clement IV, did not live long enough to read the texts, and Bacon was condemned in 1278 for heretical views on astrology, and lived out most of the rest of his life in prison, dying in 1292.

Roger Bacon is often considered a precursor of his seventeenth-century namesake Francis Bacon in his emphasis on the role of experiment in philosophy. In his main work, the *opus maius*, Roger, like Francis, attacks the sources of error: deference to authority, blind habit, popular prejudice, and pretence to superior wisdom. There are two essential preliminaries, he says, to scientific research. One is a serious study of the languages of the ancients—the current Latin translations of Aristotle and the Bible are seriously defective. The other is a real knowledge of mathematics, without which no progress can be made in sciences like astronomy. Bacon's own contribution to science focused on optics, where he followed up some of the insights of Grosseteste. It was, indeed, at one time believed that he was the first inventor of the telescope.

Bacon identifies a distinct kind of science, *scientia experimentalis*. A priori reasoning may lead us to a correct conclusion, he says, but only experience

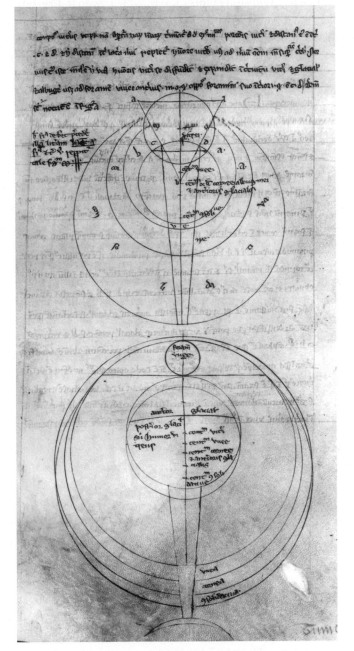

The mechanics of vision, as portrayed by Roger Bacon.

gives us certainty. Aristotelian physics may teach that fire burns, but it is the child that is actually burnt that dreads the fire. Experiment can also take us beyond the demonstrated conclusions of the scientific disciplines, as we can see if we consider the pharmacopoeia built up by the experience of practical physicians. Constructing a model of the heavens, like an astrolabe, can teach us more things about them than deductive science can.

Though Bacon believed in the possibility of the alchemical transmutation of baser metals into gold, and saw the ability to foretell the future and to work wonders as being one of the rewards of scientific research, he made a sharp distinction between science and magic. Indeed he thought that one reason for taking up science was in order to refute the false claims made for the magical arts. But before one salutes him as a protagonist in any war between science and mysticism, it is important to remember that among the 'experience' to which he attached such importance in philosophy he includes religious visions and mystical states of rapture.

Roger Bacon was one of a distinguished trio of Franciscan thinkers who graced Oxford in the thirteenth and fourteenth centuries, the other two being John Duns Scotus and William Ockham. The three are very different from each other, as we shall see, so that it would be quite wrong to think of Oxford as the home of a particular Franciscan school of thought. But all three of them had an influence that was to extend far beyond Oxford or England.

Duns Scotus

Of all the great philosophers, John Duns Scotus is the one whose life is least known and whose biography rests almost entirely on conjecture. Any account of his career has to be based on just four firm dates for which there is documentary evidence: on 17 March 1291 he was ordained priest at Northampton; on 26 July 1300 he was at Oxford, as a Franciscan friar, unsuccessfully seeking a licence to hear confessions; on 18 November 1304 he was commended by the Franciscan minister-general for a position of authority in Paris; on 30 February 1308 he was a lector in theology at Cologne. Even the date of his death is uncertain; the date traditionally given is 8 November 1308.

From these fragments of evidence scholars have built up skeleton biographies: what follows is only one of several possible reconstructions.[6] John was born, we are told, at Duns, a town on the Scottish border a few miles inland from Berwick upon Tweed. Working back from his ordination, we can guess a birth date of early 1266. Some time in his teens he seems to have become a novice in the Franciscan house at Dumfries, under his uncle Elias Duns, head of the Scottish friars who had recently achieved a degree of self-government under the English branch of the order. During the 1280s he was sent to Oxford, where he studied philosophy in the Franciscan house, Greyfriars, which was already large enough to contain some seventy students. Scotus began theological studies in the university in 1288: the course lasted thirteen years and culminated with three years of obligatory lecturing, two on the *Sentences* of Peter Lombard and one on the Bible. In 1300–1 he obtained his baccalaureate in theology, a status equivalent to that of assistant professor.

For reasons that can only be guessed, the Franciscan authorities decided that instead of taking an Oxford doctorate Scotus should go as a bachelor to Paris. Possibly he had shown such brilliance as a lecturer that they felt he should be given a chance to shine in the premier university of the age— one with which Oxford was only just now catching up. However, the Franciscan convent in Paris, home of Alexander of Hales and Bonaventure, did not provide a peaceful environment. After a year of lecturing on the *Sentences*, Scotus, along with eighty other friars, was banished from France for supporting the papal side in the dispute between Philip the Fair and Boniface VIII.[7] He left in June 1303, and returned to England, spending some time at Cambridge, where there was a Franciscan graduate house.

After the death of Pope Boniface in late 1303 relations between the Holy See and the French kingdom improved, and the ban on the Franciscans was revoked. Scotus returned to Paris, completed his lecture series on the *Sentences*, proceeded to his doctorate, and was regent master during the year 1306–7. Once again he was forced to leave Paris at a time of political unrest, and he spent the last year of his life—the forty-second—at Cologne. He died there and was buried in the Franciscan church with the

---

[6] My account of Scotus' life owes much to a detailed study, sadly still unpublished, by Antoon Vos.

[7] Perhaps best known through Dante's account of the French mistreatment of Boniface in Anagni (*Purgatorio*, 20).

epitaph 'Scotland bore me | England taught me | France received me | Cologne now keeps me'. He was beatified by Pope John Paul II in 1993.

Many manuscripts of Scotus' writings survive, but their nature and order present as much of an enigma as the details of his biography. Most of them were in a fragmentary and incomplete form at the time of his death, and they were collected and polished by the devoted labours of disciples over several generations. The canon thus established was published in twelve volumes by Luke Wadding in 1639, an edition republished in 1891–5 by the Paris firm of Vives. The centrepieces of this edition were two commentaries on the *Sentences*, entitled *Opus Oxoniense* and *Reportata Parisiensia*; the collection also contained a series of commentaries on Aristotle, a set of quodlibetical questions, and a number of monographs, notably *De Rerum Principio*, *De Primo Principio*, and *Grammatica Speculativa*. Scholars were dependent on the Vives–Wadding edition until the latter part of the twentieth century, and it still provides the only printed text for a number of Scotus' works.

The work of scholars in the twentieth century, however, has completely refashioned the canon. Most of the commentaries on Aristotle turned out to be the work of other, later, hands. There remain, as authentic, commentaries on the *Categories*, the *De Interpretatione*, and the *Sophistici Elenchi*, plus a commentary on Porphyry. These logical works most probably date from Scotus' first period in Oxford in the early 1290s.[8] So too do a set of questions on Aristotle's *De Anima*, and probably a commentary on the *Metaphysics*, though this appears to have undergone revision quite late in Scotus' career. Two of the most heavily studied monographs in the Vives–Wadding edition, the *De Rerum Principio* and the *Grammatica Speculativa*, turned out, on critical inspection, to be inauthentic.

In the mid-1920s manuscripts were discovered of a text which, after some controversy, is now accepted as Scotus' own notes for his lectures on the first two books of the *Sentences* in Oxford in the years 1298–1300. In 1938 the Franciscan order set up a scholarly commission in Rome to produce a critical edition of Scotus' works, and between 1950 and 1993 this important text was published by the Vatican Press under the title *Lectura I–II*. *Lectura III*, published in 2003, is most probably the course given by Scotus during his

---

[8] The philosophical works of Scotus are being published, since 1999, in a critical edition by a team of editors operating first in St Bonaventure, NY, and later at the Catholic University of America in Washington DC.

period in Oxford during exile from Paris in 1303. The text previously known as the *Opus Oxoniense* is now seen as consisting of elements from an ongoing revision of this course, which continued throughout the Paris years. The *Reportata Parisiensia* bears testimony to a late stage of the revision from the hands of students attending the lectures. The definitive form of a medieval lecture course was attained when the lecturer compared his own drafts with his students' notes, and incorporated the material into a single, approved, text known as an *Ordinatio*. The publication of the *Ordinatio* never finally retouched by Scotus himself—has been the major task of the Scotist Commission. Between 1950 and 2001 seven volumes of this critical edition appeared, completing the commentary on *Sentences* I–II. For *Ordinatio III* and *IV* scholars still rely on the last two books of the *Opus Oxoniense* as printed by Wadding.

The Vatican editions of the *Lectura* and *Ordinatio* are the main point of reference for the study of Scotus by present-day philosophers and theologians. But two works of uncontested authenticity provide evidence of Scotus' mature thought. The quodlibetical questions undoubtedly belong to the brief period when Scotus was regent master in Paris, in 1306 or 1307. The brief monograph *De Primo Principio*, published in several editions since 1941, belongs to the last period of his life, and some scholars believe that it was written in Cologne in the year of his death. Finally, the genuineness of a work entitled *Theoremata* is still the object of scholarly dispute. The balance of opinion now seems in favour of authenticity, but if the work is genuine it testifies to a remarkable volte-face by Scotus on an important topic, the question whether God's existence can be proved by the natural light of reason.

Scotus is not an easy author to read. His language is crabbed, technical, and unaccommodating, and the structure of his arguments is often difficult to discern. He had, however, one of the sharpest minds ever to have engaged in philosophy, and he well deserved his sobriquet 'the subtle doctor'. In his brief academic career he altered the direction of philosophical thinking in many areas and set it on new courses to be followed for centuries.

On many major issues Scotus took the opposite side to Aquinas. In his own mind, if not in the light of history, equal importance attached to his disagreements with another of his seniors, Henry of Ghent. Henry taught at Paris from 1276 to 1292 and defended many of the ideas of Augustinian Neoplatonism against the radical Aristotelianism of some of the arts faculty. Scotus often situated his own positions in relation to Henry's stance, and it was through Henry's eyes that he viewed many of his predecessors.

Scotus broke with the Aristotelian tradition by maintaining that the concepts of being and of other universally applicable predicates such as 'good' were not analogous but univocal, and could be used about God in exactly the same sense as about creatures.[9] Metaphysics was the science that studied the univocal concept of being and its fundamental properties. Aristotle had defined metaphysics as the science that studies Being *qua* being. Scotus makes great use of this definition, but he understands it in a highly personal way and broadens its scope immeasurably by including within Being the infinite Christian God. Whatever belongs to any of Aristotle's categories—substance or accident—is part of Being; but Being is much greater than this, for whatever falls within the categories is finite, and Being contains the infinite. The most important division to be made within the realm of Being was the division between finite and infinite being.[10]

The existence of an infinite being is something that, for Scotus, can be philosophically proved. In this he agrees with Aquinas and the great majority of medieval thinkers. But he rejects the proofs of God's existence offered by Aquinas on the ground that they are too dependent on Aristotelian physics, and he offers an elaborate metaphysical proof of his own to establish the existence of God as first efficient cause, ultimate final cause, and most excellent of all beings. Unlike Aquinas, he thinks that divine attributes such as omniscience and omnipotence can be known only by revelation and cannot be established by natural reason alone.[11]

Scotus makes use of the apparatus of Aristotelian hylomorphism, using familiar terms like 'matter', 'form', 'substance', and 'accident'. But he gives many of these terms a new and radical interpretation. In particular he recasts the Aristotelian concepts of actuality and potentiality, treating potential beings as if they are entities that possess all the detailed individuality of actual beings. This comes out, for instance, in his treatment of place and time: unlike Aristotle he held that there can be vacuous space and motionless time. Where, for Aristotle, the presence of a body is needed in

---

[9] Scotus' theory of univocity is discussed in Ch. 3 below.
[10] Scotus' metaphysics is treated in more detail in Ch. 5 below.
[11] Scotus' natural theology is discussed in Ch. 9 below.

order to create a space, for Scotus the mere possibility of a body is enough
to keep the walls of a vacuum apart. Where, for Aristotle, there must be
motion if there is to be time, since time is the measure of motion, for
Scotus there can be time without motion, time that measures the mere
potential for motion.[12] In treating possibilities as shadowy, but definite,
individuals, Scotus betrays the influence of Avicenna; but he explores the
area with a degree of elaboration that entitles him to be regarded as the
begetter of the philosophy of possible worlds.

In Aristotelian tradition matter was the principle of individuation: two
humans, Peter and Paul, were distinct from each other not on account of
their form but on account of their matter. Scotus rejected this: it was not
matter that made the difference between Peter and Paul, but a unique
identifying feature that each alone possessed, a *haecceitas*, or thisness. Thus,
in an individual such as Socrates there was both a common human nature
and an individuating principle. The common nature and the individual
difference were, he maintained, really identical, but distinguished from
each other by a distinction of a special kind, the 'formal distinction'. By this
means Scotus hoped to preserve the validity of universal terms without
falling into Platonism: the common nature was real enough, and was not
merely created by the human intellect, but it could never occur in reality
except in company with an individuating element.

By comparison with Aquinas, Scotus extended the scope of the human
intellect in two directions. Aquinas had held that there was no purely
intellectual knowledge of individuals, because an immaterial faculty could
not grasp matter, which was the principle of individuation. For Scotus,
each thing has within it an intelligible principle of individuality, and
therefore the intellect can grasp the individual in its singularity. Aquinas
maintained that the proper object of the intellect, in this life, was the
knowledge of the nature of material things. Scotus said that if we were to
take the future as well as the present life into consideration, we must say
that the proper object of the intellect was as wide as Being itself. To
define the object of the intellect as Aquinas had, he maintained, was like
defining the object of sight as what could be seen by candlelight.

Scotus definitively rejected the thesis—dear to the Augustinian tradition
and revived by Henry of Ghent—that a special divine illumination was

---

[12] See N. Lewis, 'Space and Time', in *CCDS*.

needed to enable the human intellect to grasp universals. God, however, is not totally excluded from his epistemology. God's power is absolute: he can do anything that does not involve contradiction. Accordingly, God could create in a human mind a conviction of the presence of an individual entity without that entity being present. Fortunately, while having absolute power, God acts only in accordance with his orderly power, power guided by wisdom. Hence, he would not exercise the absolute power that would deceive us in the manner suggested. Here Scotus, like Descartes centuries later, can exclude radical scepticism only by appealing to the doctrine that the good God is no deceiver.

In philosophy of mind Scotus innovated in his description of the relationship between the intellect and the will. Whereas for Aquinas the will was essentially a rational appetite which derived its freedom from the flexible nature of practical reasoning, Scotus saw the will as a sovereign power whose activity could not be caused by anything except its own self-determination. The will was indeed a rational power, a power capable of being exercised in more than one way, but this did not mean that its exercise was under the direction of reason. The intellect, by contrast, was a natural power, a power which, given the appropriate natural conditions for its operation, could act only in one way. Whereas for most Aristotelian scholastics the ultimate end of human beings is an intellectual operation, the beatific vision of God, for Scotus the union of the blessed with God in heaven consists essentially in a free act of the will.[13]

In both humans and in God, Scotus assigns to the will a much broader scope than any of his predecessors had done. The human will is a power for opposites, not just in the sense that it can will different things at different times, but that at the very time of willing one thing it retains a power for willing its opposite at the same time. A created will that existed only for a single moment could still make a free choice between opposites. Again, the divine will, for Scotus, enjoys a freedom far wider than that attributed to it by previous theologians. God was free, for instance, to dispense with or cancel many of the moral precepts commonly believed to belong to the natural law.

Duns Scotus is important in the history of philosophy not so much for founding a school—though there have been devoted Scotists in every

---

[13] Scotus' philosophy of mind is discussed in Ch. 7 below.

generation up to the present—but because many of his philosophical innovations came to be accepted as unquestioned principles by thinkers in later generations who had never read a word of his works. The Reformation debates between Luther and Calvin and their Catholic adversaries took place against a backcloth of fundamentally Scotist assumptions. The framework within which Descartes laid out the foundations of modern philosophy was in all its essentials a construction erected in Oxford around the year 1300. The quarter of a century that separated Aquinas' *Summa Theologiae* from Scotus' *Lectura* was one of the most momentous periods in the history of philosophy.

Scotus is not widely read outside professional circles: he is a philosophers' philosopher. But one of those who had the most vivid appreciation of his genius was the Victorian poet Gerard Manley Hopkins. In his poem 'Duns Scotus' Oxford' Hopkins placed him on a pedestal above Aquinas, Plato, and Aristotle, saluting him as

> Of realty the rarest-veined unraveller; a not
> rivalled insight, be rival Italy or Greece.

What most impressed Hopkins was the concept of haecceity, which he took as anticipating his own concept of inscape, the unique characteristic of each individual, which he celebrated in many of his poems, notably 'As kingfishers catch fire'.

> Each mortal thing does one thing and the same:
> Deals out that being indoors each one dwells;
> Selves—goes itself; *myself* it speaks and spells,
> Crying *What I do is me: for that I came.*

In the decades immediately after his death Scotus did not receive such applause in Oxford, and even among his fellow Franciscans there was strong opposition to his views.

William Ockham

William Ockham arrived in Oxford shortly after Scotus had left it for the last time. He took his surname from his birthplace, the village of Ockham in Surrey. He was born in the late 1280s and joined the Franciscan order around 1302. It was probably at Greyfriars in London that he received his philosophical training. At the end of the decade he went to Oxford to commence the study of theology. By the time of his lectures on the *Sentences* in 1317–19 a school of Scotists was building up in Oxford, and Ockham defined his own position partly in contrast to them. He was soon criticized by fellow Franciscans, and also regarded with suspicion by the university's chancellor, Thomas Lutterell, who was a Thomist. He left Oxford without proceeding to the doctorate, and lived in London in the early 1320s, probably again at Greyfriars.[14] He became a lecturer in philosophy and held a number of quodlibetal disputations. He also wrote up his Oxford lectures, composed a systematic textbook of logic, a number of commentaries on the logical and physical works of Aristotle, and an influential treatise on predestination and future contingents. He is best remembered for something he never said, namely 'Entities are not to be multiplied beyond necessity', the famous 'Ockham's razor'.

In his works Ockham took up a number of positions in logic and metaphysics either in development of, or in opposition to, Scotus. Though his thought is less sophisticated than Scotus', his language is mercifully much clearer. Like Scotus, he treated 'being' as a univocal term, applicable to God and creatures in the same sense. He sharply reduced, however, the number of created beings, reducing the ten Aristotelian categories to two, namely substances and qualities. Ockham's most significant disagreement with Scotus concerned the nature of universals. He rejected outright the idea that there was a common nature existing in the many individuals we call by a common name. No universal exists outside the mind; everything in the world is singular. Universals are not things but signs, simple signs representing many things.

According to Ockham, there are two kinds of signs: natural signs and conventional signs. Natural signs are the thoughts in our minds, and conventional signs are the words that we coin to express these thoughts. The concepts in our minds form a language system, a language common to all humans and prior to all the different spoken languages such as English

---

[14] Ockham's premature departure from Oxford without a doctorate may be the reason why his medieval nickname was *venerabilis inceptor*—'the venerable beginner'. This seems more likely than the alternative explanation, that he was regarded as an admirable innovator. But at all events, the title involves complicated wordplay, since 'incept' was, in medieval jargon, the word for actually taking the doctorate, something that Ockham never did. His other title, 'the invincible doctor', needs less explanation.

and Latin. Ockham's denial of real universals is often called 'nominalism': but the names which, according to him, are the only true universals are not only spoken and written names, but also the inward names of our mental language. Accordingly, when we are making a contrast between Ockham's teaching and the realism of his opponents it would be more apt to call him a conceptualist than a nominalist.[15]

At different times Ockham gave different accounts of the way in which the names of mental language are related to objects in the world. According to his earlier theory, the mind fashioned mental images, or 'fictions', that resembled real things, and that provided the terms of mental propositions, as proxies for the corresponding realities. Fictions were universals in the sense of having an equal likeness to many different things in

The palace of the Popes at Avignon, where Ockham was tried and whence he fled to the Emperor.

[15] Ockham's nominalism is discussed in Ch. 3 below.

the world. Later, partly as a result of criticism by his Franciscan colleague Walter Chatton, Ockham gave up belief in fictions. Names in mental language, he came to think, were simply acts of thinking, items in an individual person's mental history.

Ockham accepted Scotus' distinction between intuitive and abstractive knowledge; it is only by intuitive knowledge that we can know whether a contingent fact obtains or not. However, Ockham makes explicit a consequence of the theory that is only implicit in Scotus. By his almighty power, Ockham maintains, God can do directly whatever he currently does by means of secondary causes. In the ordinary way, God makes me know that a wall is white by making the white wall meet my eye; but if he normally acts thus via normal sensory causation, he can make me have the same belief in the whiteness of the wall without there being any white wall there at all. This thesis obviously opens wider the breach in epistemology that had been opened by Scotus, and broadens the road to scepticism.[16]

These and other views of Ockham quickly gave rise to concern among his Franciscan brethren, and in 1323 he was asked to explain to a provincial chapter of the order his teaching about the Aristotelian categories. A year later, in response to a denunciation from Oxford, Ockham had to face a commission at the papal court in Avignon set up to examine his *Sentences* for heresy. The commission, which consisted mainly of Thomists, and included the former Oxford chancellor Lutterell, failed, after many months of work, to produce a convincing case against him.

However, Ockham's stay in Avignon did give his philosophical career a wholly new turn. The pope of the time, John XXII, was in conflict with the Franciscan order on two issues concerning poverty: the historical question whether Christ and his Apostles had lived in absolute poverty, and the practical question whether the Franciscan order could legitimately own any property. St Francis had held up an extreme ideal of poverty: the friars were to own nothing, never touch money, and depend on alms for food, clothing, and shelter. St Bonaventure, the reforming general of the order, made a distinction between ownership (*dominium*, or lordship) and use (*usus*). Franciscans could use property, but they could not own it, whether as individuals or collectively as a religious order. In 1279 Pope Nicholas III

---

[16] Ockham's epistemology is discussed in Ch. 4 below.

relieved the Franciscan order of the ownership of all the property made use of by the friars, and assumed it into the patrimony of the papacy.

At the end of 1322 John XXII overturned this compromise, denouncing the distinction between ownership and use—so far as concerned consumables, at least—as a hypocritical fudge. In the following year he also rejected the Franciscan teaching that Jesus and the Apostles had renounced all ownership during their lives. Ockham was asked by Michael of Cesena, the head of the Franciscan order, who was also in Avignon, to study the papal decrees containing these denunciations. He came to the conclusion that they were immoral, absurd, and heretical, and publicly denounced them. With Michael he fled from Avignon in 1328, shortly before a papal bull was issued condemning their doctrines as heretical. The pair escaped to Munich, where they came under the protection of Ludwig of Bavaria, an enemy of John XXII, who had opposed his election as emperor.

Ludwig, excommunicated in 1324, had appealed to a general council, using the quarrel with the Franciscans as a reason for denouncing the Pope as a heretic. In 1328 he entered Rome, had himself crowned as emperor, burnt John in effigy, and installed an antipope. In Rome, Ludwig was joined by another philosophical ally, Marsilius of Padua, former rector of the University of Paris. Marsilius had been forced, like Ockham, to flee to the protection of Ludwig because he had written a book containing a sustained attack, not just on John XXII but on the papacy as an institution.

The work, *Defensor Pacis* ('The Defender of the Peace', 1324), became a classic text of political philosophy. It begins with a denunciation of papal interference in the affairs of secular polities. The disorder, corruption, and warfare endemic in Italy, Marsilius maintains, are all the result of papal arrogance and ambition. In the course of the work he moves from local issues to general principle.

The state is a 'perfect' society, that is to say, one that is both supreme and self-sufficient within its own sphere. There are two types of government: rule by the consent of the ruler's subjects, and rule against their will. Only the former is legitimate and the latter is a form of tyranny. The laws of the state derive their legitimacy neither from the will of the ruler nor directly from God: they are given authority by the citizens themselves. The actual task of legislation may be delegated to particular bodies and institutions, which may reasonably differ from state to state. The prince is the executive head of state: the citizens' consent to his rule is best expressed if he is chosen by election, but there are other systems by which consent may legitimately be manifested. An irregular or incompetent prince should be removed from office by the legislature.

Marsilius' book was extraordinarily influential. No writer on the papal side was able to counter it at a similar level of philosophical sophistication. It influenced Orthodox Catholics and heretics alike, right up to the Lutheran reformation. Ockham was among the first philosophers to exhibit its influence, in a series of political treatises that he wrote during the 1330s. These works are less systematic, and also less radical, than the *Defensor Pacis*.

The first was the *Work of Ninety Days*, a lengthy tract written in haste in 1332. This was later followed by a *Letter to the Franciscans* and a set of *Dialogues* on the relations between Church and State. Though polemical in intent, these works are 'recitative', that is to say, they state ('recite') arguments used by papal opponents in a manner that does not necessarily commit Ockham himself to agreement with their conclusions. But by comparing them with other works written in the first person ('assertive' works) we can piece together Ockham's own opinions.

The philosophical core of Ockham's position on Franciscan poverty is a theory of natural rights. He distinguishes between two classes of rights: those that may be legitimately renounced (such as the right to private property) and those that are inalienable (such as the right to one's own life). In the garden of Eden there was no such thing as property; after the fall property rights were established by human law. Private ownership is not in itself wrong, but, *pace* Pope John, it must be distinguished from use. A host allows his guests to use the food and drink at his table, but he does not confer the ownership of these things on his guests. The Franciscans have a right to use the necessities of life, but this does not involve them in any ownership, because it is only a moral right, not enforceable in any court of law (*OND* 6. 260–71).

While Marsilius' conceptions of government were shaped by conditions in the Italian city-states of his time, Ockham's are more influenced by the structure of the Holy Roman Empire. The emperor, he says, derives his power not from the pope, but from the people via the college of imperial electors. The right to choose one's ruler is one of the natural rights of human beings. These rights can be exercised by setting up a hereditary monarchy; but the tenure of a hereditary monarch depends on good conduct, and if he abuses his power the people are entitled to depose him.

Despite his quarrel with Pope John XXII, Ockham was much less hostile than Marsilius to the papacy as an institution. However tyrannically they behaved in practice, the popes, he maintained, did have a supremacy deriving from divine law. They should, however, be regarded as constitutional, not absolute, monarchs. They were answerable to general councils, which should themselves be constituted by locally elected churchmen.

Ockham was never reconciled with the papacy of his time. In 1331 John XXII, in his late eighties, began to preach a doctrine that was universally regarded as heretical: namely, that the souls of those who depart life in good standing do not enjoy the beatific vision of God until they rejoin their bodies after the Last Judgement. This, of course, placed a new weapon in the hands of his Franciscan opponents, and the Pope was forced to recant on his deathbed in 1334. The new pope, Benedict XII, defined that the souls of the just, as soon as they die, or after a period in purgatory, see God face to face. But Benedict did not repeal the condemnation of the dissident Franciscans, and Ockham died during the Black Death, still under the ban of the Church, in Munich in 1349.

The Reception of Ockham

Paris and Oxford were the two great universities of the high Middle Ages. While Paris was undoubtedly the senior partner in the thirteenth century, Oxford took the lead in the fourteenth century. It is a matter of scholarly dispute how far Ockham's influence was felt in either university. Certainly it is an exaggeration to say that there was ever, even in Oxford, an Ockhamist school, but on the other hand a number of Parisian thinkers followed up and developed specific themes from his writings.

Gregory of Rimini, for instance, an Augustinian friar who taught in Paris in the 1340s, accepted Ockham's natural philosophy while dissenting from his logic. Jean Buridan, a member of the arts faculty who was rector of the Sorbonne in 1328 and 1340, shared Ockham's nominalism, but he was much more confident than Ockham that progress could be made in the scientific exploration of the world. He reintroduced Philoponus' theory of impetus, and was the teacher of a distinguished generation of philosophical physicists, including Nicole Oresme, who explored, without endorsing, the hypothesis that the earth revolved daily on its axis. Like Ockham, Buridan is

best known for something he never said. In discussing the freedom of the
will to choose between alternatives he is alleged to have said that a donkey
faced between two equally attractive bales of hay would be unable to eat
either: hence 'Buridan's Ass' became a byword for indecision.

Two other French thinkers were much influenced by Ockham's epistemology: the Cistercian John of Mirecourt, and a secular canon Nicholas of
Autrecourt, both of whom lectured in Paris in the 1340s, and both of whom
incurred academic and ecclesiastical censure for their radical opinions. In
1347 forty-one propositions taken from John's writings were condemned by
the chancellor of the Sorbonne, and more than fifty of Nicholas' theses
were condemned by the papal legate. John defended his writings in an
apology; Nicholas recanted and continued his career.

John of Mirecourt's epistemology was based on a development of
Ockham's theory of assent. Assents may be evident or they may be given
with fear of error. Central truths of logic enjoy a supreme degree of
evidence, but there is also natural evidence, based on experience of the
world. Natural evidence cannot produce absolute certainty, except in the
case of one's own existence, which cannot be denied without self-contra-
diction. One cannot attain similar certainty about the existence of any other
entity. Even God's existence cannot be proved with certainty, since the
arguments for his existence are based on facts in the world involving only
natural evidence. Moreover, even if nothing other than myself existed, God
could, by a miracle, make it appear that there is a real world out there.

It will be seen that John came very close, in anticipation, to the position
Descartes reached at the beginning of his Second Meditation. Nicholas of
Autrecourt adopted an even more radical form of scepticism. If we define
intuitive awareness as involving a 'judgement that a thing exists, whether
or not it does exist', then we can never be certain that what appears to the
senses is true. We cannot be certain of the existence of the objects of the five
senses. One of the condemned propositions that he was made to recant ran
thus: 'virtually no certainty can be obtained about things by natural
appearances'. However, Nicholas qualified this sceptical claim with the
remark that a modicum of certainty could be achieved in a short time if
only people turned their mind to things themselves and not to the reading
of Aristotle and his commentators (DB 553 ff.).

Unlike John, Nicholas did not see 'I think, therefore I am' as offering a
way out of the sceptical impasse—it certainly did not prove the existence of

any substantive ego. Even 'Here is an intellectual thought: therefore some intellect exists' was, he said, a far from evident argument. No form of causal argument could bring certainty of the existence of anything of any kind. Only the principle of non-contradiction, Nicholas concluded, will provide a solid basis for knowledge: and such a basis will not let one get very far in philosophy. 'The existence of one thing', ran one of his condemned propositions, 'can never be inferred or proved with the appropriate degree of evidence from the existence of some other thing, nor can the non-existence of one thing from the non-existence of another.' Here it is not Descartes, but Hume, who is brought to the mind of a reader of modern philosophy.

Rightly or wrongly, the scepticism of Nicholas of Autrecourt was often held up in later ages as an example of the horrible excess to which the teaching of Ockham could lead. With equally dubious justice, he was sometimes hailed by twentieth-century logical positivists as a distinguished predecessor.

The immediate reception of Ockham in England was not uniformly favourable. Even his close associates, such as Adam Wodeham and Walter Chatton, adapted his teachings to make them more conformable to mainstream scholasticism. Walter Burley, whose career overlapped with that of Ockham, was one of the most significant English thinkers of the time. He took his MA at Oxford in 1301 and his doctorate in theology at the Sorbonne in the early 1320s; he was a fellow of Merton and a diplomat in the service of Edward III. He is best remembered for his treatise *The Pure Art of Logic* (1328), which was one of the finest logical texts to survive from the medieval period. In that work he defended the traditional view of signification and supposition against the criticisms of Ockham.[17]

The Oxford Calculators

The second quarter of the fourteenth century saw the development among Oxford philosophers of a school that had a remarkable influence on the history of physics. Foremost among the school was Thomas Bradwardine (1295–1349), who was a fellow successively of Balliol and

[17] See Ch. 3 below.

Merton colleges, later confessor to Edward III, and eventually archbishop of Canterbury. Other members of the school, such as William Heytesbury and Richard Swineshead, were, like Bradwardine, fellows of Merton, so that members of the group are sometimes known as the Mertonians. They shared a taste for solving philosophical and theological problems by mathematical methods, and so they are also called the Oxford Calculators, after a treatise by Swineshead called the *Liber Calculationum* (1350).

Bradwardine, in 1328, published a work entitled *De Proportionibus Velocitatum in Motibus* ('On Proportions of Velocity in Motions'). In it he developed a theory of ratios which he used to present a theory of how forces, resistances, and velocities were to be correlated in motion. This theory quickly superseded Aristotle's laws of motion, and it was influential not only in Oxford, but also in Paris, where it was adopted by Oresme. Other Calculators, too, produced work of importance for natural philosophy, but they devoted their mathematical talents to the solution of logical and theological problems rather than to physical research. Questions about maxima and minima, for instance, were the germ of development towards the differential calculus; but they were first raised in connection with the question what was the minimum, and what the maximum, length of time to be spent in prayer to fulfil a command to pray night and day. The question of how to measure non-quantitative qualities, such as heat and cold, was first worked out in the analysis of the growth of grace in the souls of the faithful and in measuring the capacity for happiness of souls in heaven.

Many of the developments in physics originated as solutions to logical puzzles, or *sophismata*. These were propositions whose content was ambiguous or paradoxical, set as problems to be resolved by logic students, and solved, or determined, by masters in the arts faculty. One of the most ingenious sets of these *sophismata* was produced, around 1328, by Richard Kilvington, not himself a Mertonian, but closely associated with the other Calculators as part of a research group assembled by Richard of Bury, bishop of Durham and lord chancellor. Kilvington was not himself a mathematician, but his *sophismata* were quickly given a mathematical form by Heytesbury in his *Regulae Solvendi Sophismata* (1335), in which he worked out the theory of uniform acceleration.

Sophismata fell into disrepute at the Renaissance, but they came into fashion again in the twentieth century. At a time when France was a republic, Bertrand Russell inquired about the truth-value of 'The king of

France is bald'. His investigation led to a very influential logical analysis of definite descriptions. Similarly, Kilvington in his *sophismata* sets out a scenario, for instance, that Socrates is as white as it is possible to be, and that Plato, hitherto not white, is at this moment beginning to be white. He then inquires into the truth-value of 'Socrates is whiter than Plato begins to be white'. A natural reaction might be to say that this sentence, so far from being either true or false, is not even well-formed; but Kilvington patiently spells out what one might mean by it, and in the course of expounding it and similar puzzle questions offers an analysis of concepts of degree, ratio, and proportion.

The doyen of the Calculators, Thomas Bradwardine, was also a heavy-weight theologian. He was the leading representative of another Oxford fourteenth-century tendency, a revival of Augustinianism. Of course, throughout the whole medieval period Augustine had been an authority to be treated with reverence and quoted no less frequently than Aristotle. But these neo-Augustinians like Bradwardine and his Irish contemporary Richard Fitzralph (chancellor of Oxford in 1333 and later archbishop of Armagh) began to pay more attention to the historical context of Augustine's work and to take greater interest in his later writings against the Pelagians. Bradwardine, in his massive *De Causa Dei*, presented an Augustinian treatment of the issues surrounding divine foreknowledge, future contingent propositions, and human freedom.

John Wyclif

The most distinguished figure of this Augustinian renaissance was John Wyclif (1330?–1384), who was also a leader of the realist reaction against the nominalism of the Ockhamists. In the middle years of the century he was by far the most prominent figure in the university. His life exhibited a pattern that recurs in the history of Oxford and is illustrated also by John Wesley and John Henry Newman. In the middle of the fourteenth, the eighteenth, and the nineteenth centuries the most significant event in the religious history of the university was the defection of a favourite son from the religious establishment.[18]

---

[18] See R. A. Knox, *Enthusiasm* (Oxford: Oxford University Press, 1948), 66.

John Wyclif, as shown in an illuminated initial of a 1472 Bohemian MS.

Like Wesley and Newman, Wyclif was a fine flower of the Oxford schools, a man who stood out among his contemporaries for learning and austerity of life. Like them, he formed around himself a group of disciples, and seemed likely to dominate, by his personal influence and reputation, the course of the university's thought and practice. Like them, he took a doctrinal step which alienated his closest theological allies and vindicated the suspicions of his critics. Exiled from Oxford as they were exiled, he carried on his religious mission elsewhere, casting only a rare nostalgic glance at the distant spires of the home of his youth and promise.

Wyclif went to Oxford in the 1350s and though from time to time distracted by public service—at one time engaged in an embassy, at another offering an expert opinion to parliament—he spent his life mainly in teaching, preaching, and writing. Between 1360, when he was master of Balliol, and 1372, when he took his DD, he produced a philosophical *Summa* whose most important volume is a treatise on universals, designed to vindicate realism against nominalist sophistry. In his maturity he wrote a theological *Summa* which began with two books of banal orthodoxy, moved through several books of hardy innovation, passed into overt heresy, and ended in barren polemic. The volumes of this work covered the whole range of medieval theology. Three of them dealt with issues of law and property, and proposed the controversial theses that evil clerics should be disendowed and that even laymen, if sinners, had no right to ownership of property. Several other volumes, on Church, king, and papacy, analysed the structure of the Christian Church and society, castigated abuses, and proposed reforms. In one of his latest works, on the Eucharist, he presented a novel interpretation of the Mass, the centre of medieval spirituality.

One of Wyclif's most startling innovations was his proposal for communism, based on his theory of *dominium*, or ownership. He argued thus. On the one hand, someone who is in sin has no right to property. You can only possess something justly if you can use it justly; but no sinner can use anything justly because all his actions are sinful. On the other hand, if you are in a state of grace, as an adoptive son of God you inherit the whole realm of God. But if each Christian in grace is lord of all, he must share his lordship with all other Christians in grace.

All the goods of God should be common. This is proved thus. Every man should be in a state of grace; and if he is in a state of grace, he is lord of the world and all it contains. So every man should be lord of the universe. But this is not consistent with there being a number of men, unless they ought to have everything in common. Therefore all things should be in common.

Surprisingly, Wyclif's writings on dominion, radical though they were, did not seem to have caused him trouble with the authorities during his lifetime. The secular authorities used them in support of the taxation of the clergy, and ignored their implications with regard to the laity.

However, the increasing hardihood of Wyclif's speculations made his position in Oxford less and less tenable. When he denounced the popes and questioned papal claims, he could find sympathizers—at a time when a disgraceful schism was splitting Christendom in two—even among the higher clergy. When he, a secular priest enjoying several benefices, called for the disendowment of the Church, many laymen and begging friars found his words congenial. But when, in 1379, he denounced the doctrine of transubstantiation, and said that the bread and wine at Mass were Christ's body only in the same way that paper and ink in the Bible were God's Word, then friars, noblemen, and bishops all turned against him. He was condemned by a provincial synod and expelled from Oxford. He ended his life, at liberty but in disgrace, in a country living at Lutterworth in Northamptonshire.

Wyclif's influence after his death was greater than in his life. In subsequent decades his English followers, the Lollards, were disseminating a vernacular version of the Bible over his name. It is a matter of dispute how far he had himself been involved in the translation, but it is for that Bible, rightly or wrongly, that he has been most famous up to recent times. Abroad, in Bohemia, his memory was kept green by the followers of Jan Hus. The official Church, once the schism had finally ended at the Council of Constance in 1415, burnt Hus as a heretic, and condemned 260 propositions attributed to Wyclif. At home his body was exhumed and burnt.

Because of his association with the Lollard Bible, and because of his attacks on transubstantiation and the papacy, Wyclif was hailed by Protestant hagiographers as the Morning Star of the Reformation. His works have not been much read by philosophers: Protestant thinkers were repelled by the scholasticism from which the Reformation, it was believed, had delivered us all, while Catholic scholars felt they could ignore the texts of a heretic when there were holy men of genius still awaiting critical editions. But in recent years philosophers who have looked at his work have come to realize that he is a considerable thinker, worthy to make a third to his two great Oxford predecessors: the Evening Star, in fact, of scholasticism.

Beyond Paris and Oxford

Wyclif's career coincided with a period when Oxford became more isolated from the rest of Europe. Scotus and Ockham were both well known in Paris as well as in Oxford, and lived long periods on the Continent. Wyclif remained in England except for one brief visit abroad. Latin continued in use as the medium of academic exchange, but vernacular literature began to thrive in all the countries of Europe and Latin was no longer the chosen medium of the best writers among Wyclif's contemporaries, such as Chaucer and Langland. The Hundred Years' War between England and France placed a barrier between Oxford and Paris. The two universities went on their separate ways, impoverished.

By the end of the fourteenth century, however, new universities had begun to flourish in various parts of Europe. The Charles University of Prague dated its foundation to 1347; by 1402 the debates in its schools between Ockhamists and Wycliffites were reverberating throughout Europe. The University of Heidelberg was founded by papal bull in 1385, with a former rector of Paris, Marsilius of Inghen, as its first rector. In 1399 the University of Padua received its first buildings. In 1400 the Jagiellonian University was chartered at Cracow. St Andrews, the oldest Scottish university, was founded in 1410, at a time when Scotland and England belonged to the allegiance of two different schismatic popes. The first university in the Low Countries was Louvain, founded in 1425.

Replacing the old close partnership of Paris and Oxford a new international network of universities grew up. In the decades around 1500, for instance, a group of Scottish scholars, of whom the central figure was John Major or Mair, later principal of the University of Glasgow, studied together at the University of Paris. They made significant contributions to logic and epistemology which one recent scholar has not hesitated to compare to the Scottish Enlightenment of the eighteenth century.[19]

Simultaneously, a quite different kind of philosophizing was being practised outside the universities. The split between two styles of philosophy was to have serious long-term consequences for the non-academic world. In Paris in the early years of the fourteenth century, while Duns Scotus was lecturing, lectures were also being given by another philosopher of genius, the German Dominican Meister Eckhardt. Eckhardt went on to acquire a great reputation as a preacher and lecturer in the University of Cologne; and if Scotus can be seen as the first protagonist of the analytic tradition of philosophizing in the fourteenth century, Eckhardt can be regarded as the founding father of an alternative, mystical tradition.

The devotional writings of the thinkers of this tradition—the *Devotio Moderna* of Eckhardt's pupils John Tauler and Henry Suso—are not part of

---

[19] See A. Broadie, *The Circle of John Mair* (Oxford: Oxford University Press, 1985) and *Notion and Object* (Oxford: Oxford University Press, 1989).

the history of philosophy. What does concern the historian of philosophy is the anti-intellectual attitude that became associated with the school. A Dutchman called Gerard Groote (1340–84) founded, in Deventer, a pious association named The Brotherhood of the Common Life. The rules that he drew up for the confraternity included an attack on the entire academic system. Only a libertine could be happy in a university, and disputations and degrees served only to foster vainglory.

The Deventer brotherhood gave birth to a new congregation of canons regular, based at Windesheim. The best known of the Windesheim canons is Thomas à Kempis, who is in all probability the author of *The Imitation of Christ*, one of the best-known classics of Christian devotion, written around the time of Wyclif's posthumous condemnation. This work contains a fierce denunciation of scholastic philosophy and theology.

What doth it profit thee to discuss the deep mystery of the Trinity, if thou art from thy lack of humility displeasing to the Trinity. . . . I would rather choose to feel compunction than to know its definition. . . . Vanity of vanities, all is vanity save to love God and serve him only ... Have no wish to know the depths of things, but rather to acknowledge thy own lack of knowledge.

The tradition of Deventer and Windesheim thrived well into the sixteenth century, and it was one of the forces that led, in that century, to the downgrading of scholasticism. The young Erasmus was a pupil of the Brothers of the Common Life, and for a while a reluctant canon of the Windesheim congregation. Luther, too, was influenced by this mystical anti-intellectualism, and it helped to fuel his attacks on medieval Aristotelianism.

One person, in the fifteenth century, straddles the analytical–sceptical tradition and the mystical–fideistic tradition. This is Nicholas of Cusa (1401–64). He was born at Cusa, near Koblenz on the Moselle. He too was a pupil of the Deventer community, and subsequently studied at Heidelberg and Padua. He was a delegate to the Council of Basel in 1432, which marked the high point of the assertion of the authority of general councils against the ecclesiastical supremacy of the pope. Later, he adhered to the papal party and became a diplomat in the service of Pope Eugenius IV. Created a cardinal in 1448, he was papal legate in Germany in 1451–2. He died at Todi, in Umbria, in 1464.

Nicholas was a pious and charitable man, a dedicated Church reformer and a devoted ecumenist. Throughout his life he sought reconciliation:

between the conciliarists and the papalists within the Roman obedience, between the Latin Church and the Greek Church, between scholastic and mystical theology, and between Christian and pagan thought. He held that the names that Jews, Greeks, Latins, Turks, and Saracens applied to God were equivalent to each other, reconcilable in the Tetragrammaton which was the name God himself had revealed (Sermo 1. 6. 14).

Like the Oxford Calculators, Nicholas wrote on mathematical subjects, but his best-known philosophical work, and also his earliest, was the *De Docta Ignorantia* ('On Learned Ignorance') of 1440. The leading idea of this work is that God is the *coincidentia oppositorum*, a supreme and infinite synthesis of opposites. Whenever we apply a predicate to God we can with equal propriety attach its opposite. If God is the greatest being, he is also the least being: he is both maximum and minimum, because nothing can be greater than him, but he also lacks any size or volume. The fact that opposites coincide in God shows how impossible it is for us to have any real knowledge of him. Rational attempts to reach the ultimate truth are like a polygon inscribed in a circle: however many sides we add to the polygon, it will never coincide with the circumference, however closely it approaches it.[20]

Renaissance Platonism

Nicholas of Cusa is often described as a transitional figure between the Middle Ages and the Renaissance. The composition of *On Learned Ignorance* did indeed coincide with one of the seminal events of the Renaissance: the Council of Florence of 1439. The Byzantine Greek Empire of Constantinople, threatened by the overwhelming military power of the Ottoman Turks, sought help from Western Christians. The Pope, the Venetian Eugenius IV, made theological unity a condition of a crusade, and the emperor John VIII and the patriarch of Constantinople attended a council in Ferrara and Florence in order to reunite the Latin and Greek Churches. Their presence in Florence has been immortalized by Benozzo Gozzoli's frescoes of the adoration of the Magi in the Palazzo Medici-Ricardi, which contains portraits of the main participants. The union between the

---

[20] Nicholas' theology is studied in Ch. 9 below.

Churches, proclaimed in the decree *Laetentur Caeli*, agreed by Pope, emperor, and patriarch in 1439, proved as short-lived as its predecessor of 1270. But the effects of the Council on the history of philosophy were more long-lasting.

Florence was already home to a revival of ancient classical learning: of 'humanism', not in the sense of a concern with the human race, but in the sense of a devotion to 'humane letters'. One of the earliest manifestations of this was an admiration for the style of classical Roman authors and a corresponding distaste for scholastic Latin. Leonardo Bruni, a senior Florentine civil servant in the 1430s, retranslated important texts of Aristotle into more elegant Latin. Along with a desire for new translations of Greek classics, many educated men felt a hunger to learn Greek itself and to read Plato, Aristotle, and other ancient thinkers in the original language. From 1396 Greek had been regularly taught in Florence to a select few.

The presence of Eastern scholars at the Council of Florence gave a fillip to this movement. Those in attendance at the Council included Georgios Gemistos Plethon (1360–1452), a leading Platonist, his pupil Bessarion (1403–72), and the Aristotelian George of Trebizond (1395–1484). Of this trio only Plethon, an opponent of Church union, returned to Greece after the Council: the others stayed in Rome, George becoming a papal secretary and Bessarion a cardinal.

During the Council, Plethon lectured on the comparative merits of Plato and Aristotle. Latin philosophers, he said, greatly overvalued Aristotle. Plato was much to be preferred: he believed in a creator God, not just a prime mover; and he believed in a truly immortal soul. Aristotle was wrong about Ideas, wrong in thinking virtue was a mean, and wrong in equating happiness with contemplation.

Plethon's onslaught drew replies from both Greeks and Latins. George Scholarios, an admirer of Aquinas and a supporter of union at Florence, later became disillusioned and returned to Constantinople, where he eventually became patriarch. In 1445 he wrote a *Defence of Aristotle* against those who preferred Plato. Though Aristotle thought the world was eternal, nonetheless he did think God was its efficient cause; he believed that the human soul was immortal and indestructible. He was a much clearer and more systematic philosopher than Plato. Scholarios believed—perhaps rightly—that Plethon was not a Christian at all, but a Neoplatonist pagan, and after he died he had his works publicly burnt.

A tempestuous defence of Aristotle was made by George of Trebizond, who was at this time translating, for Pope Nicholas V, works of both Plato and Aristotle as well as many Greek Fathers. His *Comparison of Plato and Aristotle* (1458) makes Aristotle a Christian hero and Plato a heretical villain. George claims that Aristotle believed in creation out of nothing, in divine providence, and in a Trinity of divine persons. Plato, on the other hand, propounded disgusting doctrines such as the beauty of pederasty and the transmigration of souls into animals, and encouraged gymnastics for both sexes together in the nude. Devotion to Plato had led the Greek Church into heresy and schism; Latin Aristotelians had combined philosophy with orthodoxy. Only scholars who were more concerned with style than content could prefer Plato to Aristotle.

Two cardinals entered the debate to redress the balance. Nicholas of Cusa, for whom George had translated Plato's *Parmenides*, wrote a dialogue, *On the Not Other*, in which he stressed the limitations of both Aristotelian logic and Platonic metaphysics, while endeavouring to build on both of them in attaining knowledge of God, the divine Not-Other. More soberly, Bessarion wrote a treatise, published in both Greek and Latin, entitled *Against the Calumniator of Plato*. He pointed out that many Christian saints had been admirers of Plato. While neither Plato nor Aristotle agreed at all fully with Christian doctrine, the points of conflict between them were few, and there were as many points of similarity between Plato and Aristotle as between Aristotle and Christianity.

Aristotle, he said, *pace* George of Trebizond, did not believe that God freely created the world out of nothing, and Plato was much closer to the Christian belief in divine providence. Aristotle, again, did not prove that individual human souls were immortal. The way in which Aristotle explains concept-formation by the influence of the agent intellect is very close to Plato's theory of human links to the Ideas in recollection. Bessarion balances George's citation of licentious passages from the dialogues with others in which Plato exhorts to continence and virtue. Both Plato and Aristotle were outstanding thinkers, sent by providence to bring humans to the truth by different paths. Plato's anthropology, Bessarion maintains, is closer to what life would have been without original sin; Aristotle gives a more realistic account of fallen humanity.

By the 1460s it was universally accepted that the study of Plato was appropriate for Catholic scholars in the West. The fall of Constantinople to

Portraits of Cardinal Bessarion are rare. In this painting by Gentile Bellini he is almost crushed under the fine reliquary he is presenting to a Venetian confraternity.

the Turks in 1453 led to an influx of refugees, bringing with them not only their own knowledge of classical Greek but also precious manuscripts of ancient authors. These were welcomed both in Rome and in Florence. Cosimo de' Medici commissioned his court philosopher, Marsilio Ficino, to translate the entire works of Plato. The work was completed around 1469, when Cosimo's grandson Lorenzo the Magnificent succeeded as head of the Medici clan. Lorenzo collected Greek manuscripts in his new Laurenziana library, just as Pope Nicholas V and his successors had been doing in the refounded Vatican library.

Marsilio Ficino gathered round him, at Careggi near Florence, a group of wealthy students of Plato, whom he called his Academy. He translated, in addition to Plato, works of Proclus and Plotinus, and the *Corpus Hermeticum*, a collection of ancient alchemical and astrological writings. He wrote commentaries on four major dialogues of Plato and on the *Enneads* of Plotinus. He also wrote a number of short treatises himself, and one major work, the *Theologia Platonica* (1474), in which he set out his own Neoplatonic account of the soul and its origin and destiny. His aim was to combine the Platonic element in the scholastic tradition with a literary and historical appreciation of its origins in the ancient world. He regarded the pagan Platonic tradition as itself divinely inspired, and believed that its incorporation in theological teaching was essential if the Christian religion was to be made palatable to the new humanistic intelligentsia. Thus he equated the charity which St Paul speaks of in 1 Corinthians with the Eros of the *Phaedrus*, and identified the Christian God with the *Republic*'s Idea of the Good.

The most distinguished of Ficino's Platonic associates was Giovanni Pico, count of Mirandola (1463–94). Well educated in Latin and Greek, Pico learnt Greek and Hebrew at an early age, and in addition to the Hermetic Corpus he made a serious study of the Jewish mystical cabbala. He wanted to combine Greek, Hebrew, Muslim, and Christian thought into a great eclectic Platonic synthesis. He spelt this out in 900 theses and invited all interested scholars to discuss these with him in a public disputation in Rome in 1487. Pope Innocent VIII forbade the disputation, and appointed a committee to examine the theses for heresy. Among the propositions condemned was 'there is no branch of science which gives us more certainty of Christ's divinity than magic and cabbala'.

The oration which Pico prepared to introduce the aborted disputation survives under the title *On the Dignity of Man*. Pico draws equally on Genesis and on Plato's *Timaeus* in describing the creation, and imagines God as addressing the newly created human being in the following terms:

The nature of other beings is limited and constrained within the bounds of laws prescribed by Us. Thou, constrained by no limits, in accordance with thine own free will, in whose hand We have placed thee, shalt ordain for thyself the limits of thy nature. We have set thee at the world's centre that thou mayest from thence more easily observe whatever is in the world. We have made thee neither of heaven nor of earth, neither mortal nor immortal, so that with freedom of choice and with honour, as though the maker and moulder of thyself, thou mayest fashion thyself in whatever shape thou shalt prefer. Thou shalt have the power to degenerate into the lower forms of life, which are brutish. Thou shalt have the power, out of thy soul's judgement, to be reborn into the higher forms, which are divine.[21]

Pico sees the human, at birth, as a totipotential being, containing the seeds of many forms of life. Depending on which seed you cultivate, you may become a vegetable, a brute, a rational spirit, or a son of God. You may even withdraw into yourself and become one with God in solitary darkness.

Pico's consistent aim in his writings was to exalt the powers of human nature. To this end he defended the use of alchemy and symbolic rituals: these were legitimate magic, to be sharply distinguished from the black magic that invoked the aid of demons. But not all the scientific claims of the ancients were to be believed. Pico wrote twelve books against astrology: the heavenly bodies could affect men's bodies but not their minds, and no one could know the stars' movements and powers well enough to cast a horoscope. Astrology was to be opposed because the determinism it proclaimed limited human freedom; white magic was to be pursued because it made man the 'prince and master' of creation.

Pico's evocation of human dignity was an ancestor of Hamlet's paean:

What a piece of work is a man, how noble in reason, how infinite in faculty, in form and moving how express and admirable, in action how like an angel, in apprehension how like a god—the beauty of the world, the paragon of animals.

In spite of his unorthodox views and difficulties with the Church authorities, Pico was much admired by St Thomas More, who as a young man

---

[21] E. Cassirer *et al.*, *The Renaissance Philosophy of Man* (Chicago: Chicago University Press, 1959), 225.

wrote a life of him, holding him up as a model of piety for the layman. Pico did, indeed, make a pious end. When, after the Medici had been expelled from Florence, Savonarola turned the city into a religious republic, Pico became one of his followers, and considered becoming a friar. But before he could carry out this plan, he died at the age of 31. At his death he was working on a volume reconciling Platonic and Aristotelian metaphysics.

Renaissance Aristotelianism

In the 1490s, while the Platonists were showing an irenic spirit towards Aristotle, a vigorous revival of Aristotelianism was under way at Padua. This took two forms, Averroist and Thomist. In 1486 the Dominican order had replaced the *Sentences* of Peter Lombard with the *Summa Theologiae* of St Thomas as the basic text to be lectured on in their schools, and this initiated a Renaissance revival of Thomism. But at Padua, initially, the Averroist faction was dominant. The two leading lecturers, Nicoletto Vernia (d. 1499) and his pupil Agostino Nifo (1473–1538), both produced editions of Averroes' commentary, and maintained the Averroist position that there is only a single immortal intellect for all individual human beings. In 1491, however, there arrived in Padua one of the greatest Thomists of all time: the Dominican Thomas de Vio, known always as Cajetan, from the Latin form of Gaeta, the town where he was born and of which he later became bishop.

Cajetan commented on several works of Aristotle, including the *De Anima*, but he is best known for his commentaries on St Thomas, beginning with one on the *De Ente et Essentia* written at Padua in the early 1590s, and including a commentary on the whole *Summa Theologiae*. Though not always easy to read, these are highly valued by Thomists to this day. Particularly influential was a small tract on analogy, which systematized and classified the different kinds of analogy to be found in scattered remarks in Aristotle and St Thomas. Between 1495 and 1497 Cajetan held the post of professor of Thomist metaphysics at Padua.[22] Though a sympathetic commentator, Cajetan was not afraid to disagree with St Thomas, and he came to believe

---

[22] A chair of Scotism had also been founded in Padua, held at this time by the Franciscan Antonio Trombetta.

that Aristotle did not maintain individual immortality, and that such immortality could not be known by natural reason alone.[23]

Such was also the view of the cultured and erudite scholar who emerged as the head of the Paduan Aristotelians, Pietro Pomponazzi. He was the author of a work, *De Immortalitate Animae*, which argued that if one took seriously the Aristotelian doctrine that the human soul was the form of the human body, it was impossible to believe that it could survive death.[24] Pomponazzi considered himself a Christian, and was prepared to accept personal immortality as an article of faith: but he and his Paduan associates soon found themselves the object of ecclesiastical hostility.

In 1512 the warrior pope Julius II, battered in conflict and ailing in health, summoned a general council to meet at the Lateran, with a view to the emendation of a Church by now universally agreed to be in great need of reform. Shortly after the summoning of the Council, Julius died and was replaced by the Medici pope Leo X. Leo showed little enthusiasm for reformation, and the Council achieved almost nothing in practical terms apart from a useful decree declaring that those who ran pawnshops were not necessarily guilty of the sin of usury. Some ecclesiastical abuses were prohibited, but the decrees remained a dead letter, until the issues were brought back by Luther to haunt the papacy. In the meantime, Pope Leo found it helpful to turn the minds of the Council members to less embarrassing issues of philosophy, such as the Paduan teaching on immortality.

A bull issued in December 1513 lamented that the devil had recently sown a pernicious error in the field of the Lord, namely, the belief that the rational soul was either mortal or single in all men, and that some rash philosophers had asserted that this was true 'at least in philosophy'. It proclaimed, on the contrary that the soul, by itself and essentially, was the form of the human body, that it was immortal, and that it was multiplied in proportion to the multitude of the bodies into which it was infused by God. Moreover, since truth could not contradict truth, any assertion contrary to the revealed truth was damned as heretical.

---

[23] Cajetan was called to Rome in 1501, and became successively head of the Dominican order, cardinal, and papal legate to Germany, in which capacity he held a famous debate with Luther at Augsburg in 1518.

[24] Pomponazzi's arguments are set out in greater detail in Ch. 7 below.

Raphael shows Plato and Aristotle amicably dividing the empire of philosophy into separate realms.

The immortality of the soul had been Christian teaching for many centuries, and the religious teaching had already been combined with Aristotelian hylomorphism at the Council of Vienna in 1311. What is noteworthy about the Lateran Council's declaration is its insistence on the relationship between revealed and philosophical truth, and its claim that the immortality of the soul is not only true, but provable by reason. The Church, for the first time, was laying down the law not just on religious truth, but also on religious epistemology. This decree, like the reforming decrees, seems to have had little practical effect. A couple of years later Pomponazzi published his treatise on the soul: it was topped and tailed with professions of faith and submission to the Holy See, but the meat of the work consists of a battery of arguments against personal immortality.

It was while the Lateran Council was in session that Raphael painted in the Vatican, first for Pope Julius and then for Pope Leo, the Stanza della Segnatura, on whose walls and ceilings are represented the disciplines of theology, law, philosophy, and poetry. The fresco *The School of Athens* contains some of the most loving representations of philosophers and philosophical topics in the history of art. Here the reconciliation of Plato and Aristotle is given spatial and colourful form. The two philosophers, side by side, preside over a resplendent court of thinkers, Greek and Islamic. Plato, wearing the colours of the volatile elements air and fire, points heavenwards; Aristotle, clothed in watery blue and earthly green, has his feet firmly on the ground. The two are reconciled, in Raphael's vision, by being assigned different spheres of influence. Aristotle, standing under the aegis of Minerva on the side of the fresco next to the law wall, dominates a group of ethical and natural philosophers. Plato, under the patronage of Apollo, stands above a throng of mathematicians and metaphysicians. Surprisingly, perhaps, he, who banished the poets from his Republic, is given his place next to the wall dedicated to poetry and dominated by Homer. Facing, across the room, is *The Disputation of the Sacrament*, where sit the great Christian philosophers: Augustine, Bonaventure, and Aquinas. The whole is a masterpiece of reconciling genius, bringing together the two truths which, so the Lateran fathers were proclaiming, no man should put asunder.

3

Logic and Language

Augustine on Language

In his account of his childhood in his *Confessions* Augustine describes the learning of language. One passage of his account has become famous:

When they (my elders) named some object, and accordingly moved towards something, I saw this and I grasped that the thing was called by the sound they uttered when they meant to point it out. Their intention was shewn by their bodily movements, as it were the natural language of all peoples: the expression of the face, the play of the eyes, the movement of other parts of the body, and the tone of voice which expresses our state of mind in seeking, having, rejecting or avoiding something. Thus, as I heard words repeatedly used in their proper places in various sentences, I gradually learnt to understand what objects they signified, and after I had trained my mouth to form these signs, I used them to express my own desires. (*Conf.* I. 8. 13)

This passage was placed by Wittgenstein at the beginning of his *Philosophical Investigations*[1] to represent a certain fundamentally mistaken view of language: the view that naming is the foundation of language and that the meaning of a word is the object for which it stands. The passage quoted lays great stress on the role of ostension in the learning of words, and makes no distinction between different parts of speech. Despite this Augustine is a curious choice as a spokesman for the thesis attacked by Wittgenstein, since in many respects what he says resembles Wittgenstein's own views rather than the views that are Wittgenstein's target.

Like Wittgenstein, Augustine believes that the setting-up of linguistic conventions presupposes a uniformity among human beings in their

[1] (Oxford: Blackwell, 1953).

natural, pre-conventional reactions to such things as pointing fingers—
'the natural language of all peoples'. Ostensive definition by itself will not
teach a child the meaning of a word: a child must also 'hear the words
repeatedly used in their proper places in various sentences'. The whole
learning process is started by the child's own efforts to express its sensations
and needs pre-linguistically. Just before the quoted passage he says, 'by cries
and various sounds and movements of my limbs I tried to express my inner
feelings and get my will obeyed'. He thus makes a point, much stressed by
Wittgenstein, that 'words are connected with the primitive, the natural,
expressions of a sensation and used in their place'.[2]

The account of language in the *Confessions* was preceded by a much
ampler account in an early work, *On the Teacher*. The theme of the work,
which is a dialogue between Augustine and his son Adeodatus, is narrower
than its title suggests: it is not concerned with education in general,
but focuses on the teaching and learning of the meaning of words. It
begins with a lively review of the varied uses for which we employ
language. We use it not solely for the communication of information,
but for many other purposes also, from praying to God to singing in the
bath. We can use speech without sound when we form words in our minds:
in such a case we use them as means to recall to memory the objects that
they signify.

Augustine does not leave unexamined the facile assumption that words
are signs. He quotes a line of Vergil,

> If naught of such a city is left by heav'n to stand,

and asks Adeodatus what each of the three first words signifies. What does
'if' stand for? The best Adeodatus can offer is that it expresses doubt.
'Naught' means nothing, so it cannot be true that every word means
something. What of 'of'? Adeodatus proposes that it is a synonym for
'from', but Augustine suggests that this is simply replacing one sign with
another—it does not take us from sign to reality (*DMg* 2. 3–4).

Ostensive definition seems to offer a way out of the impasse, at least for
some words. If I ask what 'wall' means, you could point to it with your
finger. Not only material objects, but colours, can be ostensively defined in
this way. But there are two objections to this as a general account. First of

---

[2] *Philosophical Investigations*, I. 244.

all, words like 'of' cannot be ostensively defined; and, more fundamentally, the gesture of pointing, no less than the utterance of a word, is only a sign, not the reality signified (*DMg* 3. 5–6).

Augustine responds to these objections that there are some words, like 'walk', 'eat', and 'stand', which can be explained by producing an instance of the very thing signified: I ostensively define 'walk' by walking. But suppose I am already walking when someone asks me what 'walk' means: how do I define it? I suppose I walk a little faster, says Adeodatus. But this shows that even in this favoured case ostensive definition is incurably ambiguous: how do I know whether the meaning that is offered is that of 'walk' or of 'hurry'?

Eventually Augustine concludes from the failure of ostensive learning that the meaning of words is not something that is taught by any human teacher, but by a teacher within us whose home is in heaven (*DMg* 14. 46). This is a Christian version, in the special case of language learning, of Plato's thesis in the *Meno* that all learning is really recollection. On the way to this conclusion, however, Augustine discusses a number of important issues in philosophy of language.

First, he classifies signs in a rudimentary semiotic. All words are signs, but not all signs are words: for instance, there are letters and gestures. All names are words, but not all words are names: besides words like 'if' and 'of' there are pronouns, which stand in for nouns, and verbs, that is to say, words with tenses (*DMg* 4. 9, 5. 13).

It is important to keep in mind the distinction between a sign and what it signifies (what Augustine calls its 'significable'). No one is likely to confuse a stone with a word for a stone: but some words are words for words, and here there is a real danger of confusion between sign and significable.

In modern English we minimize the risk of such confusion by employing quotation marks. Adeodatus is human, and there are two syllables in 'human'. In antique Latin, with no quotation marks, there is no such clear distinction between the normal case when we use the word as a predicate, and the special case where we use it in order to mention itself. Adeodatus has to be on his guard to avoid the trap set by his father: you are not composed of two syllables, therefore, you are not human (*DMg* 8. 22). Augustine devotes several pages to explaining that while, at one level, not all words are names, at another level every word is a name since it can be used to name itself. Even 'verb' is a name. The problems he spells out in this dialogue were discussed at great length by the medieval scholastics who developed the theory of supposition.[3]

Augustine himself, however, made no contribution to the discipline of formal logic. He never made a serious study of Aristotle, whom he describes rather condescendingly in *The City of God* as 'a man of outstanding intellect, no match for Plato in style, but well above the common herd'. He was, for a while, very interested in the Stoics, but it was the natural and ethical, not the logical, branch of their philosophy that principally engaged him.

In his youth, indeed, Augustine had read Aristotle's *Categories*, at the bidding of his rhetoric teacher in Carthage. In the *Confessions* he boasts that he mastered the text very quickly, but complains that it did him no good. The book, he says, was very clear on the topic of substance and the items that belong to them, but it is useless from a theological perspective.

What help was this to me when the book got in my way? Thinking that everything whatever was included in the ten categories, I tried to conceive you also, my God, wonderfully simple and immutable as you are, as if you too were a subject of which magnitude and beauty are attributes. I imagined them as inhering in you as a subject like a physical body, whereas you yourself are your own magnitude and your own beauty. (*Conf.* IV. 16. 28–9)

Among the works traditionally attributed to Augustine, at least from the time of Alcuin, is a Latin paraphrase of the *Categories*.[4] The work, however, is not mentioned by Augustine in his *Retractationes*, an exhaustive catalogue of his *Nachlass*, and it is nowadays the universal opinion of scholars that the work is not authentic. However, the attribution to Augustine secured the attention of early medieval scholars to this part of Aristotle's logic. Another work, *De Dialectica*, long thought spurious, has recently been restored to the canon.[5] It shows signs of Stoic influence but is concerned more with grammar than with logic or philosophy of language.

---

[3] See below, p. 130.

[4] It was edited by L. Minio-Paluello as the first volume of the *Aristoteles Latinus* (Bruges: Desclée, De Brouwer, 1953–).

[5] Edited by Darrell Jackson (Dordrecht: Reidel, 1985).

The Logic of Boethius

The close connection between logic and language is emphasized by Boethius, the most significant Latin logician of the first millennium. 'The whole art of logic', he wrote, 'is concerned with speech.' Boethius translated most, perhaps all, of the books of Aristotle's logical corpus, and he prefaced his translation of the *Categories* with a commentary (indeed a pair of commentaries) on the *Isagoge*, or *Introduction*, of Porphyry (c.233–309). Porphyry, the disciple and biographer of Plotinus, had introduced the logic of Aristotle into the curriculum of the Neoplatonic schools, and his *Isagoge* became the standard introductory text. Thanks to the work of Boethius, it retained that position well into the high Middle Ages.

An important feature of Porphyry's *Isagoge* was the theory of predicables, or the kinds of relation in which a predicate might stand to a subject. He listed five heads of classification: species, genus, *differentia*, property, and accident. All of these are terms that occur in Aristotle's *Topics*, but the theory of predicables differs from Aristotle's theory of categories, though the two classifications are related to each other. 'Stigger is a Labrador' tells us the species to which Stigger belongs; 'Stigger is a dog' tells us his genus. The *differentia* indicates the feature which marks off the species within the genus, e.g. 'Stigger is golden-haired and a retriever'. Humans, it was commonly explained, formed a species of the genus *animal* marked off by the *differentia rational*.

The predicates 'human', 'animal', when used of an individual human, Socrates, are predicated in the category of substance—they indicate, wholly or partly, the basic kind of entity that Socrates is. The predicate 'rational', the *differentia*, seems to straddle the distinction between substance and accident: as part of the definition it seems to belong in the substance category, but on the other hand rationality is surely a quality, and qualities are accidents. A property (*proprium*) is an attribute which is peculiar to a particular species, though not definitive of it: the ability to see jokes was standardly taken in medieval times to be a property of the human race. An accident is a predicate that may or may not belong to a given individual, without prejudice to that individual's existence.

The theory of predicables permits us to construct hierarchies within categories. The distinction between genus and species is relative: what is a species relative to a superior genus is a genus relative to an inferior species. But there are ultimate species that are not genera—such as the human species. And there are ultimate genera that are not species of any higher genus: such as the ten categories (which are not species of some superior genus such as 'being'). If we take the category of substance as basic, we can derive two genera from it, body and spirit, by adding the *differentia* 'material' or 'immaterial' respectively. From the genus body, we can then derive two further genera, living beings and minerals, by adding the *differentia* 'animate' or 'inanimate'. The genus of living beings will, by a similar fission, generate the genera of vegetable and animal, and the genus animal will, with the *differentia* 'rational', produce the final species human, which includes the

In this fourteenth century MS of the *Consolation of Philosophy* Boethius is represented as a medieval professor of logic.

individuals Peter, Paul, and John. A branching hierarchy of this kind, set out in a diagram, is a 'Porphyry's Tree'.

In the *Isagoge* Porphyry uses his branching strategy to pose three questions about species and genera. Species and genera are not individual entities like Peter and Paul: they are in some sense universal. Do such things, Porphyry asked, exist outside the mind, or are they merely mental? If they are outside the mind, are they corporeal or incorporeal? If they are incorporeal, do they exist in things perceptible by the senses, or are they separate from them? Porphyry left these questions unanswered; but they set an agenda for many medieval discussions. They became the canonical statement of the Problem of Universals.

Boethius himself answered these questions thus: they exist outside the mind; they are incorporeal; they are not separable except in thought from individuals. A species or a genus is a similarity abstracted from particulars, as we collect the likeness of humanity (*similitudo humanitatis*) from individual humans. This, Boethius says, was Aristotle's view; but for purposes of formal logic it is not necessary to rule out the Platonic thesis of universals existing in separation (PL 64. 835A).

Boethius wrote commentaries on Aristotle's *Categories* and *De Interpretatione*. These commentaries show that he had some acquaintance also with Stoic logic, though he never regards it as trumping Aristotle. For example, he says that the Stoics were wrong about future contingents: when *p* is a future-tensed proposition about a contingent matter, 'Either *p* or not-*p*' is true, but neither '*p*' nor 'not-*p*' need be definitely true. Thus 'Either there will be a sea-battle tomorrow or there will not be a sea-battle tomorrow' is true; but neither 'There will be a sea-battle tomorrow' nor 'There will not be a sea-battle tomorrow' need be definitely true today.

Besides commenting on Porphyry and Aristotle, Boethius wrote textbooks on syllogistic reasoning, one on categorical syllogisms and one on hypothetical syllogisms. A hypothetical syllogism must contain at least one hypothetical premiss, that is to say, a molecular proposition constructed from atomic categorical propositions by means of the connectives 'if', 'or', or 'since'. Some hypothetical syllogisms contain categorical premisses as well as hypothetical ones: one example is the *modus ponens* already familiar in Stoic logic:

If it is day, the sun is shining; but it is day; therefore the sun is shining.

Boethius, however, is more interested in syllogisms where all the premisses and the conclusion too are hypothetical, such as

If it's A, it's B; if it's B it's C; so if it's A it's C.

He elaborates schemata including negative premisses as well as affirmative ones and premisses involving conjunctions other than 'if', e.g. 'Either it is day or it is night'. Hypothetical syllogisms, he maintains, are parasitic on categorical syllogisms, because hypothetical premisses have categorical premisses as their constituents, and they depend on categorical syllogisms to establish the truth of their premisses. Once again, Boethius is siding with Aristotle against the Stoics, this time about the relationship between predicate and propositional logic.

In discussing hypothetical syllogisms Boethius makes an important distinction between two different sorts of hypothetical statement. He uses 'consequentia' ('consequence') as a term for a true hypothetical; perhaps the nearest equivalent in modern English is 'implication'. In some consequences, he says, there is no necessary connection between the antecedent and the consequence: his example is 'Since fire is hot, the heavens are spherical'. This appears to be an example of what modern logicians have called 'material implication'; Boethius' expression is 'consequentia secundum accidens'. On the other hand, there are consequences where the consequent follows necessarily from the antecedent. This class includes not only the logical truths that modern logicians would call 'formal implications' but also hypothetical statements whose truth is discovered by scientific inquiry, such as 'If the earth gets in the way, there is an eclipse of the moon' (PL 64. 835в).

True consequences can be derived, Boethius believes, from a set of supreme universal propositions which he calls 'loci', following Cicero's rendering of the Aristotelian Greek 'topos'. The kind of proposition he has in mind is illustrated by one of his examples: 'Things whose definitions are different are themselves different'. He wrote a treatise, De Topicis Differentiis, in which he offered a set of principles for classifying the supreme propositions into groups. The work, though it appears arid to a modern reader, was influential in the early Middle Ages.[6]

---

[6] De Topicis Differentiis, trans. Eleonore Stump (Ithaca, NY: Cornell University Press, 1978).

Abelard as Logician

Boethius' work as writer and commentator provided the background to the study of logic until the reception of the full logical corpus of Aristotle in the high Middle Ages. After that time the logic he had handed down was referred to as the 'old logic', in contrast to the new logic of the universities. The old logic culminated in the work of Abelard in the first years of the twelfth century: such was the genius of Abelard that his logic contained a number of insights that were missing from the writings of later medieval logicians.

Abelard's preferred name for logic is 'dialectic' and *Dialectica* is the title of his major logical work. He believes that logic and grammar are closely connected: logic is an *ars sermocinalis*, a linguistic discipline. Like grammar, logic deals with words—but words considered as meaningful (*sermones*) not just as sounds (*voces*). Nonetheless, if we are to have a satisfactory logic, we must begin with a satisfactory account of grammatical parts of speech, such as nouns and verbs.

Aristotle had made a distinction between nouns and verbs on the ground that the latter, but not the former, contained a time indication. Abelard rejects this: it is true that only verbs are tensed, but nouns too contain an implicit time-reference. Subject terms stand primarily for things existing at the present time: you can see this if you consider a proposition such as 'Socrates was a boy', uttered when Socrates was old. If time belonged only to the tensed verb, this sentence would mean the same as 'A boy was Socrates'; but of course that sentence is false. The true corresponding sentence is 'Something that was a boy is Socrates'. This brings out the implicit time-reference in nouns, and this could be brought out in a logically perspicuous language by replacing nouns with pronouns followed by descriptive phrases: for example, 'Water is coming in' could be rewritten 'Something that is water is coming in'.

The defining characteristic of verbs is not that they are tensed but that they make a sentence complete; without them, Abelard says, there is no completeness of sense. There can be complete sentences without nouns (e.g. 'Come here!' or 'It is raining') but no complete sentences without verbs (*D* 149). Aristotle had taken the standard form of sentence to be of the form 'S is P'; he was aware that some sentences, such as 'Socrates drinks', did not contain the copula, but he maintained such sentences

123

could always be rewritten in the form 'Socrates is a drinker'. Abelard, on the other hand, takes the noun-verb form as canonical, and regards an occurrence of 'is' as merely making explicit the linking function that is explicit in every verb. We should take '...is a man' as a unit, a single verb (*D* 138).

The verb 'to be' can be used not only as a link between subject and predicate, but also to indicate existence. Abelard paid considerable attention to this point. The Latin verb 'est' ('is'), he says, can appear in a sentence either as attached to a subject (as in 'Socrates est', 'Socrates exists') or as third extra element (as in 'Socrates est homo', 'Socrates is human'). In the second case, the verb does not indicate existence, as we can see in sentences like 'Chimera est opinabilis' ('Chimeras are imaginable'). Any temptation to think that it does is removed if we treat an expression like '...is imaginable' as a single unit, rather than as composed of a predicate term 'imaginable' and the weasel word 'is'.

Abelard offers two different analyses of statements of existence. 'Socrates est', he says at one point, should be expanded into 'Socrates est ens', i.e. 'Socrates is a being'. But this is hardly satisfactory, since the ambiguity of the verb 'esse' carries over into its participle 'being'. Elsewhere—in one of his non-logical works—he was better inspired. He says that in the sentence 'A father exists' we should not take 'A father' as standing for anything; rather, the sentence is equivalent to 'Something is a father'. 'Exists' thus disappears altogether as a predicate, and is replaced by a quantifier plus a verb. In this innovation, as well as in his suggestion that expressions like '...is human' should be treated as a single unit, Abelard anticipated nineteenth-century insights of Gottlob Frege which are fundamental in modern logic.[7]

To Abelard's contemporaries, the logical problem which seemed most urgent was that of universals. Dissatisfied with the theories of his two first teachers, the nominalist Roscelin and the realist William of Champeaux, Abelard offered a middle way between them. On the one hand, he said, it was absurd to say that Adam and Peter had nothing in common other than the word 'human'; the noun applied to each of them in virtue of their likeness to each other, which was something objective. On the other hand,

[7] The transformation of existential propositions into quantified propositions was regarded by Bertrand Russell as a logical innovation that gave the death blow to the ontological argument for God's existence; see below, p. 293.

it is absurd to say that there is a substantial entity, the human species, which is present in its entirety in each and every individual; this would imply that Socrates must be identical with Plato and that he must be in two places at the same time. A resemblance is not a substantial thing like a horse or a cabbage, and only individual things exist.

When we maintain that the likeness between things is not a thing, we must avoid making it seem as if we were treating them as having nothing in common; since what in fact we say is that the one and the other resemble each other in their being human, that is, in that they are both human beings. We mean nothing more than that they are human beings and do not differ at all in this regard. (*LI* 20)

Their being human, which is not a thing but, Abelard says, a status, is the common cause of the application of the noun to the individual.

Both nominalism and realism depend on an inadequate analysis of what it is for a word to signify. Words signify in two ways: they mean things, and they express thoughts. They mean things precisely by evoking the appropriate thoughts, the concepts under which the mind brings the things in the world. We acquire these concepts by considering mental images, but they are something distinct from images (*D* 329). It is these concepts that enable us to talk about things, and turn vocal sounds into significant words. There is no universal *man* distinct from the universal noun 'man'—that is the degree of truth in nominalism. But, *pace* Roscelin, the noun 'man' is not a mere puff of breath—it is turned into a universal noun by our understanding. Just as a sculptor turns a piece of stone into a statue, so our intellect turns a sound into a word. In this sense we can say that universals are creations of the mind (*LNPS* 522).

Words do signify universals in that they are the expression of universal concepts. But they do not mean universals in the way that they mean individual things in the world. There are different ways in which words mean things. Abelard makes a distinction between what a word signifies and what it stands for. The word 'boy', wherever it occurs in a sentence, has the same signification: young human male. When the word stands in subject place in a sentence, as in 'A boy is running up the road', it also stands for a boy. But in 'This old man was once a boy', where it occurs as part of the predicate, it does not stand for anything. Roughly speaking, 'boy' stands for something in a given context only if it makes sense to ask 'Which boy?'

We can ask not just what individual words signify, but also what whole sentences signify. Abelard defines a proposition as 'an utterance signifying truth or falsehood'. Once again, 'signify' has a double sense. A true sentence *expresses* a true thought, and it *states* what is in fact the case (*proponit id quod in re est*). It is the second sense of 'signification' that is important when we are doing logic, for we are interested in what states of affairs follow from other states of affairs, rather than in the sequence of thoughts in anybody's mind (*D* 154). The enunciation of the state of affairs (*rerum modus habendi se*) that a proposition states to be the case is called by Abelard the *dictum* of the proposition (*LI* 275). A *dictum* is not a fact in the world, because it is something that is true or false: it is true if the relevant state of affairs obtains in the world; otherwise it is false. What is a fact is the obtaining (or not, as the case may be) of the state of affairs in question.

Abelard, unlike some other logicians, medieval and modern, made a clear distinction between predication and assertion. A subject and predicate may be put together without any assertion or statement being made. 'God loves you' is a statement; but the same subject and predicate are put together in 'If God loves you, you will go to heaven' and again in 'May God love you!' without that statement being made (*D* 160).

Abelard defines logic as the art of judging and discriminating between valid and invalid arguments or inferences (*LNPS* 506). He does not restrict inferences to syllogisms: he is interested in a more general notion of logical consequence. He does not use the Latin word 'consequentia' for this: in common with other authors he uses that word to mean 'conditional proposition'—a sentence of the form 'If p then q'. The word he uses is 'consecutio', which we can translate as 'entailment'. The two notions are related but not identical. When 'If p then q' is a logical truth, then p entails q, and q follows from p; but 'If p then q' is very often true without p entailing q.

For p to entail q it is essential that 'If p then q' be a necessary truth; but for Abelard this is not sufficient. 'If Socrates is a stone, then he is a donkey' is a necessary truth: it is impossible for Socrates to be a stone, and so impossible that he should be a stone without being a donkey (*D* 293). Abelard demands not just that 'If p then q' be a necessary truth, but that its necessity should derive from the content of the antecedent and the consequent. 'Inference consists in a necessity of entailment: namely, that what is meant by the consequence is determined by the sense of the antecedent' (*D* 253).

But the necessity of entailment does not demand the existence of the things that antecedent and consequent are talking about: 'If x is a rose, x is a flower' remains true whether or not there are any roses left in the world (*LI* 366). It is the *dicta* that carry the entailments, and *dicta* are neither thoughts in our heads nor things in the world like roses.

In modal logic Abelard's most helpful contribution was a distinction (which he claimed to derive from Aristotle's *Sophistici Elenchi* 165^{b}26) between two different ways of predicating possibility. Consider a proposition such as 'It is possible for the king not to be king'. If we take this as saying that 'The king is not the king' is possibly true, then the proposition is obviously false. Predication in this way Abelard calls predication *de sensu* or *per compositionem*. We can take the proposition in a different way, as meaning that the king may be deposed; and so taken it may very well be true. Abelard calls this the sense *de re* or *per divisionem*. Later generations of philosophers were to find this distinction useful in various contexts; they usually contrasted predication *de re* not with predication *de sensu* but with predication *de dicto*.

The Thirteenth-Century Logic of Terms

In the latter half of the twelfth century the complete *Organon*, or logical corpus, of Aristotle became available in Latin and formed the core of the logical curriculum henceforth, supplemented by Porphyry's *Isagoge*, two works of Boethius, and a single medieval work—the *Liber de Sex Principiis* of an unknown twelfth-century author. This presented itself as a supplement to the *Categories*, discussing in detail those categories that Aristotle had treated only cursorily. Partly because of its novel availability, the work of Aristotle most energetically studied at this period was the *Sophistici Elenchi*. Sophisms—puzzling sentences that needed careful analysis if they were not to lead to absurd conclusions—became henceforth a staple of the medieval logical diet. Among the most studied sophisms were versions of the liar paradox: 'I am now lying', which is false if true, and true if false. These were known as *insolubilia*.

The rediscovery of Aristotle's logical texts had as one consequence that the work of Abelard, who had been unacquainted with most of the *Organon*, fell into disrepute and was neglected. This was unfortunate, because in

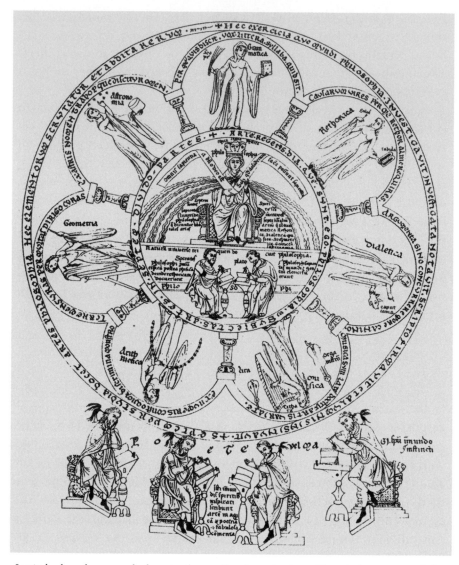

Logic had an honoured place in the medieval curriculum. Here it forms part of the crown of Lady Philosophy presiding over a disputation between Plato and Socrates, and surrounded by the seven liberal arts.

several important features Abelardian logic was superior to Aristotelian logic. Some of his insights reappear, unattributed, in later medieval logic; others had to wait until the nineteenth century to be rediscovered independently.

In the middle of the thirteenth century there appeared two logical manuals that were to have long-lasting influence. One was the *Introductiones in Logicam* written by an Englishman at Oxford, William of Sherwood; the other was the *Tractatus*, later called *Summulae Logicales*, written by Peter of Spain, a Paris master who may or may not be identical with the man who became Pope John XXI in 1276. There was no set order in which writers dealt with logical topics, but one possible pattern corresponded to the order of treatment in the *Organon*—*Categories, De Interpretatione, Prior Analytics*. There was a certain propriety in studying in turn the logic of individual words ('the properties of terms'), of complete sentences (the semantics of propositions), and the logical relations between sentences (the theory of consequences).

Terms include not only words, written or spoken, but also the mental counterparts of these, however these are to be identified. In practice concepts are identified by the words that express them, so the medieval study of terms was essentially the study of the meanings of individual words. In the course of this study logicians developed an elaborate terminology. The most general word for 'meaning' was 'significatio', but not every word that was not meaningless had signification. Words were divided into two classes according to whether they had signification on their own (e.g. nouns) or whether they only signified in conjunction with other, significant, words. The former class were called categorematic terms, the latter were called syncategorematic (*SL* 3). Conjunctions, adverbs, and prepositions were examples of syncategorematic terms, as were words such as 'only' in 'Only Socrates is running'. Categorematic words give a sentence its content; syncategorematic words are function words that exhibit the structure of sentences and the form of arguments.

As a first approximation one can say that the signification of a word is its dictionary meaning. If we learn the meaning of a word from a dictionary, we acquire a concept that is capable of multiple application. (What constitutes the precise relation between words, concepts, and extra-mental reality will depend on what theory of universals you accept.) Categorematic terms, in addition to signification, could have a number of other semantic properties, depending on the way the words were used in particular contexts. Consider the four sentences 'A dog is scratching at the door', 'A dog has four legs', 'I will buy you a dog for Christmas', and 'The dog has just been sick'. The word 'dog' has the same signification in each of these sentences—it corresponds to a single dictionary entry—but its other semantic properties differ from sentence to sentence.

These properties were grouped by medieval logicians under the general heading of 'suppositio' (*SL* 79–89). The distinction between signification and supposition had some of the same functions as the distinction made by modern philosophers between sense and reference. The most basic kind of supposition is called by Peter of Spain 'natural supposition': this is the capacity that a significant general term has to supposit for (i.e. stand for) any item to which the term applies. The way in which this capacity is exercised in different contexts gives rise to different forms of supposition.

One important initial distinction is between simple supposition and personal supposition (*SL* 81). This distinction is easier to make in English than in Latin, because in English it corresponds to the presence or absence of an article before a noun. Thus in 'Man is mortal' there is no article and the word has simple supposition; in 'A man is knocking at the door' the word has personal supposition. But personal supposition itself comes in several different kinds, namely, discrete, determinate, distributive, and confused.

There are three different ways in which a word can occur in the subject place of a sentence: these correspond to discrete, determinate, and distributive supposition. In 'The dog has just been sick' the word 'dog' has discrete supposition: the predicate attaches to a definite single one of the items to which the word applies. This kind of supposition attaches to proper names, demonstratives, and definite descriptions. Determinate supposition is exemplified in 'A dog is scratching at the door': the predicate attaches to some one thing to which the word applies, a thing that is not further specified. In 'A dog has four legs' (or 'Every dog has four legs') the supposition is distributive: the predicate attaches to everything to which the word 'dog' applies. To distinguish determinate from distributive supposition one should ask whether the question 'Which dog?' makes sense or not.

A word can, however, have personal supposition not only when it occurs in a subject place, but also if it appears as a predicate. In 'Buffy is a dog' (or in 'A dachshund is a dog') the name 'confused' was given to the supposition of the word 'dog'. In confused supposition, as in distributive supposition, it makes no sense to ask 'Which dog?' (*SL* 82).

All the kinds of supposition we have listed—simple supposition and the various forms of personal supposition—are examples of 'formal supposition'. Formal supposition, naturally enough, contrasts with material supposition, and the underlying idea is that the sound of a word is its matter, while its meaning is its form. The Latin equivalent of ' "Dog" is a monosyllable' would be an instance of material supposition, and so is the equivalent of ' "dog" is a noun'. This is, in effect, the use of a word to refer to itself, to talk about its symbolic properties rather than about what it means or stands for. Once again, modern English speakers have the advantage over medieval Latinists. In general it takes no philosophical skill to identify material supposition, because from childhood we are taught that when we are mentioning a word, rather than using it in the normal way, we must employ quotation marks and write ' "dog" is a monosyllable'. But in more complicated cases confusion between signs and things signified continues to occur from time to time even in the works of trained philosophers.[8]

Supposition was the most important semantic property of terms, but there were others, too, recognized by medieval logicians. One was appellation, which is connected with the scope of terms and sentences. Consider the sentence 'Dinosaurs have long tails'. Is this true, now that there are no dinosaurs? If we take the view that a sentence is made true or false on the basis of the current contents of the universe, then it seems that the sentence cannot be true; and we cannot remedy this problem simply by changing the tense of the verb to 'had'. If we wish to regard the sentence as true, we shall have to regard truth as something to be determined on the basis of all the contents of the universe, past, present, and future. The medievals posed this problem as being one about the appellation of the term 'dinosaur'.

---

[8] The reader should be warned that though most logicians made the distinctions identified above, there is considerable variation in the terminology used to make them. Moreover, in the interests of simplicity I have abbreviated some of the technical terms. What I have called 'confused supposition' should strictly be called 'merely confused' and what I have called 'distributive' should be called 'confused and distributive'. See Paul Spade in *CHLMP* 196, and W. Kneale, in *The Development of Logic* (Oxford: Oxford University Press, 1962), 252.

Two schools of thought adopted different approaches to the problem. One school, to which William of Sherwood belonged, held that the standard, or default, appellation of terms was only to presently existing objects. If one wishes a term to supposit for something no longer extant, one has to apply to the term a procedure called *ampliation*. The other view, to which Peter of Spain subscribed, held that the standard appellation of terms included all things to which they applied, whether present, past, or future. If one wished to restrict the supposition of a term to the current contents of the universe, one had to apply a procedure called *restriction* (*SL* 199–208). Both schools drew up complicated rules to indicate when the context imposed ampliation, or restriction, as the case may be.

Propositions and Syllogisms

If we turn from the logic of terms to the logic of propositions, we find that just as the medievals regarded nouns as expressing concepts in the mind, so they regarded sentences as expressing beliefs in the mind. Following Aristotle, they distinguished between simple thoughts (expressed in single words) and complex thoughts (expressed in combinations of words). There were, they said, again following Aristotle, two different operations of the intellect: one, the understanding of non-complexes, and the other, the composition and division of a proposition (cf. Aquinas, I *Sent.* 19. 5 ad 1). A proposition, we are regularly told, is a combination of words that expresses something that is either true or false.

There are a number of difficulties in reconciling these accounts of the nature of the proposition. First of all, once we have distinguished (with Abelard) between predication and assertion, it is clear that a complex consisting of a subject and predicate need not be an assertion nor express a belief. (Some medieval logicians marked the distinction by saying that not every proposition was an enunciation.)[9] Secondly, 'composition and division' in Aristotle appears to mean the same as 'positive and negative judgements'—but are not the subject and predicate put together in a single complex in a negative judgement no less than in a positive one? Thomas Aquinas offered the following answer to this problem:

---

[9] L. de Rijk, *Logica Modernorum* (Assen: van Gorcum, 1962–6), II. 1. 342.

If we consider what takes place in the mind by itself then there is always combination where there is truth and falsehood; for the mind cannot produce anything true or false unless it combines one simple concept with another. But if the relation to reality is taken into account, then the mind's operation is called sometimes 'combination' and sometimes 'division': 'combination' where the mind so places one concept beside another as to represent the combination or identity of the things *of* which they are the concepts; 'division' where it so places one concept beside another as to represent that the corresponding realities are distinct. We talk in the same way of sentences too: an affirmative sentence is called 'a combination' because it signifies that there is a conjunction in reality; a negative sentence is called 'a division' because it signifies that the realities are separate. (*In I Periherm.* 1. 3, p. 26)

A proposition, whether asserted or not, will be true or false; that is to say, it will, as a matter of fact, correspond or not with reality. The same is true of the corresponding thought, whether it is a belief or the mere entertainment of a conjecture. But only the speech-act of asserting, or the corresponding mental act of judging, commits the thinker or speaker to the truth of the proposition.

Against this background, we may raise the question, What do propositions signify? If we take 'signify' as equivalent to 'express', then it is easy to give an answer: spoken and written propositions express thoughts in the mind. But there is then a further question: What do mental propositions signify? Here 'signify' has to be closer to 'mean' than to 'express'. Propositions, it seems, cannot signify anything in the world, because a proposition must signify the same whether it is true or false; and if the proposition is false, there is nothing in the world to correspond to it. The most popular answer to this question in the thirteenth century was essentially that given by Abelard: it is the state of affairs which, if it obtains, makes the sentence true. Abelard had called this a *dictum*; others called it an *enuntiabile*; but most people found it difficult to give a clear account of its metaphysical status. One author said that *enuntiabilia* were neither substances nor qualities, but stood in a class of their own—not to be found in Aristotle's categories. They were not tangible entities but could be grasped only by reason.[10] As we shall see, the existence of such entities was called in question in the fourteenth century.

---

[10] Ibid. II. 1. 357–9. There was a particular problem about the signification of tensed propositions, a problem that constantly recurred in treatments of divine foreknowledge. See Ch. 9 below.

There is a further, related, question: What kind of thing is it that is true or false? Sentences, thoughts, and *dicta* can all be called true. But which of these is the primary bearer of truth-values? The question is particularly pointed when we consider the relation between truth and time. Some philosophers believe that all that we say in natural languages by the use of tensed sentences could be said in a logical language that contained no tenses but whose sentences contained timeless verbs plus an explicit temporal reference or quantification over times. Thus, a sentence 'It will rain' uttered at time *t*1 would on this view have to be understood as expressing a proposition to the following effect: at some time *t* later than *t*1 it rains (timelessly). It is still a matter of debate whether such a translation of tensed sentences into timeless propositions can be carried out without loss of content.

In the Middle Ages there was little enthusiasm for such translation. Most commonly, *enuntiabilia* no less than sentences were regarded as tensed. Consequently, both sentences and *enuntiabilia* could change their truth-values. Aristotle was frequently quoted as saying that one and the same sentence 'Socrates is sitting' is true when Socrates is sitting and false when he gets up.[11] The nearest approximation to timeless propositions in the thought of medieval logicians was a disjunction of tensed propositions. Thus it was sometimes suggested that there was a single object of faith in which Hebrew prophets and Christian saints alike believed, namely, the proposition 'Christ will be born or Christ is born or Christ has been born'.[12]

The thirteenth-century logic manuals contained, in addition to discussions of terms and propositions, substantial sections on the theory of

Medieval students learned their logical mnemonics in a classroom such as this.

[11] This issue was discussed particularly in connection with God's timeless knowledge of events in time; see Ch. 9 below.

[12] See G. Nuchelmans, 'The Semantics of Propositions', in *CHLMP* 202.

inference. The core of their treatment was Aristotle's syllogistic. The logicians provided doggerel verses to make the rules of syllogistic memorable and easy to operate. The best-known such verse is the following:

> Barbara celarent darii ferio baralipton
> Celantes dabitis fapesmo frisesomorum;
> Cesare campestres festino baroco; darapti
> Felapton disamis datisi bocardo ferison.

Each word represents a particular mood of valid syllogism, with the vowels indicating the nature of the three propositions that make it up. The letter 'a' stands for a universal affirmative proposition, and the letter 'i' a particular affirmative proposition (these letters being chosen because they are the first two vowels in 'affirmo', 'I affirm'). The letter 'e' stands for a universal negative, and 'o' for a particular negative. (The Latin for 'I deny' is 'nego': hence the choice of vowels.) Thus a syllogism in Barbara contains three universal propositions (e.g. 'All kittens are cats; all cats are animals; so all kittens are animals'). A syllogism in Celarent, by contrast, has as premisses one universal negative and one universal affirmative, with a universal negative conclusion (e.g. 'No cats are birds; all kittens are cats; so no kittens are birds').

The first four moods of syllogism were regarded as the most perspicuous forms of valid argument. Accordingly the mnemonic words for the later moods contain instructions for transforming themselves into arguments in one or other of the first four moods. The letter at the beginning of each mood's name indicates which of the four it is to be converted into. 'C' at the beginning of 'Cesare' shows that it is to be converted into a syllogism in Celarent. Other letters show how to do this: the 's' after the first 'e' in Cesare shows that the order of the terms in that premiss are to be switched. Thus 'No birds are cats; all kittens are cats; so no kittens are birds', a syllogism in Cesare, is converted, by switching the terms in the first premiss, into the syllogism in Celarent, illustrated above.

The occurrence of the letter 'c' within the body of a mnemonic word indicates that the conversion into the preferred mood has to be undertaken in a particularly complicated and difficult manner, which need not be illustrated here. But the operation left such a mark on students of logic that of the two words containing such a 'c', Baroco gave its name to a highly elaborate style of architecture while Bocardo gave its name to the prison in which delinquent Oxford students were incarcerated. Mnemonics such as these, ingenious though they are, were mocked by Renaissance writers as being, literally, barbaric; and they contributed to the disrepute of medieval logic in early modern times.

Aquinas on Thought and Language

Thomas Aquinas made little contribution to formal logic, but he reflected upon the nature of language and the relationship of language to thought: he offers various classifications of speech-acts, and of what we might call the corresponding thought-acts. He begins from a text of Aristotle which makes a distinction between two kinds of intellectual activity.

There are, as Aristotle says in the *De Anima*, two kinds of activity of our intellect. One consists in forming simple essences, such as what a man is or what an animal is: in this activity, considered in itself, neither truth nor falsehood is to be found, any more than in utterances that are non-complex. The other consists in putting together and taking apart, by affirming and denying: in this truth and falsehood are to be found, just as in the complex utterance that is its expression. (*DV* 14. 1)

The distinction between these two types of thought is linked to the difference in language between the use of individual words and the construction of complete sentences. This is brought out when Aquinas explains that any act of thinking can be regarded as the production of an inner word or inner sentence.

The 'word' of our intellect . . . is that which is the terminus of our intellectual operation. It is the thought itself, which is called an intellectual conception: which may be either a conception which can be expressed by a non-complex utterance, as when the intellect forms the essences of things, or a conception expressible by a complex utterance, as when the intellect composes and divides. (*DV* 4. 2c)

As we have seen, the notion of intellectual 'composition and division' is not a straightforward one. The paradigm example of such composition and division is the making of affirmative and negative judgements. But there are other types of complex thought. Besides judging that *p* and judging that not-*p* I may wonder whether *p*, or simply entertain the idea that *p* as part of a story. Consider any proposition, for example 'Smoking causes deafness' or 'Saudi Arabia possesses nuclear weapons'. With respect to propositions such as these a judgement, affirmative or negative, may be made or withheld; if made, it may be made truly or falsely, with or without hesitation, on the basis of argument, or on grounds of self-evidence.

Aquinas classes exercises of the intellectual powers on the basis of these different possibilities: the withholding of judgement is doubt (*dubitatio*); tentative assent, allowing for the possibility of error, is opinion (*opinio*); unquestioning assent to a truth on the basis of self-evidence is understanding (*intellectus*); giving a truth unquestioning assent on the basis of reasons is knowledge (*scientia*); unquestioning assent where there are no compelling reasons is belief or faith (*credere, fides*). All of these are instances of *compositio et divisio*.

What of the other intellectual activity, the conception of non-complexes? Aquinas seems, in different places, to give two different accounts of this. Sometimes he seems to equate it with the mastery of the use of a word. In that case someone would have a concept of *gold* if she knew the meaning of the word 'gold'. But in other places Aquinas equates a concept with the knowledge of the quiddity or essence of something: in this sense only a chemist, who could link the properties of gold with its atomic number and its place in the periodic table, would have a real concept of *gold* (*ST* 1a 3. 3 and 1a 77. 1 ad 3). He was well aware of the difference between the two types of concept: he points out, for instance, that we can know what the word 'God' means, but we do not and cannot know God's essence (e.g. *ST* 1a 2. 2 ad 2).

How close, for Aquinas, is the link between language and thought: what is the relationship between these varied intellectual operations and the corresponding speech-acts? Aquinas believed that any judgement that can be made can be expressed by a sentence (*DV* 2.4). It does not follow from this, nor does Aquinas maintain, that every judgement that is made *is* put into words, either publicly or in the privacy of the imagination. Again, even though every thought is expressible in language, only a small minority of thoughts are *about* language.

On the question of universals, Aquinas' starting point is a rejection of Platonism, a doctrine that he described as follows:

Plato, to save the fact that we can have certain intellectual knowledge of the truth, posited in addition to ordinary bodily things, another class of things free of matter and change, which he called *species* or Ideas. It was by participation in these that all particular tangible objects get called 'human' or 'horse' or whatever. Accordingly,

Plato held that definitions, and scientific truths, and all other things pertaining to the operation of the intellect, are not about ordinary tangible bodies, but about those immaterial things in another world. (*ST* 1a 84. 1c)

Plato was misled, Aquinas thought, by the doctrine that like can be known only by like, and so the form of what is known must be in the knower exactly as it is in the known. It is true that the objects of thought in the intellect are universal and immaterial; but universals of this kind do not exist anywhere outside an intellect.

Aquinas was prepared to agree with Plato that there are forms that make things what they are: there is, for instance, a form of humanity that makes Socrates human. But he denied that there was any such form existing apart from matter. There is not, outside the mind, any such thing as human nature as such, human nature in the absolute. There is only the human nature of individual human beings like Peter and Paul. There is no human nature that is not the nature of some individual, and there is not, in heaven or earth, such a thing as the Universal Man (*ST* 1a 79c). Human nature exists in the mind in abstraction from individuating characteristics, related uniformly to all the individual humans existing outside the mind. There is no Idea of Human, only people's ideas of humanity. Plato's Ideas are rejected in favour of Tom, Dick, and Harry's concepts (*DEE* 3. 102–7).

The humanity of an individual, as Aquinas put it, was 'thinkable' (because a form) but not 'actually thinkable' (because existing in matter). To make it actually thinkable it had to be operated upon by a special intellectual power, the 'agent intellect'. We will follow Aquinas' account of this operation when we examine his philosophy of mind; at present we may ask what are the implications of Aquinas' anti-Platonic account of universals for the semantics of names and predicates.

Aquinas spells out the consequences in respect of one kind of universal, namely, a species. The species *dog* does not exist in reality, and it is no part of being a dog to be a species, even though dogs are a species. But if being a species were part of what it was to be a dog, then Fido would be a species. When we say that dogs are a species, we are not really, if Aquinas is right, saying anything about dogs: we are making a second-order statement about our concepts. First, we are saying that the concept *dog* is universal: it is applicable to any number of dogs. Secondly, we are saying that it is a composite concept that has other concepts as constituents: for instance, *animal*. Genus and species are defined in terms of predication, and predicates are things that minds make up, in forming affirmative and negative propositions (*DEE* 3. 133–5).

One of Aquinas' best-known contributions to the logic of language is his treatment of analogical discourse. He introduces the topic most commonly when discussing the possibility of discourse about God, but it is one of wide application. Drawing on a number of cryptic passages in Aristotle, he distinguishes two different kinds of analogy. The first kind (which some scholastics called 'analogy of attribution') can be illustrated by reference to the term 'healthy'. Strictly speaking, only living things such as animals and plants can be healthy; but a diet or a complexion may naturally be described as healthy. 'We use the word "healthy" of both a diet and a complexion because both of them have some relation to health in a human, the former as a cause, the latter as a symptom' (1a 13. 5). The other kind of analogy (which some scholastics called 'analogy of proportionality') may be illustrated with reference to the analogous term 'good'. A good knife is a knife that is handy and sharp; a good strawberry is a strawberry that is soft and tasty. Clearly, goodness in knives is something quite different from goodness in strawberries; yet it does not seem to be a mere pun to call both knives and strawberries 'good', nor does one seem to be using a metaphor drawn from knives when one calls a particular batch of strawberries good.

Analogy and Univocity

Aquinas maintained that the words by which we describe God and creatures are not used in the same sense about each. Similarly, to adapt one of his examples, we do not mean quite the same thing when we call the sun 'bright' and when we call the colour of a patch of paint 'bright'. On the other hand, if we say that God is wise and that Socrates is wise, we are not making a pun or talking in metaphor. 'This way of using words', Aquinas says, 'lies somewhere between pure equivocation and simple univocity, for the word is used neither in the same sense, as with univocal usage, nor in totally different senses, as with equivocation'. (*ST* 1a 13. 5).

This theory of analogy was rejected by Duns Scotus, both in itself and in its application to religious language. If it is to be possible to talk about God at all, Scotus argued, there must be some words that have the same meaning when applied to God and creatures. Not all of our theological discourse can be analogical; some of it must be univocal. Scotus focused on words such as 'good'—words that he called 'transcendental' terms, because they transcended the boundaries of the Aristotelian categories, applying across all of them. As Aristotle himself had pointed out, we can talk of good times and good places as well as good men or good qualities (*NE* 1. 5. 1096^{a}23–30). Scotus maintained that such transcendental terms were all univocal: they had a single sense whether they were applied to different kinds of creatures, or whether they were applied to creatures and to God himself. The most important transcendental term was 'ens', 'being'. Substances and accidents, creatures and creator, were all beings in exactly the same sense.

Scotus' target in his discussion of analogy and univocity was not Aquinas but Henry of Ghent. Henry had maintained that our unreflective concept of being masks two distinct concepts, one that applies to the infinite being of God, and another that applies to the creatures that fall within the different categories. Reflection reveals that there is no single, univocal, concept that applies both to God and to creatures; there is, however, a similarity between the two concepts sufficient to enable us to make analogical predications about God, describing him not just as a being, but as good, wise, and so on.

Scotus rejects the idea that there can be a half-way house between univocity and equivocation. Certainly, if we are dealing with simple concepts that have no constituent parts, there cannot be such a thing as the sense of a word being *partly* the same and *partly* different. If the terms we apply to God are equivocal—are used in a quite different sense from the one they have when applied to creatures—then we cannot draw any conclusions about God from the properties of creatures. Any attempt to use an analogical predicate as the middle term of a syllogism would be guilty of the fallacy of equivocation (*Lect.* 16. 266).

A concept is univocal, Scotus tells us, when

it possesses sufficient unity in itself so that to affirm and deny it of one and the same thing would be a contradiction. It also has sufficient unity to serve as the middle term of a syllogism, so that whenever two extremes are united by a middle term that is one in this way, we may conclude to the union of the two extremes among themselves. (*Ord.* 3. 18)

To show that there can be a univocal concept of being that applies both to God and to creatures, Scotus argues as follows. If you can be certain that S is P while doubting whether S is Q, then P and Q must be different concepts. But you can be certain that God is a being, while doubting whether he is an infinite or a finite being. Hence the concept of being differs from that of infinite being and that of finite being—Henry's two primitive concepts—and is univocal, applying to both finite and infinite in the same sense (*Ord.* 3. 29). Concepts like 'being', 'good', 'one', and the like are thus, for Scotus, transcendental not just in transcending the boundaries of the categories, but also in transcending the gap between finite and infinite.

Scotus does not deny that there are concepts that apply analogously to God and creatures. His claim is that these are built upon, and could not exist without, more basic concepts that are univocal.

Take, for example, the formal notion of 'wisdom' or 'intellect' or 'will'. Such a notion is considered first of all simply in itself and absolutely. Because this notion includes formally no imperfection or limitation, the imperfections associated with it in creatures are removed. Retaining this same notion of 'wisdom' and 'will' we attribute these to God—but in a most perfect degree. Consequently, every inquiry regarding God is based upon the supposition that the intellect has the same univocal concept which it obtains from creatures. (*Ord.* 3. 26–7)

Perhaps the disagreement between Aquinas, Henry, and Scotus is not as sharp as it at first appears, because the notions *the same sense* and *the same concept* are themselves not sharp. Two words have different senses, we might suggest, if a dictionary would give two separate definitions of them. But when Aquinas says that 'good' is an analogous term, he need not be suggesting that every different application of 'good' creates a new lexical item. Different creatures have different good-making properties, but that does not mean that the meaning of 'good' in 'good horse' is different from the meaning of 'good' in 'good time'. Indeed, someone who did not realize that 'good' was, in Aquinas' terms, analogous, would not understand its meaning in the language at all. Scotus is right, on the other hand, that when we learn to apply 'good' to a new object, we do not learn a new vocabulary lesson.

Whether 'being' is analogous or univocal is a murky question not because of difficulties about analogy but because of the almost universal opacity of the medieval notion of *being*. If we are talking about existence, as expressed, say, in the sentence 'There is a God', then the question whether being is an analogous or univocal predicate does not arise since attributing existence to something is not a matter of attaching a predicate to a subject. But, in Scotus at least, 'to be', period, seems equivalent to a vast disjunction of predicates: 'to be a horse, or a colour, or a day, or...' and so on ad infinitum. So understood, 'to be' seems clearly univocal. Suppose that there were only three items in the universe, A, B, and C. The predicate '... is either A, or B, or C' seems to attach in exactly the same sense to each of the three items.

Modistic Logic

Scotus did not make any substantial contribution to formal logic, though his metaphysical ideas on the nature of power and potentiality were to have a significant long-term effect on modal logic. He was, however, long credited with an interesting work on the borders of logic and linguistics, a *Grammatica Speculativa* that the young Martin Heidegger took as the subject of his doctoral thesis. The work is now regarded as inauthentic by scholars, and attributed not to Scotus but to his little-known contemporary Thomas of Erfurt, writing about 1300.

The work is important as representative of a new approach to logic, adopted by Radulphus Brito (d. 1320) and a number of thinkers in the late thirteenth century, known as 'modistic logic' in contrast to the 'terminist logic' which we have seen in the works of Peter of Spain and William Sherwood. Rather than studying the properties of individual terms, these modist logicians studied general grammatical categories—nouns, verbs, cases, and tenses, for instance—which they called *modi significandi*, or ways of signifying.

Meaning, according to the modists, was conferred on sounds by human convention, which they called 'imposition'. The unit element of meaning was the *dictio*, 'diction'. A single diction might embrace many different verbal forms: the cases of a Latin noun, for instance, plus the adjectives and adverbs associated with it. A favourite example was the diction for *pain*, which included the noun 'dolor' in its different cases, the verb for feeling pain 'doleo', and the adverb 'dolenter', meaning 'painfully'. The basic convention setting up the diction for pain was called by the modists first imposition; further conventions, by a second imposition, established these *modi significandi* that linked different word forms to different types of use.[13]

Some *modi significandi* were more fundamental than others. The essential one defined a word as a particular part of speech—noun or verb, for example. Other accidental ones allotted to it such features as case, number, tense, or mood. Complicated rules were worked out to determine which words, with which *modi significandi*, could combine together to make a well-formed sentence.

Broadly speaking, it can be said that the study of *modi significandi* was a study of syntax, while the focus of semantics was the *ratio significandi*, or signifying relation conferred by the first imposition. The speculative grammarians did, however, seek to find a semantic element associated with the modes of signifying. The sense of an expression is fixed by the combination of *ratio* and *modi*: this was called its 'formal meaning', its meaning in virtue of language (*virtus sermonis*). In modern terminology we might call this its lexical meaning, its meaning as determined by the dictionary.

In a context of actual use, however, an expression also has a reference determined by its sense. Faced with the Latin sentence 'Homo appropinquat' we may be told that this consists of the nominative singular of the masculine noun 'homo', meaning man, plus the third-person singular of the verb 'appropinquo', meaning approach. This information is given us by the *virtus sermonis*: but we may ask, in a real-life context, *which man* is approaching; and this fact opens up a new area of inquiry. The modist logicians had various suggestions to offer here, but they were not taken up by later generations of thinkers. Instead, there was a revival of terminist logic, which had developed the theory of supposition to deal precisely with issues of the relationship between sense and reference.

Ockham's Mental Language

One of the most important of the terminist logicians of the fourteenth century was William Ockham. Ockham offers a novel system: a terminist

---

[13] See J. Pinborg, 'Speculative Grammar', in *CHLMP* 254–69.

This doodle in a Cambridge MS is the earliest known representation of Ockham.

logic that is nominalist, not realist. All signs, Ockham maintained, represent individual things, because there are no such things in the world as universals for them to represent. He offers a series of metaphysical arguments against the idea that a universal is a real common nature existing in individuals. If individuals contained universals, then no individual could be created out of nothing, for the universal part of it would be already in existence. On the other hand, if God annihilated an individual, he would destroy simultaneously all other individuals of the same species by wiping out the common nature (*OPh*. 1. 15).

A universal is a singular thing, and is universal only by signification, being a single sign of many things. There are two kinds of universal: natural and conventional. A natural universal is a thought in our mind (*intentio animae*); conventional signs are universal by our voluntary decision, being words coined to express these thoughts and to signify many things. The signs in our mind are put together to make mental propositions in the same way as spoken signs are put together to make a vocal proposition (*OPh*. 1. 12).

Ockham regarded these mental concepts as forming a language system. Besides the spoken, conventional, languages like English and Latin, all human beings share a common, natural language. It is from this universal

144

language that regional languages derive their significance. The mental language contains some, but not all, of the grammatical features studied by the modists. Thus Mental contains nouns and verbs, but not pronouns and particles. The nouns have cases and numbers, and the verbs have voices and tenses, but there are not different declensions of nouns and conjugations of verbs as in Latin grammar. If two Latin expressions, or two expressions in different languages, are synonymous with each other, then, according to Ockham, they will correspond to one, not two, elements of Mental. It follows that in Mental itself there is no such thing as synonymy.

Other logicians in later ages have from time to time endeavoured to construct ideal languages in which there is no ambiguity or redundancy. Modern formal logics can be looked at as such idealizations of certain fragments of natural language: the propositional connectives like 'and', 'or', and 'if', the quantifiers like 'all' and 'some', and various expressions concerned with tense and moods. Ockham deserves credit for being a pioneer in pointing out the idealization that is involved in applying formal logic to natural language, even if we may smile at his readiness to transfer idiomatic features of medieval Latin into the universal language of the mind.

It is one thing when a logician constructs an ideal language for a particular purpose, as an object of comparison to draw attention to features of natural languages that are ambiguous or invite confusion. It is another matter when logicians—medieval or modern—maintain that their ideal language is somehow already present in our use of natural language, and contains the ultimate explanation of the meaningfulness of the way we use words in everyday speech. If this was Ockham's intention, then his invention of Mental was futile, for it serves no such explanatory purpose.

In the first place, there is a problem about the nature of the mental entities corresponding to spoken and written nouns. Ockham himself seems to have worried about this, and to have changed his mind on the topic at least once. Initially he identified the names of mental language with mental images or representations. These were creations of the mind—'fictions' that serve as elements in mental propositions, going proxy for the things they resembled. Fictions could be universal in the sense of having an equal likeness to many different things.

What is the status of these fictions? Ockham, at this stage, maintains that they do not have real existence, but only what he calls 'objective existence', that is to say, existence as an object of thought. There are fictions, after all, not only of things that really exist in the world, but also of things like chimeras and goat-stags which are, in the ordinary modern sense, fictional. When we think a thought, there are two things to be distinguished: our act of thinking, and what we think of, that is to say, the content or object of our thought. It is the latter that is the fiction and that features as a term in a mental proposition.

Later Ockham came to regard this distinction as spurious. There is no need to postulate objects of thought: the only elements needed to support mental language are the thoughts themselves. Unlike a chimera, my-thinking-of-a-chimera is a real entity—a temporary quality of my soul, an item in my psychological history. When mental names occur in mental sentences, it is as elements in the thinking of the sentence. Ockham does not seem to have made up his mind whether they were successive stages in the thinking of the sentence, or a set of simultaneous thoughts, or a single complex thought.

There is good reason for Ockham's hesitation here, because the analogy between speech and thought breaks down when we consider temporal duration. Spoken words take time to utter, and one word comes out after another. The case is the same with mental images of words, as when one recites a poem to oneself in imagination. But thoughts are quite different: the whole content of a judgement must be present at once if a judgement is to be made at all, and there can be no question of the temporal sequence of the elements of a thought.[14]

However mental names are conceived, in Ockham's view they all refer to, supposit for, individual objects, since in reality there are no such things as universals. These individual objects, however, may include individual thoughts. Ockham's nominalism means that he has to modify the theory of supposition that we have seen in earlier logicians such as Peter of Spain.[15] Ockham redefines the principal forms of supposition: simple supposition and personal supposition.

Simple supposition had been defined as a word standing for what it signifies; and this was taken to imply that in a sentence such as 'Man is

---

[14] See P. T. Geach, *Mental Acts* (London: Routledge & Kegan Paul, n.d.), 104–5.
[15] See p. 130 above.

mortal' the subject 'man' stood for a universal. But for Ockham, simple supposition occurs when a word stands for a mental entity, as in 'man is a species', in which 'man' stands for a mental term, the only kind of thing that can be a species. This is not a case of a word standing for what it signifies, for the term 'man' signifies nothing other than individual men.

In personal supposition it is indeed true that a term stands for what it signifies. In 'Every man is an animal' the word 'man' stands for what it signifies, because men are the very thing it signifies—not something that is common to them, but the very men themselves. But there can be personal supposition even when a term is not standing for a thing in the world. 'Personal supposition is where a term stands for what it signifies, whether that is an extra-mental reality, or a word, or a concept in the mind, or something written, or whatever is imaginable' (*OPh.* 1. 64).

Personal supposition is basic for Ockham, and it can apply to predicates as well as subjects. A predicate signifies, and supposits for, whatever it is true of. Thus, if Peter and Paul and John are all the men there are, then both in 'Every man is mortal' and in 'Every Apostle is a man' the word 'man' supposits for Peter, Paul, and John. This seems to mean that the first sentence is equivalent to 'Peter and Paul and John are mortal' and the second to 'Every Apostle is either Peter or Paul or John'. A general term, in other words, is equivalent to a list of proper names—a conjunctive list in the first case, and a disjunctive list in the second.

Truth and Inference in Ockham

Ockham uses the notion of supposition to define truth. A proposition like 'Socrates is human' is true if and only if the subject term 'Socrates' and the predicate term stand for the same thing. This is sometimes called a two-name theory of truth: an affirmative categorical proposition is true if it puts together, as subject and predicate, two names of the same thing. But Ockham's theory is a little more complicated than that, at least if we are thinking of names as being proper names. As we have seen, for Ockham a general term is not a proper name, but is equivalent to a list of proper names; and the truth condition he lays down in terms of identity of supposition amounts to the requirement that for an affirmative categorical to be true one and the same proper name must occur in both the subject list and the predicate list.

The simple two-name theory is easily shown to break down. If 'Socrates is a philosopher' is true because Socrates can be called both 'Socrates' and 'philosopher', it is not easy to see how to explain the truth conditions of 'Socrates isn't a dog'. In order to know that 'dog' is not a name of Socrates, we have to know what it *is* a name of: and there does not seem any answer to the question 'Which dog is it that Socrates isn't?' The more complicated theory of Ockham does have an answer to this difficulty: the list corresponding to 'dog' and the (one-item) list corresponding to 'Socrates' do not have a common term. But it falls into a corresponding difficulty of its own. If every general term is an abbreviation for a list of proper names, then every proposition must be either necessarily true or necessarily false. 'Socrates is human' surely is not simply a redundant identity statement. But that is what it is if it means 'Socrates is either Socrates or Plato or Aristotle'.[16]

Ockham devoted great attention to the logical relationships between different propositions: the theory of *consequentiae*, as it came to be called in the fourteenth century. Earlier writers had used the word in the sense of 'conditional proposition'. So understood, an example of a *consequentia* would be

If Socrates is a man, Socrates is an animal,

with 'Socrates is a man' as the antecedent and 'Socrates is an animal' as the consequent.

Consequentiae, so understood, could be true or false, and could be necessary or contingent. Logicians were particularly interested in *consequentiae* that were, like the example above, necessary truths. In such cases one can construct a corresponding argument, namely,

Socrates is a man. Therefore, Socrates is an animal.

Here we have not one but two propositions, the antecedent here being a premiss and the consequent being a conclusion. Arguments are not, like propositions, true or false; they are good or bad, that is to say, valid or invalid, depending on whether the conclusion does or does not follow from the premisses.

---

[16] See Kneale and Kneale, *The Development of Logic*, 268.

Fourteenth-century treatises on *consequentiae* were concerned with sorting out good from bad arguments, rather than with assigning truth-values to the corresponding conditional propositions. Arguments could contain any number of premisses: Aristotelian syllogisms, which contain only two premisses, were just a single class of *consequentiae*. Premisses and conclusions could be of various forms: they could include singular propositions, and not only quantified propositions such as occurred in syllogisms.

Ockham begins by distinguishing 'simple consequences' from 'consequences as of now'. A simple consequence holds if the antecedent can never be true without the consequent being true, e.g. 'No animal is running, therefore no man is running'. An as-of-now consequence holds if the antecedent cannot now be true without the consequent being true, even if at some other time that might be the case. An example would be 'Every animal is running, therefore Socrates is running', where, once Socrates is dead, the antecedent can be true without the consequent (*OPh*. III. 3. 1)

A second distinction that Ockham makes is between consequences whose validity is internal (*per medium intrinsecum*) and those whose validity is external (*per medium extrinsecum*). A consequence is valid externally if its validity does not depend on the meaning of any of the terms in the premiss and conclusion. In such a case the consequence can be stated in schematic form, using only variables: e.g. 'If only As are Bs, then all Bs are As'. A consequence is valid internally if its validity depends upon the meaning of one of the terms: e.g. the validity of 'Socrates is running, therefore a man is running' depends on the fact that Socrates is a man. There is no general principle 'If X is running, therefore an A is running' (*OPh*. III. 3. 1).

Finally, Ockham distinguishes between material and formal consequences. From the examples he gives it appears that he regards as formal consequences both those that are externally valid and those that are internally valid. In material consequences, on the other hand, the impossibility of the antecedent's being true without the consequent depends not on any connection, external or internal, between the content of the antecedent and the content of the consequent. It arises either from the antecedent's being necessarily false, or from the consequent's being necessarily true. Thus 'If a man is an ass, then God does not exist' and 'If a man is running, then God exists', are both valid material consequences (*OPh*. III. 3. 1).

The first of these is an instance of a general rule, 'Anything whatever follows from what is impossible', and the second is an instance of 'What is necessary follows from anything whatever'. Ockham formulates a set of such rules that apply to inference of very varied kinds. They include the following six:

1. What is false does not follow from what is true.
2. What is true may follow from what is false.
3. Whatever follows from the consequent follows from the antecedent.
4. Whatever entails the antecedent entails the consequent.
5. The contingent does not follow from the necessary.
6. The impossible does not follow from the possible.

Many of Ockham's rules derive from earlier philosophers, but he was the first to set them out systematically, and they were generally accepted by later logicians.

Walter Burley and John Wyclif

In *The Pure Art of Logic* of Walter Burley the theory of consequences is given even more prominence, and Aristotelian syllogistic is treated perfunctorily. A very wide variety of inferences is brought under the rubric of 'hypothetical consequences'. The premisses of such inferences include not only conditional sentences (containing 'if...then') but also conjunctive and disjunctive sentences (with 'and' or 'or') and exclusive and exceptive sentences (e.g. 'Only Peter is running' and 'Everyone is running except Peter'). An important class, studied also by Burley's colleagues among the Oxford Calculators, were sentences of the form 'A begins to φ' and 'A ceases to φ'.

Burley accepts Ockham's distinctions between different types of consequence, and adds further subdivisions of his own. In all this, he is continuing, sympathetically, work begun by Ockham. But when we turn from the theory of consequences to the more old-fashioned topic of the properties of terms, the picture is very different. Burley rejects the nominalism that Ockham had built into his logic, and restates the theory of signification and supposition in a manner closer to its traditional realist form.

First, he rejects Ockham's claim that a noun signifies all the things to which it applies.

This noun 'man' has a primary signification, and its primary signification is not Socrates or Plato. If that were so, someone hearing the word and knowing what it signified would have a determinate and distinct thought of Socrates, which is false. Therefore this noun 'man' does not have anything singular as its primary signification. So its primary signification is something common, and that common thing is the species. Whether this common thing is something outside the soul, or is a concept in the soul, I do not much mind at this point. (*PAL.* 7)

With 'signification' thus defined, Burley can restore the traditional definition of simple supposition: a term stands for what it signifies. The final sentence of the quoted paragraph leaves it open for his definition to coincide in practice with Ockham's definition of simple supposition, namely that in simple supposition a term stood for a concept in the mind.

Burley not only defended, but also extended, the traditional theory of supposition. As Ockham had done before him, he identified well-formed sentences that were not covered by the types of personal supposition listed by Peter of Spain and William Sherwood. One such sentence was 'Every man loves himself': the classification hitherto devised would not bring out the fact that this entails 'Socrates loves Socrates'. Burley said that in such a sentence 'himself' had a special form of personal supposition, half-way between confused and distributive supposition, to which he gave a new and complicated technical name. Another sentence which was ill served by the traditional apparatus is 'A horse has been promised to you'. In order to distinguish between the case where you have been promised a particular horse and the case where any old horse will be a fulfilment of the promise, Walter had again to introduce new modes of supposition to assign to the word 'horse' here.

As a critic of Ockham's nominalism, Burley was soon outpaced by John Wyclif, whose treatise *On Universals* is a sustained defence of realism. The key to understanding universals, Wyclif believed, is a grasp of the nature of predication. The most obvious form of predication is that in which subject and predicate are linguistic items, parts of sentences. This is the most discussed form of predication, and modern writers think there is no other. In fact, Wyclif said, it is modelled on a different kind of predication, real predication, which is 'being shared by or said of many things in common' (*U* 1. 35).

Real predication is not a relation between terms—like the relation between 'Banquo' and 'lives' in 'Banquo lives'—but a relation between realities, namely Banquo, and whatever in the world corresponds to 'lives'. But what is the extra-mental entity that corresponds to 'lives'? Indeed *is* there anything in the world that corresponds to predicates? Wyclif's answer to the second question is that, if not, then there is no difference between true and false sentences. His answer to the first question is his theory of universals.

His argument for realism is simple. Anyone who believes in objective truth, he maintains, is already committed to belief in real universals. Suppose that one individual A is perceived to resemble another individual B. There must be some respect C in which A resembles B. But seeing that A resembles B in respect of C is the same thing as seeing the C-ness of A and B; and that involves conceiving C-ness, a universal common to A and B. So anyone who can make judgements of likeness automatically knows what a universal is.

Consider, as examples of universals, the species *dog* and the genus *animal*. A realist can define genus simply as what is predicated of many things that are different in species. A nominalist has to entangle himself in some circumlocution such as this: 'A genus is a term that is predicable, or whose counterpart is predicable, of many terms that signify things that are specifically distinct'. He cannot say that it is essential to a term to be actually predicated: perhaps there is no one around to do any verbal predicating. He cannot say that any particular term—any particular sound or image or mark on papers—has to be predicable; most signs do not last long enough for multiple predication. That is why he has to talk of counterparts, other signs that are of the same kind. He cannot say that the term is predicated of terms differing in species: the *word* 'dog' does not differ in species from the *word* 'cat'—they are both English nouns on this page. So the nominalist has to say that the terms signify things that differ specifically. But of course in doing this he gives the game away: he is making specific difference something on the side of the things signified, not something belonging purely to the signs. So the nominalist's gobbledygook does not really help him at all.

Wyclif's argument is clearly directed at a nominalist of a much more radical type than Ockham. The 'names' of Ockham's system were not uttered sounds or marks on paper: they were terms in a mental language. But Wyclif's attack does hit at Ockham's weakest point: namely, the failure to give any explicit account of the relation between the terms of his imagined mental language and actual signs in the real world. Ockham seems to have felt that he explained the features of Latin grammar by postulating a mental counterpart; but the only reason for thinking Mental has any explanatory force is that its operations occur in the ghostly medium of the mind. Wyclif, by forcing the conversation on to flesh and blood sounds and pen and ink marks, was anticipating Wittgenstein's method of philosophizing by turning latent nonsense into patent non-sense.

Three-Valued Logic at Louvain

One final medieval development was the adumbration of a three-valued logic. The possibility of a third value between truth and false is aired in a number of discussions of Aristotle's treatment of the sea-battle. In one case, however, the issue aroused a quarrel that reverberated across Europe.

In 1465 a member of the arts faculty at the young University of Louvain, Peter de Rivo, was asked by his students to discuss the question: after Christ had said to St Peter 'Thou wilt deny me thrice', was it still in Peter's power not to deny Christ? Yes it was, said Peter de Rivo, but that is not compatible with accepting that what Christ said was true at the time he said it. We must instead maintain that such predictions were neither true nor false, but had instead a third truth-value, neutral.

The theology faculty reacted strongly. Scripture, they said, was full of future-tensed propositions abut singular events, namely prophecies. It was no good saying that these were going to come true at a later date: unless they were already true when made, the prophets were liars. Peter responded by saying that anyone who denied the possibility of a third truth-value must fall into the heresy of determinism. He was backed up by the university authorities at Louvain.

The theologians sought advice from friends in Rome. A Franciscan logician, Francesco della Rovere, worked out some of the logical relationships involved in a system of three-valued logic. The contradictory of a true proposition, obviously enough, is a false proposition; but the contradictory of a neutral proposition, he maintained, is not false but is itself neutral. However, those who denied future-tensed articles of the Creed could only

TEMPLA DOMVM EXPOSITIS:VICOS FORA MOENIA PONTES:
VIRGINEAM TRIVII QVOD REPARARIS AQVAM.
PRISCA LICET NAVTIS STATVAS DARE COMMODA PORTVS:
ET VATICANVM CINGERE SIXTE IVGVM:
PLVS TAMEN VRBS DEBET:NAM QVAE SQVALORE LATEBAT:
CERNITVR IN CELEBRI BIBLIOTHECA LOCO.

Francesco della Rovere, Pope Sixtus IV, here accepts the homage of the Vatican
Librarian, Platina (Melozzo da Forli, Pinacoteca Vaticana).

be fairly condemned as heretics if they were uttering a falsehood. Hence, the articles they contradicted must be true, not neutral.

Fortified by this advice, the theologians delated to the Vatican the following propositions:

For a proposition about the future to be true, it is not enough that what it says should be the case: it must be unpreventably the case. We must say one of two things: either there is no present and actual truth in the articles of faith about the future, or what they say is something that not even divine power can prevent.

The propositions were condemned by the Pope in 1474.

It was not until the twentieth century that the notion of three-valued logic was seriously explored by logicians. But the episode illustrates how impossible it is, in the history of philosophy, to draw a sharp line between the Middle Ages and the Renaissance. For the logician who intervened in this eminently scholastic debate was none other than the pope who issued the condemnation of 1474: the paradigmatically Renaissance figure of Sixtus IV, who gave his name to the Sistine Chapel.

4

Knowledge

Augustine on Scepticism, Faith, and Knowledge

During the time prior to his conversion to Christianity, Augustine, under the influence of Cicero, took an interest in the sceptical arguments of the New Academy. The first of the philosophical treatises that he wrote at Cassiciacum was *Contra Academicos*, in which he defended the possibility of attaining knowledge of various kinds. We know logical truths, such as the principle of excluded middle, namely, that either *p* or not *p* (*CA* 3. 10. 23). We also know truths about immediate appearance. The sceptic cannot refute a person who says 'I know this thing seems white, this sound is delightful, this smell is pleasant, this tastes sweet, that feels cold' (*CA* 3. 11. 26). Such claims cannot be erroneous. But don't the senses deceive us, as when a straight oar looks bent in water? There is no deceit here: rather, if the oar in the water looked straight, that would be a case of my eyes deceiving me. But of course an oar's looking bent to me is not at all the same as my making a judgement that it is bent.

There are many propositions, however, that stand somewhere between truths of logic and immediate reports of experience, and throughout his life Augustine returned to the classification and evaluation of such propositions. One of his fullest defences of the possibility of certainty occurs in a late work, *De Trinitate* ('On the Trinity'). Here he is prepared to admit, for the sake of argument, that the senses may be deceived, when the eye sees the oar as bent or navigators see landmarks in apparent motion. But I cannot be in error when I say 'I am alive'—a judgement not of the senses, but of the mind. 'Perhaps you are dreaming.' But even if I am asleep, I am alive. 'Perhaps you are insane.' But even if I am insane I am alive. Moreover, if

I know that I am alive, I know that I know that I am alive, and so on ad infinitum. Sceptics may babble against the things that the mind perceives through the senses, but not against those that it perceives independently. 'I know that I am alive' is an instance of the second kind (*DT* 15. 12. 21).

Those who have read Descartes cannot help being reminded here of the Second Meditation; and indeed arguments akin to 'I think, therefore I am' are found in several of Augustine's works. In *The City of God*, for instance, in response to the Academic query 'May you not be in error?', Augustine replies, 'If I am in error, I exist.' What does not exist cannot be in error; therefore if I am in error, I exist (*DCD* IX. 26). Each of us knows not only our own existence, but other facts too about ourselves. 'I want to be happy' is also something I know, and so is 'I do not want to be in error'.

But the mature Augustine accepts the truth of many propositions besides the Cartesian certainties. We should not doubt the truth of what we have perceived through sense; it is through them that we have learnt about the heavens and the earth and their contents. A vast amount of our information is derived from the testimony of others—the existence of the ocean, for instance, and of distant lands; the lives of the heroes of history and even our own birthplace and parentage (*DUC* 12. 26). Throughout his life Augustine gave a place of honour to the truths of mathematics, which he classes as 'inward rules of truth': no one says that seven and three ought to be ten, we just know that they *are* ten (*DLA* 2. 12. 34).

Whence and how do we acquire our knowledge of mathematics, and our knowledge of the true nature of the creatures that surround us? In the *Confessions* Augustine emphasizes that knowledge of the essences of things cannot come from the senses.

My eyes say 'if they are coloured, we told you of them'. My ears say 'if they made a noise, we passed it on'. My nose says 'if they had a smell, they came my way'. My mouth says 'if they have no taste, don't ask me'. Touch says 'if it is not bodily, I had no contact with it, and so I had nothing to say'. The same holds of the numbers of arithmetic: they have no colour or odour, give out no sound, and cannot be tasted or touched. The geometer's line is quite different from a line in an architect's blueprint, even if that is drawn thinner than the threads of a spider's web. Yet I have in my mind ideas of pure numbers and geometrical lines. Where have they come from? (*Conf.* X. 11. 17–19)

Plato, in his *Meno*, had sought to show that our knowledge of geometry must date from a life before conception: what looks like learning geometry is in fact recalling our buried memories of what we have always known. Early in life Augustine was tempted by this explanation (cf. *Ep.* 7. 1. 2), but in his mature writings he cools to the idea that the soul pre-existed the formation of the body. Even if there were such a previous life, he argues in *On the Trinity*, it would not explain the learning of geometry, because we can hardly suppose that every one of us was a geometer in a previous life.

> We ought rather to believe that the nature of the intellectual mind was so formed that by means of a unique kind of incorporeal light it sees the intelligible realities to which, in the natural order, it is subordinate—just as the eye of the flesh sees the things that surround it in this corporeal light. (*DT* 12. 15. 24)

What Augustine here calls 'intelligible realities' he elsewhere calls 'incorporeal and eternal reasons'. They are unchangeable, and are therefore superior to the human mind; and yet they are in some way linked to the mind, because otherwise it would not be able to employ them as standards to judge of bodily things (*DT* 12. 2. 2).

We employ them in this way when, for example, we decide that a particular cartwheel is not a perfect circle, or if we apply Pythagoras' theorem when measuring a field. But it is not only arithmetical and geometrical standards that we apply in this way: there are also intellectual canons of beauty. Augustine recalled a particular traceried arch he had seen in Carthage. His judgement that this was aesthetically pleasing was, he tells us, based on a form of eternal truth that he perceived through the eye of the rational mind (*DT* 9. 6. 11).

Augustine's 'intelligible realities' are clearly very close to Plato's Ideas. In rejecting the account of the *Meno*, Augustine is disagreeing not about the existence of eternal standards, but about the nature of human access to them. Following the lead of Neoplatonic thinkers such as Plotinus,[1] he locates the Ideas in the divine mind.

Augustine's Christianization of Plato is most explicit in the treatise *De Ideis*, which is the forty-sixth question in his *Eighty-Three Different Questions*. He offers three Latin words for Ideas: 'formae', 'species', and 'rationes'. The Ideas cannot be thought to exist anywhere but in the mind of the creator. If creation was a work of intelligence, it must have been in accord with eternal reasons. But it is blasphemous to think that God, in creating the world in accordance with Ideas, looked up to anything outside himself.

---

[1] See vol. i, p. 313.

Hence, the unique, eternal, unchanging Ideas have their existence in the unique, eternal, unchanging Mind of God. 'Ideas are archetypal forms, stable and immutable essences of things, not created but eternally and unchangeably existent within the divine intellect' (*83Q* 46. 2).

Augustine on Divine Illumination

Human beings acquire their own ideas not by recollection (as Plato thought) nor by abstraction (as Aristotle thought) but by divine illumination. 'Illuminated by God with intelligible light, the soul sees, by means not of bodily eyes but of the intellect which is its crowning excellence, the reasons whose vision constitutes its ultimate bliss' (*83Q* 46, end).

Much has been written about Augustine's theory of illumination. Is illumination necessary for all knowledge, or only for the a priori knowledge of logic and mathematics? If Ideas are the contents of the divine mind, how can a finite mind come in contact with them without seeing God himself? How is the vision of God which on this account is necessary for the basic understanding of geometry to be distinguished from the vision of God which is the final and exclusive prerogative of the blessed in heaven?

In my view, such discussions are unrewarding. Augustine does not have a thought-out theory of illumination, such as some of his medieval followers later developed. He is simply using a metaphor, which even as a metaphor is never worked out in a coherent and systematic manner.

Representing intellectual operation in terms of bodily operations is a natural and universal feature of human languages. In English we speak of *grasping* a concept, or of a proposition as *ringing true* or *smelling fishy*; but of all our bodily senses it is vision with which the action of the intellect is most often compared. When we assent to a proposition without being led to it by argument or persuasion, we may say that we simply *see* it to be true: using the same metaphor, we speak of *intuitive* knowledge. Augustine can speak quite naturally in this way of intellectual vision or of the eye of reason.

Talk of illumination, however, adds an extra feature to this natural metaphor. It implies that when we understand, there is some medium through which we understand, just as light is the medium of our vision when we see colours. It implies that there is a source from which this medium originates, in the way that the sun and lesser luminaries are the source of the light by which we see. And it implies that there are objects of vision that may be concealed by darkness as well as revealed by light.

It is hard to flesh out Augustine's account of illumination in a way that gives a coherent set of counterparts to the items involved in the metaphor. The clearest element, of course, is that God is the source of intellectual illumination, just as the sun is the source of visible light. This divine illumination is supposed to explain how we humans possess ideas corresponding to the Platonic archetypes. But the Ideas are not shady entities that need lighting up: they are supposed to be the most luminous entities there are. If we accept that there are such things as Ideas, why is any medium needed to access them? Why not say—as Descartes was later to say—that God simply creates replicas of them within our minds when he brings our minds into existence?

In evaluating Augustine's account, let us forget what we know, or think we know, of the physics of light; let us simply consider the banal facts of (literal) illumination, facts that were as familiar to him as they are to us. Light helps us to see things when light shines on the object to be seen. Light shining directly in our eyes—above all the light of the sun—does not help but hinder vision. Yet the divine illumination, as represented by Augustine, shines not upon the objects of intellectual vision, but on the eyes of our reason. Intellectual inquiry, as this metaphor represents it, seems as hopeless a venture as driving a car at night with the headlights turned backward to shine through the windscreen.

The language of illumination also throws into confusion the distinction, so important for later Christian philosophers, between faith and reason. It became customary to distinguish between what could be known about God in this life by unaided natural reason, and what could only be believed about him, in response to revelation and supernatural grace. Illumination, in Augustine, is clearly intended to be something distinct from creation, which makes it appear to be supernatural rather than natural. On the other hand, illumination seems to be necessary to enable the mind to grasp not only mysteries like the Trinity but also the most basic truths of everyday experience.

Augustine has much to say about faith (*fides*) but he does not restrict the word to the later, technical, use in which it means belief in a proposition on the basis of the revealed word of God. At one point he offers a definition of faith as 'thinking with assent' (*DPS* 2. 5). This definition became classical,

S·BONA·VEN·TVRA

In this fresco by Fra Angelico in St Nicholas' chapel in the Vatican, Bonaventure – represented improbably with a beard – looks up to heaven for illumination.

but it seems inadequate in two ways. First of all, we think with assent whenever we call to mind a belief on any topic, whether religious or not. Secondly, as Augustine himself often points out, at any moment there are many things we believe even though we are not thinking about them at all. A thought, that is to say a thinking (*cogitatio*), is a dateable event in our mental life; belief (including the special kind of belief that is faith) is something different, a disposition rather than an episode.

When Augustine talks of faith, he is less concerned to expound its epistemic status than to emphasize its nature as a gratuitous virtue, one of the Pauline triad of faith, hope, and charity, infused in us by God. And when he is most eloquent in expounding its role, his language once again uses the metaphor of light, but in a manner that goes contrary to his explanation of our knowledge of eternal truths. Thus, we read in *The City of God*, 'The human mind, the natural seat of reason and understanding, is enfeebled by the darkening effect of inveterate vice. It is too weak to bear, let alone to embrace and enjoy, the changeless light. To be capable of such bliss it needs daily medication and renovation. It must submit to be cleansed by faith' (*DCD* IX. 2).

Bonaventure on Illumination

The relation of faith to reason occupied a principal place in the epistemology of Augustine's successors in the high Middle Ages. St Bonaventure, like Augustine, preferred Plato's philosophy to that of Aristotle, but he believed that even Plato's greatest successors, Cicero and Plotinus, were grievously in error about the true nature of human happiness. Without faith, no one can learn the mystery of the Trinity or the supernatural fate that awaits humans after death (I *Sent*. 3. 4). But, for Bonaventure, the philosopher, however gifted, is in a position worse than that of mere ignorance: he is in positive error about the most important things there are to know. 'Philosophical science is the way to other sciences; but he who wishes to stop there, falls into darkness' (*De Donis*, 3. 12).

A Christian philosopher, enlightened by the grace of faith, can make good use of the arguments of philosophers to broaden his understanding of saving truth. This Bonaventure himself does, offering various proofs of the existence of God: defective being implies perfect being, he argues, dependent being implies independent being, mobile being implies immobile being, and so on. These proofs he interprets, in Platonic manner, as being mere stimuli to bring to full consciousness a knowledge of God's existence that is implanted by nature in the human mind (*Itin.*, c. 1). He offers his own version of Anselm's ontological argument to show that nothing more than reflection on what is already in our minds is needed to produce an explicit awareness of God's existence.[2] Reflection on the desire for happiness, which every human being has, will show that it is a desire that cannot be satisfied without possession of the supreme Good, which is God (*De Myst. Trin.* 1. 17, *conclusio*).

For Bonaventure, the inborn notion of God was a special case. He did not believe, in general, that our ideas were innate; he agreed with Aristotle that the mind was initially a tabula rasa, and that even the most general intellectual principles were only acquired subsequent to sense-experience (II *Sent.* 24. 1. 2. 4). The notion of God was, uniquely, innate because the mind itself was an image of God, a mirror in which God's features could be dimly seen. (*De Myst. Trin.* 1. 1). Somewhere between the inborn knowledge of God and the acquired knowledge of intellectual principles stands our knowledge of virtue: not an innate idea nor an abstraction from the senses, but a natural capacity to tell right from wrong (I *Sent.* 17. 1).

The knowledge acquired from the changeable and perishable objects of sense-perception is itself subject to doubt and error. If we are to acquire stable certainties, we need assistance from the unchangeable truth which is God. The Ideas in God's mind, the 'eternal reasons', are not, in this life, visible to us; but they exercise an invisible, causal, influence on our thought. This is the divine illumination that enables us to grasp the stable essences that underlie the fleeting phenomena of the world (*Itin.* 2. 9).

Aquinas on Concept-Formation

So, following a long line of predecessors, Bonaventure appeals to the supernatural to explain how the human mind works. His contemporary, Aquinas, rejects this approach. Aquinas does use the metaphor of light to explain the working of the intellect: the agent intellect provides light,

---

[2] See Ch. 9 below.

which turns potentially thinkable individual objects in the world into actually thinkable objects in the mind. But Aquinas insists that the agent intellect is a natural faculty within the individual human being, not—as in the tradition of Avicenna and Averroes—a supernatural entity operating on the mind from outside.[3]

In the *Summa Theologiae* 1a 79. 3–4 Aquinas states with great emphasis that the agent intellect is something in the human soul. To be sure, there is an intellect superior to the human intellect, namely the divine intellect; but for human thought there needs to be a human power derived from that superior intellect. God enlightens every man coming into the world, as St John says, but only as the universal cause who gives the human soul its characteristic powers (4 ad 1).

Aquinas sets out his attitude to theories such as Bonaventure's in question 84 of the First Part, where he asks whether the intellectual soul knows material things 'in their eternal natures' (*in rationibus aeternis*). In the *Sed contra* we are told:

Augustine says: If we both see that what you say is true, and we both see that what I say is true, then where do we see that? Not I in you, nor you in me, but both of us in that unalterable truth that is above our minds (*Conf.* XIII. 25. 35). But the unalterable truth is in the eternal natures. Therefore the intellectual soul knows all things in their eternal natures.

In his usual courteous style, Aquinas in the sequel rejects the doctrine of divine illumination, but phrases his rejection in such a way as not to criticize St Augustine more than is absolutely necessary.[4]

There is no doubt that Aquinas is not an empiricist: that is to say, he denies that sensory experience is sufficient by itself for intellectual thought (*ST* 1a 84. 6c). In addition to sense-experience, there is needed the action of the agent intellect. But if Aquinas is not an empiricist, he is not an illuminist either. The agent intellect by itself is insufficient for the acquisition of intellectual knowledge. 'Beside the intellectual light within us, there is a need for thinkable species taken from outward things, if we are to have knowledge of material things' (*ST* 1a 84. 6c). The human intellect, in this life, is a faculty for the understanding of material objects. Without

---

[3] See Ch. 7 below.

[4] I am here taking issue with the account in R. Pasnau, *Thomas Aquinas on Human Nature* (Cambridge: Cambridge University Press, 2001), from which I have learnt much.

the senses no object would be given to us; without the agent intellect no object would be thinkable. Thoughts without phantasms are empty; phantasms without species are darkness to the mind.

The agent intellect is not, for Aquinas, something supernatural: it is part of human nature. When he discusses the nature of teaching (*ST* 1a 111. 1), Aquinas says: 'There is within each human being a principle of knowledge, namely the light of the agent intellect, by means of which from the beginning there are known certain universal principles of all sciences.' Aquinas compares the role of the agent intellect in teaching to the role of our bodily nature in medicine. The doctor's art imitates nature, which heals a patient by temperature control, by digestion, and by the expulsion of noxious matter. When a pupil is learning, the teacher is assisting him to make use of his intellect's natural light in order to progress to new knowledge. The analogy is telling: the action of the agent intellect is no more supernatural than the action of the digestive system. Both of them, equally, are products of the creator God; but if being a creature of God makes something supernatural, then the whole world is supernatural, and the distinction between nature and supernature loses its point.

But does not God, as creator of the agent intellect, infuse a special insight in a way in which he does not in creating other things? In the *Summa contra Gentiles* 3. 47 Aquinas distinguishes between the likeness of God that is present in every creature and the special likeness in the intellect because of its capacity for the knowledge of truth. There are some truths on which all human beings agree, the first principles of speculative and practical reasoning. It is the presence of these truths in the mind that makes the mind an image of God. These truths are not inborn, nor are they acquired from experience or induction. What is inborn is the faculty for recognizing them when experience presents us with their instances.

The agent intellect is essentially a concept-forming capacity, which operates upon phantasms. It turns the potentially thinkable data of sense-experience into the actually thinkable species. The formation of concepts involves the application of principles such as that of non-contradiction: possession of the concept of X involves the ability to distinguish what is X from what is not X. In that sense the agent intellect can be said to be aware of such principles: but of course, by itself without any sensory input, such an awareness contributes nothing to the knowledge of the essence of material objects which is the intellect's proper task in our present life.

It is the agent intellect itself that is the reflection, the mirroring, of the uncreated light of the divine intellect. When the agent intellect employs its principles in forming concepts out of sense-experience, it needs no further divine illumination, as Thomas emphasizes.

In all awareness of the truth, the human mind needs the divine operation. But in the case of things known naturally it does not need any new light, but only divine movement and direction (*IBT* 1. 1c).

St Thomas did, of course, believe that there was a supervenient, super-natural divine illumination of the human mind: this was the grace that produced faith in those fortunate enough to possess it. But he carefully distinguishes this from the innate, natural light that is the agent intellect. 'Whatever we understand and judge, we understand and judge in the light of the primary truth, in so far as any light of our intellect—whether it be the product of nature or of grace—is an impression of the primary truth' (*ST* 1a 88. 3 ad 1).

Aquinas on Faith, Knowledge, and Science

A sharp distinction between truths knowable by natural light, and those accessible only by the supernatural light of faith, is indeed one of St Thomas' principal contributions to medieval epistemology. Natural reason, he believed, was capable of reaching a limited number of truths about God: that he existed, was omniscient, omnipotent, benevolent, and so on. Doctrines such as the Trinity and the Incarnation were known only by revelation and unprovable by unaided reason. Faith, in the theological sense, is belief in something on the word of God. Faith is different from the kind of belief in the existence of God which a successful philosophical proof would produce. The faithful believer takes God's word for many things, but one cannot take God's word for it that he exists. Belief in God, in this sense, is not part of faith, but is presupposed by it. Thomas calls it a 'preamble' of faith.

Truths about God that are reached by natural reason are the province of natural theology; the mysteries of faith are the subject of revealed the-ology. But there is an ambiguity in the expression 'unaided reason'. It may mean that in arguing for its conclusions, natural theology rests only on premises derived from experience or reflection, and that it has no need to call in aid any premises derived from sacred texts or special revelation. In another sense it may mean that the natural theologian reaches his conclusions without the aid of divine grace. When we talk about 'unaided reason' in the first sense, we are talking about the premises from which reason reaches its conclusion, and we are talking about logical relationships. On the other hand, when we contrast unaided reason with the aid of grace, we have moved from the realm of reasons to that of causes: we are talking about the causal, not the logical, antecedents of the reasoning process.

Even those truths that are in principle open to reason, such as the existence of God and the immortality of the soul, must, according to Aquinas, in practice be accepted by many people on authority. To establish them by philosophical argument demands more intelligence, leisure, and energy than can be expected from the majority of humankind. In setting out the structure of natural theology, St Thomas makes a distinction between the beliefs of the learned and the beliefs of the simple. The simple believer need not be capable of following proofs such as the Five Ways which, in the philosopher, produce (if successful) knowledge that God exists. The simple believer only *believes* that there is a God. This belief is not faith, for the reason given; it is a belief on human, not divine, authority. But it is perfectly reasonable, provided that arguments for the existence of God are available to the believing community, even if intelligible only to the learned members of it (*ScG* 1. 3–6).

Aquinas' distinction between faith and reason and between natural and revealed theology marked a turning point in medieval epistemology. Epistemology is the philosophical discipline that studies knowledge and belief: what kinds of things we can know, and how we can know them; what kinds of things we should believe, and why we should believe them. Aquinas' work sharpened the distinction between knowledge and belief; more than any of his predecessors he emphasized that a Christian's grasp of the mystery of the Trinity was a matter not of knowledge or understanding, but of faith. Within the realm of belief he made a distinction between faith and opinion on the basis of degrees of certitude: faith, but not opinion, involves a commitment to the truth of the proposition believed parallel to that of knowledge. Corresponding to this difference of certitude, there is a difference in the type of justification: faith depends on supernatural testimony, opinion rests on everyday evidence.

Having distinguished it from faith, Aquinas gives an account of knowledge (*scientia*) that is heavily influenced by the ideal of a deductive science that Aristotle set out in his *Posterior Analytics*. Every truth that is capable of being strictly known, he maintained, is a conclusion that can be reached by syllogistic reasoning from self-evident premisses. There are some propositions that have only to be understood in order to command assent: such are the law of non-contradiction and other similar primary principles. The ability to grasp and exercise these principles is the fundamental endowment of the intellect: it is called *intellectus* in the strictest sense. The human intellect also has the power to deduce conclusions from these self-evident principles by syllogistic processes: this is called the *ratio*, or reasoning faculty. First principles are related to the conclusions of reason as axioms to theorems. The grasp of first principles is called the *habitus principiorum*; the knowledge of theorems deduced from them is the *habitus scientiae* (*ST* 1a 2ae. 57. 2).

St Thomas nowhere gives a list of the self-evident principles that are the premisses of all scientific knowledge, nor does he try, like Spinoza, to exhibit his own philosophical theses as conclusions from self-evident axioms. But he tells us that the findings of any scientific discipline constitute an ordered set of theorems in a deductive system whose axioms are either theorems of a higher science or the self-evident principles themselves. A theorem may be provable in more than one system: that the earth is round, for instance, can be shown both by the astronomer and by the physicist. Sciences differ from each other if they have different formal objects: the astronomer and the geometer, we might say, know about a single material object, the sun, under two different formal descriptions: *qua* heavenly body or *qua* spherical solid. Conclusions derivable from different sciences will be deduced from syllogisms with different middle terms. More than one chain of reasoning may lead from the first principles to a particular theorem; but from any theorem at least one chain must lead back to the axioms. The ideal of science thus set out seemed most obviously realized by Euclid's formalization of geometry.

Such a theory of *scientia* is clearly inadequate as a general epistemology. In the first place, many of the things that we are commonly, and rightly, said to know are not propositions of any deductive system. It may be claimed that this point is simply an issue of translation: the Latin verb 'scire' and the noun 'scientia' are concerned not with knowledge but with science. In fact, Aquinas often uses the verb as equivalent simply to 'know'; but it is true that he has a pair of terms, the verb 'cognoscere' and the noun 'cognitio' which have a much broader and less technical scope. These words are used in a variety of contexts to refer to very different things: sense-perception as well as intellectual understanding; knowledge by description as well as knowledge by acquaintance; acquiring concepts as well as making use of them. Careful attention to context is needed to find the appropriate translation in different contexts. Sadly, some medievalists in recent years have abandoned translation for transliteration, which not only produces ugly English but leads to intellectual confusion. The pseudo-verb 'cognize' looks like an episode verb; and so all kinds of different cognitive states, activities, and acts are made to look as if they referred to a momentary event of which there could be a mental snapshot. But it remains true that if we are to look for a rewarding epistemology in Aquinas we should examine his practice with 'cognitio' rather than his theory of *scientia*.

However, let us look for a moment at Aquinas' theory as an account of science, rather than as a general epistemology. It is important to realize that it is not intended as an account of scientific method: we are not meant to understand that the scientist starts with self-evident principles and proceeds to conclusions about the world by rolling out a priori deductions. The procedure goes in the opposite direction: the scientist starts with a phenomenon—an eclipse of the moon, say—and looks for the cause of it. Finding the cause is the same thing as finding the middle term in a syllogism which will have as its conclusion the occurrence of the eclipse. The task of science is only completed when this syllogism, in turn, is traced back, through other syllogisms, to arrive at first principles. But the first principle thus arrived at forms the conclusion, not the starting point, of the scientific inquiry.[5] The chain of deduction is not the vehicle, but the output, of the venture.

The serious problem with Aquinas' theory is that it leaves quite unclear what is the role of experience and experiment in science. True, 'scientia' is broad enough to include mathematics and metaphysics; but it is clear from Aquinas' examples that his account is meant to cover disciplines such as

---

[5] Aquinas clearly distinguishes the two procedures in *ST* 1a 79. 8, but rather confusingly he calls the deductive process 'inquiry' and the process of inquiry 'judgement'. But in his commentary on the *Posterior Analytics* he makes clear that that work is concerned with 'judgement'. See Eleonore Stump, *Aquinas* (London: Routledge, 2003), 525, to which I am much indebted.

astronomy and medicine. *Scientia*, he tells us, concerns universal and necessary truths: but how can the fluctuating world we encounter in sense-experience provide any such truths? How can it be that—as Aquinas himself says (*ST* 1a 101. 1)—human beings depend on the senses for the acquisition of *scientia*?

The role that Aquinas assigns to the senses in the scientific enterprise concerns the acquisition of concepts and the understanding of principles, rather than the establishment of any contingent laws of nature. He describes how the deliverances of the senses are necessary for the abstraction of universal concepts, and he shows how we grasp universal principles by reflecting on particular instances of them. In each case he used the word 'inductio' to describe this process (*CPA* 1. 30, 2. 30). But the word, like so many of Aquinas' Latin technical terms, is a false friend. In *inductio* individual instances provide an illustration of, not an argument for, a proposition which, once clearly understood, is self-evidently true. This is something quite different from induction as understood since the time of Bacon, in which instances provide statistical support for a scientific generalization.

Since early modern times, epistemology has often taken the form of a response to scepticism: what reasons do we have for relying on the evidence of our senses, for accepting the existence of an external world, for believing in the existence of other minds? Aquinas shows very little interest in epistemology as thus understood. He accepts the general reliability of our senses, regards the nature of material objects as the proper object of the human intellect as we know it, and argues about the nature

Duns Scotus, as imagined by a fifteenth-century illuminator.

and number, rather than the existence, of human and superhuman minds. In the intellectual climate of his time there was not a clear distinction to be drawn between psychology and epistemology, that is to say between the description and the vindication of the activities of our mental faculties. Aquinas himself did not seek to develop such a distinction, in a manner parallel to the way in which he sharpened the dichotomy between faith and reason. A reader, therefore, who wishes to follow further his discussion of the operation of the senses and the intellect should turn to the chapter on philosophy of mind (Chapter 7).

The Epistemology of Duns Scotus

It is arguable that epistemology, as understood in modern times, makes its first appearance in the writings of Duns Scotus. This may seem a surprising claim. At first sight, Scotus is much further removed than Aquinas is from any concern with scepticism. Whereas Aquinas thought that the proper object of the intellect, in this life, was the nature of material objects, Scotus believed the intellect was powerful enough to include all things in heaven and earth, ranging over the full scale of being, infinite as well as finite. Moreover, while Aquinas believed that material individuals were the subject of sensory rather than intellectual knowledge, Scotus was willing to attribute to the intellect a direct knowledge of individuals in themselves (*Quodl.* 13 p. 32). But while Scotus thus extended the scope of the intellect, he diminished the degree of certainty it could attain.

A particular individual, Scotus argues in his commentary on the *De Anima* (22. 3), is something capable of being grasped by the human intellect, even in the present life when its faculties are dimmed by sin. If it were not, we would never be able to attain knowledge of universals by induction, and we would not be able to have a rational love for a human individual. But our knowledge of individuals is obscure and incomplete. If two individuals did not differ at all in their sensory properties, the intellect would not be able to tell one from the other, even though they would have two different haecceities and thus be two different individuals. This obscurity in our knowledge of individuals must carry with it also a clouding of our knowledge of universals; for 'it is impossible to abstract universals from the singular without previous knowledge of the singular; for in this case the intellect would abstract without knowing from what it was abstracting' (ibid.).

For Scotus, knowledge involves the presence in the mind of a representation of its object. Like Aquinas, he describes knowledge in terms of the presence of a species or idea in the knowing subject. But whereas for Aquinas the species was a concept, that is to say an ability of the intellect in question, for Scotus it is the immediate object of knowledge. For knowledge, he says, 'the real presence of the object in itself is not required, but something is required in which the object is represented. The species is of such a nature that the object to be known is present in it not effectively or really, but by way of being displayed.' (*Ord.* 3. 366).

For Aquinas the object of the intellect was itself really present, because it was a universal, whose only existence was exactly such presence in the mind. But Scotus, because he believes in intellectual knowledge of the individual, conceives of intellectual knowledge on the model of sensory awareness. When I see a white wall, the whiteness of the wall has an effect on my sight and my mind, but it cannot itself be present in my eye or my mind; only some representation of it.

Scotus made a distinction between intuitive and abstractive cognition. 'We should know that there can be two kinds of awareness and intellection in the intellect: one intellection can be in the intellect inasmuch as it abstracts from all existence; the other intellection can be of a thing in so far as it is present in its existence' (*Lect.* 2. 285). The distinction between intuitive and abstractive cognition is not the same as that between sense and intellect—the word 'abstractive' should not mislead us, even though Scotus did believe that intellectual knowledge, in the present life, depends on abstraction. There can be both intellectual and sensory intuitive knowledge; and the imagination, which is a sensory faculty, can have abstractive knowledge (*Quodl.* 13, p. 27). Scotus makes a further distinction between perfect and imperfect intuitive knowledge: perfect intuitive knowledge is of an existing object as present, imperfect intuitive knowledge is of an existing object as future or past.

Abstractive knowledge is knowledge of the essence of an object which leaves in suspense the question whether the object exists or not (*Quodl.* 7, p. 8). Remember that, for Scotus, essences include individual essences; so that abstractive knowledge is not just knowledge of abstract truths. The notion is a difficult one: there cannot, surely, be knowledge that p if p is not the case. Perhaps we can get round this by insisting that 'knowledge' is not the right translation of 'cognitio'. We are, however, left with a state of mind, the *cognitio* that *p*, which (*a*) shares the psychological status of the knowledge that *p* and (*b*) is compatible with *p*'s not being the case. Moreover, the question arises how we can tell whether, in any particular case, our state of mind is one of intuitive or abstractive cognition. Are the two distinguishable by some infallible inner mark? If so, what is it? If not, how can we ever be sure we really know something?

Intuitive and Abstractive Knowledge in Ockham

These problems with the notion of abstractive knowledge open a road to scepticism, which troubled Scotus himself (*Lect.* 2. 285). Because the distinction between two kinds of knowledge was extremely influential in the years succeeding Scotus' death, the road which it opened was travelled, to ever greater lengths, by his successors. We may begin with William Ockham.

In introducing the notions of intuitive and abstractive knowledge Ockham makes a distinction between apprehension and judgement. We apprehend single terms and propositions of all kinds; but we assent only to complex thoughts. We can think a complex thought without assenting to it, that is to say without judging that it is true. On the other hand, we cannot make a judgement without apprehending the content of the judgement. Knowledge involves both apprehension and judgement; and both apprehension and judgement involve knowledge of the simple terms entering into the complex thought in question (*OTh.* 1. 16–21).

Knowledge of a non-complex may be abstractive or intuitive. If it is abstractive, it abstracts from whether or not the thing exists and whatever contingent properties it may have. Intuitive knowledge is defined as follows by Ockham: 'Intuitive knowledge is knowledge of such a kind as to enable one to know whether a thing exists or not, so that if the thing does exist, the intellect immediately judges that it exists, and has evident awareness of its existence, unless perchance it is impeded because of some imperfection in that knowledge' (*OTh.* 1. 31). Intuitive existence can concern not only the existence but the properties of things. If Socrates is white, my intuitive knowledge of Socrates and of whiteness can give me evident awareness that Socrates is white. Intuitive knowledge is fundamental for any knowledge of contingent truths; no contingent truth can be known by abstractive knowledge (*OTh*. 1. 32).

On first reading, one is inclined to think that by 'intuitive knowledge' Ockham means sensory awareness. It is then natural to take his thesis that contingent truths can be known only by intuitive knowledge to be a forthright statement of empiricism, the doctrine that all knowledge of facts is derived from the senses. But Ockham insists that there is a purely intellectual form of intuitive knowledge. Mere sensation, he says, is incapable of causing a judgement in the intellect (*OTh*. 1. 22). Moreover, there are many contingent truths about our own minds—our thoughts, affections, pleasures, and pains—that are not perceptible by the senses. Nonetheless, we know these truths: it must be by an intellectual intuitive knowledge (*OTh*. 1. 28).

In the natural order of things, intuitive knowledge of objects is caused by the objects themselves. When I look at the sky and see the stars, the stars cause in me both a sensory and an intellectual awareness of their existence. But a star and my awareness of it are two different things, and God could destroy one of them without destroying the other. Whatever God does through secondary causes, he can do directly by his own power. So the awareness normally caused by the stars could be caused by him in the absence of the stars.

However, Ockham says, such knowledge would not be *evident* knowledge. 'God cannot cause in us knowledge of such a kind as to make it appear evidently to us that a thing is present when in fact it is absent, because that involves a contradiction. Evident knowledge implies that matters are in reality as stated by the proposition to which assent is given' (*OTh*. 9. 499). Whereas, for most writers, only what is true can be known, for Ockham, it seems, one can know truly or falsely; but only what is true can be *evidently* known. If God makes me judge that something is present when it is absent, Ockham says, then my knowledge is not intuitive, but abstractive. But that seems to imply that I cannot even tell (short of a divine revelation) which bits of my knowledge are intuitive and which are abstractive.[6]

[6] The relation in Ockham between intuitive knowledge, assent, and truth is a matter of much current controversy. For two contrasting opinions, see Eleonore Stump, 'The Mechanisms of Cognition', and E. Karger, 'Ockham's Misunderstood Theory of Intuitive and Abstractive Cognition', in *CCO*.

If intuitive knowledge is our only route to empirical truth, and intuitive knowledge is compatible with falsehood, how can we ever be sure of empirical truths? To be sure, my deception about the existence of the star could only come about by a miracle; and Ockham adds that God could work a further miracle, suspending the normal link between intuitive knowledge and assent, so that I could refrain from the false judgement that there is a star in sight (*OTh*. 9. 499). But that seems little comfort for the revelation that I never have any way of telling whether a piece of intuitive knowledge is evident or not, or even whether a piece of knowledge is intuitive or abstractive.

It is to be remarked that Ockham's position is quite different from that of some later empiricists who have sought to preserve the link between knowledge and truth by saying that the immediate object of intuitive awareness is not any external object, but something private, such as a sense-datum. Ockham says explicitly that if the sensory vision of a colour were preserved by God in the absence of the colour, the immediate object both of the sensory and of the intellectual vision would be the colour itself, non-existent though it was (*OTh*. 1. 39).

5

Physics

Augustine on Time

In the eleventh book of the *Confessions* there is a celebrated inquiry into the nature of time. The peg on which the discussion hangs is the question of an objector: what was God doing before the world began? Augustine toys with, but rejects, the answer 'Preparing hell for people who look too curiously into deep matters' (*Conf.* XI. 12. 14). The difficulty is serious: if first God was idle and then creative, surely that involves a change in the unchangeable one? The answer Augustine develops is that before heaven and earth were created there was no such thing as time, and without time there can be no change. It is folly to say that innumerable ages passed before God created anything; because God is the creator of ages, so there were no ages before creation. 'You made time itself, so no time could pass before you made time. But if before heaven and earth there was no such thing as time, why do people ask what you were doing then? When there was no time, there was no "then" ' (*Conf.* XI. 13. 15). Equally, we cannot ask why the world was not created sooner, for before the world there was no sooner. It is misleading to say even of God that he existed at a time earlier than the world's creation, for there is no succession in God. In him today does not replace yesterday, nor give way to tomorrow; there is only a single eternal present.

In treating time as a creature, it may seem as if Augustine is treating time as a solid entity comparable to the items that make up the universe. But as his argument develops, it turns out that he regards time as fundamentally unreal. 'What *is* time?' he asks. 'If no one asks me, I know; if I wish to explain to an inquirer, I know not.' Time is made up of past, present, and future. But the past is no longer, and the future has not yet come. So the only real time is the present: but a present that is nothing but present is not time, but eternity (*Conf.* XI. 14. 17).

We speak of longer and shorter times: ten days ago is a short time back, and a hundred years is a long time ahead. But neither past nor future are in existence, so how can they be long or short? How can we measure time? Suppose we say of a past period that it was long: do we mean that it was long when it was past, or long when it was present? Only the latter makes sense, but how can anything be long in the present, since the present is instantaneous? A hundred years is a long time: but how can a hundred years be present? During any year of the century, some years will be in the past and some in the future. Perhaps we are in the last year of the century: but even that year is not present, since some months of it are past and some future. The same argument can be used about days and hours: an hour itself is made up of fugitive moments. The only thing that can really be called 'present' is an indivisible atom of time, flying instantly from future into past. But something that is not divisible into past and future has no duration (*Conf.* XI. 15. 20).

No collection of instants can add up to more than an instant. The stages of any period of time never coexist; how then can they be added up to form a whole? Any measurement we make must be made in the present: but how can we measure what has already gone by or has not yet arrived?

Augustine's solution to the perplexities he has raised is to say that time is really only in the mind. His past boyhood exists now, in his memory. Tomorrow's sunrise exists now, in his prediction. The past is not, but we behold it in the present when it is, at the moment, in memory. The future is not; all that there is is our present foreseeing. Instead of saying that there are three times, past, present, and future, we should say that there is a present of things past (which is memory), a present of things present (which is sight), and a present of things future (which is anticipation). A length of time is not really a length of time, but a length of memory, or a length of anticipation. Present consciousness is what I measure when I measure periods of time (*Conf.* XI. 27. 36).

This is surely not a satisfactory response to the paradoxes Augustine so eloquently constructed. Consider my present memory of a childhood event. Does my remembering occupy only an instant? In which case it lasts no time and cannot be measured. Does it take time? In which case, some of it must be past and some of it future—and in either case, therefore, unmeasurable. If we waive these points, we can still ask how a current memory can be used to measure a past event. Surely we can have a brief memory of a long, boring event in the past, and on the other hand we can dwell long in memory on some momentary but traumatic past event.

Augustine's own text reveals that he was not happy with his solution. Our memories and anticipations are signs of past and future events; but, he says, that which we remember and anticipate is something different from these signs and is not present (*Conf.* XI. 23. 24). The way to deal with his paradoxes is not to put forward a subjective theory of time, but rather to untangle the knots which went into their knitting. Our concept of time makes use of two different temporal series: one that is constructed by means of the concepts of earlier and later, and another that is constructed by means of the concepts of past and future. Augustine's paradoxes arise through weaving together threads from the two systems, and can only be dissolved by untangling the threads. It took philosophers many centuries to do so, and some indeed believe that the task has not yet been satisfactorily completed.[1]

Augustine's interest in time was directed by his concern to elucidate the Christian doctrine of creation. 'Some people', he wrote, 'agree that the world is created by God, but refuse to admit that it began in time, allowing it a beginning only in the sense that it is being perpetually created' (*DCD* IX. 4). He has some sympathy with these people: they want to avoid attributing to God any sudden impetuous action, and it is certainly conceivable that something could lack a beginning and yet be causally dependent. He quotes them as saying 'If a foot had been planted from all eternity in dust, the footprint would always be beneath it; but no one would doubt that it was the footprint that was caused by the foot, though there was no temporal priority of one over the other' (*DCD* X. 31).

Those who say that the world has existed for ever are *almost* right, on Augustine's view. If all they mean is that there was no time when there was no created world, they are correct, for time and creation began together. It is as wrong to think that there was time before the world began as it is to think that there is space beyond where the world ends. So we cannot say

---

[1] See A. N. Prior, 'Changes in Events and Changes in Things', in his *Papers on Time and Tense* (Oxford: Oxford University Press, 1968).

that God made the world after so and so many ages had passed. This does not mean that we cannot set a date for creation, but we have to do so by counting backwards from the present, not, impossibly, counting forward from the first moment of eternity. Scripture tells us, in fact, that the world was created less than six thousand years ago (*DCD* IX. 4, 12. 11).

Philoponus, Critic of Aristotle

There was a well-known series of arguments, deriving from Aristotle, to the effect that the universe cannot have had a beginning. Augustine was aware of some of these arguments, and attempts to counter them, but a definitive attack on Aristotle's reasoning was first made by John Philoponus.

Philoponus' work *Against Aristotle, On the Eternity of the World* survives only in quotations gleaned from the commentaries of his adversary Simplicius, but the fragments are substantial enough to enable his argumentation to be reconstructed with confidence.[2] The first part of the work is an attack on Aristotle's theory of the quintessence, namely the belief that in addition to the four elements of earth, air, fire, and water with their natural motions upward and downward, there is a fifth element, ether, whose natural motion is circular. The heavenly and sublunar regions of the universe, he argues, are essentially of the same nature, composed of the same elements (books 1–3).

Aristotle had argued that the heavens must be eternal because all things that come into being do so out of a contrary, and the quintessence has no contrary because there is no contrary to a circular motion (*De Caelo* 1. 3. 270^a 12–22). Philoponus pointed out that the complexity of planetary motions could not be explained simply by appealing to a tendency of celestial substance to travel in a circle. More importantly, he denied that everything comes into being from a contrary. Creation is bringing something into being out of nothing; but that does not mean that non-being is the material out of which creatures are constructed, in the way that timber is the material out of which ships are constructed. It simply means that there is no thing out of which it is created. The eternity of the world,

---

[2] The reconstruction has been carried out by Christian Wildberg, who has translated the reconstructed text as *Philoponus: Against Aristotle on the Eternity of the World* (London: Duckworth, 1987).

Philoponus says, is inconsistent not only with the Christian doctrine of creation, but also with Aristotle's own opinion that nothing could traverse through more than a finite number of temporal periods. For if the world had no beginning, then it must have endured through an infinite number of years, and worse still, through 365 times an infinite number of days (book 5, frag. 132).

In his commentary on Aristotle's *Physics* (641. 13 ff.) Philoponus attacked the dynamics of natural and violent motion. Aristotle encountered a difficulty in explaining the movement of projectiles. If I throw a stone, what makes it move upwards and onwards when it leaves my hand? Its natural motion is downwards, and my hand is no longer in contact with it to impart its violent motion upwards. Aristotle's answer was that the stone was pushed on, at any particular point, by the air immediately behind it; an answer that Philoponus subjected to justified ridicule. Philoponus' own answer was that the continued motion was due to a force within the projectile itself—an immaterial kinetic force impressed upon it by the thrower, to which later physicists gave the technical term 'impetus'. The theory of impetus remained influential until Galileo and Newton proposed the startling principle that *no* moving cause, external or internal, was needed to explain the continued motion of a moving body.

Philoponus applied his theory of impetus throughout the cosmos. The heavenly bodies, for instance, travel in their orbits not because they have souls, but because God gave them the appropriate impetus when he created them. Though the notion of impetus has been superannuated by the discovery of inertia, it was itself a great improvement on its Aristotelian predecessor. It enabled Philoponus to dispense with the odd mixture of physics and psychology in Aristotle's astronomy.

Natural Philosophy in the Thirteenth Century

Nonetheless, Aristotle's natural philosophy remained influential for centuries to come. Both in Islamic and in Latin philosophy the study of nature was carried out within the framework of commentaries on Aristotle's works, especially the *Physics*. Individuals such as Robert Grosseteste and Albert the Great extended Aristotelian science with detailed studies of particular scientific topics; but the general conceptual framework

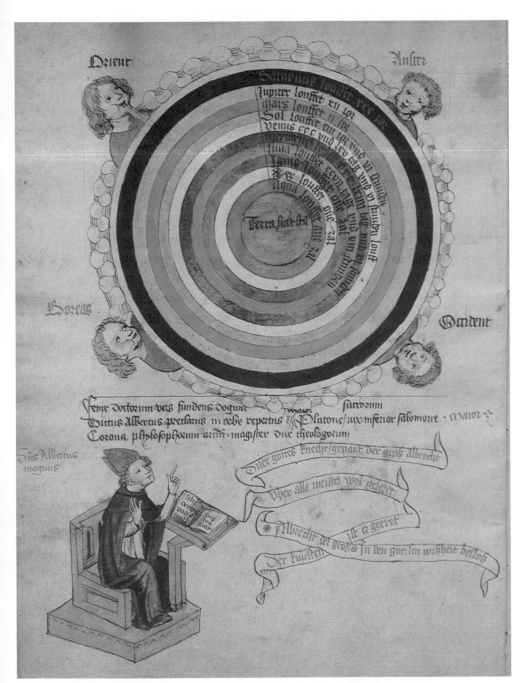

Albert the Great teaching astronomy, from a MS in the University library of Salzburg

remained Aristotelian until the fourteenth century. We may illustrate this by considering the concepts of motion, time, and causation.

Aristotle had defined motion as 'the actuality of what is in potentiality, in so far as it is in potentiality'.[3] Arabic commentators struggled to relate this definition to the system of categories. Avicenna placed motion in the category of *passio*: all changes in nature were due to the action of the heavenly intelligences, who as it were stirred the forms around in the broth of the natural world. Averroes emphasized the variety of types of change covered by Aristotle's term 'motion': there was local motion, which was change in place, growth, which was change in size, and there were qualitative changes of many kinds. Any instance of motion belonged in the same category as its terminus: location, quantity, or quality. So far from being the passive result of the operation of the heavenly intelligences, any change in a natural body, animate or inanimate, was the action of an internal agent (a *motor conjunctus*).

Albert the Great, with support from Aristotelian texts, sought to combine the two Islamic accounts: a motion was simultaneously an action of an agent and a *passio* of a recipient: when a gardener turns the soil, the turning of the soil is at one and the same time an action of the gardener and an event that happens to the soil. He agreed with Averroes that motion was an analogical term, which ranged across several categories; but he thought that Averroes had not fully grasped Aristotle's distinction between perfect and imperfect actualities. A movable body at point A has a potentiality to be at point B. Arrival at B is the perfect actuality of this potentiality; but motion towards B is the imperfect actuality, when the moving body is not yet at B but only on the way to B. Albert maintains that Aristotle's broad definition of motion—the actuality of what is in potentiality in so far as it is in potentiality—can be applied, extending its analogical sense to generation (substantial change) and to creation (bringing into being out of nothing).[4]

For Aristotle time and motion are closely linked: time is the measure of motion, and time derives its continuity from the continuity of motion. The question whether motion and time had a beginning was a subject of keen debate among Christian philosophers in the thirteenth century in connection with the provability of God's existence. Following al-Kindi and the

---

[3] See vol. i, p. 184.
[4] See J. Weisheipl, 'The Interpretation of Aristotle's *Physics*', in *CHLMP* 526–9.

kalam philosophers, and utilizing arguments from Philoponus, some theologians thought that philosophy could prove that the natural world had a beginning, and therefore there was needed a supernatural agent, God, to bring it into existence. Others thought that the beginning of the world, though taught in Genesis, was not something that could be established by pure philosophical reasoning.

Aquinas, who took the second view, sums up the arguments on both sides in the forty-sixth question of the First Part of the *Summa Theologiae*. In the first article he presents ten arguments that purport to show that the world ('the universe of creatures') has existed for ever; in the second he presents eight arguments to show that it had a beginning. He offers a refutation of each of the arguments on either side, and concludes that while the world did have a beginning, that is not something that can be proved or scientifically known, but is purely an article of faith.

Here is a sample argument to show that the world must have existed for ever: it takes the form of a *reductio ad absurdum*.

Whatever begins to be, was, before it existed, possible to be; otherwise it would have been impossible for it to come into being. So if the world began to be, before it began, it was possible for it to be. But what has the possibility of being is matter, which is in potentiality both to being (through form) and to non-being (through deprivation of form). So, then, if the world began to be, there was matter before the world began. But matter cannot exist without form; but the matter of the world, plus form, is the world. So the world already was before it began to be; which is impossible. (46. 1, obj. 1)

To which Aquinas replies that before the world existed, its possibility was not the passive possibility that constitutes matter. The pre-existent possibility consisted of two elements: the logical possibility of the existence of a world, plus the active power of the omnipotent God.

One of Aquinas' arguments on the other side is one that had already had a long history: 'If the world has always existed, then an infinite number of days has preceded today. But it is not possible to traverse anything infinite. Therefore today could never have been reached; which is obviously false' (46. 2, obj. 6). His answer is brief, but decisive. A traverse has to be from one terminus to another. But whatever earlier day you designate as the *terminus a quo* of the traverse is only a finite number of days ago. The objection assumes that you can designate a pair of termini with an infinite number of days between them.

In addition to answering individual arguments for and against the world's having existed for ever, Aquinas offers general reasons why we can never know, by pure reason, whether it had a beginning. We reason about the world by the use of universal concepts, and universals abstract from times and places, and so they cannot tell us about beginnings and endings. Reasoning about God will not help either: reason may teach us necessary truths about him, but not the inscrutable decrees of his sovereign freedom (46. 2c).

While admirably agnostic about the limits of philosophical cosmogony, Aquinas was unduly credulous about the causal structure of the universe as it actually exists. On the one hand, he accepted the Aristotelian theory that the heavenly bodies were quite different in nature from anything to be found on earth; on the other hand, he believed that the same heavenly bodies were directly causally responsible for the natural activities of all complex entities here below. The four elements, and their physical prop-erties such as heat and cold, he maintained, were quite insufficient to explain the rich variety of natural phenomena on earth. Accordingly, he says, citing Aristotle's *De Generatione*,

we must posit some active principle in motion, which by its presence and absence causes the variations in generation and corruption of bodies on earth. Such a principle is provided by the heavenly bodies. So whatever brings into existence others of its kind on earth operates as the instrument of a heavenly body. Thus it is said in the second book of the *Physics* that man and the sun beget man. (1a 115a 3 ad 2)

In a later article Aquinas spells out how he understands this obscure Aristotelian dictum. Semen, he says, has an active power, derived from the soul of the man producing it. The active power has as its vehicle the froth in the semen, which has a special heat of its own, derived not from the soul of the male, but from the action of the heavenly bodies. Thus, in the earliest stage of the generation of a human being, there is a concurrence of the human power and the heavenly power (1a 118. 1 ad 2).

Despite his belief in the intimate involvement of heavenly bodies in earthly processes, Aquinas does not believe in all the claims made by astrologers. He does not deny that the heavenly bodies may affect human conduct—after all, a hot sun may make me take off my over-coat—but he insists that they do not do so in such a way as to determine human choice and make astrological prediction possible. If the human intellect and will were purely bodily faculties, then the stars would indeed be able to act on them directly; but since these faculties are spiritual, they escape their fatal influence. To those who claim that astrologers are successful in predicting the outcome of wars, Aquinas replies that this is because the majority of humans fail to exercise their free will and yield instead to their bodily passions. Hence astrologers can make statistically reliable predictions, but they cannot foretell the fate of an individual. Astrologers themselves admit, he says, that the wise man can overcome the stars (1a 115. 4).

Actual and Potential Infinity

Most medieval philosophers accepted the position of Aristotle that the notion of an actually infinite number was incoherent. Matter, he maintained, was divisible to infinity: but this meant, not that matter had infinitely many parts, but that however often it had been divided it could always be divided further. The infinite, he maintained, had only a potential existence.

Aristotle himself objected only to a synchronic actual infinite. The universe, he believed, had existed for ever, and that must mean that an infinite number of periods of time had already passed. However, his theorem was applied by medieval philosophers not only to the divisibility of the continuum, but also to the duration of the created universe.

Those who wished to prove that the world had been created in time often argued that belief in an eternal universe entailed belief in an actual infinite. Thus Bonaventure argues as follows:

It is impossible for any addition to be made to what is infinite. This is clear, because whatever is added to becomes greater, but nothing is greater than the infinite. But if the world had no beginning, it has lasted for infinity; therefore, no addition can be made to its duration. But it is clear that this is false; every day a new solar revolution is added to all the past revolutions. Perhaps you will say that it is infinite with respect to the past, but actually finite with respect to the present that now obtains, and it is only with respect to the current, finite, part that one can find something greater. But we can show that with respect to the past a greater can be found. It is an unquestionable truth that if the world is eternal, there have been infinite revolutions of the sun, and moreover that there have been twelve revolutions of the moon for every one of the sun. Hence, the moon has gone round more often than the sun. But the sun has gone round an infinite number of times; therefore it is possible to find something exceeding what is infinite in the very respect in which it is infinite. But this is impossible.[5]

If there were actual infinities, even if not synchronic, they would be countable, in the way that years and months are countable. But if there were countable infinities, there would be unequal infinities, and surely this was a scandal.

Medieval philosophers responded to the scandal in different ways. Some denied that 'equal to' and 'greater than' applied to infinite numbers at all. Others accepted that there could be equal and unequal infinities, but denied that the axiom 'the whole is greater than its part' applied to infinite numbers.

The infinitely divisible continuum, as envisaged by Aristotle, did not raise the problem of unequal infinities, because the parts of the continuum were only potentially distinct from each other, and potential entities were not countable in the same way as actual entities. In the fourteenth century, however, some thinkers began to argue that the continuum was composed of indivisible atoms, which were infinite in number. Notable among these was Henry of Harclay, who was chancellor of Oxford University in 1312.

Aristotle had argued that a continuum could not be composed of points that lacked magnitude. Since a point has no parts, it cannot have a boundary distinct from itself; two points therefore could not touch each other without becoming a single point. But Henry tried to argue that they could touch—they would indeed touch whole to whole, but they could differ from each other in position, and thus add to each other. This theory was difficult to understand, and Bradwardine was able to show that it made nonsense of Euclidean geometry. If you take a square and draw parallel lines from each atom on one side to each atom on the opposite side, these will meet the diagonal in exactly as many atoms as they meet the sides. But this is incompatible with the diagonal's being incommensurable with the sides.

Ockham took a much more radical stance against Henry. As part of his general reductionist programme, he argued that points had no absolute existence. Not even God could make a point exist in independence from all other entities. So far from a line being constructed out of points, as it was for Henry, a point was nothing other than a limit or cut in a line.

---

[5] II *Sent.* 1. 1. 1. 2; cited by J. Murdoch, 'Infinity and Continuity', in *CHLMP* 570.

A point is not an absolute thing distinct from substance and quality and the other quantities listed by modern writers, because if it was, it would be something other than a line. But this is false. Is it part of a line, or not? Not a part, because, as Aristotle tries to show, a line is not made up out of points. If it is not part of a line—and a line is manifestly not part of a point—then they are two wholly distinct things, neither a part of the other. (*OPh*. 2. 207)

Ockham agrees with Aristotle about the impossibility of an actual infinite, and uses the theorem to show that a point is not an indivisible entity really distinct from anything divisible. If points were such atoms, there would be infinitely many of them actually existing. In any piece of wood you can designate any number of lines, each ending in a point. If the points are real, then there will be infinitely many actually existing entities, which is impossible and contrary to all philosophy (*OPh*. 2. 209–10).

Fourteenth-century logicians and natural philosophers took an interest not only in the spatial continuum, but in the continua of time and motion. One of Richard Kilvington's *sophismata* (no. 13) sets a problem about traversing a distance. When Socrates traverses a distance A, should we say that he traverses it at any time he is in the process of traversing, or only when he has completed the process? There seems a problem either way. If we take the second option, then Socrates is only traversing A when he has ceased to do so; if we take the first option, then Socrates traverses A infinitely many times, since the motion is infinitely divisible; yet he only traverses it once.

Kilvington deals with his puzzle sentence 'Socrates will traverse distance A' by drawing a distinction between two ways of spelling out the verb 'will traverse'.

In one way it is expounded as follows: 'Socrates will traverse distance A'—that is, 'Socrates will be in the process of traversing distance A'. And in this way the sophisma is true. Moreover, the last conclusion—that in this way infinitely often will Socrates traverse distance A—is granted; for infinitely often will Socrates be in the process of traversing distance A. The sophisma can be expounded in another way as follows: 'Socrates will traverse distance A'—that is, 'Distance A will have been traversed by Socrates'. Speaking in this way, before C [the moment of reaching the terminus] Socrates will not traverse distance A. (*Sophismata*, 328[6])

The method of 'expounding' verbs had been popular with logicians since the time of Peter of Spain. Favourite 'exponible' verbs were 'begin' ('inci-

---

[6] Introd., trans., and comm. Norman Kretzmann and Barbara Ensign Kretzmann (Cambridge: Cambridge University Press, 1990).

pere') and 'cease' ('desinere'). Kilvington and his colleagues offered to expound such verbs in order to deal with such problems as whether there were first and last moments of motion. The common answer was that there were not: only a last moment before a motion began, and a first moment after motion ceased.

Walter Burley wrote a whole treatise *On the First and Last Instant*, dividing up entities and processes of various kinds, some of which had a first instant and no last instant, others no first instant but a last instant, and so forth. He also extended the notions of continuity and divisibility to changes in quality as well as in quantity. His book *On the Intension and Remission of Forms* discussed the nature and measurement of continuous change in properties such as heat and colour.

Scholastic philosophers discussing the heating of bodies customarily took one of two positions. On one view, when a body grew hotter, it was by the addition of an element of heat. On another view, change in temperature was to be explained as an admixture of heat and cold. Burley introduced a third alternative: he introduced the notion of degrees of heat, on a single scale which he called a 'latitude'. Heat and cold were to be considered not two qualities, but a single quality. At one end of the latitude would be maximum heat, and at the other end maximum cold. He thus introduced our modern concept of temperature and laid the foundation for important developments in physics.

6

Metaphysics

In the writings of the late Neoplatonists and of Augustine there is no lack of metaphysical thinking. However, in their work it is so bound up with consideration of the divine nature that it is difficult to disentangle from their natural theology, and in this volume it is considered in the chapter on God. This situation changes dramatically when we come to the philosophy of Avicenna, who was beyond doubt the greatest metaphysician of the first millennium AD.

Aristotle, it will be recalled, gives two definitions of first philosophy: one, that it was the science of divine substance, the other that it was the science that theorizes about being *qua* being. Both definitions, I have argued, coincide. The second describes metaphysics in terms of the field it is to explain, namely whatever there is. The first describes metaphysics in terms of the principle of explanation it offers: reference to the divine unmoved mover. Thus theology and the science of being *qua* being are one and the same first philosophy.[1]

Avicenna on Being, Essence, and Existence

Commentators on Aristotle, however, have commonly taken the two definitions as offering different, competing, accounts of the nature of metaphysics. Avicenna accepts the thesis that metaphysics studies being *qua* being, but rejects the idea that the object of metaphysics is God. The reason he gives is this. No science can demonstrate the existence of its own

---

[1] See vol. i, p. 227.

subject matter. But metaphysics, and only metaphysics, demonstrates the existence of God. So God cannot be the subject matter of metaphysics (*Metaph.* 1. 5–6).

Being, the object of metaphysics, is something whose existence does not have to be proved. Metaphysics studies being as such, not particular types of being, such as material objects. It studies items in the Aristotelian categories, which are as it were species of being. It treats of topics such as the one and the many, potentiality and actuality, universal and particular, the possible and the necessary—topics that transcend the boundaries between natural, mathematical, and ethical disciplines. It is called a divine science because it treats of 'things that are separate from matter in their definition and being' (*Metaph.* 1. 13–15).

According to Avicenna, the first ideas that are impressed on the soul are *thing*, *being*, and *necessary*; these cannot be explained by any ideas that are better known, and to attempt to do so involves a vicious circle. Every thing has its own reality which makes it what it is—a triangle has a reality that makes it a triangle, whiteness has a reality that makes it whiteness: this can be called its being, but a more appropriate technical term is its 'quiddity'.[2] This is a better word because 'being' also has the other sense of 'existence'.

The most important division between types of being is that between necessary being and possible being (there is no such thing as impossible being). Possible being is that which, considered in itself, has no necessity to be; necessary being is that which, considered in itself, will be necessary to be. What is necessary of itself has no cause; what is of itself possible has a cause. A being which had a cause would be, considered in abstraction from that cause, no longer necessary; hence it would not be that which is necessary of itself.

Whatever, considered in itself, is possible has a cause both of its being and its not being. When it has being, it has acquired a being distinct from non-being. But when it has ceased to be, it has a non-being distinct from being. It cannot be otherwise than that each of these is acquired either from something other than itself or not from something other than itself. If it is acquired from something other than itself, that other thing is its cause. If it is not acquired

---

[2] The Arabic term is derived from the interrogative 'What?'; the Latin translators formed a corresponding word, 'quiddity', to indicate that which answers the question 'What (*quid*) is an X?' One could form an English term 'whatness', but 'quiddity' has become sufficiently Anglicized over the centuries.

from something other than itself, then it must be derived from its own quiddity. If the quiddity is sufficient on its own for the acquisition, then it is not a possible but a necessary being. If the quiddity is not sufficient, but needs external aid, then that external element is the real cause of the being or not being of the possible being. (*Metaph.* 1. 38)

Avicenna makes use of this argument to show the existence of a first cause that is necessary of itself, and goes on to list the attributes of this necessary being: it is uncaused, incomparable, unique, and so on. But it is important to pause here and reflect on the passage just cited.

The passage supposes that there can be a subject, one and the same subject, that first possesses non-being and then, at a later stage, possesses being: an X such that first X does not exist and then X exists. This is obviously something quite different from an underlying matter that first has one form and then another, as when, in the Aristotelian system, a piece of clay takes different forms or one element is transmuted into another (cf. *Metaph.* 1. 73). But exactly what kind of metaphysical entity we are being offered is unclear. Is the subject that passes from non-being to being (and vice versa) the universe, or a species, or an individual? When we read this passage, does Avicenna want us to have in mind 'Once the universe did not exist' or 'There used to be dinosaurs, but now there aren't' or 'First there wasn't Socrates, but then there was'? Each of these thoughts raises metaphysical problems, but let us concentrate on the last of the three, which is both the clearest and the most problematic.

Surely, before Socrates existed, there was no such subject to have predicates attached to it, or, if you like, there was no Socrates around to be doing the non-existing. It seems difficult to talk about non-existent individuals, because of the impossibility of individuating what does not exist. Well, how do we individuate what *does* exist? Aristotle believed that one individual of a particular species was distinct from another because it was a different parcel of matter. But what does not exist is not a part of the material universe and hence cannot be individuated by matter. But need Avicenna accept that matter is the sole individuating feature?

To answer this, we need to look at what Avicenna tells us about the relationship between universals and particulars. A concept can be universal, he says, in different ways. It can be something that is, in actual fact, truly predicated of many things, such as *human*. It may be something that it is logically possible to predicate of many things, but which in fact is not truly predicated of many things. Here there are two possible cases. The concept *heptagonal house*, he tells us, is not truly predicated of anything, but there is nothing to stop that universal being instantiated many times. The concept *sun*, however, is truly predicated of only one thing, and cannot be truly predicated of more than one thing; but this impossibility, he says, is a matter of physics, not of logic. Individuals are quite different. 'An individual is something that cannot be conceived as being predicated of more than one thing, like the essence of Zayd here, which cannot be conceived as belonging to anything other than himself' (*Metaph*. 5. 196).

Consider the concept *horse*. We can consider this in three ways: we can consider it as it has being in individuals, or in respect of the being it has in the mind, or we can consider it absolutely, in the abstract, without reference to either being.

The definition of *horseness* bypasses the definition of *universal*, and universality is not contained in the definition of horseness. Horseness has a definition which has no need of universality; universality is something extra. Horseness is itself nothing but horseness; in itself it is neither one nor many, in itself it does not exist either in perceptible individuals nor in the soul...Horseness is common, in that many things share its definition; but if you take it with particular properties and designated accidents, it is individual. But horseness in itself is nothing but horseness. (*Metaph*. 5. 196)

Avicenna is not saying, in Platonic style, that there exists such a thing as horseness in itself, apart from any individual horse. Horseness is something that occurs in individual horses, Bellerophon or Eclipse, and we can study it by examining it in these individuals. We can consider also the concept as it occurs in the mind: as when we say that the concept *horse* is a concept easily attained. But we can also consider in the abstract what is involved in being a horse, and this is considering horseness in itself (*Metaph*. 5. 207).

Horseness in an individual horse, and humanity in a particular human, will be accompanied by 'particular properties and designated accidents', Avicenna says. For Aristotle, it would be these designated accidents—the ones that mark out a particular parcel of matter—that would be what individuated Socrates. But for Avicenna the humanity in an individual human is itself individuated. Though the humanity of Zayd and the humanity of Amr do not differ from each other, it is quite wrong to think that they are numerically the same: they are not one but two humanities. For Avicenna, there are individual as well as generic essences.

The invention of individual essences holds out the possibility of the individuation of non-existent entities. Just as the coming into existence of steam out of water can be looked on as the addition of the form of steam to the pre-existent matter that was previously water, so the coming into being of Socrates can be looked upon as the addition of existence to an essence that previously lacked it. The pre-existent essence can be regarded as a potentiality whose actuality is existence. Thus essence and existence appear as a third potentiality–actuality pair alongside matter–form and sub-stance–accident. Existence, Avicenna sometimes seems to say, is an acci-dent added to essence.[3]

In the case of a being that is necessary of itself, there is no question of having being after non-being, and so the distinction between essence and existence does not arise. But in all other entities, on Avicenna's view, the two are distinct. Since Avicenna's time some philosophers have agreed that in all cases except that of God there is a real distinction between essence and existence; other philosophers have denied this, but all have treated the issue as important. But the significance of the issue depends on whether, in this context, 'essence' means generic essence or individual essence.

If we take 'essence' in the generic sense, then the distinction between existence and essence corresponds to the distinction between the question 'Are there Xs?' and 'What are Xs?' That there are quarks is not at all the same thing as what quarks are. If this is what the distinction amounts to, then it is undeniable.[4] But if we take the distinction to be one about individual essences, then it seems to entail the possibility of individual essences not united to any existence; individual essences of possible, but non-existent individuals. The essence of Adam, say, is there from all eternity; when God creates Adam, he confers actuality on this already present potentiality.

The postulation of individual essences, though it was to be influential down to the present day, was a recipe for philosophical confusion. Let us ask how an individual humanity—say the humanity of Abraham—is itself individuated. It is not individuated *qua* humanity: that is something shared by all humans. It is not individuated by belonging to Abraham: *ex hypothesi*, it

---

[3] So at least he was often understood in the Latin Middle Ages; see *CHLMP* 393.

[4] Though if this interpretation is accepted, then the doctrine that in God essence and existence are not distinct amounts to saying that the answer to the question 'What is God?' is 'There is one'. Some theologians appear happy to accept this.

An autograph manuscript of Aquinas, from the Ambrosian library in Milan.

could exist, and be the same individual, even if Abraham had never been created but remained a perpetual possibility. It can only be identified, as Avicenna says, by the properties and accidents that accompany it—that is to say, by everything that was true of the actual Abraham—that he migrated from Ur of the Chaldees, obeyed a divine command to sacrifice his son, and so on. Of course, since Abraham's essence was there before Abraham existed, it could not be individuated by the actuality of these things, but only by their possibility.

But, prior to Abraham's conception, there was no one and nothing to be the subject of these possibilities. There was only the abstract possibility that there should be *an* individual who migrated from Ur, sacrificed his son, and so on; it was not the possibility of *this* individual. Similarly, before Noah was conceived, there was not the possibility that *he* would build the Ark, but only the possibility that *someone* would build an Ark. Avicenna rightly insisted against Plato that there was no actualization without individuation—there were no actual universals in existence. It was a pity that he did not accept the converse principle that there can be no individuation without actualization.

Aquinas on Actuality and Potentiality

The ideas of Avicenna were powerful throughout the high Middle Ages. Traces of his thought are often to be found in the work of Thomas Aquinas, whose early metaphysical manifesto *On Being and Essence* begins with a quotation from Avicenna to the effect that being and essence are the first things grasped by the intellect. As his thought matured, Aquinas developed his own version of Aristotelian metaphysics, but he never wholly shook off Avicenna's influence.

The key concepts in Aquinas' metaphysics are those of actuality and potentiality. He derives the notions, obviously, from Aristotle and from Aristotle's commentators; but he applies them in new areas and with new degrees of sophistication. Already in Aristotle the simple pairing of the concepts had been modified by a distinction between first and second actuality: Aquinas developed this distinction into a stratification of levels of potentiality and actuality, in particular making a systematic study of the notion of *habitus*, or disposition. In Aristotle the two principal instances of the potentiality–actuality structure are the relationships of subject to accident and matter to form. Aquinas accepts and elaborates Avicenna's addition of a third instantiation of the dichotomy: essence and being.

Aquinas devoted five questions of the *Summa Theologiae, Prima Secundae*, to the notion of *habitus*. The immediate purpose of this treatise (which, though Aristotelian in spirit, is largely original work) is to introduce the notion of virtue. But the concept of *habitus* has much wider application: indeed it is an essential element in the characterization of peculiarly human behaviour and experience, even though great philosophers have sometimes seemed almost unaware of this fact. Aquinas has the merit of having grasped the importance of the concept and of having been the first great philosopher to attempt a full-scale analysis of it.

Examples of *habitus* include—as well as virtues like temperance and charity—sickness and health, beauty and toughness, knowledge of logic and science, beliefs of any kind, and the possession of concepts. The variety of examples shows that the word 'habit' will not do as a translation; the nearest contemporary philosophical term is 'disposition'. The notion of *disposition* is best approached via the notions of *capacity* and *action*. Human beings have many capacities that animals lack: the capacity to learn languages, for instance, and the capacity for generosity. These capacities are realized in action when particular human beings speak particular languages or perform generous actions. But between capacity and action there is an intermediate state possible. When we say that a man can speak French, we mean neither that he is actually speaking French, nor that his speaking French is a mere logical possibility. When we call a man generous, we mean more than that he has a capacity for generosity in common with the rest of the human race; but we need not mean that he is currently doing something generous. States such as knowing French and being generous are dispositions. A disposition, Aquinas says, is half-way between a capacity and an action, between pure potentiality and full actuality (*ST* 1a 2ae 50. 4).

Not every activity, for Aquinas, is an exercise of a disposition. God's thought and the motion of planets are activities that spring from no dispositions. Natural agents need no dispositions in order to perform their natural activities. By nature fire heats and water wets: these are the natural activities of fire and water and the only activities for which they have capacities. Where capacity and activity are identical as in God, or where capacity can be realized only in a single activity, as with the planets and natural agents, there is no room for a third term between capacity and activity.

Dispositions are qualities: they fall into one of the nine Aristotelian categories of *accident*. Accidents inhere in substances, and that goes also for dispositions. All attributes, Aquinas stresses, are in the last analysis attributes of substances, and all a person's dispositions are dispositions of a human being. What believes, or is generous, or is healthy is, strictly speaking, a man and not his mind or his heart or his body (1a 2ae 50. 2). Still, it is not senseless to ask, say, whether skill in writing history is principally a gift of memory or of imagination. To ask whether something is a disposition of mind or of body is to ask whether it belongs to a human being *qua* intelligent being or *qua* animal of a particular constitution.

Once again, in attaching dispositions to particular faculties as well as to the substance in which as accidents they ultimately inhere, Aquinas is applying a network of stratification to the original Aristotelian dichotomy of actuality and potentiality. The results are sometimes surprising. No human activity, he maintains, issues from a purely bodily disposition. Bodily activities are either subject to voluntary control or they are not. If they are not, then they are natural activities and as such need no disposition to account for them. If they are, then the dispositions that account for them must be located primarily in the soul. Thus, for Aquinas, the ability to run a marathon is a disposition of the soul no less than the ability to read Hebrew (1ae 2ae 50. 1).

In general, Aquinas' treatment of the relation between substance and accident is a natural development of his Aristotelian original. But one highly innovative application of the concepts is Aquinas' account of the Eucharist, the sacrament in which Catholics believed that bread and wine were changed, by the words of the priest at Mass, into Christ's body and blood. The substance of bread, he maintained, gave way to the substance of Christ's body—that was *transubstantiation*—and what remained, visible and tangible on the altar, were the mere accidents of bread and wine. The shape, colour, and so on of the bread remain without a substance to inhere in (*ST* 3a 75–7).

It is hard to decide whether the concept of accidents inherent in no substance is a coherent one. On the one hand, the idea of the Cheshire cat's grin without the cat seems absurd; on the other hand, the blue of the sky is not the blue of anything real and so perhaps is an accident without a substance. But St Thomas' account seems to fail in its purpose of explaining the presence of Christ on the altar: for one of the Aristotelian accidents is location, and so 'is on the altar', like 'is white and round', simply records the presence of an accident inhering in no substance and tells us nothing about the location of Christ. At all events, this particular application of the concepts of substance and accident would certainly have taken Aristotle by surprise.

But if Aristotle would be unlikely to countenance accidental forms existing apart from a substance, he left his followers in some doubt about the possibility of substantial forms existing apart from matter. Aquinas, like Aristotle, frequently objects to Plato's postulation of separated forms; but, unlike Bonaventure, he rejects universal hylomorphism and regards angels as pure forms. Unlike the Ideal Bed or the Idea of Good, angels such as Michael and Gabriel are living, intelligent beings; but so far as metaphysical status goes, there seems little difference between Plato's Forms and Aquinas' angels. Typical of the ambiguity in Aquinas' position is the following passage from his treatment of creation:

Creation is one way of coming into being. What coming into being amounts to depends on what being is. So those things properly come into being and are created, which properly have being. And those are subsistent objects.... That to which being properly belongs, is that which has being—and that is a subsistent thing with its own being. Forms, and accidents, and the like, are not called beings because they themselves are, but because by them something else is what it is. Thus whiteness is only called a being because by it something *is* white. That is why Aristotle says that an accident not so much *is* but *is of*. So, accidents and forms and the like, which do not subsist, are rather coexistent than existent, and likewise they should be called concreated rather than created. What really gets created are subsistent entities. (*ST* 1a. 45. 4c)

The passage as quoted is admirable as a statement of forthright Aristotelianism against any Platonic reification of forms, whether substantial or accidental. But in that very passage, in a sentence that I deliberately omitted, Aquinas divides the subsistent entities, which alone really have being and are created, into two classes: hylomorphic material substances on the one hand, and separated substances on the other. But separated substances— angelic spirits and the like—are, as understood by Aquinas, forms that are not forms *of* anything, and his way of conceiving them seems open to all the objections an Aristotelian would make against a Platonist. It seems difficult to render Aquinas' teaching coherent on this topic, other than by saying that he is an Aristotelian on earth, but a Platonist in heaven.

The most important way in which Aquinas, for better or worse, amplifies the Aristotelian system of potentiality and actuality is by applying it to the pair of concepts *essence* and *existence*, which he took over from Avicenna. For Aquinas, as for Avicenna, there are not just generic essences, such as *humanity*, but also the individual humanities of Peter and Paul. There are also two different kinds of existence, or two different senses of 'esse', the Latin verb 'to be' when it is used as equivalent to 'exist'. There is, first, generic existence, the existence of a kind of thing: as in 'Angels exist' or 'There are angels'. There is also the individual existence of particular objects as in 'The Great Pyramid still exists, but the Pharos of Alexandria does not'. (In Latin the use of 'est' and 'non est' is quite natural in such contexts; but in English 'Rome is, but Troy is not' has an archaic flavour.) Generic existence is the kind of existence that philosophers, since Kant, have insisted 'is not a predicate'; it is expressed in modern logic by the use of the particular quantifier (for some x, x is an angel). Individual existence, on the other hand, is a perfectly genuine predicate.[5]

With regard to generic existence, Aquinas' teaching is quite clear. A classic text is from *De Ente et Essentia*:

Whatever [belongs to a thing and] is not part of the concept of an essence or quiddity is something that arrives from outside and is added to the essence; because no essence can be conceived without the elements which are parts of the essence. But every essence or quiddity can be conceived without anything being understood with respect to its existence; for I can understand what a human being is, or what a phoenix is, and yet be ignorant whether they have existence in the nature of things. Hence it is clear that existence is different from essence or quiddity . . . (*DEE* 4. 94–105)

Whether there are things of a certain kind is quite a different issue from what things of that kind are: whether there are any angels is not at all the same question as what 'angel' means. If this is what is meant by saying that essence and existence are really distinct, then the doctrine is undoubtedly correct.

---

[5] In my book *Aquinas on Being* (Oxford: Oxford University Press, 2002) I have listed twelve different senses of 'esse' in Aquinas.

It is not so easy to work out what, for Aquinas, is the relation between individual essences and individual existence. Is there a real distinction between Peter's existence and Peter's essence—or between either of these and Peter himself? Surely not: it seems that Peter, Peter's humanity, and Peter's existence all have exactly the same duration; they all begin, roughly speaking, a few months before Peter's birth and end with Peter's death.

But perhaps one could argue for a real distinction between essence and existence in the following way. While it is true that any creature's existence persists for exactly the same length of time as its essence, there is this difference, that its existence at one time does not have consequences for its existence at a later time in the way that its essence at one time may have consequences for its existence at a later time. A human being tends to go on living for a certain time; a radioactive element tends to go out of existence at a certain rate. These tendencies are part of the relevant essences: it is because of the kind of thing they are that these creatures tend to continue or to cease to exist. Essence, therefore, would be distinct from existence, as a cause—a formal cause, in this case— is distinct from its effect.

Aquinas' teaching on the relation of essence and existence is obscure partly because the word 'esse', in addition to meaning 'existence' in both of its senses, has a variety of meanings in which it corresponds to the word 'being'. Sometimes, for instance, St Thomas tells us that all the things of different kinds in the universe—mice and men, storms and seasons, virtues and vices, times and places—have it in common that they *are*. Being in this sense is a very thin and universal predicate. (Gilbert Ryle once characterized it as 'like breathing, only quieter'.) At other times the verb 'to be' is used to mark a transition from potentiality to actuality. A caterpillar has the capacity to become a butterfly, but as long as it remains a caterpillar it *is* not a butterfly. Only when the magic day comes can we say: now it *is* a butterfly.

These senses of 'be' are important in Aquinas' system only when he uses them in order to clarify his thesis that in God, unlike creatures, there is no distinction between being and essence. God is, he claims, pure Being. Not only the distinction between essence and existence, but also the distinctions between other forms of potentiality and actuality—substance and accident, matter and form—have no place when we want to give an account of God, for he is pure actuality. These doctrines will be analysed in the final chapter of this book, on philosophy of religion.

The Metaphysics of Duns Scotus

In the system of Duns Scotus, metaphysics occupies a fundamental place. It is a metaphysics stated in Aristotelian terms, but given a very personal interpretation. Like Aristotle, Scotus defines metaphysics as the science that studies being *qua* being; but whereas in Aristotle, to study something *qua* being was a special way of studying, in Scotus, being *qua* being is a special object for study. Being *qua* being is indeed the broadest possible object of study, including finite and infinite being, actual and possible being.

In Scotus as in Aquinas it is a principal concern of metaphysics to establish the existence and attributes of God, so that natural theology is a branch of the discipline. But for Scotus the scope of natural theology, and therefore of metaphysics, is both broader and narrower than it is for Aquinas. It is broader, because Scotus believed that the terms that signify the fundamental properties of being *qua* being—such as 'good', 'true', 'one', and so on—applied not just analogously, but univocally to God as well as to creatures. But it is narrower, because many truths about God that Aquinas had treated as accessible to natural reason are regarded by Scotus as graspable only by faith. Aquinas had thought that reason could prove that God was omnipotent, immense, omnipresent, and so on. Scotus, on the contrary, thought that reason was impotent to prove that God was omnipotent. A Christian, he argued, knows that among the powers of an omnipotent God is the power to beget a Son; but this is not a power that pure reason can show God to possess. Thus many topics that, for Aquinas, were within the scope of the metaphysician are by Scotus assigned to the dogmatic theologian.

It was commonplace among scholastics to say that 'being' was a transcendental term that applied across the Aristotelian categories, and to say further that every being of every kind had properties like goodness and unity. Scotus' innovation in this respect was the claim that transcendental predicates such as 'being' and 'good' were univocal, not analogical.[6] But there is a different kind of transcendental to which Scotus attached great importance: the transcendental disjunction. He drew up a list of pairs of terms of which one or other must apply to whatever there is: every being must be either actual or potential, finite or infinite, necessary or contingent.

[6] See Ch. 3 above.

'Necessary' is not a term that applies to every being: but the disjunction 'necessary or contingent' does apply, right across the board (*Ord.* 3. 207).

Not only did Scotus lay a new emphasis on the necessary–contingent disjunction, he introduced a fundamentally new notion of contingency. It was generally believed by scholastics that many matters of fact were contingent. It is contingent that I am sitting down, because it is possible for me to stand up—a possibility that I can exemplify by standing up at the very next moment. Scotus, like other scholastics, accepted such a possibility: but he went further and claimed that at the very moment when I am sitting down there exists a possibility of my standing up at that same moment. This involves a new, more radical, form of contingency, which has been aptly named 'synchronic contingency' (*Lect.* 17. 496–7).

Of course, Scotus is not claiming that at one and the same moment I can be both sitting down and standing up. But he makes a distinction between 'moments of time' and 'moments of nature'. At a single moment of time there can be more than one moment of nature. At this moment of time I am sitting down: but at this same moment of time there is another moment of nature in which I am standing up. Moments of nature are synchronic possibilities.

Scotus is not talking about mere logical possibility: an instant of nature is a real possibility that is distinct from mere logical coherence. It is something that could be possible while the nature of the physical world remains the same. Synchronic possibilities need not be compatible with each other, as in the case just discussed; they are possible, a modern philosopher might say, in different possible worlds, not in the same possible world.

Scotus' instants of nature are indeed the ancestor of the contemporary philosophical concept of a possible world. His own account of the origin of the world sees God as choosing to actualize one among an infinite number of possible universes. Later philosophers separated the notion of possible worlds from the notion of creation, and began to take the word 'world' in a more abstract way, so that any totality of compossible situations constitutes a possible world. This abstract notion then came to be used as a means of explicating every kind of power and possibility. Credit for the introduction of the notion is often given to Leibniz, but, for better or worse, it belongs to Scotus.

The introduction of the notion of synchronic contingency involves a radical refashioning of the Aristotelian concepts of potentiality and actuality. For Scotus, unlike Aristotle or Aquinas, but like Avicenna, non-existent items can possess a potentiality to exist: a potentiality that Scotus calls *objective* potentiality, to contrast it with the Aristotelian potentiality, which he calls subjective potentiality.

There are two ways in which something can be called a being in potentiality. In one way it is the terminus of a power, that to which the power is directed—and this is called being in potentiality objectively. Thus Antichrist is now said to be in potentiality, and other things can be said to be in potentiality such as a whiteness that is to be brought into existence. In the other way something is said to be in potentiality as the subject of the power, or that in which the power inheres. In that way something is said to be in potentiality subjectively, because it is in potentiality to something but is not yet perfected by it (like a surface that is about to be whitened). (*Lect.* 19. 80)

Non-existent items, Scotus explains, are individuated by their objective potentiality: non-existent A differs from non-existent B because if and when they do exist A and B differ from each other.

Other terms of the Aristotelian metaphysical arsenal are likewise re-interpreted. The relationship between matter and form, for instance, is expounded by Scotus in a novel way. For Aristotle, matter was a funda-mental item in the analysis of substantial change. Substantial change is the kind of change exemplified when one element changes into another—e.g. water into steam (air)—or a living being comes into or goes out of existence—e.g. when a dog dies and its corpse decays. When a substance of one kind changes into one or more substances of another kind, there is, for Aristotle, a form that determines the nature of the substance that precedes the change, and a different form or forms determining the nature of the substance(s) subsequent to the change. The element that remains constant throughout the change is matter: matter, as such, is not one kind of substance rather than another, and has, as such, no properties. While form determines what *kind* of thing a substance is, it is matter that determines *which thing* of that kind a substance is. Matter is the principle of individuation, and form, we might say, is the principle of specification.

Scotus rejects both the notion of matter lacking properties and the thesis that matter is the principle of individuation. Matter, according to him, has properties such as quantity, and further, prior to such properties, it has an essence of its own, even if it is virtually impossible for human beings to know what this essence is (*Lect.* 19. 101). Matter, indeed, can exist without any form at all. Matter and form are really distinct, and it is well within the power of God to create and conserve both immaterial form and formless matter, each of them individuated in their own right.

Actual material substances are composed of both matter and form: here Scotus agrees with Aristotle and Aquinas. Socrates, for instance, is a human individual, composed of individual matter and an individual form of humanity. Scotus gives a novel account, however, of the way in which the individual substance and its matter and form are themselves individuated. For Aquinas, the form of humanity is an individual form because it is the human form *of Socrates*, and Socrates is individuated by his matter, which in turn is individuated by being designated, or marked off as a particular parcel of matter (*materia signata*). For Scotus, on the other hand, the form is an individual in its own right, independently of the matter of Socrates and the substance Socrates (*Ord.* 7. 483).

What individuates Socrates is neither his matter nor his form but a third thing, which is sometimes called his *haecceitas*, or *thisness*. In each thing, Scotus tells us, there is an *entitas individualis*. 'This entity is neither matter nor form nor the composite thing, in so far as any of these is a nature; but it is the ultimate reality of the being which is matter or form or a composite thing' (*Ord.* 7. 393).

According to Aristotelian orthodoxy, forms themselves neither come into existence nor go out of existence: it is substances, not forms, that are the subjects of generation and corruption. Strictly speaking we should say not that the wisdom of Socrates comes into existence: that is only a complicated way of saying that Socrates becomes wise. With regard to the independently individuated substantial forms, in Scotus' system, by contrast, one can raise the question how they come into existence, and whether they come out of nothing. Are they created, or do they evolve from something pre-existing? Scotus rejects both these options. Forms do not evolve from embryonic forms, or *rationes seminales*, as Augustine, followed by Bonaventure, had thought. Postulating such entities does not answer the question of the origin of forms, since the question would simply rearise concerning whatever is the new element that distinguishes a fully fledged form from an embryonic one. On the other hand, we do not want to say that forms are created; but we can avoid saying that if we redefine 'creation' not as bringing something into existence out of nothing, but as bringing something into existence in the absence of any precondition (*Lect.* 19. 174).

Aquinas had maintained that in all material substances, including human beings, there was only a single substantial form. Scotus denied this: and in this denial he had, for once, the majority of medieval scholastics on his side. He agreed with Aquinas that non-living entities had only a single substantial form: a chemical compound did not retain the forms of the elements of which they were composed. But living bodies—plants, animals, and humans—possessed, in addition to the specific forms belonging to their kinds, a common form of corporeality that made them all bodies. He argued for this on the basis that a human body immediately after death is the same body as it was immediately before death, even though it is no longer an ensouled human being. Similar considerations hold with regard to animals and plants.

Though Scotus held that the soul is not the only substantial form of humans, he did not, like some of his predecessors, believe that there were three different souls coexisting in each human being, an intellectual, sensitive, and vegetative soul. If there were any forms in human beings other than the soul and the form of corporeality, they were forms of individual human organs—a possibility that Scotus once considered.[7] But in addition to the matter and the forms in a substance there is another item which is neither matter nor form, the haecceity that makes it the individual it is. For the individuality of the matter and the individuality of the form are between them not sufficient to individuate the composite substance (*Lect.* 17. 500).

How do all these items—matter, forms, haecceity—fit together in the concrete material substance? It is wrong to think of a material substance as being an aggregate of which all these items are parts; for the parts could, on Scotus' account, all exist separately. Moreover, the whole substance has properties that are different from any of the properties of the parts listed: for instance, the property of being a unified whole. In addition to those parts, Scotus believed, we had to add an extra item: the relationship between them—something which he is prepared to look on as yet another part. But even after we have added this, we have to say that an individual

---

[7] See R. Cross, *The Physics of Duns Scotus: The Scientific Context of a Theological Vision* (Oxford: Clarendon Press, 1998), 68.

material substance is an independent entity distinct from its matter, forms, and relations (or any pair or triple of these items) (*Oxon.* 3. 2. 2 n. 8).

How are these different entities—the whole and its several parts—distinguished from each other? Scotus maintains that there is a real distinction between the substance and its matter and form and the relationship between them. By saying that these items are really distinct he means that it is at least logically possible for any of them to exist without any of the others. He adds, for good measure, that if we say that the essence or quiddity of a substance equals its matter plus its form, we must say that the essence, no less than the substance itself, is really distinct from its components.

What is the relation, we may ask, between the essence and the haecceity—are these, too, really distinct from each other? In an individual such as Socrates we have, according to Scotus, both a common human nature and an individuating principle. The human nature is a real thing that is common to both Socrates and Plato; if it were not real, Socrates would not be any more like Plato than he is like a line scratched on a blackboard. Equally, the individuating principle must be a real thing, otherwise Socrates and Plato would be identical. The nature and the individuating principle must be united to each other, and neither can exist in reality apart from each other: we cannot encounter in the world a human nature that is not anyone's nature, nor can we meet an individual that is not an individual of some kind or other. Yet we cannot identify the nature with the haecceitas: if the nature of donkey were identical with the thisness of the donkey Brownie, then every donkey would be Brownie.

To solve this enigma, Scotus introduces a new complication. Any created essence, he says, has two features: replicability and individuality. My essence as a human being is replicable: there can be, and are, other human beings, essentially the same as myself. But it is also individual: it is *my* essence, because it includes an individuating haecceity. The distinction (*Ord.* 2. 345–6) between the essence and the haecceity is not a real distinction, but it is not a mere fiction or creation of the mind. It is, Scotus says, a special kind of formal distinction, a *distinctio formalis a parte rei*, a formal distinction 'on the side of reality'. The essence and the haecceity are not really distinct, in the way in which Socrates and Plato are distinct, or in the way in which my two hands are distinct. Nor are they merely distinct in thought, as Socrates and the teacher of Plato are. Prior to any thought about them, they are, he says, formally distinct: they are two distinct formalities in the same thing. It is not clear to me, as it was not to many of Scotus' successors, how the introduction of this terminology clarifies the problem it was meant to solve. One of the problems about understanding exactly how Scotus meant his distinction to be understood is that the illustrations he gives of its meaning, and the contexts in which he applies it, are all themselves drawn from areas of great obscurity: the relationships between the different divine attributes, and the distinction between the vegetative, sensitive, and rational souls in human beings.

Ockham's Reductive Programme

William Ockham was one of the first to reject Scotus' formal distinction on the side of reality. He argued.

Where there is a distinction or non-identity, there must be some contradictories true of the items in question. But it is impossible that contradictories can be true of any items unless they—or the items for which they supposit—are distinct things, or distinct concepts, or distinct *entia rationis*, or a thing and a concept. But if the distinction is from the nature of things, then they are not distinct concepts, nor a pair of a thing plus a concept: therefore they are distinct things. (*OTh.* 2. 14)

But this assumes that the only candidates for being the terms of a distinction are (a) things, (b) *entia rationis*, (c) concepts. This begs the question against Scotus, who accepted a much less restricted ontology. But the move is characteristic of Ockham's reductionist drive.

'Entia non sunt multiplicanda praeter necessitatem'—'Entities are not to be multiplied beyond necessity.' This is the famous 'Ockham's razor', designed to shave off philosophers' superfluous woolliness. The remark is not, in fact, to be found in his surviving writings.[8] He did say similar things such as 'it is futile to do with many what can be done with few' and 'plurality is not to be assumed without necessity', but he was not the first person to make such remarks. However, the slogan does sum up his reductionist attitude towards the technical philosophical developments of his predecessors.

[8] It seems to have been attributed to him first in a footnote to the Wadding edition of Scotus in 1639.

One of the first superfluous entities to be subjected to the razor are Scotus' haecceities, or individuating principles. Scotus had argued that in addition to the human nature of Socrates there must be something to make it *this* nature; because if his human nature were itself *this*, then every human nature would be *this*, that is to say would be the nature of Socrates. Ockham believed neither in the common nature nor in the individuating principle. All that exists in reality are individuals, and they just are individual—they need no extra principle to individuate them. It is not individuality, but universality, that needs explaining—indeed, explaining away.

But Ockham's nominalism is only part of his programme of metaphysical deflation. In addition to universals, Ockham wanted to shave off large classes of individuals. For his medieval predecessors there were individuals in every category—not only individual substances like Socrates and Brownie the donkey, but individual accidents of many kinds, such as Brownie's whereabouts and Socrates' relationship to Plato. Ockham reduced the ten Aristotelian categories to two. Only substances and qualities were real.

Belief in individuals of other kinds, Ockham maintained, was due to a naive assumption that to every word there corresponded an entity in the world (*OTh.* 9. 565). This was what led people to invent 'when-nesses' and 'wherenesses'—they might as well, he says, have invented also 'andnesses' and 'butnesses'. Medieval philosophers did not, in fact, have a great deal invested in some of the later categories of the Aristotelian catalogue. What was serious in Ockham's innovation was the denial of the reality of the categories of quantity and of relation.

Ockham was not denying the distinction between the different categories: what he was denying was that the distinction was more than a conceptual one.

Substance, quality and quantity are distinct categories, even though they do not signify an absolute reality distinct from substance and quality, because they are distinct concepts and words signifying the same things but in a different manner. They are not synonymous names, because 'substance' signifies all the things it signifies in one manner of signifying, namely directly; 'quantity' signifies the same things but in a different manner of signifying, signifying substance directly and its parts obliquely; for it signifies a whole substance and connotes that it has parts distant from other parts. (*OTh.* 9. 436)

Ockham's principal philosophical argument against the reality of quantity is derived from the phenomena of expansion and contraction, rarefaction and condensation. If a piece of metal is heated and expands from being 80 cm long to being 90 cm long, then, on the theory he is attacking, it changes from possessing an accident of 80-cm-longhood to possessing another accident of 90-cm-longhood. Ockham argues that it is difficult to give a convincing account of where the second accident has come from, and what has become of the first accident. Moreover, if the change is a continuous one, so that the metal has expanded through lengths of 81 cm to 82 cm and so on, then there will be an infinite number of fleeting accidents coming into and going out of existence. This, Ockham claims, strains our credulity. The local motion by which one part moves away from another part is quite sufficient to explain such phenomena. Accordingly, real accidents of quantity are quite superfluous, and should be eliminated from philosophical consideration.

One might think that similar considerations might be used to show that qualities, too, were not real accidents. Aristotle had listed four kinds of quality: (a) dispositions like virtue and health, (b) inborn capacities, (c) sensory properties like colour, taste, heat, (d) shapes. Ockham was willing to eliminate some of the qualities in the first class, like health and beauty, and he applied his razor very explicitly to qualities in the fourth class.

When a proposition is true of reality, if one thing is sufficient to make it true, it is superfluous to posit two. But propositions like 'this substance is square' 'this substance is round' are true of reality; and a substance disposed in such and such a way is quite sufficient for its truth. If the parts of a substance are laid out along straight lines and are not moved locally and do not grow or shrink, then it is contradictory that it should be first square and then round. So squareness and roundness add nothing to a substance and its parts. (OTh. 9. 707)

But he maintained that other qualities, notably colour, were different.

It is impossible for something to pass from one contradictory to another without gaining or losing something real, in cases where this is not accounted for by the passage of time or by change of place. But a man is first non-white, and afterwards white, and this change is not accounted for by change of place or the passage of time. Therefore, the whiteness is really distinct from the man. (OTh. 9. 706)

One might think, however, that a gradual change of colour was quite parallel to a gradual change of size: the implausibility of an infinite series of

After the heyday of scholasticism, Augustine's influence revived in the later middle ages. Here in a fresco in the upper church in Assisi he is shown dictating to a Dominican friar.

fleeting accidents can be urged in this case too. What makes the difference between the two cases, for Ockham, seems to be simply whether local motion can be called in to explain the change to be explained.

Ockham's arguments on the topic of relations are more powerful than his arguments against real quantity. If a relation were a real entity distinct from the terms of the relation, it would be capable of existing even if the terms were not. Suppose Socrates is the father of Plato, and Plato is the son of Socrates. Then there is a relation of paternity between Socrates and Plato. It is absurd to say either that this relation could exist without Socrates ever having begotten Plato, or that, Socrates having begotten Plato, God could remove from Socrates the relation of paternity (*OTh.* 4. 368).

210

The relation of likeness is an important one for Ockham, because of its connection with real qualities: everything that has a certain real quality P is like everything else that has that quality. A white wall is like every other white wall. A painter who paints a wall white in Rome makes it like each of the white walls in London. But if the relation of likeness was a real thing, then the painter in Rome would be bringing into existence numerous entities in London. Indeed if God made a thousand worlds and an agent produced whiteness in one of them, he would produce likenesses in each one of them (*OTh*. 1. 291, 9. 614). What is true of likeness is true of position. If I move my finger, its position is changed in relation to everything else in the world. If relations of position are real things, then by moving my finger I create a gigantic number of converse relations throughout the universe.

Ockham is not saying that a relation is identical with its foundation. 'I do not say that a relation is really the same as its foundation; but I say that a relation is not the foundation but only an intention or concept in the soul, signifying several absolute things' (*Ord*. 1. 301). Relative terms signify the absolute things that are the bearers of the relation, but they are connotative terms that signify one term of the relation, connote the other, and connote the way in which the two exist. Thus, when we say that A is next to B, we are not talking about a real entity of 'nextness'; we are signifying A, connoting B, and saying that there is nothing getting in the way between them (*OTh*. 4. 285, 312).

This, Ockham says, is what natural reason teaches: that there are no such entities as relations. But, rather ignominiously, he is prepared to accept the existence of such relations in certain cases because he believes that certain Christian doctrines—the Trinity, the Incarnation, the Eucharist—demand the existence of such relations. This naturally led to the suspicion that he was a proponent of a double truth: that something could be true in theology that was false in philosophy.

Wyclif and Determinism

In the generation after Ockham, as we have seen, there was a reaction against his nominalism and his general reductive programme. In Oxford this took the form of a revival of Augustinianism, which in turn led to a renewed interest in problems of predestination and determinism. John

Wyclif was a leader of the realist reaction. After his death Wyclif acquired the reputation of being a thoroughgoing determinist. One of the propositions attributed to him and condemned at the Council of Constance was 'All things happen by absolute necessity'.

In fact, at least in his youth, Wyclif developed a highly subtle and nuanced theory of the relationship between different types of necessity and contingency. He distinguished no less than seven types of necessity, which we may crudely catalogue as: logical necessity, natural necessity, eternal truth, sempiternal truth, inevitable truth, duress, and irresistible impulses. He insisted that there were some events—e.g. human choices—that were exempt from every one of these types of necessity.

In defending this, Wyclif had to deal with the following difficulty that he puts to himself:

Just as no one can prevent the world's having been, so no one can prevent any effect coming to be at the appropriate time. For the following argument is valid: God ordains A; therefore A will necessarily come to pass at the appropriate time. The antecedent is outside any created power and is accordingly altogether unpreventable. Therefore, so is everything which formally follows from it. (*U* XIV. 322–7)

Wyclif's solution to this is to propose that the relationship between the divine volition and events in the world is a two-way one: if God's volition causes things to happen here below, so, in a sense, events here below cause God's volition.

On this it is to be noted that the volition of God, with respect to the existence of a creature, can be understood as a relationship, a mental entity with its basis in God's willing the thing to be in accordance with its mental being—which is something absolutely necessary—and with its terminus in the existence of the creature in its own kind. And such a relationship depends on each of the terms, since if God is to will that Peter or some other creature should be it is requisite that it should in fact be. And thus the existence of the creature, even though it is temporal, causes in God an eternal mental relationship, which is always in process of being caused, and yet is always completely caused. (*U* XIV. 328–44)

The objection that if God's ordaining is outside our power, then all that follows from his ordaining is outside our power, is answered in a dramatic fashion. Wyclif simply denies the antecedent: God's ordaining is not outside our power.

It cannot be said that Wyclif's solution resolves the problem of the relationship between determinism and freedom. When he distinguished God's decrees into complex relational volitions, one simply wants to restate the objection in terms of the absolute mental volitions that are one element of the complex, an element that seems quite beyond human control. But no other medieval theologian succeeded in giving a satisfactory answer to the antinomy of divine power and earthly contingency, and perhaps no satisfactory answer will ever be possible. But it is clear that it is a great mistake to regard Wyclif as the arch-determinist. Where he departs from his colleagues is not in imputing extra necessity to human actions, but in assigning unusual contingency to divine volitions.

7

Mind and Soul

Philosophers of mind, throughout history, can be grouped into two main classes: introvert and extrovert. Introvert philosophers believe that the way to understand the nature of the human mind is to look within oneself and to pay close attention to the phenomena of introspective consciousness. Extrovert philosophers start from the observable behaviour of human beings and inquire into the criteria by which we ascribe to others mental capacities, states, and activities. In the second millennium we could point to Descartes and Hume as paradigms of the introvert school, and Aquinas and Wittgenstein as illustrating, in different degrees, the extrovert approach. Extroverts look, in the ancient world, to Aristotle as their champion; the introvert school can claim Augustine as its founding father, and to this day one of its most eloquent members.

Augustine on the Inner Life

Augustine often speaks of the 'inward man' and the 'outward man'. This is not to be confused with the distinction between soul and body. Not only the body, but certain aspects of our soul, belong to the outward man, namely, whatever we have in common with dumb animals, such as the senses and the sensory memory. The inward man is our better part: the mind, whose tasks include recollection and imagination, as well as rational judgement and intellectual contemplation (*DT* 12. 1–3).

The outward man perceives bodies with the five senses of sight, hearing, smell, taste, and touch. Augustine takes vision as the paradigm sense. When we see something—a rock, or a flame—there are three things to be taken into consideration: the object seen, the seeing of the object, and a third item that Augustine calls 'intentio animi', namely, our mental focus on the object. This third element, Augustine tells us, is something proper to the mind alone—sight is called a sense of the body only because the eyes are part of the body (*DT* 11. 2). The mental element can remain, as a striving to see, when vision itself is not possible.

Vision is the product both of the object and the sense: the body when seen impresses a form upon the sense, and that is called vision. This is a likeness of the thing seen.

We do not, by the same sense, make any distinction between the form of the body that we see, and the form that comes into existence from it in the sense of the one who sees, because the connection between them is so close that there is no room for distinguishing them. But by our reason we conclude that it would have been utterly impossible for us to perceive anything, unless some likeness of the body that was seen came into existence in our sense. (*DT* 11. 2. 3)

The image is different from the body, even though it does not remain when the body is removed; just as if a ring is placed in liquid, the displacement of the fluid is something different from the shape of the ring, even if it disappears once the ring is removed. After-images testify to the distinction between the shape of the object seen and the impression it makes on the eye; so too does the possibility of producing double vision by pressing on the eyeball. The impressed form 'is so closely united with the species of the thing which we saw that it could not be discerned at all, and this was vision itself' (*DT* 11. 2. 3).

It is a matter of debate among commentators whether this thesis commits Augustine to a representational theory of sense-perception. Most likely it does not, if a 'representational theory' is one according to which the immediate object of perception is an image or sense-datum. The image formed is not, according to Augustine, at all obvious; its existence has to be proved by argument. Probably Augustine postulates it as something that is necessary to explain the causation of memory by sensation (*DT* 11. 9. 16)[1].

The senses are sources of information about objects in the world; but of course they are not the only way in which we acquire such information.

---

[1] See Gareth Matthew, 'Knowledge and Illumination', in *CCA* 176. For an opposite view, see Paul Spade in *IHWP* 63–4.

A blind man cannot see, but can find out, by asking others, the things that they have learnt by sight. What makes the difference between sense-perception and information-gathering? In answer to this question, Aristotle long ago invoked the concept of pleasure. 'Where there is sense-perception there is also both pain and pleasure, and where they occur there is also of necessity desire.' (*De An.* 2. 413^{b}23). The information acquired through the senses, and the discriminations performed with their aid, may be acquired and performed by means other than the senses, and indeed by agents other than human beings. We can obtain through optical instruments visual information to classify different human beings, and catalogue visual features of lunar landscapes through distant probes. Such operations are not sense-perception because they occur without pleasure or pain: the human beings inventoried with their statistics are not perceived as beautiful or ugly, the landscapes strike neither terror nor awe.

Augustine shows himself well aware of this dual aspect of our concept of sense, and indeed emphasizes the hedonic rather than the epistemic component of sense-perception. In *On Free Will* he remarks that 'pleasure and pain fall within the jurisdiction of the bodily senses'. Sight judges whether colours are harmonious or clash with each other, and hearing judges whether voices are melodious or harsh (*DLA* 2. 5. 12. 49). In book X of the *Confessions* he gives a colourful listing of the different types of sensual pleasure that may offer us temptation. We must distinguish, he says, between two different employments of the senses: to bring pleasure and to satisfy curiosity. The second element too, of course, can bring temptation: we can sin through the lust for experience and knowledge (*Conf.* X. 35. 54).

Among the objects of the outer senses, Augustine makes the usual distinction between those that can be perceived by one sense only (e.g. colour and sound) and those that can be perceived by more than one sense (e.g. size and shape). Besides the five outward senses, Augustine believes that there is an inner sense. In the case of animals, he says, the sense of sight is a different thing from the sense to shun or to seek what is seen, and so with the other senses, whose objects are sometimes accepted with pleasure and sometimes shunned with disgust. This sense cannot be identified with any one of the five senses, but must be some other sense that presides over all the other senses. While it is only by reasoning that we identify this separate faculty, it is not itself a part of reason, because it is possessed not only by rational humans but also by irrational beasts (*DLA* 2. 2. 8).

In his description of our mental faculties, Augustine dwells longest on the memory, and indeed he often uses 'memory' in a very broad sense, almost equivalent to 'mind' itself. He describes some of memory's powers in *Confessions* X. 13. Even in darkness and silence I can produce colours at will in my memory, and distinguish between white and black. With tongue motionless and throat silent, I can sing whatever song I wish.

Memory is something we take for granted: Augustine urges us to remind ourselves what a very remarkable faculty it is. People gaze with wonder on mountain peaks, towering waves, and broad waterfalls, on the encompassing ocean and the rotating starry skies. But they take no notice of themselves and of their memory, which contains sky, sea, and land and much else besides. I could not speak, Augustine says, of any of the wonders of nature unless I could see inwardly the mountains and waves and rivers and stars—and even the ocean that I have never seen but know about only from the tales of others. 'I see them inwardly with dimensions just as great as if I saw them in the outer world' (*Conf.* X. 8. 15).

Augustine describes memory as a huge cavern, full of dark and mysterious nooks and crannies: true to the introvert tradition he imagines the inward man exploring this vast storehouse. Within it, I can call for an item that I want to recall; fetching it may take a shorter or longer time.

Some memories rush out to crowd the mind, and while I am looking and asking for something quite different, they leap out in front of me saying 'Are we what you want?' With the hand of my heart I chase them away from the face of my memory until what I want is freed from the murk and comes out of its hiding place. (*Conf.* X. 8. 12)

Augustine has a gift for vivid phenomenological description of experiences of calling to mind and forgetting—remembering the face but not the name, being unable to recall a letter read absent-mindedly, being obsessed with an unwelcome memory one would prefer to forget (*DT* 11. 5. 9). When he comes to give a philosophical analysis of memory, it is modelled very closely on his account of outer vision. Just as when we see there is the object seen, the seeing itself, and the mental focus, so, when we remember, there is the memory recalled, the actual recalling, and the gaze of thought. The difference between a merely dispositional memory (something that we have learnt and not forgotten) and an episode of remembering is treated by Augustine as parallel to that between an object out of sight and object in full view (*DT* 11. 8). Remembering is treated very literally as inward seeing, and in the case of both inner and outer vision Augustine lays great stress on the voluntary nature of the activity. In talking of mental focus, and the gaze of thought, Augustine is thinking of the operation of the will (*DT* 11. 2. 3).

The will can choose whether to concentrate on the outer or inner eye. If it makes the latter choice, it can produce likenesses of bodies so vivid 'that not even reason itself can distinguish whether a body itself is seen without, or something similar thought within'. Terrifying imaginations can make one cry out, and sexual fantasies can cause erections. But not all such experiences are under voluntary control: in sleep and in frenzy images can force themselves upon the mental gaze by some secret force 'through certain spiritual mixings of a spiritual substance' (*DT* 11. 4. 7).

I can remember only what I have seen; but I can think of many more things. Thus I can remember only one sun, but I can think of two or three suns. I can think of the sun as larger or smaller than it is; I can think of it standing still or travelling to anywhere I will. I can think of it as square and green. Augustine clearly regards thoughts of this kind as inner seeings: he insists that what we actually see with our inner eye is derived from our memory of the one and only sun. But what of when we listen to another person's narrative? We cannot then turn our mind's eye back to memory. What happens is that we follow the story by calling up the ideas corresponding to the words of his story. But this too depends on memory.

I would never have been able to understand a storyteller the first time I had heard his words put together, unless I had remembered generically the individual things that he described. A man who describes to me a mountain rising out of a forest and clothed with olive trees is speaking to one who remembers mountains, forests, and olives. If I had forgotten them, I should not at all know what he was saying, and so could never have followed his narrative. (*DT* 11. 8. 14)

What is true of listening to another's narrative is true of inventing a story for oneself. I can combine remembered images with others and say 'O that this or that were so'. Whatever we imagine is constructed out of elements supplied by memory: thus Augustine models his idea of the walls of Alexandria, which he has never seen, on his memory of the walls of Carthage, which are familiar to him. No doubt anyone who really knew Alexandria, if they could look into Augustine's mind and see his image of it, would find it highly inadequate (*DT* 8. 6. 9). Anticipating later empiricist philosophers, Augustine says that it is impossible to have any idea of a colour one has never seen, a sound one has never heard, or a flavour one has never tasted.

The loftiest part of the mind, the reason or intellectual soul, has, for Augustine, two elements. The superior part of reason is concerned with the eternal truths, accessible to intellect alone. The inferior part controls our dealings with temporal and bodily things. It is, Augustine says, a deputy of the superior reason: a minister for contingent affairs, as it were. Both inferior and superior reason belong to the inward man (*DT* 13. 1). When God created Adam, he found among the beasts no fit companion for him; so too, in the human soul, those parts that we have in common with dumb animals are not enough to make the intellect at home in the world we live in. So God has endowed us with a faculty of practical reason, formed out of rational substance just as Eve was formed from Adam's body, intimately united with the superior reason just as Adam and Eve were two in one flesh (*DT* 12. 3).

The operation of the lower reason is called by Augustine 'scientia', which he defines as 'the cognition of temporal and changeable things that is necessary for managing the affairs of this life' (*DT* 12. 12. 17). The functions of this reason are very close to those assigned by Aristotle to *phronesis*, or practical wisdom, and the translation 'science' would give a very misleading impression of what is meant. Science, as we understand it, hardly figures in Augustine's catalogue of mental activities, and from time to time he makes disparaging remarks about the pursuit of knowledge for its own sake. *Scientia*, like *phronesis*, is indispensable if we are to possess moral virtues (*DT* 14. 22).

The superior reason's function is called 'sapientia'. Once again, the obvious translation, 'wisdom', would be misleading, since the English word is more appropriate to the virtue of practical reason than to the virtue of theoretical reason. *Sapientia*, we are told, is contemplation: the contemplation of eternal truths in this life and the contemplation of God in the life of the blessed (*DT* 12. 14). Contemplation is not for the sake of action, but is pursued for its own sake. Augustine goes out of his way to tell us that the part of the human mind that is concerned with the consideration of eternal reasons is something 'which, as is evident, not only men but also women possess' (*DT* 12. 7. 12).

Augustine on the Will

Augustine devoted much of *On the Trinity* to seeking, in human beings, replicas of the divine trinity of Father, Son, and Holy Spirit. He identified many different triads, but the supreme image of God is in the trinity of memory, intellect, and will (9. 12, 15. 3). How is this to be related to the anatomy of the mind we have just summarized? When he is most concerned to draw the theological parallel, Augustine presents his human trinity as consisting of the mind's existence, its knowledge of itself, and its love of itself (9. 12). But he uses the terms of his mental trinity in a broad variety of contexts, which we can summarize as follows. The memory is the ability to think thoughts of all kinds; the intellect (whose activity is *sapientia*) is the ability to assent to theoretical thoughts as true; the will is the ability to consent to thoughts as plans of action.

Augustine makes great play with the notion of the will, and some commentators have alleged that in doing so he was inventing a concept that was lacking in the ancient world. The allegation can only be made by a philosopher starting from an introspective stance on philosophy of mind. Philosophical discussion of the will may start by considering it as an introspectible phenomenon, an item of consciousness that makes the difference between voluntary and involuntary actions. Or it may start with the observable behaviour of agents and ask for external criteria by which we distinguish between the voluntary and involuntary actions of others. In the ancient world Augustine is the outstanding exponent of the introspective approach; Aristotle, on the other hand, had adopted an extrovert stance, which has led introvert philosophers to deny that he had any concept of the will at all.[2]

In fact, there are considerable similarities between the two philosophers. For Augustine as for Aristotle, all fully human choice originates in the pursuit of happiness, and for both of them individual decisions are to be seen as the selection of means to that end. Suppose, Augustine says, I want to see a scar as evidence of a wound, or look through a window in order to see the passers-by. 'All these and other such acts of the will have their own proper ends, which are referred to the end of that will, by which we wish to live happily and arrive at that life which is not referred to anything else, but

---

[2] See A. Kenny, *Aristotle's Theory of the Will* (London: Duckworth, 1979).

is sufficient in itself for the lover.' This is quite parallel to Aristotle's account of practical reasoning (*NE* 1112^b 18 ff.; *EE* 1. 1218^{b}8–24).

Both Aristotle and Augustine imagine the will, or practical reason, as an issuer of commands, and both of them are keenly interested in the possibility of disobedience to these commands, in the sinner (Augustine) or in the incontinent person (Aristotle, *NE* 1147^{a}32). But Augustine exploits the analogy much more fully. He regards every voluntary motion of the body as an obedience to a command of the will; and he is fascinated by the possibility of second-order volition, where the will is issuing commands to itself.

The mind (*animus*) commands the body, and obedience is instant; the mind commands itself and meets resistance. The mind tells the hand to move, and all goes so smoothly that it is hard to distinguish the command from its execution. Yet the mind is the mind, and the hand is a body. The mind tells the mind to will; one is the same as the other, and yet it does not do what it is told. (*Conf.* VIII. 9. 21)

What is really happening in such a case, when, for instance, a man wants to will to be chaste and yet does not really will to be chaste? How can the will command itself and yet not obey? The command to will, Augustine says, is half-hearted: if it were wholehearted, the will to be chaste would already be there. In his own case, he says, while he was hesitating about the service of God 'I who was willing to serve was the same I who was unwilling; I was neither wholly willing nor wholly unwilling'. Such self-conflict, such inner dissociation, is possible only because we are the descendants of Adam, inheriting his sin.

It is the consideration of Adam that leads Augustine to differ significantly from Aristotle on an important point. Aristotle accepted that a man may act against the dictates of the rational will, but he envisaged this as happening through the stress of animal passion. But Adam fell into sin in Eden, at a time when he had no disordered passions; again, Lucifer and his angels fell into sin, though they had no animal bodies. So Augustine is led to postulate uncaused acts of evil will. 'If you look for an efficient cause of such an evil volition, you will find nothing. What is it that makes a will evil, when it is doing an evil deed? The evil will is the efficient cause of the evil deed, but of an evil will there is no efficient cause' (*DCD* XII. 6). However one tries to trace back the cause of an evil action, sooner or later one will arrive at a sheer act of evil will. Suppose that we imagine two people alike in mind and body, each hitherto innocent, and each subjected to the same temptation. One gives in, the other does not. What is the cause of the sinner's sin? We cannot say it is the sinner himself: *ex hypothesi* both people were equally good up to this point. We have to say that it is a causeless evil choice (*DCD* XII. 6). Thus Augustine expounds what was later to be called 'contra-causal freedom'—which, paradoxically, he combines

The *City of God* was one of the most read and most copied texts of the Middle Ages. Here, in a sketch in the margin of a twelfth century Bohemian MS we see a copyist distracted from his work by a "bad, bad mouse".

with a strong version of determinism, as we shall see in a later chapter when we consider his theory of predestination.

The Agent Intellect in Islamic Thought

During the latter part of the first millennium the most interesting developments in philosophy of mind concerned not the will but the intellect, and took place not in Christendom but in the Muslim schools of Baghdad. Al-Kindi and al-Farabi both devoted themselves to the elucidation of the puzzling passage in Aristotle's *De Anima* which tells us that there are two different intellects: an agent intellect 'for making things' and a receptive intellect 'for becoming things'.

Al-Farabi, following al-Kindi, explained this in terms of his own version of Aristotelian astronomy. Each of the nine celestial spheres, he believed, had a rational soul; it was moved by its own incorporeal mover, which acted upon it as an object of desire. These incorporeal movers, or intelligences, emanated one from another, in a series originating ultimately from the Prime Mover, or God. From the ninth intelligence (which governs the moon) there emanates a tenth intelligence; and this is nothing other than the agent intellect, the one that Aristotle says is what it is by virtue of making all things.

The agent intellect, according to al-Farabi, is needed in order to explain how the human intellect passes from potentiality to actuality. In his account of human psychology we find in fact three intellects, or three stages of intellect. First there is the receptive or potential intellect, the inborn capacity for thought. Under the influence of the external agent intellect, this disposition is exercised in actual thinking, and the human intellect thus becomes an intellect in actuality ('the actual passive intellect'). Finally, Al-Farabi tells us, a human being 'perfects his receptive intellect with all intelligible thoughts'. The intellect thus perfected is called the acquired intellect.[3]

Can we separate al-Farabi's psychology from its antiquated astronomical context? We may begin to make sense of it if we ask why anyone should

---

[3] See H. A. Davidson, *Alfarabi, Avicenna and Averroes on Intellect* (Oxford: Oxford University Press, 1992), ch. 3.

think that an agent intellect was required at all. The Aristotelian answer would be that the material objects of the world we live in are not, in themselves, fit objects for intellectual understanding. The nature and characteristics of the objects we see and feel are all embedded in matter: they are transitory and not stable, individual and not universal. They are, in Aristotelian terms, only potentially thinkable or intelligible, not actually so. To make them actually thinkable, it is required that abstraction be made from the corruptible and individuating matter, and concepts be created that are actually thinkable objects. That is the function of the agent intellect.

Al-Farabi compares the action of the agent intellect upon the data of sensory experience to the action of the sun on colours. Colours, which are only potentially visible in the dark, are made actually visible by the sunlight. Similarly, sense-data that are stored in our imagination are turned by the active intellect into actually intelligible thoughts. The agent intellect structures them within a framework of universal principles, common to all humans. (Al-Farabi gives as an instance 'two things equal to a third are equal to one another'.) Thus far al-Farabi's account seems philosophically plausible. The difficult point—and one that was to be debated for centuries—is whether the agent intellect is to be identified with some separate, superhuman entity, or whether it should simply be regarded as a species-specific faculty that differentiates humans from non-language-using animals.

Al-Farabi's Muslim successors emphasized, to an ever greater degree, the superhuman element in intellectual thought. For Avicenna, as for al-Farabi, the First Cause is at the summit of a series of ten incorporeal intelligences, each giving rise to the next in the series by a process of emanation, of which the tenth is the agent intellect. The agent intellect, however, has for Avicenna a much more elaborate function than it has for al-Farabi: it is a veritable demigod. First it produces by emanation the matter of the sublunar world, a task that al-Farabi had assigned to the celestial spheres; that is to say, it is responsible for the existence of the four elements. Next, the agent intellect produces the more complex forms in this world, including the souls of plants, animals, and humans. Indeed the 'giver of forms' is one of Avicenna's favourite titles for the agent intellect. Once again, we encounter emanation: forms that are undifferentiated within the agent intellect are transmitted, by necessity, into the world of matter. Only at a third stage does the agent intellect exercise the function that it had in al-Farabi, of being the cause that brings the human intellect from potentiality into actuality.[4]

Avicenna on Intellect and Imagination

According to Avicenna, when a piece of matter has developed to a state in which it is apt to receive a human soul, the agent intellect, the giver of forms, infuses such a soul into it. The soul, however, is something more than the form of the human body. To show this Avicenna uses an original argument, which was later to be reinvented by Descartes.

Let someone imagine himself as wholly created in a single moment, with his sight veiled so that he cannot see any external object. Imagine also that he is created falling through the air, or in a vacuum, so that he would not feel any pressure from the air. Suppose too that his limbs are parted from each other so that they neither meet nor touch. Let him reflect whether, in such a case, he will affirm his own existence. He will not hesitate to affirm that he himself exists, but in so doing he will not be affirming the existence of any limb, or external or internal organ such as heart or brain, or any external object. He will be affirming the existence of himself without ascribing to it any length, breadth, or depth. If in this state he were able to imagine a hand or some other bodily part, he would not imagine it being a part of himself or a condition for his own existence. (*CCMP* 110)

Avicenna argues that since intellectual thoughts do not have parts, they must belong to something that is indivisible and incorporeal. Hence he concludes that the soul is an incorporeal substance that cannot be regarded simply as a form or faculty of the body.

Avicenna distinguishes four different possible conditions of the human intellect. When a human baby is born, it has an intellect that is empty of thoughts, the soul's mere capacity for thought. In the second state, the intellect has been furnished with the basic intellectual equipment: it understands the principle of contradiction, and general principles such as that the whole is greater than the part. Avicenna compares this to a boy who has learnt how to use pen and ink and can write individual letters. In the third state, the person has accumulated a stock of concepts and beliefs, but does not actually have them present in thought. This is like an

---

[4] See ibid. 74–83.

accomplished scribe, who is capable of writing any text at will. All these three states are potentialities, but each of them nearer to actuality than the previous one: the third state is called by Avicenna 'perfect potentiality'. The fourth state is when the thinker is actually thinking a particular thought (one at a time)—this is like the scribe actually writing down a sentence.

In each of these transitions from potentiality towards actuality there is, for Avicenna, a direct causal influence exercised on the human intellect by the superhuman agent intellect. Experience, he argues, cannot be the source either of the first principles or the universal scientific conclusions reached by the intellect. Experience can provide only inductive generalizations such as 'All animals move their lower jaw to chew', and such generalizations are always falsifiable (as that one is falsified by the crocodile). So first principle and universal laws must be infused in us from outside the natural world.

It is hard to conceive exactly how this causality operates; it appears to be something like involuntary telepathy. Perhaps, to use a metaphor unavailable to Avicenna, the agent intellect is like a radio station perpetually broadcasting, on different wavelengths, all the thoughts that there are. The human intellect's movement from potentiality to act is the result of its being tuned in on an appropriate wavelength. To explain how a human being does the tuning in, Avicenna presents an elaborate theory of interior sensation.

In addition to the five familiar external senses, Avicenna believed that we have five internal senses:

(1) the common sense, which collects impressions from the five exterior senses;
(2) the retentive imagination, which stores the images thus collected;
(3) the compositive imagination, which deploys these images;
(4) the estimative power, which makes instinctive judgements, e.g. of pleasure or danger;
(5) the recollective power, which stores the intuitions of the estimative power.

We have met some of these faculties in Aristotle and in Augustine,[5] but Avicenna treats them in a much more detailed and systematic fashion.

[5] See vol. i, p. 245, and p. 216 above.

They are faculties that are common to humans and animals, and they have specific locations in ventricles of the brain.

Now while the brain is an appropriate storehouse for the deliveries of outer and inner sense (including, for example, the sheep's instinctive knowledge that the wolf is dangerous), it cannot be regarded as the repository of intellectual thoughts. When I am not actually thinking them, the thoughts I think are available only outside myself, in the agent intellect; my memory of those thoughts, my ability to recall them, is my ability to tune in, at will, to the ever-continuing transmission of the agent intellect.[6]

The exercise of the ability to acquire or retain intellectual thoughts does involve the senses, but only in a way parallel to that in which the development of matter in the embryo triggers the infusion of the soul. The role of the compositive imagination is here crucial: when it is preparing the human soul for intellectual thought it is called by Avicenna the 'cogitative faculty'. This faculty works on images retained in memory, combining and dividing them into new configurations: when these are in appropriate focus for a particular thought, the human intellect makes contact with the agent intellect and thinks that very thought.

Avicenna describes the interplay between imagination and intellect in the case of syllogistic reasoning. A human intellect wishes to know whether all As are B. His cogitative power rummages among images and produces an image of C, which is an appropriate middle term to prove the desired conclusion. Stimulated by this image, the human intellect contacts the agent intellect and acquires the thought of C. The acquisition of this thought from the agent intellect is an *insight*; and Avicenna explains that in favoured cases the intellect may have an insight—see the solution to an intellectual problem—without having to go through the elaborate introspectible process of cogitation.

Avicenna calls the state of somebody actually thinking an intellectual thought 'acquired intellection'. The term is appropriate, since for him every intellectual thought, even of the most everyday kind, is not the work of the human thinker, but a gift from the agent intellect. However, he also

---

[6] Avicenna embellishes his already elaborate structure with a detailed analysis of the situation where a person is certain he can answer a question he has never answered before—a discussion that is interestingly parallel with Wittgenstein's discussion of the 'Now I know how to go on' phenomenon in *Philosophical Investigations*, I. 151.

uses a very similar term for an intellect that has achieved the possession of all scientific truth, and the ability to call it to mind at will. This might perhaps be more appropriately called 'perfected intellect'. For one who has reached such a stage, the senses are no longer necessary; they are a distraction. They are like a horse that has brought one to the desired destination and should now be let loose.

Is such a perfect state possible in this life—and if not, is there any afterlife? Avicenna's answer to the first question is unclear, but he has much to tell us in answer to the second. The destruction of the body does not entail the destruction of the soul, and the soul as a whole, not just the intellect, is immortal. Souls cease to make use of some of their faculties once they are separated from their bodies, but they remain individuated, and they do not transmigrate into other bodies.

Immortal souls, after death, achieve very different grades of well-being. One who has achieved perfect intellection so far as that is possible in this life enters into the company of celestial beings and enjoys perfect happiness. Those who fall short of this, but have achieved reasonable competence in science and metaphysics, will enjoy happiness of a decent but more modest kind. Those who are qualified for philosophical inquiry but have failed to take the opportunity for it in this life will suffer the most terrible misery. They will indeed suffer much greater misery than those philosophers who (like Avicenna himself) have over-indulged their bodily appetites. For the unfulfilled bodily appetites, when the soul survives alone, will soon wither away and lose their capacity to tease, whereas the pain of unfulfilled philosophical desire never comes to an end because intellectual curiosity is of the essence of the soul (*PMA* 259–62).

So much for the afterlife of intellectuals. But many people are what Avicenna calls 'simple souls', who have no notion of intellectual desire or intellectual satisfaction. After death these will neither enjoy the pleasures of satisfied intellect nor suffer the pains of intellect dissatisfied. They will live for all eternity in a kind of peace. If in their earthly life they have been led to believe that they will be rewarded for virtue by sensual pleasure (e.g. in a garden with dark-eyed maidens) or be punished for vice by bodily pains (e.g. in a hellish fire), then at death they will go into the appropriate dream, which will seem just as vivid to them as the reality.

Like al-Farabi, Avicenna in his psychological system assigns a significant role to prophecy. At the highest level, prophecy is the supreme level of

Averroes' psychology was both admired and attacked in the thirteenth century. Here a manuscript of that period shows him in conversation with the Greek logician Porphyry.

insight, in which the human mind makes contact with the agent intellect without effort, and grasps conclusions without having to reason them out. At a lower level, the compositive imagination of a prophet recasts the prophetic knowledge in figurative form, which makes it suitable for communication to unlearned people. The ability to work miracles is, for Avicenna, a sub-category of prophecy: the prophet has a specially powerful motive faculty in his body which enables him to bring about material effects, such as the healing of the sick and the bringing of rain, by sheer operation of the will.

What are we to make of Avicenna's philosophy of mind? Taken as a system, it is clearly quite incredible. Leaving aside its link with antiquated astronomy, it contains a number of internal inconsistencies. How can the whole soul be immortal when the interior senses are shared with brute beasts? How can a disembodied soul dream when dreaming is an activity of the brain? Examples could be multiplied.

Nonetheless, Avicenna's philosophical psychology is important in the history of philosophy because he was the original begetter of many concepts and structures that played a part in the systems of more sober philosophers. Many others accepted his anatomy of the interior senses; those who disagreed with him about the nature of the agent intellect agreed in their description of the tasks it was needed to perform. Others, of various faiths, have been happy to accept (wittingly or not) his rationalization of the delights and sorrows held out by religion in the afterlife.

The Psychology of Averroes

At the beginning of his philosophical career Averroes accepted a theory of intellect quite close to Avicenna's. Each individual human, he believed, had a material or receptive intellect that was generated by congress between the inborn human disposition for thought and the activity of the transcendent agent intellect. After a period of lengthy reflection, however, Averroes put forward a radically different view. He reached the conclusion that neither the agent intellect nor the receptive intellect is a faculty of individual human beings. The receptive intellect, no less than the agent intellect, is a single, eternal, incorporeal substance.

He argues for this conclusion as follows. Aristotle told us that the receptive intellect receives all material forms. But it cannot do this if in itself it possesses any material form. Accordingly it cannot be a body nor can it be in any way mixed with matter. Since it is immaterial, it must be indestructible, since matter is the basis of corruption, and it must be single and not multiple, since matter is the principle of multiplication. The receptive intellect is the lowest in the hierarchy of incorporeal intelligences, located one rung below the agent intellect. Paradoxically, though itself incorporeal, it is related to the incorporeal agent intellect in a manner similar to that in which the matter of a body is related to the form of a body; and so it can be called the material intellect.

How then can my thoughts be *my* thoughts if they reside in a superhuman intellect? Averroes replies that thoughts belong to not one, but two, subjects. The eternal receptive intellect is one subject: the other is my imagination. Each of us possesses our own individual, corporeal, imagination, and it is only because of the role played in our thinking by this individual imagination that you and I can claim any thoughts as our own.

The method by which the superhuman intellect is involved in the mental life of human individuals is highly mysterious. Though it is an entity far superior to humankind, it appears to be to some extent under the control of mortal men. The initiative in any given thought rests with the imagination, not with the receptive intellect. The process has been well described as follows:

The eternity of the material intellect's thought of the physical world is, accordingly, not a single continuous fiber, nor does it spring from the material intellect. It is wholly dependent on the ratiocination and consciousness of individual men, the complete body of possible thoughts of the physical world being supplied at any given moment by individuals living at that moment, and the continuity of the material intellect's thought through infinite time being spun from the thoughts of individuals alive at various moments.[7]

Averroes' psychology strikes any modern reader as bizarre: and yet philosophers in the twentieth century have held positions that were not wholly unrelated. There is good reason for thinking that the contents of the imagination possess a degree of privacy and individuality that the contents of the intellect do not, though it is usually in the social rather than in the celestial realm that the reason for this is sought by modern philosophers. And all of us are inclined to talk, with a degree of awe, of Science as containing a body of coherent and lasting truth which cannot possibly all be within the mind of any mortal scientist.

Because, for Averroes, the truly intellectual element in thought is non-personal, there is not, he believed, any personal immortality for individual humans. After death, souls merge with each other. Averroes argues for this as follows:

Zaid and Amr are numerically different but identical in form. If, for example, the soul of Zaid were numerically different from the soul of Amr in the way Zaid is numerically different from Amr, the soul of Zaid and the soul of Amr would be numerically two, but one in their form, and the soul would possess another form. The necessary conclusion is therefore that the soul of Zaid and the soul of Amr are identical in their form. An identical form inheres in a numerical, i.e. a divisible multiplicity, only through the multiplicity of matter. If then the soul does not die when the body dies, or if it possesses an immortal element it must, when it has left the body, form a numerical unity.

At death the soul passes into the universal intelligence like a drop of water into the sea.

---

[7] Davidson, *Alfarabi, Avicenna and Averrroes on Intellect*, 292–3.

One of the first and severest critics of Averroes' philosophy of mind was Albert the Great. In a special treatise he listed thirty Averroist arguments in favour of the single agent intellect, and answered each in turn; on the other side he offered thirty-six arguments of his own. He insisted that both the receptive intellect and the agent intellect were faculties of the individual soul: there were as many agent intellects as there were human beings. Otherwise the intellectual soul would not be the form of the body and our thoughts would not be our own. The role of the human agent intellect is to complete the abstraction of a universal concept from the data of sense.

There are, for Albert, four grades of abstraction. There is already a degree of abstraction in sensation itself, even though the object is present, for instead of the material form of what is perceived, there is a separate *intentio* in our sense-faculty. The second grade of abstraction is when the *intentio* thus acquired is retained in our imagination, now divorced from the presence of the object, but still in all its particularity. The image of the man will retain the same posture, colour, age, and so on as the original. The third degree takes place in the phantasy, which Albert distinguishes from the imagination: one would expect this to be an image which is vague enough to represent more than one thing, but Albert tells us that it includes some non-sensible properties of the individual, such as whether he is good company or not, and who his father was. The fourth degree is the operation of the agent intellect producing a universal concept, applicable to all instances of a kind (*CHLMP* 603–4; *De An.* 2. 3. 4).

In keeping with his interest in empirical science, Albert is keen to locate these different activities in particular parts of the brain. The internal senses, such as the imagination and the phantasy, are located in pockets of animal spirits, or fluids, which vary in subtlety in accordance with the degrees of abstraction associated with them.

However, while emphasizing the material vehicle of all but the most intellectual forms of thought, Albert retains a vestige of the theories of Avicenna and Averroes in that he does recognize a direct divine causal influence on human intelligence. If the universal concepts and beliefs that are the work of our agent intellect are to be retained in the form of knowledge in our receptive intellect, there is need of a special light emanating from the uncreated agent intellect. Such illumination is especially necessary if we are to have knowledge of immaterial objects such as angels and God: here phantasms and abstraction are of no help.

Aquinas on the Senses and the Intellect

Aquinas rejected the need for a special divine illumination to explain normal human concept-formation and the pursuit of natural science.[8] For him the intellect—both the agent intellect and the receptive intellect—are faculties of the individual human being, standing at the summit of the hierarchy of capacities and abilities that constitute the human soul.

Following Aristotle, Aquinas accepts three different kinds of soul: a vegetative soul in plants, a sensitive soul in animals, and a rational soul in human beings. In human beings there is only one soul, the rational soul, but this soul, in addition to its own special intellectual powers, has powers that correspond to those of the other two souls: vegetative powers to grow and reproduce, and sensory and locomotive powers such as animals have. At the animal and rational level there are two kinds of powers, cognitive or information-gathering powers, and appetitive or goal-oriented powers. At the animal level there is the power to perceive and the power to desire; at the rational level there is the power to think and the power to will (ST 1a 78. 1 and 2).

In studying Aquinas' philosophy of mind it is important to remember that he does not, as many modern philosophers have done, identify the mind with consciousness. For him the mind was essentially the faculty, or set of faculties, that set off human beings from other animals. Dumb animals and human beings can all see and hear and feel, but only human beings can think abstract thoughts and take rational decisions. It is the possession of intellect and will that set them off from animals, and it is these two faculties that essentially constitute the mind, the rational soul.

Nonetheless, to understand Aquinas' account of the mind it is important to consider what he says about the senses, for on his view the activity of the two faculties, rational and sensory, are tightly interwoven. The operation of the senses is essential for both the origin and the exercise of intellectual concepts. Moreover, much of what a modern philosopher would consider as mental activity is, for Aquinas, the operation of a sense of a particular kind, namely, the imagination, which is one of the inner senses.

---

[8] See Ch. 4 above.

Aquinas accepted the traditional list of five outer senses: sight, hearing, touch, taste, and smell. Senses are distinguished from each other not by having different organs but by having different objects: sight and hearing differ not because eyes differ from ears, but because colours differ from sounds. Senses are essentially discriminatory powers, such as the power to tell hot from cold, black from white, and so on. Each sense has its proper object, an object that only it can detect; but there are also objects common to more than one sense, such as shape, which can be both seen and felt (*ST* 1a 78. 3. 3).

A sense, according to Aquinas, is a capacity to undergo a special kind of change caused by an external object. When we see, the form of colour is received in the eye without the eye becoming coloured. Normally, when the form of F is received by a material object, the object becomes F, as when a stone receives the form of heat and becomes hot. That is the standard form of change, material change. To the kind of change that takes place when a colour is seen, Aquinas gives the name 'intentional' change. The form of colour exists intentionally in the eye, or, as he sometimes says, the intention (*intentio* or *species*) of colour is in the eye (1a 84. 1).

An *intentio* is not a representation, even though Aquinas sometimes calls it a likeness, or *similitudo*, of the object perceived. Some philosophers believe that in sense-experience we do not directly observe objects or properties in the external world, but rather perceive private sense-data from which we infer the nature of external objects and properties. In Aquinas there are no such intermediaries between perceiver and perceived. In sensation the faculty does not come into contact with a likeness of the object; it becomes itself like the object by taking on its form. This is summed up in the slogan taken over from Aristotle: the sense-faculty in operation is identical with the sense-object in action (*sensus in actu est sensibile in actu*).[9]

Aquinas' teaching on intentionality is not meant to offer an arcane mechanism as a theory to explain sensation. It is meant to be a philosophical truism to help us to see clearly what is happening. The Aristotelian slogan means no more than this: if I pop a sweet in my mouth, my tasting its sweetness (the operation of my sense-faculty: *sensus in actu*) is one and the same thing as its tasting sweet to me (the operation of the sensory

---

[9] See vol. i, p. 244.

property: *sensibile in actu*). The importance of the truism is precisely to rule out the naive representationalism that is tempting in this area.

In addition to the five outer senses, Aquinas believed that there were inner senses, and took over a list of them from Avicenna: the general sense, the memory, the imagination, and a fourth faculty, which in animals is called the *vis aestimativa* and in humans the *vis cogitativa*. The *vis aestimativa* seems to correspond to our notion of 'instinct': animals' inborn appreciation of what is useful or dangerous, expressed in such activities as nest building or fleeing from predators. Aquinas does not succeed in making clear what he regards as the equivalent human capacity (*ST* 1a 78. 4).

Many philosophers besides Aquinas have classified memory and imagination as inner senses. They have regarded these faculties as senses because they saw their function as the production of imagery; they regarded them as inner because their activity, unlike that of the outer senses, was not controlled by external stimuli. Aquinas, indeed, thought that the inner senses, like the outer ones, had organs—organs that were located in different parts of the brain.

It seems to be a mistake to regard the imagination as an inner sense. It has no organ in the sense in which sight has an organ: there is no part of the body which can be voluntarily moved so that we can imagine better, in the way that the eyes can be voluntarily moved so that we can see better. Moreover, it is not possible to be mistaken about what one imagines in the way that one can be mistaken about what one sees: others cannot check up on what I say I imagine as they can check up on what I claim to see. These are crucial differences between imagination and genuine senses.

Fortunately much of what Aquinas has to say about the role of the imagination and its relation to the intellect is unaffected by this excessive assimilation to the five senses. Calling it a sense—and therefore, for Aquinas, a faculty wholly within the realm of the material—has the great advantage of distinguishing it from the intellect. Many philosophers have conceived the mind as an immaterial and private world, the locus of our secret thoughts, the auditorium of our interior monologues. This is a profound mistake. Of course it is undeniable that human beings can keep their thoughts secret and talk to themselves without making any noise and call images before their mind's eye. But this ability, for Aquinas, is not the mind: it is not the intellect but the imagination.

'Intellectus' is one of the few technical terms in Aquinas that means roughly the same as its English equivalent, 'intellect'. The cognate verb 'intelligere', however, does not have an equivalent 'intellege' and fortunately no medievalist has had the idea of coining such a word to match 'cognize'. The Latin verb is often translated 'understand', but in Aquinas' use it has a very broad sense, rather like the English 'think'. We have seen that Aquinas divides the acts of the intellect into two classes: the grasp of non-complexes, on the one hand, and composition and division on the other.[10] These correspond to two kinds of thought: thoughts *of* (such as the thought of a hawk), and thoughts *that* (such as the thought that a hawk is not a handsaw). It is not quite faithful to Aquinas, however, to equate the intellect with the capacity for thought, because he believed that animals, who do not have intellects, could have simple thoughts. It is more accurate to identify the intellect with the capacity for the kind of thought that only language-users can have.

For Aquinas, the intellect thinks in universals, and a grasp of universals is not within the capacity of animals: a universal can neither be sensed nor imagined. Nonetheless, Aquinas believed that in human beings the operation of sense and imagination was essential both for the acquisition and for the exercise of universal concepts. In the present life, he maintained, the proper object of the human intellect was the essence, or quiddity, of material objects; and this, he said, the intellect understood by abstraction from phantasms (*phantasmata*). By 'phantasms' Aquinas means the deliverances of sense and imagination, and without them Aquinas thinks that intellectual thought is impossible. But he does not believe, as empiricist philosophers have believed, that ideas are derived from sense-experience by abstraction from, or selective inattention to, features of that experience. If that were so, then animals no less than humans would be able to frame universal concepts, whereas Aquinas believed that such conceptualization demanded a species-specific human faculty, the agent intellect. On the other hand, Aquinas does not believe, as rationalist philosophers have believed, that there are individual ideas inborn in every human being. The human intellect, at birth, is for him a tabula rasa. (*ST* 1a 85).

The human intellect, for Aquinas, consists of two powers with a double function. Beside the agent intellect, which is the capacity to abstract

---

[10] See Ch. 3 above.

universal ideas from particular sense-experience, there is in humans a receptive intellect, which is the storehouse of ideas abstracted from sense and beliefs acquired from experience. At birth this storehouse is empty: the receptive intellect is the initially blank page on which the agent intellect writes. But phantasms, Aquinas maintains, are necessary not only for the acquisition of concepts, but also for their exercise: not only to place ideas in the mental storehouse, but also to take them out again and put them to use (*ST* 1a 79).

This latter thesis is important when we consider the application of universal ideas to individuals in the world. Some philosophers have thought that an object could be individuated by listing the totality of its properties, that is to say, by listing the universals under which it falls. But Aquinas rejected this: however long a list we draw up, it is always possible that it might apply to more than one individual. Given that the intellect thinks in universals, it is therefore impossible for there to be purely intellectual knowledge of individuals.

It is only indirectly, and by a certain kind of reflection, that the intellect can know an individual. Even after it has abstracted ideas it cannot make use of them in intellectual operation unless it turns towards the phantasms in which it grasps the intellectual idea, as Aristotle says. Thus, what the intellect grasps directly by the intellectual idea is the universal; but indirectly it grasps individuals to which phantasms belong. And that is how it forms the proposition 'Socrates is human'. (*ST* 1a 86c)

If I know someone well there will be many descriptions I can give of him; but unless I bring in reference to particular times and places there may be no description that could not in theory be satisfied by someone else. Only by pointing, or taking you to see him, or reminding you of an occasion when you met, can I make clear to you which person I have in mind; and pointing and vision and memory are outside the realm of pure intellectual thought.

The indirect nature of intellectual thought about individuals follows from two theses that Aquinas held: first, that matter is the principle of individuation, and secondly, that the immediate object of all knowledge is form. The senses perceive accidental forms such as colour and shape; the intellect grasps substantial forms, such as humanity. Both thought and sensation are cases of the intentional occurrence of forms; but whereas in sensation the forms are individual (the smell of *this rose*), in thought the form is universal (the idea of *a rose*). It is because of this conception of the nature of thought that to this day we speak of being *informed* about a matter and call the gaining of knowledge the acquisition of *information*.

The intentionality of the intellect, like the intentionality of sensation, is expressed in a slogan: *Intellectus in actu est intelligibile in actu*: 'The actuality of the power of thinking is the very same thing as the actuality of the object of thought'. When I have a universal thought, my thinking the universal idea is one and the same thing as the idea occurring to my mind. On the one hand, the intellect just is the capacity for thinking universal ideas; and on the other hand, the universal as such, the object of thought, is something whose only existence is its occurrence in thoughts.

Aquinas on the Will

Besides the intellect, in Aquinas' system, the other great power of the mind is the will. The intellect is a cognitive power of a specifically human kind; the will is an appetitive power of a specifically human kind. It is the power to have wants that only the intellect can frame. The will is the highest form of appetition, the topmost point on a scale whose lower rungs are the teleological tendencies of inanimate bodies (e.g. the tendency of fire to rise) and the conscious, but non-rational, desires of animals (e.g. the desire of a dog for a bone). Humans share these tendencies—*qua* heavy bodies they tend to fall if not supported; *qua* animals they want food and sleep—but they also have specifically human wants, paradigmatically the desire for happiness and for the means to happiness. In humans, moreover, even the animal wants are subject to the control of the intellectual part of the soul, the will.

In other animals the appetite of desire or aggression is acted upon immediately: thus a sheep, in fear of a wolf, runs away immediately, for it has no higher appetite to intervene. But a human being does not react immediately in response to an aggressive or impulsive drive, but waits for the command of a higher appetite, the will. (*ST* 1a 81. 3)

Aquinas frequently compares the performance of a voluntary action to obedience to an interior command. There are, he says, two sorts of acts of will. There are immediate acts (*actus eliciti*): acts such as enjoying, intending, choosing, deliberating, and consenting (1a 2ae 1. 1 ad 2); and there are commanded acts (*actus imperati*), voluntary motions of the body such as walking and speaking, whose execution involves the exercise of some other power in addition to the will.

There is no need to think that Aquinas is teaching that every time I go for a walk I utter to myself under my breath the command 'Go for a walk!' nor that there are such things as interior acts of pure willing. The Latin word 'actus' need not mean any sort of action: an act of the will is in fact standardly a tendency, not an episode (1a 2ae 6. 4). A tendency can be operative without being present to consciousness, as one's desire to reach a destination can govern one's behaviour on a journey without being constantly in one's thoughts.

For Aquinas voluntary action is action that issues from a rational consideration of the action. The minimum of rational consideration seems to be that the action should issue from a consideration of it as answering to a certain linguistic description—e.g. jumping out of the way when someone shouts 'Get out of my way'. But the kind of case Aquinas is more interested in is when we have reasons for action: when the action can be presented as the conclusion of a piece of practical reasoning. The reasons for an action need not have been consciously rehearsed before acting; but if an act is to be fully voluntary one should, on request, be able to give reasons—which might take the form of showing the goodness of the act itself or of showing that it was a means to a desirable end. In calling voluntary behaviour 'commanded action' Aquinas is drawing attention to the analogy between the logical relationship between command and execution and the relationship of willing to acting.

A volition, in the case of human beings, is a state of mind that is defined by the linguistic description of the action or state of affairs that would fulfil it. I want it to be the case that *p*. The proposition *p* both specifies my state of mind and demarcates the state of affairs that stands to it in the relationship of fulfilment to want. But suppose that instead of my wanting it to be the case that *p*, you command me to bring it about that *p*: the proposition has an analogous role. The metaphor of the will issuing commands is appropriate and fruitful.[11]

---

[11] The analogies are very close, as I have tried to spell out in my book *Will, Freedom and Power* (Oxford: Blackwell, 1975).

Practical reasoning is a difficult topic, and its logic has to this day not been fully worked out. One way in which it differs from theoretical reasoning is that it is, in the lawyer's jargon, *defeasible*. What that means is this. In theoretical deductive reasoning, if a conclusion follows from a given set of premisses it follows also from any larger set containing those premisses: the argument cannot be defeated by the addition of an extra premiss. But with practical reasoning it is different. A pattern of reasoning that would justify a certain course of action on the basis of certain wants and beliefs may well cease to justify it if further wants and beliefs are brought into consideration.

Aquinas recognized the defeasibility of practical reasoning, and indeed he saw it as the underlying ground of the freedom of the will. In human beings, unlike animals, he says,

Because a particular practical evaluation is not a matter of inborn instinct, but a result of weighing reasons, a human being acts upon free judgement, and is capable of going various ways. In contingent matters reason can go either way . . . and what to do in particular situations is a contingent matter. So in such cases the judgement of reason is open to alternatives and is not determined to any one course. Hence, humans enjoy free decision, from the very fact of being rational. (*ST* 1a 83. 1c)

When we look at a piece of practical reasoning—reasoning about what to do—we find, where the analogy of theoretical reasoning would lead us to expect necessitation, merely contingent and defeasible connections between one step and another. Aquinas believed that this contingency was the fundamental ground of human freedom.

Aquinas does not generally employ a Latin expression corresponding to our 'freedom of the will': he talks instead of the will (*voluntas*) and of 'free choice' (*liberum arbitrium*). Choice is an expression of both the intellect and the will: it is an exercise of the intellect because it is the fruit of reasoning; it is an exercise of the will because it is a form of appetition. Following Aristotle, Aquinas tells us that it is both appetitive intelligence, and ratiocinative appetite (*ST* 1a 83c).

Intellect and will are the two great powers of the rational soul, the soul that is peculiar to human beings. Besides being the soul that only human beings have, it is the only soul that human beings have. Against those contemporaries who thought that humans had also animal and vegetable souls, plus a form of corporeality, Aquinas maintained that the rational soul was the one and only substantial form of a human being. If there had been a plurality of forms, he argued, one could not say that it was one and the same human being who thought, loved, saw, heard, drank, slept, and had a certain weight and size.

Aquinas believed that the human soul was immaterial and immortal. The argument that the soul is pure form, uncontaminated with matter, is presented thus:

The principle of the operation of the intellect, which we call the human soul, must be said to be an incorporeal and subsistent principle. For it is plain that by his intellect a human being can know the nature of all corporeal things. But to be able to know things, a knower must have nothing of their nature in his own nature. If it did, what it had in its nature would hinder it from knowing other things, as a sick person's tongue, infected with a bilious and bitter humour, cannot taste anything sweet because everything tastes sour to it. If, then, the intellectual principle had in itself the nature of any corporeal thing, it would not be able to know all corporeal things. (*ST* 1a 75. 2)

The thesis of the immateriality of the soul goes hand in hand with the thesis of the intentional existence of the objects of thought. 'Prime matter receives individual forms, the intellect receives pure forms,' Aquinas says. That is to say, the shape of the Great Pyramid is *its* shape, and not the shape of any other pyramidal object; but the intellectual idea of a pyramid in my mind is the idea purely of pyramid and not the idea of any particular pyramid. But if the mind had any matter in it, the idea would become individual, not universal (1a 75. 5c).

This argument, if successful, shows that the soul does not contain matter. But does it mean that it can exist in separation from matter—in separation, for instance, from the body of the person whose soul it is? Aquinas believes that it does. Intellectual thought is an activity in which the body has no share; but nothing can act on its own unless it exists on its own; for only what is actually existent can act, and the way it acts depends on the way it exists. 'Hence we do not say that heat heats, but that a hot body heats. So the human soul, which is called the intellect or mind, is something non-bodily and subsistent' (1a 75. 2c).

One problem with this argument is that elsewhere Aquinas insists that just as it is strictly incorrect to say that heat heats, so it is strictly incorrect to say that the soul, or the mind, thinks. Aristotle had said, 'It is better not to say that the soul pities, or learns, or thinks, but that it is the human being that does these things with his soul' (*De An.* 408^{b}15), and Aquinas echoes this when he says, 'It can be said that the soul thinks, just as the eye sees, but it is better to say that the human being thinks with the soul.' If we take this comparison seriously, we must say that just as an eye, outside a body, is not really an eye at all any more, so a soul, separated from a body, is not really a soul any more.

Aquinas goes some way to accepting this, but he does not treat it as a *reductio ad absurdum*. He agrees that a person's disembodied soul is not the same thing as the person whose soul it is. St Paul wrote, 'if in this life only we have hope in Christ we are of all men most miserable' (1 Cor. 15: 19). St Thomas, in commenting on this passage, wrote: 'A human being naturally desires his own salvation; but the soul, since it is part of the body of a human being, is not a whole human being, and my soul is not I; so even if a soul gains salvation in another life, that is not I or any human being.' Whether or not Aquinas' belief in the possibility of disembodied souls is coherent, it is remarkable that he refuses to identify such a soul, even if beatified, with any self or ego. He refuses to identify an individual with an individual's soul, as many theologians before him, and many philosophers after him, were willing to do.

Scotus versus Aquinas

Duns Scotus' philosophy of mind differed profoundly from that of Aquinas, in accordance with the differences in their metaphysical systems. Aquinas believed that there was no purely intellectual knowledge of individuals, because individuation was by matter, and intellectual thought was free of matter. But for Scotus there exists an individual element, or *haecceitas*, which is an object of knowledge: it is not quite a form, but is sufficiently like a form to be present in the intellect. And because each thing has within it a formal, intelligible, principle, the ground is cut beneath the basis on which Aquinas rested the need for a species-specific agent intellect in human beings.

Individuals, unlike universals, are things that come into and go out of existence. If the proper objects of the intellect include not only universals but individual items like a *haecceitas*, then there is a possibility of such an object being in the intellect without existing in reality. The possibility that one and the same object might be in the intellect and not exist in reality was the possibility that Aquinas' intentionality theory was careful to avoid. An individual form, for Scotus, may exist in the mind and yet the corresponding individual not exist. Hence the individual form present in the intellect can be only a representation of, and not identical with, the object whose knowledge it embodies. Hence a window is opened at the level of the highest intellectual knowledge, a window to permit the entry of the epistemological problems that have been familiar to us since Descartes.

The differences between Aquinas and Scotus, so far as concerns the intellect, are not so much a matter of explicit rejection by Scotus of positions taken up by Aquinas. It is rather that a consideration of the Scotist position leads one to reflect on its incompatibility at a deep level with the Thomist anthropology. But when we turn from the intellect to the will, things are very different. Here Scotus is consciously rejecting the tradition that precedes him; he is innovating in full self-awareness. He regards Aquinas as having misrepresented the nature of human freedom and the relation between the intellect and the will.

For Aquinas, the root of human freedom was the will's dependence on the practical reason. For Scotus, the will is autonomous and sovereign. He puts the question whether anything other than the will effectively causes the act of willing in the will. He replies, nothing other than the will is the total cause of volition. What is contingent must come from an undetermined cause, which can only be the will itself, and he argues against the position which he attributes to 'an older doctor' that the indetermination of the will is the result of an indetermination on the part of the intellect.

You say: this indetermination is on the part of the intellect, in so representing the object to the will, as it will be, or will not be. To the contrary: the intellect cannot determine the will indifferently to either of contradictories (for instance, this will be or will not be), except by demonstrating one, and constructing a paralogism or sophistical syllogism regarding the other, so that in drawing the conclusion it is deceived. Therefore, if that contingency by which this can be or not be was from the intellect, dictating in this way by means of opposite conclusions, then nothing would happen contingently by the will of God, or by God, because he does not construct paralogism, nor is he deceived. But this is false. (*Oxon.* 2. 25)

Scotus' criticism of the idea that the indeterminism of the will arises from an indeterminism in the intellect is based on a misunderstanding of the theory that he is attacking. The intellect in dictating to the reason does not say 'This will be' or 'This will not be', but rather 'This is to be' or 'This is not to be', 'This is good' or 'This is not good'. If what is in question is a non-necessary means to a chosen goal, it is possible for the intellect, without error, to dictate both that something is good and that its opposite is good. Moreover, in making the will the cause of its own freedom, Scotus' theory runs the danger of leading to an infinite regress of free choices, where the freedom of a choice depends on a previous free choice, whose freedom depends on a previous one, and so on for ever.

Scotus was not unaware of this danger, and in opposition to the position he attacks, he develops his own elaborate analysis of the structure of human freedom, in a way that he believes holds out the possibility of avoiding the regress. In any case of free action, he says, there must be some kind of power to opposites. One such power is obvious: it is the will's power to will after not willing, or its power to enact a succession of opposite acts. Of course, the will can have no power to will and not will at the same time—that would be nonsense—but while A is willing X at time t, A has the power to not will X at time $t + 1$.

But beside this obvious power, Scotus maintains, there is another, non-obvious power, which is not a matter of temporal succession (*alia, non ita manifesta, absque omni successione*). He illustrates this kind of power by imagining a case in which a created will existed only for a single moment. In that moment it could only have a single volition, but even that volition would not be necessary, but would be free. Now while the lack of succession involved in freedom is plainest in the case of the imagined momentary will, it is there in every case of free action. That is, that while A is willing X at t, not only does A have the power to not will X at $t + 1$, but A also has the power to not will X at t, at that very moment. The power, of course, is not exercised, but it is there all the same. It is quite distinct from mere logical possibility—the fact that there would be no contradiction in A's not willing X at this very moment—it is something over and above: a real active power. It is this power that, for Scotus, is the heart of human freedom.[12]

---

[12] See the discussion of synchronic contingency in Ch. 6 above.

In defending the coherence of the concept of this non-manifest power, Scotus makes use of a logical distinction that can be traced back to Abelard. Consider the sentence 'This will, which is willing X at *t*, can not will X at *t*'. It can be taken in two ways. Taken one way ('in a composite sense') it means that 'This will, which is willing X at *t*, is not willing X at *t*' is possibly true. Taken in that way the sentence is false, and indeed necessarily false. Taken in another way ('in a divided sense') it means that it is possible that *not-willing X at time t* might have inhered in this will which is actually willing X at time *t*. Taken in this sense, Scotus maintains, the sentence can well be true (*Ord.* 4. 417–18).

Ockham versus Scotus

Ockham rejected the non-manifest power that Scotus had introduced. It was not a genuine power, he said, because it was totally incapable of actualization without contradiction. The power not to sit at time *t* should be regarded as a power existing not at *t* (when I am actually sitting) but at time *t* − 1, the last moment at which it was still open to me to be standing up at *t*.

Like Ockham, I find Scotus' occult powers incomprehensible. But Ockham's rejection of them is not sufficiently wholehearted. Scotus' mistake was to regard a power as being a datable event just like the exercise of a power. Ockham accepts the notion of a power for an instant, and simply antedates the temporal location of the power. But having a power is a state; it is not a momentary episode like an action.

It may be true, at *t*, that I have the power to do X, without that entailing that I have the power to do-X-at-*t*. Of course, it may be true that I can do X at *t*, but in order to analyse such a statement we must distinguish between power and opportunity. For it to be true that I can swim now it is necessary not only that I should now have the power to swim (i.e. know how to swim) but also have the opportunity to swim (e.g. that there should be a sufficient amount of water about). Scotus and Ockham fail to make the appropriate distinction, and their temporarily qualified powers are an amalgam of the two notions of power and opportunity. But an opportunity is not an occult power of mine: it is a matter of the states and powers of other things, and the compossibility of those states and powers with the exercise of my power.[13]

---

[13] See my *Will, Freedom and Power*, ch. 8.

In spite of their disagreements about the precise nature of freedom, Ockham is at one with Scotus in stressing the autonomy of the will. The will's action is not determined either by a natural desire for happiness, nor by any command of the intellect, nor by any habit in the sensitive appetite: it always remains free to choose between opposites.

On the cognitive side of the soul, Ockham regularly writes as if he recognizes the three sets of powers traditional in Aristotelian philosophy: outer sense (the familiar five senses), inner sense (the imagination), and intellect. However, when he discusses the intellect it is not at all clear that he is talking about the same faculty that Aristotle and Aquinas described. For Aquinas, the intellect was distinguished from the senses because its object was universal while theirs was particular; and the individual was directly knowable only by the senses. But for Ockham, both particular and universal can be known directly by both senses and intellect.

For Aquinas, a human mind's knowledge of a particular horse would be subsequent to the acquisition of the universal idea (*species*) of horse, formed out of sense-experience by the creative activity of a faculty peculiar to human beings, the agent intellect. Once this idea has been acquired, it can be applied to individuals only by a reflective activity of the intellect, reverting to sensory experience. Ockham regards all this apparatus as superfluous.

We can suppose that the intellect can be brought to the knowledge of an individual by the same process as it is led to the knowledge of a universal. If it is brought to knowledge of the universal by the agent intellect on its own, then the agent intellect on its own—we may suppose—can equally easily bring it to the knowledge of an individual. And as it can be directed by the intelligible species or by the phantasm to think of one universal rather than another, so too we can suppose that it can be directed by the intelligible species to think of this individual and not another. In whatever way after the acquisition of the universal concept the mind can be directed to think of one individual rather than another (even though the knowledge of the universal concerns all individuals equally) in just the same way it can be directed, even before the acquisition of the universal, to think of this individual rather than another. (*OTh*. 1. 493)

When Ockham claims that the intellect can know the individual, he is not basing his claim on the existence of a formal element of individuation, like the Scotist *haecceitas*. He rejected any such principle and denied the need for it. Whatever exists in the real world just is individual, and needs no principle to individuate it. His point in the quoted passage is that whatever philosophical account you give of the acquisition and employment of knowledge of the universal, exactly the same account can be given of the acquisition and employment of knowledge of the individual. If that is so, then it seems a violation of Ockham's razor to postulate two different faculties with exactly the same function.

In fact Ockham does distinguish between the senses and the intellect, but whenever he describes the operation of the intellect, it seems to be a mere double of either the inner or the outer sense. The very same object that we sense is intuitively grasped by the intellect under exactly the same description; the intellect's grasp of the object sensed is parallel to the imagination's representation of the object senses (*OTh.* 1. 494). Seeing a white object, imagining a white object, and thinking of a white object are, for Ockham, mental operations of a similar kind. The one feature which seems to be peculiar to the intellect is the act of judging that there is a white object. This judgement is an act not of the senses, nor of the will, but of the intellect alone (*OTh.* 6. 85–6).

Just as he was unconvinced by the traditional arguments for God's existence, so Ockham was unconvinced by the arguments of medieval Aristotelians to prove the immortality of the soul. If a soul is an immaterial and incorruptible form, he said,

it cannot be known evidently either by argument or by experience that there is any such form in us. Nor can it be known that thinking in us belongs to such a substance, nor that such a soul is a form of the body. I do not care what Aristotle thought of this, because he always seems to speak hesitantly. But these three things are simply objects of faith. (*OTh.* 9. 63–4)

Pomponazzi on the Soul

As the Middle Ages drew to an end, this scepticism about philosophical proofs of immortality became more widespread. The arguments for and against the immortality of individual human beings are set out in Pietro Pomponazzi's pamphlet of 1516, *On the Immortality of the Soul*. Pomponazzi begins by considering the opinion that there is a single, immortal, intellectual human soul, while each individual human being has only a mortal

A representation, from the Sala Sistina in the Vatican library, of the fifth Lateran Council, which condemned Pomponazzi's teaching on the immortality of the soul.

soul. This opinion, which he attributes to Averroes and Themistius, is, he tells us, 'widely held in our time and by almost all is confidently taken to be that of Aristotle'. In fact, he says, it is false, unintelligible, monstrous, and quite foreign to Aristotle.

To show that the opinion is false, Pomponazzi refers the reader to arguments used by St Thomas Aquinas in his *De Unitate Intellectus*. To show that it is un-Aristotelian he appeals to the teaching of the *De Anima* that, in order to operate, the intellect always needs a phantasm, which is something material. Our intellectual soul is an act of a physical and organic body. There may be types of intelligence that do not need an organ to operate, but the human intellect is not one of them.

A body, however, can function as a subject or object. Our senses need bodies in both ways: their organs are bodily and their objects are bodily. The intellect, however, does not need a body as subject, and it can perform operations (such as reflecting upon itself) which no bodily organ can do: the mind can think of itself, while the eye cannot see itself. But this does not mean that the intellect can operate entirely independently from the body.

Aquinas is again invoked in order to refute another opinion, the Platonic view that while every human has an individual immortal soul, this soul is related to his body only as mover to moved—like an ox to a plough, say. Like Aquinas, Pomponazzi appeals to experience:

I who am writing these words am beset with many bodily pains, which are the function of the sensitive soul; and the same I who am tortured run over their medical causes in order to remove these pains, which cannot be done save by the intellect. But if the essence by which I feel were different from that by which I think, how could it possibly be that I who feel am the same as I who think? (c. 6, p. 298[14])

We must conclude that the intellectual soul and the sensitive soul are one and the same in man.

In this, Pomponazzi is in agreement with St Thomas: but at this point he parts company with him. Thomas, he said, believed that this single soul was properly immortal, and only mortal in a manner of speaking (*secundum quid*). But he, Pomponazzi, will now set out to show that the soul is properly

---

[14] In E. Cassirer *et al.* (eds.), *The Renaissance Philosophy of Man* (Chicago: University of Chicago Press, 1959).

mortal, and only immortal in a manner of speaking. He continues to speak of Aquinas with great respect. 'As the authority of so learned a Doctor is very great with me, not only in divinity but also in interpretation of Aristotle, I would not dare to affirm anything against him: I only advance what I say in the way of doubt' (c. 8, p. 302).

By nature man's being is more sensuous than intellective, more mortal than immortal. We have more vegetative and sensory powers than intellectual powers, and many more people devote themselves to the exercise of those powers than to the cultivation of the intellect. The great majority of men are irrational rather than rational animals. More seriously, the soul can only be separable if it has an operation independent of the body. But both Aristotle and Aquinas maintain that the phantasm is essential for any exercise of thought: hence the soul needs the body, as object if not as subject. Souls can only be individuated by the matter of the bodies they inform: it will not do to say that souls, separate from their bodies, are individuated by an abiding aptitude for informing a particular body.

Did Aristotle believe in immortality? In the *Ethics* he seems to assert that there is no happiness after death, and when he says that it is possible to wish for the impossible, the example he gives of such a wish is the wish for immortality. St Thomas asks why, if Aristotle thought there was no survival of death, he should want people to die rather than to live in evil ways. But the only immortal intelligence Aristotle seems to accept is one that precedes, as well as survives, the death of the individual human. However, Pomponazzi says, he has no desire to seek a quarrel with Aristotle: what is a flea against an elephant? (c. 8, p. 313; c. 10, p. 334).

The Aristotelian conclusion which Pomponazzi finally accepts is this: the human soul is both intellective and sensitive, and strictly speaking it is mortal, and immortal only *secundum quid*. In all its operations the human intellect is the actuality of an organic body, and always depends on the body as its object. The human soul is what makes a human individual, but it is not itself a subsistent individual (c. 9, p. 321). This position 'agrees with reason and experience, it maintains nothing mythical, nothing dependent on Faith'. The intellect that, according to Aristotle, survives death is no human intellect. When we call the soul immortal it is only like calling grey 'white' when it is compared to a black background.

The immortality of the soul, Pomponazzi concludes, is an issue like the eternity of the world. Philosophy cannot settle either way whether the world ever had a beginning; it is equally impotent to settle whether the soul will ever have an end. His last word—sincere or not—is this. We must assert beyond doubt that the soul is immortal: but this is an act of faith, not a philosophical conclusion.

8

Ethics

Augustine on How to be Happy

Like most moralists in the ancient world, Augustine bases his ethical teaching on the premiss that everyone wants to be happy, and that it is the task of philosophy to define what this supreme good is and how it is to be achieved. If you ask two people whether they want to join the army, he says in the *Confessions*, one may say yes and the other no. But if you ask them whether they want to be happy, they will both say yes without any hesitation. The only reason they differ about serving in the army is that one believes, while the other does not, that that will make him happy (*Conf.* X. 21. 31).

In *On the Trinity* (*DT* 13. 3. 6) Augustine tells the story of a stage player who promised to tell his audience, at his next appearance, what was in each of their minds. When they returned he told them 'Each of you wants to buy cheap and sell dear'. This was smart, Augustine says, but not really correct—and he gives a list of possible counter-examples. But if the actor had said 'Each of you wants to be happy, and none of you wants to be miserable', then he would have hit the mark perfectly.

The branch of philosophy that Greeks call 'ethics' and which Latins call 'moral philosophy', Augustine says, is an inquiry into the supreme good. This is the good that provides the standard for all our actions; it is sought for its own sake and not as a means to an end. Once we attain it, we lack nothing that is necessary for happiness (*DCD* VIII. 8). So far, Augustine is saying nothing that had not been said by classical moralists: and he is following precedent too in rejecting riches, honour, and sensual pleasure as candidates for supreme goodness. The Stoics, among others, held out a similar renunciation, and maintained that happiness lay in the virtues of the mind. They were mistaken, however, both in thinking that virtue alone was sufficient for happiness, and in thinking that virtue was achievable by unaided human effort. Augustine takes a step beyond all his pagan predecessors in claiming that happiness is truly possible only in the vision of God in an afterlife.

First, he argues that anyone who wants to be happy must want to be immortal. How can we hold that a happy life is to come to an end at death? If a man is unwilling to lose his life, how can he be happy with this prospect before him? On the other hand, if his life is something he is willing to part with, how can it have been truly happy? But if immortality is necessary for happiness, it is not sufficient. Pagan philosophers who have claimed to prove that the soul is immortal have also held out the prospect of a miserable cycle of reincarnation. Only the Christian faith promises everlasting happiness for the entire human being, soul and body alike (*DT* 13. 8. 11–9. 12).

The supreme good of the City of God is eternal and perfect peace, not in our mortal transit from birth to death, but in our immortal freedom from all adversity. This is the happiest life—who can deny it?—and in comparison with it our life on earth, however blessed with external prosperity or goods of soul and body, is utterly miserable. Nonetheless, whoever accepts it and makes use of it as a means to that other life that he longs for and hopes for, may not unreasonably be called happy even now—happy in hope rather than in reality. (*DCD* XIX. 20)

Virtue in the present life, therefore, is not equivalent to happiness: it is merely a necessary means to an end that is ultimately other-worldly. Moreover, however hard we try, we are unable to avoid vice without grace, that is to say without special divine assistance, which is given only to those selected for salvation through Christ. The virtues of the great pagan heroes, celebrated from time to time in *The City of God*, were really only splendid vices, which received their reward in Rome's glorious history, but did not qualify for the one true happiness of heaven.

Many classical theorists upheld the view that the moral virtues were inseparable: whoever possesses one such virtue truly possesses them all, and whoever lacks one virtue lacks every virtue. As a corollary, some moralists held that there are no degrees of virtue and vice, and that all sins are of equal gravity. Augustine rejects this view.[1]

---

[1] See Bonnie Kent, 'Augustine's Ethics', in *CCA* 226–9.

A woman...who remains faithful to her husband, if she does so because of the commandment and promise of God and is faithful to him above all, has chastity. I don't know how I could say that such chastity is not a virtue or only an insignificant one. So too with a husband who remains faithful to his wife. Yet there are many such people, none of whom I would say is without some sin, and certainly that sin, whatever it is, comes from vice. Hence conjugal chastity in devout men and women is without doubt a virtue—for it is neither nothing nor a vice, and yet it does not have all the virtues with it. (*Ep.* 167. 3. 10)

We are all sinners, even the most devout Christians among us; yet not everything that we do is sinful. We are all vicious in one way or another, but not every one of our character traits is a vice.

In Augustine's moral teaching, however, there is an element that has many of the same consequences as the pagan thesis of the inseparability of the moral virtues. This is the doctrine that the moral virtues are inseparable from the theological virtues. That is to say, someone who lacks the virtues of faith, hope, and charity cannot truly possess virtues such as wisdom, temperance, or courage (*DT* 13. 20. 26). An act that is not done from the love of God must be sinful; and without orthodox faith one cannot have true love of God (*DCG* 14. 45).

Augustine often says that the virtues of pagans are nothing but splendid vices: an evil tree cannot bear good fruit. Sometimes he is willing to concede that someone who lacks faith can perform individual good acts, so that not every act of an infidel is a sin. But even if pagans can do the occasional good deed, this will not help them to achieve ultimate happiness: the best they can hope for is that their everlasting punishment will be less unbearable than that of others.

Through the long history of Christianity many were to accept Augustine's picture of the dreadful future that awaits the great majority of the human race. After the disruption of the Reformation, Calvin in the Protestant camp and Jansenius in the Catholic camp were to offer visions of even darker gloom; and in the nineteenth century Kierkegaard and Newman stressed, like Augustine, how narrow was the gate that gave entry to the supreme good of final bliss. The breezy optimism that characterized many Christians in the twentieth century had little backing from tradition. But that is a matter for the history of theology, not philosophy.

Augustine on Lying, Murder, and Sex

From a philosophical point of view Augustine's contributions to particular ethical debates are of greater interest than his overall view of the nature of morality. He wrote much that repays study concerning the interpretation of three of the Ten Commandments: 'Thou shalt not kill', 'Thou shalt not commit adultery', 'Thou shalt not bear false witness against thy neighbour'.

In *The City of God* Augustine defined for future generations the way in which Christians should interpret the biblical command 'Thou shalt not kill'. In the first place, the prohibition does not extend to the killing of non-human creatures.

When we read 'thou shalt not kill' we do not take this to apply to bushes, which feel nothing, nor to the irrational animals that fly or swim or walk or crawl since they are not part of our rational society. They have not been endowed with reason as we have, and so it is by a just ordinance of the creator that their life and death is subordinate to our needs. (*DCD* I. 20)

In the second place, it is not always wrong for one human being deliberately to take the life of another human being. Augustine accepts that a public magistrate may be justified in inflicting the death penalty on a wrongdoer, provided that the sentence is imposed and carried out in accordance with the laws of the state. Moreover, he says, the commandment against killing is not broken 'by those who have waged war on the authority of God' (*DCD* I. 21).

But how is one to tell when a war is waged with God's authority? Augustine is not one to glorify war: it is an evil, to be undertaken only to prevent a greater evil. All creatures long for peace, and even war is waged only for the sake of peace: for victory is nothing but peace with glory. 'Everyone seeks peace while making war, but no one seeks war while making peace' (*DCD* XIX. 10). On the other hand, Augustine is not a pacifist, as some of his Christian predecessors had been, on the basis of the Gospel command to 'turn the other cheek'. Soldiers may take part, indeed are obliged to take part, in wars that are waged by states in self-defence or in order to rectify serious injustice. Augustine does not spell out these conditions in the way that his medieval and early modern successors did in developing the theory of the just war. He is clear, however, that even in a just war at least one side is acting sinfully (*DCD* XIX. 7). And only a state in which justice prevails has the right to order its soldiers to kill. 'Remove justice, and what are kingdoms but criminal gangs writ large'? (*DCD* IV. 4). Nonetheless, he is willing to give historical examples of wars that he considers divinely sanctioned: for instance, the defence of northern Italy against the Ostrogoths, which ended with the spectacular victory of the imperial general Stilicho at Fiesole in 405 (*DCD* V. 23).

What of killing by private citizens, in self-defence or in defence of the life of a third party? Augustine does not seem to have made up his mind whether this was legitimate, and passages in his letters can be quoted in both senses. But on one topic much contested in Hellenistic philosophy Augustine is quite firm: suicide is unlawful. The command 'Thou shalt not kill' applies to oneself as much as to other human beings (*DCD* I. 20).

The issue was topical when Augustine began writing *The City of God* because during the sack of Rome in 410 many Christian men and women killed themselves to avoid rape or enslavement. Augustine maintains that no reason can ever justify suicide. Suicide in the face of material deprivation is a mark of weakness, not greatness of soul. Suicide to avoid dishonour—such as that of the Roman Cato, unwilling to bow to the tyranny of Julius Caesar—brings only greater dishonour (*DCD* I. 23–4). Suicide to escape temptation to sin, though the least reprehensible form of suicide, is nonetheless unworthy of a Christian who trusts in God. Suicide to escape rape—an action which some other Christians, such as Ambrose, regarded as heroic—falls even more firmly under Augustine's condemnation, because to be raped is no sin and should bring no shame on an unconsenting victim (*DCD* I. 19).

Augustine is less forthright in defence of human rights other than the right to life. He asks whether a magistrate does well to torture witnesses in order to extract evidence. He spells out eloquently the evils inherent in the practice: a third-party witness suffers, though not himself a wrong-doer; an innocent accused may plead guilty to avoid torture, and even when the victim of torture is actually guilty, he may lie nonetheless and escape punishment. Overall, the pain of torture is certain while its evidential value is dubious. Nonetheless, Augustine says finally, a wise man cannot refuse to carry out the duties of a magistrate, however unsavoury. He was perhaps unaware that torture had been condemned by a synod of bishops at Rome in 384.

Unlike other Church Fathers, Augustine taught that sexual reproduction was part of God's plan for the Garden of Eden. However the Fall — as here represented in a Roman catacomb painting — made sexuality shameful and uncontrollable.

What of slavery? Unlike Aristotle, Augustine does not think that slavery is something natural. It is, he says, the result of sin: and to illustrate this he gives the example of a kind of slavery which Aristotle too regarded as immoral, namely the enslavement of the vanquished by the victors in an unjust war. However, he falls short of an outright condemnation, in this sinful world, of slavery as an institution: he is deterred from doing so by the example of the Old Testament patriarchs, and by Paul's injunctions in the New Testament to slaves to obey their masters. 'Penal slavery is ordained by the same law as enjoins the preservation of the order of nature.' As often when faced with an intractable social or political problem, Augustine takes refuge in an internalization of the issue: it is better to be slave to a good master than to one's own evil lusts, so slaves should make the best of their lot and masters should treat their slaves kindly, punishing them only for their own good (*DCD* XIX. 15–16).

It was in matters of sexual ethics that Augustine's influence on later Christian thinkers was most profound. His teaching on sex and marriage became, with little modification, the standard doctrine of medieval moral philosophers. Among the major philosophers of the Latin Middle Ages, Augustine was the only one to have had sexual experience—if we except Abelard, whose sexual history was fortunately untypical. In modern times Augustine has acquired among non-Christians a reputation as a misogynist with a hatred of sex. Recent scholarship has shown that this reputation needs re-examination.[2]

It is true that Augustine is author of the strict Christian tradition that regards sex as permissible only in marriage, that treats procreation as the principal purpose of marriage, and that sets consequential limits on the types of sexual activity lawful between husband and wife.[3] But Augustine's teaching is much less hostile to sex than that of many of his contemporaries and predecessors. Christians like Ambrose and Jerome thought that marriage was a consequence of the Fall, and that there would have been no sex in the Garden of Eden. Augustine maintained that marriage was part of God's original plan for unfallen man and that Adam and Eve, even had

---

[2] See esp. Peter Brown, *The Body and Society* (New York: Columbia University Press, 1988), 387–427.

[3] Mark D. Jordan, *The Ethics of Sex* (Oxford: Blackwell, 2002), 110, points out that the principal New Testament text on marriage, 1 Cor. 7, makes no link between marital ethics and procreation: marriage is presented as a concession to the strength of sexual desire.

they remained innocent, would have procreated by sexual union (*DCD* XIV. 18). (It is true that such union, on his account, would have lacked all the elements of passion that make sex fun: in his Eden, copulation would have been as clinical as inoculation; *DCD* XIV. 26.) Against ascetics who regarded virginity as the only decent option for a Christian, Augustine wrote a treatise defending marriage as a legitimate and honourable estate, *De Bono Conjugali*, written in 401.

Marriage, he says, is not sinful; it is a genuine good, and not just a lesser evil than fornication. Christians may enter into it in order to beget children and also to enjoy the special companionship that links husband and wife. Marriage must be monogamous, and it must be stable; divorce is not permissible and only death can part the couple (*DBC* 3. 3, 5. 5). Since the purpose of procreation is what makes marriage honourable, husband and wife must not take any steps to prevent conception. Husband and wife must honour each other's reasonable requests for sexual intercourse, unless the request is for something unnatural (*DBC* 4. 4, 11. 12). But once the need for procreation has been satisfied, husbands and wives do well to refrain from intercourse and limit themselves to continent companionship (*DBC* 3. 3). Indeed, since there is no longer a need to expand the human race—as there was in the days of the polygamous Hebrew patriarchs—lifelong celibacy, though not obligatory, is a higher state than matrimony (*DBC* 10. 10).

Marriage, for Augustine, is an institution joining unequal partners: the husband is the head of the family, and the wife must obey. He could hardly think otherwise, given the clear teaching of St Paul. He also believed that the male companionship provided by an academic or monastic community was preferable to companionship between men and women even in the intimacy of marriage. But in judging sexual morality he does not operate with a double standard biased in favour of the male. Suppose, he says, a man takes a temporary mistress while waiting for an advantageous marriage. Such a man commits adultery, not against the future wife, but against the present partner. The female partner, however, is not guilty of any adultery, and indeed 'she is better than many married mothers if in her sexual relations she did her best to have children but was reluctantly forced into contraception' (*DBC* 5. 5). Augustine was also sensitive to female property rights: he cannot think of a more unjust law, he tells us, than the Roman Lex Voconia, which forbade a woman to inherit, even if she was an only daughter (*DCD* III. 21).

Since procreation is the divine purpose for sex, it goes almost without saying that only heterosexual intercourse is permissible. 'Shameful acts against nature, like those of the Sodomites, are to be detested and punished in every place and every time. Even if all peoples should do them, they would still incur the same guilt by divine law, which did not make human beings to use each other in that way' (*Conf.* III. 8. 15). Quite recently, the emperor Theodosius had decreed the public burning of male prostitutes.

The commandment 'Thou shalt not bear false witness against thy neighbour' was often extended in Christian commentary into a more general prohibition, but it was a matter of dispute whether lying was forbidden in all circumstances. Just as Augustine opposed those Christians who justified suicide to avoid rape, so he took a rigorous line against those who justified lying in a good cause (e.g. to hide the mysteries of the faith from inquisitive pagans). He wrote two treatises on lying, which he defines as 'uttering one thing by words or signs, while having another thing in one's mind' (*DM* 3. 3). He denies that such lying, with intention to deceive, is ever permissible. Naturally he has to deal with cases in which it seems prima facie that a good person might do well to tell a lie. Suppose there is, hidden in your house, an innocent person unjustly condemned. May you lie to protect him? Augustine agrees that you may try to throw the persecutors off the scent, but you may not tell a deliberate lie. 'Since by lying you lose an eternal life, you may not ever lie to save an earthly life' (*DM* 6. 9).

Though all lies are wrong, for Augustine, not all lies are equally wrong. A lie that helps someone else without doing any harm is the most venial, a lie that leads someone into religious error is the most wicked. A false story told to amuse, without any intention to deceive, is not really a lie at all—though it may indicate a regrettable degree of frivolity. (*DM* 2. 2, 25).

Abelard's Ethic of Intention

Augustine's moral teaching lays great emphasis on the importance of the motive, or the overarching desire, with which actions are performed. But among Christian moralists the one who went to the greatest length in attaching importance to intention in morals was Abelard. In his *Ethics*, entitled *Know Thyself*, he objected to the common teaching that killing

Abelard's teaching on intention focussed on practical problems. Here, in a miniature from a twelfth century legal text, a lady who intended to marry the nobleman on the right, finds that she has married, by mistake, the serf on the left.

people or committing adultery was wrong. What is wrong, he said, is not the action, but the state of mind in which it is done. 'It is not what is done, but with what mind it is done, that God weighs; the desert and praise of the agent rests not in his action but in his intention' (AE, c. 3).

Abelard distinguishes between 'will' (*voluntas*) and 'intention' (*intentio, consensus*). Will, strictly speaking, is the desire of something for its own sake; and sin lies not in willing but in consenting. There can be sin without will (as when a fugitive kills in self-defence) and bad will without sin (as in lustful desires that one cannot help). If we take 'will' in a broader sense, then we can agree that all sins are voluntary, in the sense that they are not unavoidable and that they are the result of some volition or other—e.g. the fugitive's desire to escape (AE 17). Intention, or consent, appears to be a state of mind that is more related to knowledge than to desire. Thus, Abelard argues that since one can perform a prohibited act innocently— e.g. marry one's sister when unaware that she is one's sister—the evil must be not in the act, but in the intention or consent.

Thus, a bad intention may ruin a good act. A criminal may be hanged justly, but if the judge condemns him not out of a zeal for justice, but out of inveterate hatred, he sins. More controversially, Abelard maintained that a good intention might justify a prohibited action. The Gospel tells us that those who were cured by Jesus disobeyed his command to keep their cures secret. They did well, because their motive in publicizing the miracles was a good one. God himself, when he ordered Abraham to kill Isaac, ordered something which it was bad to do, and ordering an evil deed is itself evil. But God's intention was a good one, to test his faith; and 'this intention of God was right in an act which was not right' (AE 31).

A good intention not carried out may be as praiseworthy as a good action. Two men both resolve to build an almshouse. One succeeds, but the second is robbed of his money before he can carry out his plan. Each is as deserving as the other: otherwise we must say that one man may be more virtuous than another simply because he is richer or luckier (AE 49).

Similarly, bad intentions are as blameworthy as bad actions. Why then punish actions rather than intentions? Abelard was an early proponent of the doctrine of strict liability, the doctrine that *mens rea* is not required for an offence. Human punishment, he says, may be justified where there is no guilt. Suppose a woman, while asleep, turns over and crushes to death the infant lying beside her. There is no sin there, since she did not know what she was doing; but she may justly be punished in order to make others more careful. The reason we punish actions rather than intentions is that human frailty regards a more manifest evil as worse than a hidden one. But at the Last Judgement God will not judge thus.

Does it follow that those who persecute Christians in the belief that they serve God thereby act praiseworthily? Not necessarily, Abelard says, but they are no more guilty than a man who kills a fellow man by mistake for an animal while hunting in a forest. However, in order to have a good intention, it is not sufficient that a man should believe that he is doing well. 'The intention of the persecutors is erroneous, and their eye is not simple.'

Abelard makes no clear distinction between the persecutors' erroneous opinion about the desirability of killing Christians and their virtuous purpose in the killing, namely to serve God. Consequently, it is not clear whether his doctrine of justification by intention means that an erroneous conscience excuses from guilt, or that a good end justifies means known to be evil. Abelard never clearly distinguished between the volitional and the cognitive element in intention.

Abelard's doctrine came close to the slogan of 1960s hippies, 'It doesn't matter what you do as long as you're sincere', and it is not surprising that it was found shocking by his contemporaries, even though he believed that our grasp of natural law set a limit to the possibilities of sincere moral error. The Council of Sens condemned the teaching that those who killed Christ in good faith were free from sin; and also among the condemned propositions was 'A man does not become better or worse on account of the works he does' (DB 380).

Aquinas' Ethical System

Aquinas, like Abelard, attached considerable importance to the role of intention in ethics. However, he located the concept of intention within a much richer account of the nature of human action, in which he drew on, and improved on, the account given by Aristotle in his *Nicomachean Ethics*. Aristotle in describing human action makes use of two key concepts: that of voluntariness and that of purpose. For him, something is voluntary if it is originated by an agent free from compulsion or error; it is a purpose (*prohairesis*) if chosen as part of an overall plan of life. His concept of the voluntary was too broad and his concept of purpose too narrow to demarcate most of the moral choices of everyday life. While retaining and refining Aristotle's concepts, Aquinas introduced the concept of intention to fill the gap between the two of them.

He explains the concept as follows. There are three types of action: those that are ends in themselves, those that are means to ends, and those that we do, perhaps reluctantly, as unavoidable accompaniments of actions of the first two kinds. It is in actions of the middle kind that we exhibit intention: we intend to achieve the end by the means. Actions of the third kind are not intentional, but merely voluntary. Voluntariness, then, is the broadest category; whatever is intentional is voluntary, but not vice versa. Intention itself, while not as broad as voluntariness, is a broader concept than Aristotle's purpose (*ST* 1a 2ae 12).

Human acts, according to Aquinas, may again be divided into three categories, this time in respect of moral evaluation. Some kinds of act are good (e.g. almsgiving), some are bad (e.g. rape), and some are indifferent (e.g. taking a country walk). Each individual action in the concrete will be performed in particular circumstances with a particular end in view. For an individual action to be morally good, it must belong to a class of acts that is not bad, it must take place in appropriate circumstances, and it must be done with a virtuous intention. If any of these elements is missing, it is a bad act. Consequently, a bad intention can spoil a good act (almsgiving out of vainglory), but a good intention cannot redeem a bad act (stealing to give to the poor). We may not do evil that good may come (*ST* 1a 2ae 19–20).

Aquinas agrees with Abelard that the goodness of a good action derives from the good will with which it is performed; but he says that the will can only be good if it is willing an action of a kind reason can approve. We may have a false belief about the goodness or badness of an action; such a belief is called by Aquinas an erroneous conscience. We must follow our conscience, even if erroneous; but though an erroneous conscience always binds us, it does not always excuse us. While an error about a fact (e.g. whether this woman is or is not married to someone else) may, if not the result of negligence, excuse from guilt, an error about divine law (e.g. the belief that adultery is not sinful) does not excuse. Again, against Abelard, Aquinas insists that good will cannot be fully genuine unless it is put into action when opportunity arises. Only involuntary failure will excuse non-execution. Thus Aquinas avoids the paradoxes that brought Abelard's theory of intention into disrepute (*ST* 1a 2ae 19. 5–6).

Aquinas uses his concept of intention when discussing how the morality of an action may be affected by its consequences. For him, foresight is not the same thing as intention: a consequence may be foreseen without being intended. 'A man, crossing a field the more easily to fornicate, may damage what is sown in the field; knowingly, but without a mind to do any damage.' In a case such as this, where it is a bad deed with bad consequences, the distinction is morally unimportant since in each case the wrongdoing is aggravated by the consequences. However, the distinction is important when we are dealing with the bad consequences of otherwise good acts. In discussing the lawfulness of killing in self-defence, Aquinas explains that the act of a person defending himself may have two effects, one the preservation of his own life, the other the death of the attacker. The use of reasonable violence in self-defence is permitted, even if death results as an unintended consequence; but it is never lawful for a private citizen actually to intend to kill (1a 2ae 20. 5).

Among both his admirers and his detractors, Aquinas has a reputation as a proponent of the doctrine of natural law. The reputation is not wholly accurate. Though he was writing within a Judaeo-Christian tradition which gives prominence to divine commandments as setting the standard by which acts are to be judged lawful or sinful, Aquinas' ethical theory gives pride of place not to the biblical concept of law but to the Aristotelian concept of virtue. In the *Prima Secundae* there are twenty questions on virtue to eighteen on law, while the *Secunda Secundae* is structured almost entirely around the virtues, pagan and Christian. But though Aquinas showed comparatively little interest in law as a key to morality, he did give an important place in his moral thinking to the notion of nature.

It has been common for centuries to think of Nature as a single universal force, more or less personified according to mood and context. Such was not Aquinas' notion. As an Aristotelian he starts from the fact that humans, animals, and other living beings reproduce their kind; and the nature of each thing that lives is what makes it belong to a particular natural kind. Generative processes end with the reproduction of a nature, that is to say, the bringing into being of another specimen of the same species. The nature of a thing is the same as its essence, but its essence considered as a source of activity and reproduction.

The reproduction of a nature, which is the result of the process of generation, is also the point and purpose of that process. St Thomas believed that each nature had itself a point no less than the process that reproduced it. This must be so, it might well seem, if reproduction itself were to serve any purpose. Bringing humans into being would have no point unless being a human had some point other than bringing other humans into being. 'The nature of a thing,' St Thomas wrote, 'which is the goal of its production, is itself directed to another goal, which is either an action, or the product of an action' (*ST* 1a 49. 3). Thus it might be that the point of being a glow-worm was to shine, and the point of being a bee was to make honey. Obviously, it is a matter of great importance, if this line of reasoning is correct, to have a correct view of what is the point of being a human.

All creatures, Aquinas teaches, exist for the sake of God; intelligent and non-intelligent creatures alike, in so far as they develop in accordance with their natures, mirror divine goodness. But intelligent creatures mirror God in a special way: they find their fulfilment in the understanding and contemplation of God. Human happiness is not to be found in sensual pleasures, in honour, glory, riches, or worldly power, nor even in the exercise of skill or moral virtue: it is to be found in the knowledge of God, not as he can be known in this life by human conjecture, tradition, or argument, but in the vision of the divine essence which Aquinas believes he can show to be possible in another life by means of supernatural divine enlightenment.

In all this, Aquinas draws heavily on Aristotle's *Ethics*. In the tenth book of that work Aristotle teaches that human happiness is to be found in philosophical contemplation, but he gives inconsistent reasons for doing so. He says that the intellect is what is most human in us, but also that it is superhuman and divine. Aquinas, in 1a 2ae 5. 5, resolves this ambiguity. A full understanding of human nature shows, he maintains, that humans' deepest needs and aspirations cannot be satisfied in the human activities—even the highest philosophical activities—that are natural for a rational animal. Human beings can be perfectly happy only if they can share the superhuman activities of the divine, and for that they need the supernatural assistance of divine grace. Instead of having a natural capacity for supreme happiness, human beings have free will, by which they can turn to God, who alone can make them happy.

The nature and point of each of the virtues is to be seen in the light of this overarching goal of human existence. Because the goal is supernatural we need, besides moral virtues such as fortitude and temperance, and besides intellectual virtues such as wisdom and understanding, the theological virtues of faith, hope, and charity. Only those who share in St Thomas' faith in the beatific vision as the culmination of a virtuous life can enter fully into the moral system that he presents. But thanks largely to the Aristotelian underpinning of his moral thinking, much of his thinking on individual moral topics is highly instructive also for the secular philosopher.

Aquinas seeks to reconcile Aristotelian with biblical ethics in the following manner. For Aristotle it is reason that sets the goal of action, and provides the standard by which actions are to be regarded as virtuous or vicious; in the Bible the standard is set by a code of laws. There is no conflict, Aquinas maintains, because law is a product of reason. Reflection on the essence of human action and choice, as described by Aristotle, leads to the formation of a set of ultimate practical principles to guide the activity of virtue in which human flourishing consists. Among these ultimate principles is the biblical injunction to love one's neighbour as oneself: a principle that Aquinas regarded as the first and common precept of human nature, self-evident to human reason.[4]

Human legislators, the political community or its delegates, use their reason to devise laws for the general good of particular states. But the world as a whole is ruled by the reason of God. The eternal plan of providential government, which exists in God as ruler of the universe, is a law in the true sense. It is a natural law, inborn in all rational creatures in the form of a natural tendency to pursue the behaviour and goals appropriate to them. It is this tendency that becomes articulate in the ultimate principles of practical reason. This natural law is simply the sharing, by rational creatures, in the eternal law of God. It obliges us to love God and to love our neighbour as ourselves. It is by the application of this principle that we reach specific moral rules to govern action in areas such as homicide, sexual relations, and private property.

Aquinas as Moralist

In each of the areas identified above Aquinas laid down norms that are issues of controversy at the present time, and to illustrate his approach to moral issues we may consider examples from each in turn.

On the topic of warfare, Aquinas puts himself the question 'Is soldiering always a sin?' (2a 2ae 40. 1). Following Augustine,[5] Aquinas answers in the negative, but lays down specific conditions for war-making to be lawful (2a 2ae 40. 1). The first is authority: only a prince may lawfully make war: a private citizen should take his grievances to court. Secondly, there must be a just cause: the enemy must be guilty of fault—not necessarily military aggression, but some violation of the rights of one's community or one's allies. Thirdly, the intention of those making war must be right: they must intend to promote good or to avoid evil. This appears to mean that the forceful redress of an injury must not do more harm than leaving the

---

[4] All this is very well explained in J. Finnis, *Aquinas: Moral Political, and Legal Theory* (Oxford: Oxford University Press, 1998).

[5] And also Alexander of Hales, one of the fullest early medieval theorists of the just war. See Barnes, 'The Just War', in *CHLMP* 771–84.

injuries unaddressed. Developed by later thinkers, in particular Grotius, the theory of the just war is still influential in both theoretical and practical international debate.

Aquinas accepted the legitimacy of capital punishment, imposed by lawful authority. This is a teaching that even some of his most devoted followers find difficult to accept, claiming that it is a violation of the principle that one may not do evil that good may come. But anyone who is not a pacifist must accept that the deliberate taking of human life may sometimes be lawful. If a national community may in a just war lawfully take the life of citizens of other states, it is hard to see why it is absolutely prohibited from taking the life of one of its own citizens.

When we turn to sexual ethics we find that Aquinas' thought is much conditioned by the Aristotelian biology that he accepted. For much of his life he believed that in biological generation the female merely provided nutrition for an active principle provided by the male. Since like begets like, a female is, on this view, an anomalous or defective male. Aquinas combined this theory of the transmission of human nature with the biblical account of the creation of the first pair to provide a basis for the subordination of women in medieval Christian society. The following passage shows what he would have thought of the ordination of women:

St Paul says it is not for women to utter publicly before the whole church: partly because the female sex was made submissive to the male, as Genesis says, and public instruction and persuasion is a task for leaders not subjects; partly lest men's sexual desires be aroused and partly since women generally haven't the fullness of wisdom required for public instruction. The grace of prophecy enlightens the mind, and knows no difference of male or female, as St Paul says; but utterance concerns public instruction of others, and there sex is relevant. Women exercise what wisdom or knowledge they have in private instruction of their children, not in public teaching.

Aquinas is often invoked in contemporary discussions of the morality of contraception and abortion. In fact, he had very little to say on either topic. Contraception is discussed, along with masturbation, in a question in the *Summa contra Gentiles* concerning 'the disordered emission of semen'. Aquinas maintains that this is a crime against humanity, second only to homicide. This claim rests on the belief that only the male provides the active element in conception, so that the sperm has an individual history continuous with the embryo, the fetus, and the infant. In fact, of course, male and female gametes contribute equally to the genetic constitution of the eventual human being. An embryo, unlike the father's sperm or semen, is the same individual organism as an infant at birth. For Aquinas, the emission of semen in circumstances unsuitable for conception was the same kind of thing, on a minor scale of course, as the exposure or starvation of an individual infant. That is why he thought masturbation a poor man's version of homicide.[6]

On the topic of abortion, Aquinas has remarkably little to say directly, mentioning it at most thrice in the vast expanse of his corpus. But the relevance of his teaching to the contemporary debate centres on his teaching about the beginning of human life. He is not an ally of those at the present time who claim that human life begins at conception. The developing human fetus does not count as a human being until it possesses a human soul, and this does not occur at conception, but after pregnancy is considerably advanced. For Aquinas the first substance independent of the mother is the embryo living a plant-like life with a vegetative soul. That substance disappears and is succeeded by a substance with an animal soul, capable of nutrition and sensation. Only at a later stage is the rational soul infused by God, changing this animate substance into a human being. Aquinas clearly believed that late abortion (even if caused unintentionally) was homicide. A person who strikes a pregnant woman, he says, will not be excused from homicide (1a 2ae 64. 8). But at an earlier stage, abortion, on Aquinas' account, though wrong, is wrong only for the same reason as masturbation and contraception: it is the destruction of an individual that is potentially a human being.

The theory of three successive entities at different stages of pregnancy does not seem entitled to any great respect. It is too closely linked to the idea that only the male is the active cause of the human generative process, and to the theory that the intellectual soul is immaterial and must therefore be divinely infused. The theory obscures the fact that there is an uninterrupted history of development linking conception with the eventual life of an adult. However, there are reasons quite different from Aquinas' for denying that the life of each human individual originates at

---

[6] In *ST* 1a 118 and 119 Aquinas presents a more complicated account of the development of the fetus, according to which the mother originates the vegetative soul, the father originates the sensitive soul, and God creates the intellectual soul. But he does not seem to have applied this schema to reproductive ethics.

conception. The line of development from conception to fetal life is not the uninterrupted history *of an individual*. In its early days a single zygote may turn into something that is not a human being at all, or something that is one human being, or something that is two people or more. Fetus, child, and adult have a continuous individual development which gamete and zygote do not have.

If this is correct, the destruction of an embryo at an early stage is not necessarily a form of homicide. It is no easy matter to decide exactly at what point an embryo becomes a human being, and this is not the place to attempt to decide such a difficult issue. But it seems clear that much abortion in practice takes place at a point after this stage has been reached, and therefore involves—as contraception does not—the destruction of an individual human being. Aquinas' superannuated biology is one of the ancestors of the common modern opinion which places contraception and abortion on the same moral plane. This is an error whether it leads to the denunciation of contraception no less than abortion as a serious sin, or whether it leads to the defence of abortion, no less than contraception, as a fundamental right of women.

Though he was a member of an order that held all its property in common, Aquinas did not believe in communism outside religious communities. So far from property being theft, the theft of someone else's property was a serious sin. Moreover, there is nothing wrong with doing business for the sake of profit, provided that one intends to make a good use of the profit obtained (2a 2ae 77. 4). However, Aquinas cannot be regarded as an enthusiastic supporter of capitalism: the right to acquire and retain private property is, for him, severely limited, and the making of money is subject to strict rules.

First of all, it is sinful to accumulate more property than one needs to support oneself, relatively to one's condition in life and the number of dependants one has. Secondly, if one has money to spare one has a duty—as a matter of natural justice, and not of benevolence—to give alms to those in need. Thirdly, if you fail to relieve the poor, then they may, in urgent need, legitimately take your property without your leave. 'In cases of need, all things are common. So it does not seem to be a sin if someone takes someone else's property, for it has been made common because of the state of need' (2a 2ae 66. 7). Thomas adds a Robin Hood clause: in similar cases, one may take someone else's property to succour an indigent third party (ad 3).

Psalm 15 blesses the man "that putteth not out his money to usury". This ninth century MS of the Psalter shows the good man giving his surplus instead to Christ.

Aquinas was strongly opposed to usury, that is to say, the taking of interest, however small, on money lent. He bases his opposition both on Old Testament texts and on Aristotelian principles. Some things, he says, are consumed when they are used: the use of wine, for instance, is to drink it, and once drunk it no longer exists. Other things can be used without being consumed: one can live in a house without destroying it. If you tried to charge separately for the wine and its use, you would be selling the same thing twice; but you can rent the house out without selling the house itself. But because money is used by being spent, money is like wine, not like a house; if someone gives you back a sum of money you lent him, you cannot charge him for the use he made of it in the meanwhile (2a 2ae 78).

The profits of usury, Aquinas said, must be returned to those who have been wrongly charged interest. The duchess of Brabant asked him whether it would be lawful for her to confiscate from the Jews in her realm the money that they had made usuriously. Certainly, Aquinas replied: but in the style of Portia he added that if she did so, it would be wrong for her, no less than the Jews, to keep such ill-gotten gains. She should try to trace the

271

unfortunate people who had fallen into the hands of moneylenders, and restore to them the interest they had paid (*DRI* 1. 278).

Scotus on Divine Law

Murder, abortion, usury were all, for Aquinas, violations of the natural law of God. But he structured his ethical system not around the concept of law, but around the concept of virtue as the route to self-fulfilment in happiness. It is Duns Scotus who gave the theory of divine law the central place that it was to occupy in the thought of Christian moralists henceforth. Scotus agrees with Aristotle and Aquinas that human beings have a natural tendency to pursue happiness (which he calls the *affectio commodi*); but, in addition, he postulates a natural tendency to pursue justice (an *affectio iustitiae*). The natural appetite for justice is a tendency to obey the moral law no matter what the consequences may be for our own welfare. Human freedom consists in the power to weigh in the balance the conflicting demands of morality and happiness.[7]

In denying that humans seek happiness in all their choices, Scotus is turning his back not only on Aquinas but on a long tradition of eudaimonistic ethics, with roots going back to Plato and Aristotle. Scotus is surely right to maintain that one's own happiness is not the only possible aim in life. A person may map out his life in the service of someone else's happiness, or for the furtherance of some cause which may perhaps be unlikely to triumph during his lifetime. A daughter may forgo the prospect of marriage and congenial company and a creative career in order to nurse a bedridden parent. It is unconvincing to say that such people are seeking their own happiness in so far as they are doing what they want to do.

In the eudaimonistic tradition freedom is conceived as the ability to choose between different possible means to happiness; and wrongdoing is represented as the outcome of a failure to apprehend the appropriate means. For Scotus, freedom extends not just to the choice of means to a predetermined end, but to a choice between independent and possibly competing ultimate goals. The blame for wrongdoing is placed less on a defective understanding, more on the waywardness of an autonomous will.

---

[7] See R. Cross, *Duns Scotus* (Oxford: Oxford University Press, 1999), 88.

The rightness or wrongness of the will's choice is determined by whether it accords or does not accord with the divine law. All medieval thinkers saw wrongdoing as a violation of divine law, but for Scotus the relationship between the morality of an action and the contents of divine commands was much more direct than it was for his predecessors. According to theologians in the eudaimonist tradition, certain actions were wrong because they were in conflict with the necessary conditions for human happiness as truly understood, and it was precisely because they were obstacles to happiness that God had forbidden them. For Scotus, on the other hand, an action could be wrong simply because God had forbidden it, whether or not it had any relevance to the fulfilment or non-fulfilment of human nature.

Just as Scotus' theory extends the degree of choice available to the human will subject to the divine law, so it extends the degree of freedom possessed by God in issuing commands to the human will. Scotus explores this topic in treating of the relation between the natural law and the explicitly formulated commands of the Decalogue (*Ord* 3. d 37). St Thomas had held that all of the Ten Commandments belonged to the natural law: it followed that God could not dispense from them, could not give permission for humans to act against them. Scotus agreed that no exceptions could be permitted to commandments belonging to the natural law; but he disagreed that all ten Commandments formed part of that law.

There are, indeed, some commands that God could not possibly give: he could not, for instance, command anyone to hate him, or blaspheme against him. Truths such as 'God must be loved above all things' are necessarily true, prior to any decision of God's will. God cannot dispense from such a law, and laws of this kind are the kernel of morality, the true natural law. In maintaining this, Scotus shows that he did not accept what is sometimes called the divine command theory of morality, according to which the moral value of any action whatever consists in nothing other than its prescription or prohibition by God. But it is only commands that have God himself as their object that strictly belong to the natural law.

Scotus does, indeed, accept the divine command theory for a limited number of cases. Beyond the provisions of the basic natural law, God's freedom to command is absolute. He can dispense from the law against killing human beings: when he ordered Abraham to sacrifice Isaac, he was replacing the original universal prohibition with a new, more specific, rule. Further, God was free, in principle, never to have enacted at all the command 'Thou shalt not kill'. And God can give commands, such as the prohibition on eating the fruit of the tree in Eden, where the action commanded or prohibited has no intrinsic rightness or wrongness. In such cases the moral value of the action does consist in nothing other than its relationship to the content of the divine command.

The laws of the second part of the Decalogue, for Scotus, fall between these arbitrary commands and the commands that are part of the basic natural law. It is true, quite apart from any divine command, that murder is a bad action, but this is a contingent, not a necessary, truth. The principles that find expression in the later Commandments can be said to belong to the law of nature only in an extended sense. In giving these commands, God exhibits justice towards his creatures: but he can override them, when necessary, in the interests of a higher justice—as when he permitted polygamy to the Old Testament patriarchs. Moreover, God is under no necessity to treat his creatures justly at all: the infinite owes no obligation to the finite. The will expressed in his commands is a free will; without any contradiction he could command murder, adultery, theft, and lying (*Oxon.* 4. 4. 6. 1). The only limit on the power to command is that placed by the principle of contradiction itself: even divine commands may not be inconsistent with each other. So the totality of commands in force must make up a coherent system.

Two important consequences follow from Scotus' ethical theory. The first is a limitation on human capacity for moral reasoning; the second is an externalization of the notion of sin. The natural law is the moral law that is capable of being discovered by natural reason: but if those principles that concern human beings' relationships to each other are not part of the natural law, then, however plausibly they can be argued for, we can only be certain of them in virtue of revelation. An act in breach of divine law places one in a state of sin; but this does not, according to Scotus, effect any internal change in the sinner. Guilt is not an intrinsic property of the human offender: it is simply the external fact that God has resolved on punishment. Both of these Scotist theses were to become fundamental issues of controversy at the time of the Reformation.

The Ethics of Ockham

Ockham's ethical theory is very similar to that of Scotus, despite the disagreements between the two philosophers on metaphysical issues. Though his analysis of freedom was different from Scotus', Ockham agrees that freedom is the fundamental feature of human beings, and that the will is independent of reason. 'Every man experiences that however much reason may dictate a thing, his will can either will it or fail to will it or will its opposite' (*OTh*. 9. 88). Even the choice of the ultimate end is free: a man may refuse to make happiness his goal, in the belief that it is a state unattainable by the kind of human beings we find ourselves to be (*OTh*. 1. 443).

Like Scotus, Ockham places law, not virtue, in the centre of ethical theory. He goes further than Scotus, however, in emphasizing the absolute freedom of God in laying down the divine law. Whereas Scotus accepted that some precepts (e.g. the command to love God) were part of a natural law, and derived their force not from the free decision of God but from his very nature, Ockham taught that the moral value of human acts derived entirely from God's sovereign, unfettered, will. God, in his absolute power, could command adultery or theft, and if he did so such acts would not only cease to be sinful but become obligatory (II *Sent*. 15. 353).

Obligation is a central ethical concept for Ockham. Evil is defined as being an action performed under an obligation to do the opposite. Humans are obliged by the divine commands; but God is under no obligation to human beings. God would not be violating any obligation if he were to order a human being to hate God himself. By the very fact that God wills something, it is right for it to be done. He would not be doing anything wrong even if he directly caused such an act of hatred in a person's will. Neither God nor the human person would sin; God because he is not under any obligation, the human because the act would not be a free one and only free actions are blamable (IV *Sent*. 9).

Ockham, like his Aristotelian predecessors, says from time to time that what makes an act virtuous is that it should be in accordance with correct rational judgement and that it should be performed precisely for that reason. Again, he follows tradition in saying that a person must act in accordance with their conscience (i.e. their rational moral judgement) even if it is in error. But these Aristotelian remarks are not in conflict with the fundamentally authoritarian nature of his ethic. If we are to follow reason and conscience, this is because God has commanded us to do so (III *Sent.* 13). Presumably, God in his absolute power could order us to disobey our consciences just as he can order us to hate the divine goodness.

If God's commands are arbitrary, can the content of the divine law be known without revelation? Ockham puts the question whether in moral matters there can be a demonstrative science. In answer he makes a distinction between two kinds of moral teaching. There is positive moral theory, which contains laws, divine and human, which concern actions that are good and evil only because they are commanded or prohibited by the relevant legislator. But there is also another kind of moral theory—the kind that Aristotle talks about—that deals with ethical principles. Positive moral theory, Ockham tells us, is not deductive; but the other kind does allow conclusions to be demonstrated (*OTh.* 9. 176–7).

One might wonder, given Ockham's general theory, whether any specific conclusion could be drawn that went beyond 'Obey God's commands'. But he tells us that there are principles that rule out particular kinds of acts (II. *Sent.* 15. 352). Murder, theft, and adultery, he tells us, are by definition, not to be done. 'Murder' denotes killing, and connotes that the killer is obliged by divine command to do the opposite. This may enable one to conclude that murder is wrong; but it will not enable one to tell, without revelation, whether a particular killing—e.g. the killing of Abel by Cain—was or was not murder.

It turns out, moreover, that for Ockham, the true subject matter of morality are not public actions like murder and adultery, but rather private, interior, acts of willing. No external act can have, in itself, a moral value, because any external act is capable of being performed by a madman, who is incapable of virtuous action. An action carried out in conformity with a virtuous will has no moral value additional to the moral value of the willing. The very same act of walking to church is virtuous if done out of piety, vicious if done for vainglory. A suicide who throws himself off a cliff, but repents while falling, passes from a vicious state to a virtuous one without any change in external behaviour.

We have already met, in Abelard's moral teaching, a similar privileging of interior as against exterior action. What is remarkable in Ockham is the complete severance that is made between the interior and the exterior life. A human's willing to perform an action is an independent action only contingently connected with the actual performance of the action. Of course an external action of mine can conform, or fail to conform, to my will—but so can the actions of causes quite outside my control. My will can just as well 'command' that a candle should burn in church, or that a donkey should shit in church (*OTh.* 9. 102).

9

God

The God of Augustine

In the second book of *On Free Will* Augustine raises the question 'How do we know that we derive our origin from God?' and in answer he develops a structured argument for God's existence. His interlocutor in the dialogue, Evodius, starts from the position of a simple believer who accepts the existence of God as taught in the Bible. Augustine wants to change this position of mere belief to one of knowledge (*DLA* 2. 1. 5). His strategy is to build up a hierarchy of beings of different kinds.

We can divide the things we find in the world into three classes: lifeless things that merely exist, such as stocks and stones, living things that have sensation and not intelligence, such as dumb animals, and things that have existence, life, and intelligence, such as the rational human beings. We share with the animals the five outward senses, and we share with them also an inner sense. By this sense animals are aware of the operation of the other senses and by it they feel pleasure and pain. But the highest thing in us is 'a kind of head or eye of our soul'.

We grade these different faculties in a hierarchy—inner sense is superior to outer senses, reason is superior to inner sense—on the basis that if A makes judgements about B, then A is superior to B. Within us, nothing is superior to reason. But if we find something outside ourselves superior to reason, Augustine asks, shall we call that God? To be God, Evodius replies, it is not enough to be superior to human reason. God is that than which nothing is superior (*DLA* 2. 6. 14).

Among the highest things in the human mind are knowledge of numbers and judgements of value. The truths of arithmetic are unchangeable, unlike fragile human bodies, and they are common to all educated people, unlike the private objects of sensation. Seven and three make ten, for ever and for everyone. Our knowledge of arithmetic is not derived from the experience of counting: on the contrary, we use the rules of addition and subtraction to point out when someone has counted wrong. We are aware of rules that apply throughout the unending series of numbers, a collection more numerous than we could ever encounter in experience (*DLA* 2. 8. 22–4).

Like arithmetical truths, there are ethical truths that are the common property of all humans. Wisdom is knowledge about the supreme good: everyone wishes to be happy, and so everyone wishes to be wise, since that is indispensable for happiness. Though people may disagree about the nature of the supreme good, they all agree on such judgements as that we ought to live justly, that the worse should be subject to the better, and that each man should be given his due (2. 10. 28). These 'rules and guiding lights of virtue', Augustine says, are true and unchangeable and available for the common contemplation of every mind and reason.

What is it that unites arithmetic and wisdom? After all, some mathematicians are very unwise, and some wise men are quite ignorant of mathematics. Augustine's response is surprising.

Far be it from me to suggest that compared with numbers wisdom is inferior. Both are the same thing, but wisdom requires an eye fit to see it. From one fire light and heat are felt as if they were 'consubstantial' so to speak. They cannot be separated one from the other. And yet the heat reaches those things which are brought near to the fire, while the light is diffused far and wide. So the potency of intellect which indwells wisdom causes things nearer to it to be warm, such as rational souls. Things further away, such as bodies, it does not affect with the warmth of wisdom, but it pours over them the light of numbers. (*DLA* 2. 11. 32)

What arithmetic and wisdom have in common is that both are true and unchangeably true and contained in a single unchangeable truth.

This truth is not the property of any human individual: it is shareable by everyone. Now is this truth superior to, or equal to, or inferior to our minds? If it were inferior to our minds, we would pass judgements about it, as we may judge that a wall is not as white as it should be, or that a box is not as square as it should be. If it were equal to our minds, we would likewise pass judgement on it: we say, for instance, that we understand less than we ought. But we do not pass judgement on the rules of virtue or the truths of arithmetic: we say that the eternal *is* superior to the temporal, and that seven and three *are* ten. We do not say these things *ought* to be so. So the immutable truth is not inferior to our minds or equal to them: it is superior to them and sets the standard by which we judge them (*DLA* 2. 12. 34).

So we have found something superior to the human mind and reason. Is this God? Only if there is nothing that is superior to it. If there is anything more excellent than truth, then that is God; if not, then truth itself is God. Whether there is or is not such a higher thing, we must agree that God exists (*DLA* 2. 15. 39). Thus we have turned our initial faith in God into a form of knowledge, however tenuous, of his existence.

Can philosophy tell us more of his nature? For Augustine one of the most important things we can know about God is that he is *simple*. In a passage of *The City of God* he explains what he means by 'simple'.

A nature is called simple when there is nothing that it has that it can lose, and when there is no difference between what it is and what it has. A vessel contains liquid, a body has a colour, the atmosphere has light and heat, a soul has wisdom. The vessel is not the same as the liquid, a body is not the same as its colour, the atmosphere is not the same as its light and heat, the soul is not its wisdom. Such things can lose what they have, and change, gaining different qualities and attributes: the vessel can be emptied of its liquid, the body may lose its colour, the atmosphere become dark and cold, and the soul become foolish. (*DCD* XI. 10)

If a being is simple, then, whatever is true of it at any time is true of it at any time. But for perfect simplicity, to be unchangeable is not enough. A simple being must not only be exempt from change, it must also lack contemporaneous parts. As a young man Augustine had believed that God was corporeal: a boundless ocean, he imagined, completely permeating the created world as if it was a sponge (*Conf.* VII. 5. 7). But anything that is corporeal is extended, having parts that are spatially distinct from each other. The one simple God cannot be corporeal, cannot be extended in space.

We can go further. Something might be immutable and unextended and yet not be simple if it had a set of distinct everlasting attributes. In God, Augustine believed, all the divine attributes are in some way identical with each other and with the divine substance in which they inhere (*DCD* XI. 10).

What then is the divine substance or essence? Augustine seizes on a text of Exodus (3: 14), God's message through Moses, 'I am who am', in order to reconcile Platonic metaphysics with biblical teaching. God is he who is: that is to say, he is supreme essence, he supremely is.

To the creatures he made out of nothing he gave being; but he did not give them supreme being like his own. To some he gave to be to a greater extent, and to others less, and thus he arranged a scale of essences among natures. 'Essence' is derived from the Latin verb 'esse', to be, just as 'sapientia' (wisdom) is the noun from the verb *sapere*. (*DCD* XII. 2)

'Essentia', Augustine tells us, is a new Latin word, recently coined to correspond to the Greek 'ousia'.

God's essence is identical with his attributes: and one of the most important of his attributes is his goodness. Just as God gives being to his creatures, so too he gives them goodness. All that he created is good by nature. Where then does evil come from? In his youth Augustine had subscribed to the Manichaean view that there were two supreme principles controlling the universe, one good and one evil, in conflict with each other. As a Christian he gave up belief in the evil principle, but this did not mean that he believed that the good God was the cause of evil. Evil is only a privation of good, it is not a positive reality and does not need a causal principle. Any evil in creatures is simply a loss of good—of integrity, beauty, health, or virtue (*DCD* XII. 3).

God does not create anything evil, but he does create some good things that are better than other good things, and they remain better than other things even if they are themselves defective. Thus a runaway horse is better than a stationary stone, and a drunkard is better than the fine wine he drinks (*DLA* 3. 2. 15). There is nothing to be regretted in one creature's being less well endowed than another: the variety of endowment adds to the beauty of the universe, and God owes no debt to anyone (*DLA* 3. 15. 45).

But what of the evil of an evil will? As we have seen, when discussing the nature of the mind[1] Augustine believes that an evil human choice has no cause. The freedom of the will is of course a gift of God, and the freedom of the will carries with it the possibility of the misuse of that freedom. But nothing forces or necessitates any individual case of such misuse. That was true at least of human nature as first created by God.

[1] See Ch. 7 above.

281

Human freedom operated unhindered before the Fall: that is one reason for the gravity of Adam's sin. But when Adam fell, his sin brought with it not only liability to death, disease, and pain, but in addition massive moral debilitation. We children of Adam inherit not only mortality but also sinfulness. Corrupt humans tainted with original sin have no freedom to live well without help: each temptation, as it comes, we may be free to resist, but our resistance cannot be prolonged from day to day. We need God's grace not only to gain heaven but to avoid a life of continual sin (*DCG* 7).

The grace that enables human beings to avoid sin is allotted to some people rather than others not on the basis of any merit of theirs, whether actual or foreseen. It is awarded simply by the inscrutable good pleasure of God. No one can be saved without being predestined. The choice of those who are to be saved, and implicitly also of those who are to be damned, was made by God long before they had come into existence or done any deeds good or bad.

The relation between divine predestination and human virtue and vice was a topic that occupied Augustine's last years. A British ascetic named Pelagius, who came first to Rome, and then after its sack to Africa, preached a view of human freedom quite in conflict with Augustine's. The sin of Adam, he taught, had not damaged his heirs except by setting them a bad example; human beings, throughout their history, retained full freedom of the will. Death was not a punishment for sin but a natural necessity, and even pagans who had lived virtuously enjoyed a happy afterlife. Christians had received the special grace of baptism, which entitled them to the superior happiness of heaven. Such special graces were allotted by God to those he foresaw would deserve them.

Augustine secured the condemnation of Pelagius at a council at Carthage in 418 (DB 101–8) but that was not the end of the matter. Devout ascetics in monasteries in Africa and France complained that if Augustine's account of freedom was correct, then exhortation and rebuke were vain and the whole monastic discipline was pointless. Why should an abbot rebuke an erring monk? If the monk was predestined to be better, then God would make him so; if not, the monk would continue in sin no matter what the abbot said. In response, Augustine insisted that not only the initial call to Christianity, the first stirring of faith, was a matter of sheer grace; so too was the perseverance in virtue of the most devout Christian approaching death (*DCG* 7; *DDP*).

If grace was necessary for salvation, was it also sufficient? If you are offered grace, can you resist it? If so, then there would be some scope for freedom in human destiny. While some would end up in hell because they had never been offered grace, hell would also contain those who had been offered grace and turned it down. In the course of controversy Augustine's position continually hardened, and in the end he denied even this vestige of human choice: grace cannot be declined, cannot be overcome. There are only two classes of people: those who have been given grace and those who have not, the predestined and the reprobate. We can give no reason why any individual falls in one class rather than another.

If we take two babies, equally in the bonds of original sin, and ask why one is taken and the other left; if we take two sinful adults, and ask why one is called and the other not; in each case the judgements of God are inscrutable. If we take two holy men, and ask why the gift of perseverance to the end is given to one and not to the other, the judgements of God are even more inscrutable. (*DDP* 66)

The crabbed crusader of predestination in the monastery at Hippo is very different from the youthful defender of human freedom in the gardens of Cassiciacum. It was the former, and not the latter, whose influence was powerful after his death and cast a shadow over centuries to come.

Boethius on Divine Foreknowledge

The problem that faced Augustine in reconciling human freedom with the power of God can be solved if one is willing to jettison the doctrine of predestination. But for all those who believe that God is omniscient there remains a problem about divine foreknowledge: this concerns not God's *willing* humans to act virtuously and be saved, but simply God's *knowing* what humans will or will not do. This problem was discussed in a clear and energetic fashion in the fifth book of Boethius' *Consolation of Philosophy*.

The book addresses the question: in a world governed by divine providence, can there be any such thing as luck or chance? Lady Philosophy says that if by chance we mean an event produced by random motion without any chain of causes, then there is no such thing as chance. The only kind of chance is that defined by Aristotle as the unexpected effect of coinciding causes (*DCP* 5. 1). In that case, Boethius asks, does the causal network leave any room for free human choice or does the chain of fate bind even the motions of our minds? The difficulty is this. If God foresees all, and cannot be in error, then what he foresees must happen of necessity. For if it is possible for our deeds and desires to turn out in any way other than God has foreseen, then it is possible for God to be in error. Even if in fact all turns out as he foresaw, his foresight can only have been conjecture, not true knowledge.

Boethius admits that knowledge does not, in itself, cause what is known. You may know that I am sitting, but it is my sitting that causes your knowledge, not your knowledge that causes my sitting. But necessity is different from causality; and 'If you know that I am sitting, then I am sitting' is a necessary truth. So, too, 'If God knows that I will sin, I will sin' is a necessary truth. Surely that is enough to destroy our free will, and with it all justification for reward or punishment for human actions. On the other hand, if it is still possible for me not to sin, and God thinks that I will inevitably sin, then he is in error—a blasphemous suggestion!

Lady Philosophy accepts that a genuinely free action cannot be foreseen with certainty. But we can observe, without any room for doubt, something happening in the present. When we watch a charioteer steering his horses round a racetrack, neither our vision nor anything else necessitates his skilful management of his team. God's knowledge of our future actions is like our knowledge of others' present actions: he is outside time, and his seeing is not really a *foreseeing*. 'The same future event, when it is related to divine knowledge, is necessary; but when it is considered in its own nature can be seen to be utterly free and unconditioned ... God beholds as present those future events that happen because of freewill' (*DCP* 5. 6).

There are two kinds of necessity: plain straightforward necessity, as in 'Necessarily all men are mortal', and conditional necessity as in 'Necessarily if you know that I am walking, I am walking'. Conditional necessity does not bring with it plain necessity: we cannot infer 'If you know I am walking, necessarily I am walking'. Accordingly, the future events that God sees as present are conditionally necessary, but they are not necessary in the straightforward sense that matters when we are talking of the freedom of the will (*DCP* 5. 6).

While explaining that God is outside time, Boethius produced a definition of eternity that became canonical. 'Eternity is the whole and perfect possession, all at once, of endless life' (*DCP* 5. 6). We who live in time proceed from the past into the future; we have already lost yesterday and we have not yet reached tomorrow. But God possesses the whole of his life simultaneously; none of it has flowed into the past and none of it is still waiting in the wings.

Boethius' treatment of freedom, foreknowledge, and eternity became the classical account for much of the Middle Ages. But problems remain with his solution of the dilemma he posed with such unparalleled clarity. Surely, matters really are as God sees them; so if God sees tomorrow's sea battle as present, then it really is present already. Again, the notion of eternity raises more problems than it solves. If Boethius' imprisonment is simultaneous with God's eternity, and God's eternity is simultaneous with the sack of Troy, does that not mean that Boethius was imprisoned while Troy was burning? We cannot say that the imprisonment is simultaneous with one part of eternity, and the sack with another part, because eternity has no parts but, on the Lady Philosophy's account, happens all at once.[2]

Negative Theology in Eriugena

Scotus Eriugena, two centuries later, returned to the Augustinian problem of predestination,[3] but his principal contribution to philosophical theology lay in the extremely restrictive account which he gives of the use of language about God. God is not in any of Aristotle's categories, so all the things that are can be denied of him—that is, negative ('apophatic') theology. On the other hand, God is the cause of all the things that are, so they can all be affirmed of him: we can say that God is goodness, light, etc.—that is, positive ('cataphatic') theology. But all the terms that we apply to God are applied to him only improperly and metaphorically. This applies just as much to words like 'good' and 'just' as to more obviously metaphorical descriptions of God as a rock or a lion. We can see this when we reflect that such predicates have an opposite, but God has no opposite. Because affirmative theology is merely metaphorical it is not in conflict with negative theology, which is literally true.

[2] See my *The God of the Philosophers* (Oxford: Clarendon Press, 1979), 38–48.
[3] See above, p. 282.

hIC . TITVLVS . EST .
LIBRI . HVI° . | OISPVTA
TIO . ABBATIS . ThEODORI .
GENERE . GRECI . ARTE .
PhILOSOPhI . CV̄ . IOhE . VIRO .
ERVDITISSIMO . ROMANE
ECCLESIE . ARCHIDIACO
DO . GENERE . SCOThO .

THEODORVS

IOhANNES .

John Scotus Eriugena (on the right) disputing with a Greek abbot Theodore.

According to Eriugena, God is not good but more than good, not wise but more than wise, not eternal but more than eternal. This language, of course, does not really add anything, except a tone of awe, to the denial that any of these predicates are literally true of God. Eriugena even goes as far as to say that God is not God but more than God. So too with the individual persons of the Trinity: the Father is not a Father except metaphorically.

Among the Aristotelian categories that, according to Eriugena, are to be denied of God are those of action and passion. God neither acts nor is acted upon, except metaphorically: strictly he neither moves nor is moved, neither loves nor is loved. The Bible tells us that God loves and is loved, but that has to be interpreted in the light of reason. Reason is superior to authority; authority is derived from reason and not vice versa; reason does not require any confirmation from authority. Reason tells us that the Bible is not using nouns and verbs in their proper sense, but using allegories and metaphors to go to meet our childish intelligence. 'Nothing can be said properly about God, since he surpasses every intellect, who is better known by not knowing, of whom ignorance is the true knowledge, who is more truly and faithfully denied in all things than affirmed' (*Periphyseon*, 1).

Our knowledge of God, such as it is, is derived both from the metaphorical statements of theology and from 'theophanies', or manifestations of God to particular persons, such as the visions of the prophets. God's essence is unknown to men and angels: indeed, it is unknown to God himself. Just as I, a human being, know *that* I am, but not *what* I am, so God does not know what he is. If he did, he would be able to define himself; but the infinite cannot be defined. It is no insult to God to say that he does not know what he is; for he is not a *what* (*Periphyseon*, 2).

In describing the relation between God and his creatures Eriugena uses language which is easily interpreted as a form of pantheism, and it was this that led to his condemnation by a Pope three and a half centuries later. God, he says, may be said to be created in creatures, to be made in the things he makes, and to begin to be in the things that begin to be (*Periphyseon*, 1. 12). Just as our intellect creates its own life by engaging in actual thinking, so too God, in giving life to creatures, is making a life for himself. To those who regarded such statements as flatly incompatible with Christian orthodoxy, Eriugena could no doubt have replied that, like all other positive statements about God, they were only metaphors.

Eriugena took his ideas of negative and positive theology from pseudo-Dionysius, but he developed those ideas in a novel and adventurous way. His work reaches a level of agnosticism not to be paralleled among Christian philosophers for centuries to come. His manner of approaching the realm of religious mystery will not be seen again in the history of philosophy until we encounter Nicholas of Cusa in the fifteenth century.

Islamic Arguments for God's Existence

Meanwhile, in the Islamic world philosophers were taking a more robust attitude to natural theology. Eriugena's contemporary al-Kindi was prepared to offer a series of elaborate and systematic proofs for the existence of God, based on establishing the finite nature of the world we live in. In his *First Philosophy*, drawing on some of the arguments of John Philoponus, known to Arabs as Yahya al-Nahwi, al-Kindi proceeds as follows.

Suppose that the physical world were infinite in quantity. If we take out of it a finite quantity, is what is left finite or infinite? If finite, then if we restore what has been taken out, we have only a finite quantity, since the addition of two finite quantities cannot make an infinite one. If infinite, then if we restore what has been taken out, we will have two infinite bodies, one (the original) smaller than the other (the restored whole). But this is absurd. So the universe must be finite in space.

Similar considerations show that the universe is finite in time. Time is quantitative, and an actually infinite quantity cannot exist. If time were infinite, then an infinite number of prior times must have preceded the present moment. But an infinite number cannot be traversed; so if time were infinite we would never have got to the present moment, which is absurd.

If time is finite, then the universe must have had a beginning in time; for the universe cannot exist without time. But if the universe had a beginning, then it must have had a cause other than itself. This cause must be the cause of the multiplicity to be found in the universe, and this al-Kindi calls the True One. This, he tells us is the cause of the beginning of coming to be in the universe, and is the cause of the unity that holds each creature together. 'The True One is therefore the First, the Creator who holds everything he has created, and whatever is freed from his hold and power reverts and perishes.'[4]

Christians as well as Muslims found it convenient that philosophical arguments could be offered for the creation of the world in time, so that the believer did not need to take this simply on faith, on the authority of Genesis or the Quran. The arguments which al-Kindi brought into Islam from Philoponus returned into the Christian world in the high Middle Ages, and their validity, as we shall see, became a matter of debate among the major scholastics.

Not all Muslim philosophers agreed that the world was created in time. Avicenna believed that God created by necessity: he is absolute goodness, and goodness by its nature radiates outwards. But if God is necessarily a creator, then creation must be eternal just as God is eternal. But though the material world is coeternal with God, it is nonetheless caused by God— not directly, but via the successive emanation of intelligences that culminates in the tenth intelligence that is the creator of matter and the giver of forms.[5]

Though the world is eternal, it is still possible to prove the existence of God by a consideration of contingency and necessity. For Avicenna there is a sense in which all things are necessary, since everything is a necessary creation of an eternal God. But there is an important distinction to be made between things that exist necessarily of themselves and those that, considered in themselves, are contingent. Starting with this distinction, Avicenna offers a proof that there must be at least one thing that is necessarily existent of itself.

Start with any entity you choose—it can be anything in heaven or on earth. If this is necessarily existent of itself, then our thesis is proved. If it is contingently existent of itself, then it is necessarily existent through something else. This second entity is necessarily existent either of itself, or through something else. If through something else, then there is a third entity, and so on. However long the series is, it cannot end with something that is of itself contingent; for that, and thus the whole series, would need a cause to explain its existence. Even if the complete causal series is infinite, it must contain at least one cause that is necessarily existent of itself, because

[4] See William Lane Craig, *The Kalam Cosmological Argument* (London: Macmillan, 1979), 19–36.
[5] See above, p. 224.

if it contained only contingent causes it would need an external cause and thus not be complete.

To show that a being necessarily existent of itself is God, Avicenna has to prove that such a being (which he henceforth calls, for short, 'necessary being') must possess the defining attributes of divinity. In the seventh section of the first tractate of his *Metaphysics* Avicenna argues that there can be at most one necessary being; in the eighth tractate he develops the other attributes of the unique necessary being. It is perfect, it is pure goodness, it is truth, it is pure intelligence; it is the source of everything else's beauty and splendour (*Metaph.* 8. 368).

The most important feature of the necessary being is that it does not have an essence which is other than its existence.[6] If it did, there would have to be a cause to unite the essence with the existence, and the necessary being would be not necessary but caused. Since it has no essence other than its existence, we can say that it does not have an essence at all, but is pure being. And if it does not have an essence, then it does not belong in any genus: God and creatures have nothing in common and 'being' cannot be applied to necessary and contingent being in the same sense. Since essence and quiddity are the same, the supreme being does not have a quiddity: that is to say, there is no answer to the question 'What is God?' (*Metaph.* 8. 344–7).

Anselm's Proof of God

Avicenna's natural theology was enormously fertile: theories to be found in philosophers of religion during the succeeding ten centuries can often to be shown to be (often unwitting) developments of ideas that are first found in his writings. But one theologian whose ideas bear a remarkable resemblance to his had certainly never read him. This was Anselm, who was born four years before Avicenna's death, and who died forty years before Avicenna's works were translated into Latin.

---

[6] The Arabic word for existence, 'anniya', is translated into Latin as 'anitas'—it is what answers to the question 'An est = 'Is there a...?' just as *quidditas* is what answers to 'Quid est' = 'What is a...?' 'Anity' has never taken out English citizenship as 'Quiddity' has; if one wanted to coin a word it would have to be 'ifness'—what tells us *if* there is a God.

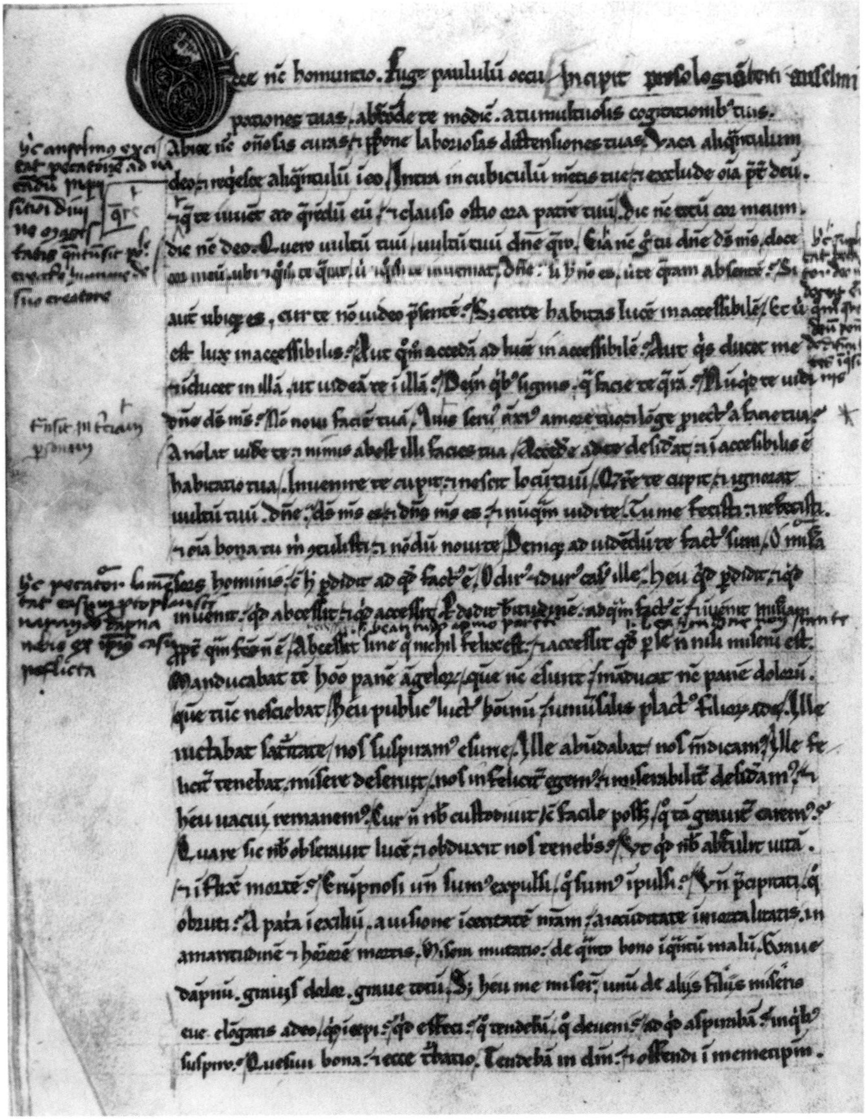

Anselm's *Proslogion,* in a twelfth century manuscript copy.

On the face of it, Avicenna's proof of the existence of a necessary being, and Anselm's 'ontological' argument for the existence of God, are very different from each other. But from a philosophical point of view they have a common structure: that is to say, they operate by straddling between the world we live in and some other kind of world. Avicenna argues from a consideration of possible worlds and argues that God must exist in the actual world; Anselm starts from a consideration of imaginary worlds and argues that God must exist in the real world. Both of them assume that an entity can be identified as one and the same entity whether or not it actually exists: they believe in what has been called, centuries later, trans-world identity. Both of them, therefore, violate the principle that there is no individuation without actualization.

The ontological argument is thus stated by Anselm:

We believe that thou art something than which nothing greater can be conceived. Suppose there is no such nature, according to what the fool says in his heart *There is no God* (Ps. 14. 1). But at any rate this very fool, when he hears what I am saying— something than which nothing greater can be conceived—understands what he hears. What he understands is in his understanding, even if he does not understand that it exists. For, it is one thing for an object to be in the understanding, and another to understand that that object exists . . . Even the fool, then, is bound to agree that there exists, if only in the understanding, something than which nothing greater can be conceived; because he hears this and understands it, and whatever is understood is in the understanding. But for sure, that than which nothing greater can be conceived cannot exist in the understanding alone. For suppose it exists in the understanding alone: then it can be thought to exist in reality, which is greater. Therefore, if that than which nothing greater can be conceived exists in the understanding alone, that very thing than which nothing greater can be conceived is a thing than which something greater can be conceived. But this is impossible. Therefore it is beyond doubt that there exists, both in the understanding and in reality, a being than which nothing greater can be conceived. (*Proslogion*, c. 2)

In presenting this argument Anselm says that he prefers it to the arguments he put forward earlier in his *Monologion* because it is much more immediate. His earlier argument—to the effect that beings dependent on other beings must depend ultimately on a single independent being—bore a certain resemblance to Avicenna's argument from contingency and necessity. But the argument of the *Proslogion* marks an advance on Avicenna's natural theology. Whereas Avicenna said that God's *essence* entailed his existence, Anselm argues that the very *concept* of God makes manifest that he exists. An opponent of Avicenna can deny the reality of both God and God's essence; but someone who denies the existence of Anselm's God seems clearly enmeshed in confusion. If he does not have the concept of God, then he does not know what he is denying; if he has the concept of God, then he is contradicting himself.

From Anselm's day to the present time, his readers have debated whether the *Proslogion* argument is valid; and highly intelligent philosophers have found it difficult to make up their mind. Bertrand Russell tells us in his autobiography that as a young man a sudden conviction of the validity of the ontological argument struck him with such force that he nearly fell off the bicycle he was riding at the time. Later, Russell would quote the refutation of the ontological argument as one of the few incontrovertible instances of progress in philosophy. 'This [argument] was invented by Anselm, rejected by Thomas Aquinas, accepted by Descartes, refuted by Kant, and reinstated by Hegel. I think it may be said quite decisively that, as a result of analysis of the concept "existence", modern logic has proved this argument invalid.'[7] But the argument was not as definitively settled as Russell thought. When a later generation of logicians developed the modal logic of possible worlds, theistic philosophers made use of this logic to resurrect the ontological argument.[8]

Criticism of Anselm's proof began in his lifetime. A monk from a neighbouring monastery, Gaunilo by name, said that if the argument was sound one could prove by the same route that the most fabulously beautiful island must exist, since otherwise one would be able to imagine one more fabulously beautiful. Anselm answered that the cases were different. The most beautiful imaginable island can be conceived not to exist, since there is no contradiction in supposing it to go out of existence. But God cannot in that way be conceived not to exist: anything, however grand and sublime, that passed out of existence would not be God.

The weak element in Anselm's argument is the one that seems most innocuous: his definition of God. How does he know that 'something than which no greater can be conceived' expresses a coherent notion? May the expression not be as misbegotten as 'a natural number than which no

---

[7] B. Russell, *History of Western Philosophy* (London: Allen & Unwin, 1961), 752.

[8] See A. Plantinga, *The Nature of Necessity* (Oxford: Oxford University Press, 1974).

greater can be found'? Of course we understand each of the words that goes into his definition, and there seems nothing wrong with its syntax. But that is not enough to ensure that the description expresses an intelligible thought. Philosophers in the twentieth century have discussed the expression 'the least natural number not nameable in fewer than twenty-two syllables'. This sounds like a readily intelligible designation of a number—until the paradox dawns on us that the expression itself names the number in twenty-one syllables.

Anselm himself seems to have sensed a problem here. He is at pains to point out that his definition does not imply that God is the greatest conceivable thing. Indeed, God is *not* conceivable: he is greater than anything that can be conceived. So far, so good: there is nothing contradictory in saying that than which no greater can be conceived is itself too great for conception. A Boeing 747 is something than which nothing larger can fit into my garage. That does not mean that a Boeing 747 will fit into my garage—it is far too large to do so.

The real problem for Anselm is in explaining how something that cannot be conceived can be in the understanding at all. In response to this difficulty, he distinguishes, in chapter 4 of the *Proslogion*, different ways in which we can think of, or conceive, a thing. We think of a thing in one way, he says, when we think of an expression signifying it; we think of it in a different way when we understand what the thing really is in itself. The fool, he implies, is only thinking of the words; the believer is thinking of God in himself. But this is not his last word, because he goes on to say that not only the fool, but every human being, fails to understand the reality that lies behind the words 'that than which nothing greater can be thought'.

Anselm's last word on this topic comes in the ninth chapter of the reply that he wrote to Gaunilo's objection:

Even if it were true that that than which no greater can be conceived cannot itself be conceived or understood, it would not follow that it would be false that 'that than which no greater can be thought' could be thought and understood. Nothing prevents something being called ineffable, even though that which is ineffable cannot itself be said; and likewise the unthinkable can be thought, even though what is rightly called unthinkable cannot be thought. So, when 'that than which no greater can be conceived' is spoken of, there is no doubt that what is heard can be conceived and understood, even though the thing itself, than which no greater can be conceived, cannot itself be conceived or understood.

Subtle as this defence is, it is in fact tantamount to surrender. The fundamental premiss of the ontological argument was that God himself existed in the fool's understanding. But if, as we now learn, all that is in the understanding of the fool (or indeed of any of us) is a set of words, then the argument cannot get started.

Omnipotence in Damiani and Abelard

A topic that exercised philosophers and theologians in the eleventh and twelfth centuries was the nature of divine omnipotence. At first, it seems easy enough to define what it means to say that God is omnipotent: it means that he can do everything. But difficulties quickly crowd in. Can he sin? Can he make contradictories true together? Can he undo the past? The discussion ranged between extremes. Peter Damiani in the eleventh century extended omnipotence as broadly as possible; Abelard in the twelfth defined it very narrowly.

St Jerome once wrote to the nun Eustochium, 'God who can do everything cannot restore a virgin after she has fallen.' In his treatise *On Divine Omnipotence* Damiani objects to this. In a discussion over dinner, he tells us, his friend Desiderio of Cassino had defended Jerome, saying that the only reason God could not restore virgins was that he did not want to. This, Damiani says, will not do. 'If God cannot do any of the things that he does not want to do, since he never does anything except what he wants to do, it follows that he cannot do anything at all except what he does. As a result we shall have to say frankly that God is not making it rain today because he cannot.' God cannot do bad things, like lying; but making a virgin out of a non-virgin is not a bad thing, so there is no reason why God cannot do it.

Damiani was taken by many to be arguing that God could change the past, to bring about (for instance) that Rome had never been built. This, it was objected, was tantamount to attributing to God the ability to make contradictories true together: Rome was built, and Rome was not built. It is possible, however, that in attributing to God the power to restore a virgin what Damiani had in mind was a physical operation rather than any genuine undoing of the past. The reason why God does not restore the marks of virginity to those who have lost them, he says, is to deter lecherous young men and women by making their sins easy to detect. He rejects the idea that God's power extends to contradiction. 'Nothing can both be and not be; but what is not in the nature of things is undoubtedly nothing: you are a hard master, trying to make God bring about what is not his, namely nothing.' But though God cannot change the past, he can bring about the past. He cannot change the present or the future either: what is, is, and what will be, will be. That does not prevent many things from being contingent, such as that the weather today will be fine or rainy (PL 145, 595 ff.).

Abelard pursued the topic further. He raised the question whether God can make more things, or better things, than the things he has made, and whether he can refrain from acting as he does. The question, he said, seems difficult to answer yes or no. If God can make more and better things than he has, is it not mean of him not to do so? After all, it costs him no effort. Whatever he does, or refrains from doing, is done or left undone for the best possible reasons, however hidden from us these may be. So it seems that God cannot act except in the way he has in fact acted. On the other hand, if we take any sinner on his way to damnation, it is clear that he could be better than he is; for if not, he is not to be blamed, still less to be damned, for his sins. But if he could be better, then God could make him better; so is something that God could make better than he has (*Theologia Scholarium*, 516).

Abelard opts for the first horn of the dilemma. Suppose it is now not raining: this must be because God so wills. That must mean that now is not a good time for rain. So if we say that God could now make it rain, we are attributing to God the power to do something foolish. Whatever God wants to do, he can, but if he doesn't want to, then he can't. It is true that we poor creatures can act otherwise than we do; but this is not something to be proud of, it is a mark of our infirmity, like our ability to walk, eat, and sin. We would be better off without the ability to do what we ought not to do.

In answer to the argument that sinners must be capable of salvation if they are to be justly punished, Abelard rejects the step from 'This sinner can be saved by God' to 'God can save this sinner'. The underlying logical principle—that '*p* if and only if *q*' entails 'possibly *p* if and only if possibly *q*'—is invalid, he claims, and encounters many counter-examples. A sound is heard if and only if somebody hears it; but a sound may be audible

Grosseteste's meticulous scholarship is shown in these marginal additions, in his handwriting, to the manuscript of a theological text.

without there being anyone able to hear it. One might object that God would deserve no gratitude from men if he cannot do otherwise than he does. But Abelard has an answer. God is not acting under compulsion: his will is identical with the goodness that necessitates him to act as he does.

Abelard's discussion—here only briefly summarized—is a remarkable example of dialectical brilliance, introducing or reinventing a number of distinctions of importance in many contexts of modal logic. However, it can hardly be said to amount to a convincing analysis or defence of the concept of omnipotence, and it certainly did not satisfy his contemporaries, in particular St Bernard. One of the propositions condemned at Sens ran: God can act and refrain from acting only in the manner and at the time that he actually does act and refrain from acting, and in no other way (DB 374).

Grosseteste on Omniscience

In the thirteenth century attention shifted from the problems of divine omnipotence to those of divine omniscience. Robert Grosseteste wrote a short but subtle tract on the freedom of the will, *De Libero Arbitrio*, which begins by setting out the following problem. Consider the argument 'Whatever is known by God either is or was or will be. A (some future contingent) is known by God. Therefore A is or was or will be. But it is not and it was not, therefore it will be.' Both premisses are necessary; therefore the conclusion is necessary, since what follows from necessary premisses is itself necessary. So A itself must be necessary, and there is no real contingency in the world.

How are we to deal with this argument? There is no doubt, Grosseteste says, that the major premiss is necessary. But is the minor a necessary truth? Some have argued that it is false on the ground that God knows only universals. But this is impious. Others have argued that it is false because knowledge is only of what is, but future contingents are not there to be known. But this would make God's knowledge subject to change: there will be things that he does not know now but will know later.

Shall we say, then, that the minor is true but contingent? If so, then there will be a case where God knows that *p*, but can fail to know that *p*. But once again, if God were able to pass from a state of knowing that *p* to not knowing that *p*, then his knowledge would be subject to variation. One might argue that it is indeed variable, in the following way: 'God knows that I will sit. Once I have sat he will no longer know that I sit, but that I have sat. So he now knows something that he will later not know' (*De Lib. Arb.* 160).

Grosseteste dismisses this sophism. It does not show that God's knowledge varies in relation to the essences of things themselves; it shows only the vicissitudes of human tenses. We must say that whatever God now knows he cannot later not know, and this is so no matter whether the object of his knowledge is now in existence or not. Neither 'Antichrist will come' nor 'God knows that antichrist will come' can change from true to false. Suppose 'Antichrist will come' now changed from being true to being false. If it is now false, it must always have been false, which conflicts with the hypothesis that it has changed. Hence it cannot change in any way other than by its coming true; and the same applies to 'God knows that antichrist will come' (*De Lib. Arb.* 165).

Considering the same question, whether God always knows what he ever knows, Peter Lombard in his *Sentences* gave a similar answer. The prophets who foretold that Christ was to be born, and the Christians who now celebrate the fact that Christ has been born, he says, are dealing with the same truth.

> What was then future is now past, so the words used to designate it need to be changed, just as at different times, when speaking of one and the same day, we designate it when it is still in the future as 'tomorrow', and when it is present as 'today', and when it is past as 'yesterday'...As Augustine says, the times have varied and so the words have been changed, but not our faith. (I *Sent.* 41. 3)

This, however, leaves Grosseteste's initial problem unresolved. In ancient Israel, for instance, someone might argue 'Isaiah has foreseen the captivity of the Jews. So he cannot not have foreseen the captivity of the Jews. So the captivity of the Jews cannot not take place.' Must we say therefore either that everything happens of necessity, or that what is necessarily entailed by necessary truths is itself merely contingent?

The solution, for Grosseteste, lies in distinguishing between two kinds of necessity. It is strongly necessary that *p* if it is not possible that it should ever have been the case that not-*p*. It is weakly necessary that *p* if it is not possible that it should henceforth become the case that not-*p*. In our argument, the minor and the conclusion are weakly necessary, but not strongly necessary. Weak necessity is compatible with freedom, so the argument does not destroy free will. On the other hand, we preserve the principle that what follows from what is necessary is itself necessary, but necessary only in the same sense as its premises are (*De Lib. Arb.* 168).

Aquinas on God's Eternal Knowledge and Power

Grosseteste's solution, subtle though it is, did not satisfy later medieval thinkers. Thomas Aquinas rejected the view, common to Grosseteste and Lombard, that 'Christ will be born' and 'Christ has been born' were one and the same proposition. He describes the supporters of this view as 'Ancient nominalists'.

The ancient nominalists said that 'Christ is born', 'Christ will be born' and 'Christ has been born' were one and the same proposition (*enuntiabile*) because the same reality is signified by all three, namely, the birth of Christ. They deduced from this that God now knows whatever he has known, because he now knows Christ born, which has the same signification as 'Christ will be born'. But this view is false, for two reasons. First of all, if the parts of speech in a sentence differ, then the proposition differs. Second, it would follow that any proposition that was once true would be forever true, which goes against Aristotle's dictum that the very same sentence 'Socrates is sitting' is true when he sits and false when he gets up. (*ST* 1a 14. 15)

So if we take the object of God's knowledge to be propositional, it is not true that whatever God once knew he now knows. But this does not mean that God's knowledge is fickle: it simply means that his knowledge is not exercised through propositions in the way that our knowledge is.

Aquinas' own solution to the problem of reconciling divine foreknowledge with contingency is presented in two stages. The first stage, which has been common currency since Boethius, appeals to two different ways in which modal propositions can be analysed.[9] The proposition 'Whatever is known by God is necessarily true' is ambiguous: it may mean (A) or (B):

(A) 'Whatever is known by God is true' is a necessary truth.
(B) Whatever is known by God is a necessary truth.

(A), in Aquinas' terminology, is a proposition *de dicto*: it takes the original statement as a meta-statement about the status of the proposition in quotation marks. (B), on the other hand, is a proposition *de re*, a first-order statement. According to Aquinas (A) is true and (B) is false; but only (B) is incompatible with God's knowing contingent truths.

So far, so good. But Aquinas realizes that he faces a more serious difficulty in reconciling divine foreknowledge with contingency in the world. In any true conditional proposition, if the antecedent is necessarily true, then the consequent is also necessarily true. 'If it has come to God's knowledge that such and such a thing will happen, then such and such a thing will happen' is a necessary truth. The antecedent, if true, is necessarily true, for it is in the past tense, and what is past cannot be changed. Therefore, the consequent is also a necessary truth; so the future thing, whatever it is, will happen of necessity.

[9] See on Abelard, p. 127 above.

Aquinas' solution to this difficulty depends on the thesis that God is outside time: his life is measured not by time, but by eternity. Eternity, which has no parts, overlaps the whole of time; consequently, the things that happen at different times are all present together to God. An event is known *as future* only when there is a relation of future to past between the knowledge of the knower and the happening of the event. But the relation between God's knowledge and any event in time is always one of simultaneity. A contingent event, as it comes to God's knowledge, is not future but present; and as present it is necessary; for what is the case is the case and is beyond anyone's power to alter (*ST* 1a 14. 13).

Aquinas' solution is essentially the same as Boethius', and he uses the same illustration to explain how God's knowledge is above time. 'A man who is walking along a road cannot see those who are coming after him; but a man who looks down from a hill upon the whole length of the road can see at the same time all those who are travelling along it.' Aquinas' solution is open to the same objection as Boethius': the notion of eternity as simultaneous with every point in time collapses temporal distinctions, on earth as well as in heaven, and makes time unreal. Aquinas cannot be said to have succeeded in reconciling contingency, and human freedom in particular, with divine omniscience.

Aquinas was more successful in defending the coherence of the notion of a different divine attribute, omnipotence. His first attempt at a definition is to say that God is omnipotent because he can do everything that is logically possible. This will not do, because there are many counter-examples that Aquinas himself would have accepted. It is logically possible that Troy did not fall, but Aquinas (unlike Grosseteste) did not think that there was any sense in which God could change the past. In fact, Aquinas preferred the formulation 'God's power is infinite' to the formulation 'God is omnipotent'. 'God possesses every logically possible power' is more coherent than the earlier formulation, but it is still only an approximation to a correct definition, because some logically possible powers— such as the power to weaken, sicken, and die—clash with other divine attributes.

Can God do evil? Can God do better than he does? Aquinas answers that God can only do what is fitting and just to do; but because of the condemnation of Abelard, he has to accept that God can do other than he does. He explains how the two propositions are to be reconciled.

The words 'fitting and just' can be understood in two senses. In the first sense 'fitting and just' is taken in primary conjunction with the verb 'is', and is thus restricted in reference to what is the case at present, and is assigned to God's power in this restricted sense. So restricted, the proposition is false: for its sense is this: 'God can only do what is fitting and just as things are'. But if 'fitting and just' is taken in primary conjunction with the verb 'can', which has an amplificatory force, and only subsequently in conjunction with the verb 'is', then the reference will be to a non-specific present, and the proposition will be true, understood in this sense: 'God can only do what, if He did it, would be fitting and just'. (1a 25. 5. 2)

If we prefer the idiom of possible worlds to the idiom of powers, we could make Aquinas' point as follows. In every possible world, what God does is fitting and just; it does not follow, nor is it true, that whatever God does is something that is fitting and just in every possible world.

Could God have made the world better? He could not have made it by any better method than he did; he made it in the wisest and best possible way. Could he have made men better? He could not have made human nature better than it is; creatures better by nature than we are would not be humans at all. But of any individual human, it is true that God could have made him better. And given any actual creature, however exalted, it is within God's power to make something better. There is no such thing as the best of all possible creatures, let alone the best of all possible worlds.

Aquinas' Proofs of God's Existence

In philosophical theology Aquinas is most often remembered not for his treatment of divine attributes such as omniscience and omnipotence, but for his endeavour to establish, by purely philosophical methods, the actual existence of God. Proofs of divine existence are to be met with in many places in his works: in the *De Potentia*, for instance, he takes, as the starting point of his proof, the taste of pepper and ginger. Wherever, he says, causes whose proper effects are diverse produce also a common effect, the additional common effect must be produced in virtue of some superior cause of which it is the proper effect. For example, pepper and ginger, besides producing their own proper effects, have it in common that they produce heat: they do this in virtue of the causality of fire, of which heat is the proper effect.

All created causes, while having their own proper effects that distinguish them one from another, also share in a single common effect which is being. Heat causes things to be hot, and a builder causes there to be a house. They have in common therefore that they cause being, and differ in that fire causes fire and a builder causes a house. There must, therefore, be some superior cause whose proper effect is being and in virtue of which everything else causes being. And this cause is God. (*DP* 7. 2c)

Better known are the Five Ways which are placed near the beginning of the *Summa Theologiae*: (1) motion in the world is only explicable if there is a first motionless mover; (2) the series of efficient causes in the world must lead to an uncaused cause; (3) contingent and corruptible beings must depend on an independent and incorruptible being; (4) the varying degrees of reality and goodness in the world must be approximations to a subsistent maximum of reality and goodness; (5) the ordinary teleology of non-conscious agents in the universe entails the existence of an intelligent universal orderer.[10]

None of the Five Ways is successful as a proof of God's existence: each one contains either a fallacy, or a premiss that is false or disputable. The first way depends on the premiss that whatever is in motion is moved by something else: a principle universally rejected since Newton. The series mentioned in the second way is not a series of causes through time (which Aquinas himself admitted could reach backwards for ever), but a series of simultaneous causes, like a man moving a stone by moving a crowbar; there is no reason why the first cause in such a series should be God rather than an ordinary human being. The third way contains a fallacious inference from 'Every thing has some time at which it does not exist' to 'There is some time at which nothing exists'. The fourth way depends on a Platonic, and ultimately incoherent, notion of Being. The fifth way is much the most persuasive of the arguments, but its key premiss, 'Things that lack awareness do not tend towards a goal unless directed by something with awareness and intelligence, like an arrow by an archer', needs, since Darwin, more supporting argument than we are given.

Many attempts have been made, and no doubt will be made, to restate the Five Ways in a manner that eliminates false premisses and fallacious reasoning. But one of the most promising recent attempts to reinstate

[10] For a detailed treatment of the Five Ways, see my book *The Five Ways* (London. Routledge, 1969).

Aquinas' proofs of God's existence takes its start not from the *Summa Theologiae* but from the *Summa contra Gentiles*.[11]

The argument runs thus. Every existing thing has a reason for its existence, either in the necessity of its own nature, or in the causal efficacy of some other beings. We would never, in the case of an ordinary existent, tolerate a blithe announcement that there was simply no reason for its existence; and it is irrational to abandon this principle when the existing thing in question is all-pervasive, like the universe.

Suppose that A is an existing natural thing, a member of a (perhaps beginningless) series of causes and effects that in its own nature is disposed indifferently to either existence or non-existence. The reason for A's existing must be in the causal efficacy of other beings. However many beings may be contributing to A's present existence, they could not be the reason for it if there were not some first cause at the head of the series— something such that everything other than it must be traced back to it as the cause of its being.

Persuasive as it is, this argument contains a key weakness. What is meant by saying that A is 'disposed indifferently to either existence or non-existence'? If it means 'disposed indifferently to going on existing or not', then the contingent beings of the everyday world, from which the argument starts, do not fit the bill. Contingent things aren't of their nature equally disposed to exist or not: on the contrary, most things naturally tend to remain in existence. On the other hand, if it means 'disposed indifferently to come into existence or not', then we lapse into absurdity: before A exists there isn't any such thing as a non-existing A to have, or to lack, a tendency to come into existence.

Duns Scotus' Metaphysical Proof of an Infinite Being

Flaws in Aquinas' proofs of God's existence were pointed out very shortly after his death. Among his critics was Duns Scotus, who offered his own proofs in their place. The one closest to the argument of the *Summa contra Gentiles* makes use of the concept of causality to prove the existence of a first cause. Suppose that we have something capable of being brought into existence. What could bring it into existence? It must be something, because

[11] See Norman Kretzmann, *The Metaphysics of Creation* (Oxford: Clarendon Press, 1999), 84–138.

nothing cannot cause anything. It must be something other than itself, for nothing can cause itself. Let us call that something else A. Is A itself caused? If not, it is a first cause, which is what we were looking for. If it is caused, let its cause be B. We can repeat the same argument with B. Then either we go on for ever, which is impossible, or we reach an absolute first cause.

Scotus, like Aquinas, makes a distinction between two kinds of causal series, one of which he calls 'essentially ordered', and the other 'accidentally ordered'. He does not deny the possibility of an unending regress of accidentally ordered causes, such as the series of human beings, each begotten by an earlier human. Such a series is only accidentally ordered. A father may be the cause of his son, but he is not the cause of his son's begetting his grandson. In an essentially ordered series, A not only causes B, which is the cause of C, but actually causes B to cause C. It is only in the case of essentially ordered series—e.g. a gardener moving earth by moving a spade—that an infinite regress is ruled out. An accidentally ordered series is, as it were, a horizontal series of causes; an essentially ordered series is a vertical hierarchy; and Scotus tells us, 'infinity is impossible in the ascending order' (*DPP* 4, p. 22).

Even after the two kinds of series have been distinguished, there seem several weaknesses in Scotus' argument, considered as a proof of the existence of God. In the first place, it seems, like the proof of the *Summa contra Gentiles* on one interpretation, to assume that it is sensible to talk of something non-existing as having, or lacking, the power of coming into existence.[12] In the second place, it is not clear why instead of a single infinite first cause the argument does not lead to a number of finite first causes.

Scotus in fact admits that he has not produced a proof of God; but the reason he gives is not either of the above. Unlike Aquinas, who took as his starting point the actual existence of causal sequences in the world, Scotus began simply with the mere possibility of causation. He did so deliberately, because he preferred to base his proof not on contingent facts of nature, but on purely abstract possibilities. If you start from mere physics, he believed, you will never get beyond the finite cosmos.

But the consequence of this is that the argument, up to this point, has proved only the possibility of a first cause: we still need to prove that it actually exists. Scotus in fact goes one better and offers to prove that it *must*

---

[12] See p. 203 above on objective possibility.

exist. A first cause, by definition, cannot be brought into existence by anything else; so either it just exists or it does not. If it does not exist, why does it not? If its existence is possible at all, there is nothing that could cause its non-existence. But we have shown that it is possible; therefore it must exist. Moreover, it must be infinite; because there cannot be anything that could limit its power. Scotus accepts that an infinite being is possible only if there is no incoherence in the notion of such an entity. It is a weakness, he thinks, in Anselm's argument that he does not show that 'that than which no greater can be thought' is a coherent concept. But if there were any incoherence between the notions of being and infinity, Scotus claims, it would long ago have been detected. The ear can quickly detect a discord, and the intellect even more easily detects incompatibilities (*Ord.* 4. 162–3).

Even if we concede to Scotus that the notion of God is coherent, his argument seems to fail, by trading on different senses of 'possible': logical possibility, epistemic possibility, and real possibility. From the mere logical possibility of God's existence, nothing follows about whether he actually exists. An agnostic may admit that perhaps, for all we know, there is a God: that is what is meant by 'epistemic possibility'. But from logical possibility and epistemic possibility, nothing follows about real possibility, still less about actuality. 'It is possible that there is a God' is not the same as 'It is possible for God to come into being'.[13] Since the concept of godhead includes everlasting existence, nothing has the power to bring any god into existence. If God exists, he must always have existed. Nor does anything have the power to prevent a god from existing, or to terminate the existence of a god. Such powers are all conceptually impossible, because of the nature of the concept *God*. But the absence of such powers shows nothing at all about whether that concept is or is not instantiated.

For Scotus, the most important element in the concept of God is infinity. The notion of infinity is simpler, more basic, than other concepts such as goodness: it is constitutive of divine being, not just an attribute of divinity. Infinity is the defining characteristic of all the divine attributes: divine goodness is infinite goodness, divine truth is infinite truth, and so on. Each divine perfection 'has its formal perfection from the infinity of the essence as its root and foundation' (*Oxon.* 4. 3. 1. 32). Scotus proves the

---

[13] The difference between the two statements is much more obvious in English than in the medieval Latin equivalent.

existence of God by proving the existence of an infinite first principle; only after establishing the infinity of God does he proceed to derive other divine attributes such as that of uniqueness and simplicity.

Scotus did not believe that all the divine attributes could be proved by natural reason. Reason could show that God was infinite, unique, simple, excellent, and perfect. Reason could not, however, show that God was omnipotent, because revelation had shown that God had the power to do things that reason could never have guessed at (e g beget a son). Reason could, however, show that God had the power to create a world out of nothing, and that in so creating he enjoyed absolute freedom.

The infinite God, reflecting on his own essence, sees it as capable of being reproduced or imitated in various possible partial ways: it is this that, before all creation, produces the essences of things, existing in the form of divine ideas. This reflection is an exercise of the divine intellect; it is not a free action of the divine will.

The divine intellect, as, in some way, that is, logically prior to the act of the divine will, produces those objects in their intelligible being and so in respect of them it seems to be a merely natural cause, since God is not a free cause in respect of anything but that which presupposes in some way his will or an act of his will. (*Ord* 1. 163)

The essences in the divine mind, as Scotus conceives them, are in themselves neither single nor multiple, neither universal nor particular. They resemble—and not by accident—Avicenna's *horseness*, which was not identical either with any of the many individual horses, nor with the universal concept of horse in the human mind. By a sovereign and unaccountable act of will, God decrees that some of these essences should be instantiated; and thus the world is created. The decree of his will is eternal, unchangeable; but the execution of the decree takes place in time (*Ord.* 1. 566). We cannot look for any reason for God's creative decree: he does not create for the sake of any good, since all good in creatures is the consequence of his creation.

Scotus, Ockham, and Valla on Divine Foreknowledge

God's knowledge of what is possible, as we have seen, precedes the act of will by which he brings chosen possible entities into existence; but his knowledge of what is actual depends solely on his knowledge of his own will. Scotus rejects Aquinas' view that God is omniscient because he sees the whole of time as present to him all at once. Anything that is present to God, Scotus argues, cannot be genuinely past or future; the way things appear to God is the way they really are. For Scotus, God knows what has been the case, what is the case, and what will be the case, because he is aware of his own decree determining what has been, what is, and what will be. It may well be thought that such an explanation of divine omniscience, and in particular of divine foreknowledge, leaves no room for the exercise of human free will. Scotus takes this complaint very seriously, but in the end rejects it.

Consider, he says, the following argument: 'God believes I will sit tomorrow; but I will not sit tomorrow; therefore God is mistaken'. This argument is clearly valid. We must surely therefore say that the following variation on the argument is also valid: 'God believes I will sit tomorrow; but it is possible that I will not sit tomorrow; therefore God can be mistaken'. We are simply employing the schema: If p and q entail r, then p and *possibly* q entail *possibly* r. Since God cannot be mistaken, the argument seems to show that it is not possible for me to do anything other than what God has foreseen I will in fact do.

Scotus' solution to this argument is to deny the validity of the schema involved. He gives a counter-example, which can be rendered as follows. Suppose there are two suitcases A and B, each of which I can carry. But suppose further that I am carrying my suitcase A. In these circumstances, to carry your suitcase B would be to carry both A and B, which is beyond my strength. 'I am carrying A and I am carrying B' obviously entails 'I am carrying A and B'. But 'I am carrying A' and 'I can carry B' do not between them entail 'I can carry A and B' (*Lect.* 17. 509).

Scotus' response is effective, and it is applicable in many contexts other than the theological one. There are many cases where I can do some action X but will not. In such cases, there will be descriptions of doing X that will describe it in terms of the fact that I am not, in fact, going to do X. Thus, let us suppose that I am going to eat my cake. I can, if I want, have my cake, but I am not going to have my cake, I am going to eat it. Given the facts of the case, to have my cake would be to have it and eat it too. But I can, if I want, have it. So, if the principle is valid, I can have my cake and eat it too. Scotus' demolition of the principle in order to show that human freedom is compatible with divine decrees provides the essential underpinning for any form of compatibilism, that is to say, the attempt to show that freedom and determinism are not the contradictory opposites that they appear at first sight to be.

Ockham rejected Scotus' method of reconciling divine foreknowledge with human freedom, just as Scotus had rejected Aquinas'. God, Scotus says, foresees future events by being aware of his own intentions, and future events are contingent, not necessary, because God's decrees about the world are themselves contingent. This, Ockham replies, may be sufficient to preserve contingency, but it does not suffice to leave the decisions of creatures free while establishing, at the same time, a basis for foreknowledge of them.[14]

Ockham's criticism of Scotus' position is forceful, but he does not himself offer in its place any solution to the problem of divine foreknowledge and human freedom. He makes clear, in fact, that he sympathizes with the position (which he wrongly attributes to Aristotle) that statements about future contingents lack a truth-value. But unless they are already true, future contingent propositions cannot be known, even by God. In spite of this philosophical reasoning, Ockham says, we are obliged to hold that God evidently knows all future contingents. A treatise exclusively devoted to the problem, *Tractatus de Praedestinatione et de Praescientia*, concludes, 'I say that it is impossible to express clearly the way in which God knows future contingent events. However, it must be held that he does know them, but contingently.'[15]

This was just one instance of the combination of devout fideism with philosophical agnosticism that is characteristic of Ockham's theology. He is critical of the arguments for God's existence to be found in Aquinas and Scotus. He agrees with Scotus that without a univocal concept of being, it would be impossible even to conceive of God (III *Sent.* 9, R); but he agrees with Aquinas that the primary object of the human mind is not being, but the nature of material substance (I *Sent.* 3. 1d).

Philosophical reason cannot prove that God is the first efficient cause of everything. There must, indeed, be a first cause, if there is not to be an infinite causal regress; but it need not be God, it could be a heavenly body

---

[14] Ockham also rejected Scotus' non-manifest power. See p. 245 above.

[15] Trans. Norman Kretzmann and Marilyn Adams (Chicago: Appleton-Century-Crofts, 1969).

or some finite spirit (*Quodl.* 2, p. 1; *OTh.* 6. 108). But even the impossibility of an infinite causal regress is open to question—why should there not be a series of begotten and begetter stretching forever backwards? Instead of asking what brings something into existence we might do better to ask what keeps it in existence; and Ockham agrees that it is implausible to think that there is an infinite series of simultaneous entities currently keeping us in existence. This can be shown, he thinks, not with absolute certainty, but by arguments that are reasonable enough (I *Sent.* 2. 10).

This is as far as Ockham is prepared to go in allowing the possibility of a proof of God's existence; and even this, he maintains, is insufficient to establish that there is only one God. A fortiori we cannot prove by natural reason that God is infinite, eternal, omnipotent, and creator of heaven and earth. With regard to God's knowledge, we cannot prove philosophically that God knows actual things other than himself, let alone their future free actions. All these truths about God have to be accepted as matters of faith.

The reconciliation of freedom and providence was a problem that occupied humanist thinkers no less than scholastics. Lorenzo Valla, Nicholas V's court philologist, wrote in 1439 a dialogue on free will, critical of Boethius' *Consolation*. It starts from a well-worn problem: 'If God foresees that Judas will be a traitor, it is impossible for him not to become a traitor'. For most of its length the dialogue follows moves and counter-moves familiar from scholastic discussions: it reads like a child's version of Scotus. But, near the end, two surprising moves are made.

First, Valla introduces two pagan gods into the discussion. Apollo predicted to the Roman king Tarquin that he would suffer exile and death. In response to Tarquin's complaints, Apollo said that he wished his prophecy were happier, but he merely predicted, he did not decide, Tarquin's fate. Any recriminations should be addressed to Jupiter. The introduction of the gods is not just a humanist flourish: it enables Valla, without blasphemy, to separate out the two attributes of omniscient wisdom and irresistible will which, in Christian theology, are inseparable in the one God.

The second surprise is that when the going gets really tough, Valla takes refuge in Scripture quotation. He turns to the passage in Paul's Epistle to the Romans about the predestination of Jacob and the reprobation of Esau. 'O the depth of the riches both of the wisdom and knowledge of God! How unsearchable are his judgements and his ways past finding out.' Rather than offer a philosophical reconciliation between divine providence and human freedom, Valla ends with a denunciation of the philosophers and above all of Aristotle. On this crucial topic of natural theology, both nominalist scholasticism and humanist scholarship reach the same dead end.

The Informed Ignorance of Nicholas of Cusa

Late medieval thought reaches a climax of agnosticism in Nicholas of Cusa's *De Docta Ignorantia*. No one since Socrates had emphasized so strongly that wisdom consists in awareness of the limits of one's knowledge. Brute ignorance is no virtue: but the process of learning is a gradually increasing awareness of how much one does not know. Truth is real enough: but we humans can only approach it asymptotically.

Truth does not admit of more or less, but stands absolute. Nothing other than truth itself can measure it with accuracy, just as a non-circle cannot measure a circle in its absolute being. Our intellect, which is not truth, can never comprehend truth so accurately that there does not remain the possibility of infinitely more accurate comprehension. Our intellect is related to the truth in the way that a polygon is to a circle: the more angles it contains, the more like a circle it is, but it never equates to the circle even if its angles are multiplied to infinity. (*DDI* 9)

What is true of the intellect's approach to truth in general is a fortiori true of its approach to the truth about God.

Cusa's paradigm of rational inquiry is measurement: we approach the unknown by measuring it against what we already know. But we cannot hope to measure the infinite, because there is no proportion between what is infinite and any finite thing. Every attempt we make to learn more about God reveals a new infinite gap between what we think and what God really is.

Our reason, guided by the principle of non-contradiction, proceeds by making distinctions. We distinguish, for instance, between great and small. But these distinctions are useless in inquiry about God. We may think, for instance, that God is the greatest of all things, the maximum. Certainly, God is something than which nothing can be greater. But God, who has no size at all, is also something than which nothing can be lesser. He is the minimum as well as the maximum. This is but one instance of a general principle: God is the union and coincidence of opposites (*DDI* 1. 4).

One of the pairs of opposites that coincide in God is the pair being–non-being. The maximum 'no more is than is not whatever is conceived to be. And it no more is not than is whatever is conceived not to be. It is one thing in such a way as to be all things, and it is all things in such a way as to be no thing. And it is maximally thus in such a way as to be also minimally thus' (*DDI* 1. 4). No doubt this all sounds very irrational. Cusa praises those philosophers who have distinguished between reason and intellect, regarding intellect as an intuitive faculty that can transcend the contradictions detected by reason. Literal language is incapable of grasping divine mystery: we must make use of metaphor and symbol. Cusa's preferred metaphors were mathematical. If we take a finite circle and gradually increase its diameter, the curvature of the circumference decreases. When the diameter reaches infinity, the circumference becomes absolutely straight. Thus a straight line (the maximum of straightness) is identical with an infinite circle (the minimum of curvature).

Other metaphors are used to describe the relation between God and the universe. All creatures are enfolded (*complicata*) in God; God is unfolded (*explicatus*) in all creatures. A creature stands in the same relation to God as my image in a mirror image is related to me—except that, with God and creatures, there is no mirror other than the image itself. Each creature not only mirrors God but images every other creature. Different creatures are closer or more distant images of God (*DDI* 2. 3).

Cusa, obviously, belongs in the tradition of the *via negativa*, going back to Dionysius the Areopagite. But his agnosticism goes further than that of his predecessors such as Eriugena. Cusa regards negative predicates as no less misleading than positive ones if they are applied to God. No name is apt for God. We cannot even call him 'the One', because for us oneness excludes otherness and plurality. If we exclude that exclusion, when calling God 'the One' what are we left with? We are still infinitely distant from naming God (*DDI* 1. 24). If we really come to grips with this reality, our informed ignorance will become sacred ignorance. That is the best that we humans can hope for here.

CHRONOLOGY

Some of these dates are approximate and others, especially in the earlier years, conjectural.

387	Conversion of St Augustine
430	Death of St Augustine
480	Birth of Boethius
525	Death of Boethius
529	Justinian closes Athens' schools
575	Death of John Philoponus
781	Alcuin meets Charlemagne
800	Charlemagne crowned in Rome
863	Eriugena's *Periphyseon*
980	Avicenna born
1077	Anselm's *Proslogion*
1140	Abelard condemned at Sens
1155	*Sentences* of Peter Lombard
1179	Averroes' *Harmony*
1188	Oxford's first faculties
1190	Maimonides' *Guide of the Perplexed*
1215	Paris University receives statutes
1225	Thomas Aquinas born
1248	Albert the Great at Cologne
1253	Death of Grosseteste
1266	*Summa Theologiae* begun
1274	Aquinas and Bonaventure die
1277	219 theses condemned at Paris
1300	Duns Scotus lecturing in Oxford
1307	Dante Alighieri begins *Divina Commedia*
1308	Duns Scotus dies
1318	Ockham lecturing in Oxford
1324	Marsilius' *Defensor Pacis*
1347	Black Death; Ockham dies

1360	Wyclif master of Balliol
1415	Council of Constance condemns Wyclif
1439	Council of Florence welcomes Greeks
1440	Nicholas of Cusa's *De Docta Ignorantia*
1469	Ficino begins *Theologia Platonica*
1474	Peter de Rivo condemned by Sixtus IV
1513	Lateran Council condemns Pomponazzi

LIST OF ABBREVIATIONS
AND CONVENTIONS

CCCM   Corpus Christianorum, Continuatio Medievalis

CCMP   A. S. McGrade, *The Cambridge Companion to Medieval Philosophy* (Cambridge. Cambridge University Press, 2003)

CCSL   Corpus Christianorum, Series Latina

CHLGP   A. H. Armstrong (ed.), *The Cambridge History of Later Greek and Early Medieval Philosophy* (Cambridge: Cambridge University Press, 1967)

CHLMP   N. Kretzmann, A. Kenny, and J. Pinborg (eds.), *The Cambridge History of Later Medieval Philosophy* (Cambridge: Cambridge University Press, 1982)

CPA   *Commentary on 'Posterior Analytics'*

CSEL   Corpus Scriptorum Ecclesiasticorum Latinorum

DB   H. Denzinger (ed.), *Enchiridion Symbolorum*, 33rd edn. (Barcelona: Herder, 1950)

IHWP   Anthony Kenny (ed.), *The Oxford Illustrated History of Western Philosophy* (Oxford: Oxford University Press, 1994)

PG   Patrologia Graeca

PL   Patrologia Latina

PMA   A. Hyman and J. J. Walsh, *Philosophy in the Middle Ages*, 2nd edn. (Indianapolis: Hackett, 1973).

Sent.   *Commentary on Lombard's 'Sentences'*; cited by book, distinction, article, and question

Abelard

AE   Abelard, *Ethics (Know Thyself)*

D   *Dialectica*

LI   *Logica Ingredientibus*

LNPS   *Logica Nostrorum Petitioni Scholarium*

Aquinas

DEE   *De Ente et Essentia* ('On Essence and Existence')

DP   *De Potentia* ('On Power')

DRI   *De Regimine Iudaeorum* ('On Jews and Government'); Leonine edn. vol. 42

DV   *De Veritate* ('On Truth')

IBT   *In Boethium de Trinitate* ('On Boethius' *De Trinitate*')

In I Periherm.	*In II Libros Perihermeneias Aristotelis Expositio*, ed. R. M. Spiazzi (Turin: Marietti, 1966)
ScG	*Summa contra Gentiles* ('On the Truth of the Catholic Faith'); cited by book and chapter
ST	*Summa Theologiae*; cited by part, question (q.), article, and (if appropriate) objection or answer

Aristotle

De An.	*De Anima* (or commentary)
EE	*Eudemian Ethics*
NE	*Nicomachean Ethics*

Augustine

References are to book, chapter, and alternative chapter number where relevant.

83Q	*De Diversis Quaestionibus LXXXIII* ('Eighty-Three Different Questions')
CA	*Contra Academicos* ('Against the Sceptics')
CCA	E. Stump and N. Kretzmann (eds.), *The Cambridge Companion to Augustine* (Cambridge: Cambridge University Press, 2001)
Conf.	*Confessiones* ('Confessions')
DBC	*De Bono Conjugali* ('On the Good of Marriage')
DCD	*De Civitate Dei* ('The City of God')
DCG	*De Correptione et Gratia* ('On Grace')
DDP	*De Dono Perseverantiae* ('On Perseverance')
DLA	*De Libero Arbitrio* ('On Free Will')
DM	*De Mendacio* ('On Lying')
DMg	*De Magistro* ('On the Teacher')
DPS	*De Praedestinatione Sanctorum* ('On Predestination')
DT	*De Trinitate* ('On the Trinity')
DUC	*De Utilitate Credendi* ('The Benefit of Belief')
Ep.	*Epistulae* ('Letters')
S	*Soliloquia* ('Soliloquies')

Averroes

HPR	*The Harmony of Philosophy and Religion*

Avicenna

Metaph.	*Metaphysics*

316

Boethius

DCP   *De Consolatione Philosophiae* ('On the Consolation of Philosophy')

Bonaventure

Brev.   *Breviloquium*
CH   *Collationes in Hexameron*
De Myst. Trin.   *De Mysterio Trinitatis*
Itin   *Itinerarium Mentis in Deum*

Walter Burley

PAL   *The Pure Art of Logic*, ed. Philotheus Boehner (St Bonaventure, NY: Franciscan Institute, 1955)

Cusanus

DDI   *De Docta Ignorantia* ('On Informed Ignorance')

Duns Scotus

CCDS   T. Williams (ed.), *The Cambridge Companion to Duns Scotus* (Cambridge: Cambridge University Press, 2003)
DPP   *De Primo Principio* ('On the First Principle')
Lect.   *Lectura*, in *Opera Omnia*, ed. C. Balic *et al.* (Vatican City, 1950–), vols. 1–3: *Ordinatio* 1–2; vols. 16–20: *Lectura* 1–3; cited by volume and page
Ord.   *Ordinatio*, in *Opera Omnia*, ed. C. Balic *et al.* (Vatican City, 1950–), vols. 1–3: *Ordinatio* 1–2; vols, 16–20: *Lectura* 1–3; cited by volume and page
Oxon.   *Opus Oxoniense*
Quodl.   *God and Creatures: The Quodlibetical Questions* (Princeton: Princeton University Press, 1975)

Eriugena

References are to book and chapter.

Robert Grosseteste

De Lib. Arb.   *De Libero Arbitrio*, in *Die philosophische Werke des Robert Grosseteste*, ed. L. Baur, Beiträge zur Geschichte der Philosophie des Mittelalters 9 (Munster: Aschendorff, 1912)
Hex.   *Hexaemeron*

317

William Ockham

CCO   P. V. Spade (ed.), *The Cambridge Companion to Ockham* (Cambridge: Cambridge University Press, 1999)

OND   *Opus Nonaginta Dierum* ('Work of Ninety Days')

OPh.   *Opera Philosophica*; cited by part and chapter

OTh.   *Opera Theologica*; cited by volume and page

Peter of Spain

SL   Peter of Spain, *Tractatus, called afterwards Summule Logicales*, ed. L. M. de Rijk (Assen: van Gorcum, 1972)

Plato

Phaedr.   *Phaedrus*

Tim.   *Timaeus*

Proclus

ET   *Elements of Theology*

John Wyclif

U   *On Universals*; cited by book and line

BIBLIOGRAPHY

General

ARMSTRONG, A. H. (ed.), *The Cambridge History of Later Greek and Early Medieval Philosophy* (Cambridge: Cambridge University Press, 1967).

CATTO, J. I., *The History of the University of Oxford*, i: *The Early Oxford Schools* (Oxford: Oxford University Press, 1984).

—— and EVANS, T. A. R., *The History of the University of Oxford*, ii: *Late Medieval Oxford* (Oxford: Oxford University Press, 1992).

COPLESTON, F. C., *A History of Philosophy*, 9 vols. (London: Burnes Oates, 1947–75).

CRAIG, WILLIAM LANE, *The Problem of Divine Foreknowledge and Future Contingents from Aristotle to Suarez* (Leiden: E. J. Brill, 1988).

DENZINGER, H. (ed.), *Enchiridion Symbolorum*, 33rd edn. (Barcelona: Herder, 1950); trans. as *The Sources of Catholic Dogma* by R. J. DeFerrari (Fitzwilliam, NY: Loreto Publications, 1955). [Texts of official Church documents.]

GEACH, P. T., *Reference and Generality: An Examination of Some Medieval and Modern Theories* (Ithaca, NY: Cornell University Press, 1980).

GRACIA, J., and NOONE, T., *A Companion to Philosophy in the Middle Ages* (Oxford: Blackwell, 2003).

GRANT, E., *God and Reason in the Middle Ages* (Cambridge: Cambridge University Press, 2001).

HUGHES, PHILIP, *A History of the Church*, iii: *Aquinas to Luther* (London: Sheed & Ward, 1947).

HYMAN, A., and WALSH, J. J., *Philosophy in the Middle Ages*, 2nd edn. (Indianapolis: Hackett, 1973).

KENNY, A., *A Brief History of Western Philosophy* (Oxford: Blackwell, 1998).

—— (ed.), *The Oxford Illustrated History of Western Philosophy* (Oxford: Oxford University Press, 1994).

KNEALE, W., and KNEALE, M., *The Development of Logic* (Oxford: Oxford University Press, 1962).

KNUUTILLA, S., *Modalities in Medieval Philosophy* (London: Routledge, 1993).

KRETZMANN, N., KENNY, A., and PINBORG, J., *The Cambridge History of Later Medieval Philosophy* (Cambridge: Cambridge University Press, 1982).

—— STUMP, E., et al., *The Cambridge Translations of Medieval Philosophical Texts*, i: *Logic and the Philosophy of Language*; ii: *Ethics and Political Philosophy*; iii: *Mind and Knowledge* (Cambridge: Cambridge University Press, 1998–).

LEFTOW, B., *Time and Eternity* (Ithaca, NY: Cornell University Press, 1991).

McGrade, A. S., *The Cambridge Companion to Medieval Philosophy* (Cambridge: Cambridge University Press, 2003).

Marenbon, John, *Later Medieval Philosophy* (London: Routledge & Kegan Paul, 1987).

—— *Early Medieval Philosophy*, rev. edn. (London: Routledge & Kegan Paul, 1988).

—— (ed.), *Aristotle in Britain during the Middle Ages* (Turnhout: Brepols, 1996).

—— (ed.), *Routledge History of Philosophy*, iii: *Medieval Philosophy* (London: Routledge, 1998).

Pasnau, Robert, *Theories of Cognition in the Later Middle Ages* (New York: Cambridge University Press, 1997).

Schmitt, C. B., and Skinner, Q., *The Cambridge History of Renaissance Philosophy* (Cambridge: Cambridge University Press, 1988).

Sorabji, R., *Time, Creation and the Continuum* (London: Duckworth, 1983).

Spade, P. V. (ed. and trans.), *Five Texts on the Medieval Problem of Universals: Porphyry, Boethius, Abelard, Duns Scotus, Ockham* (Indianapolis: Hackett, 1994).

Augustine

The City of God, trans. H. Bettenson (Harmondsworth: Penguin, 1972).

Confessions, trans. H. Chadwick (Oxford: Oxford University Press, 1991).

Confessions, text, trans., and comm. J. J. O'Donnell, 3 vols. (Oxford: Clarendon Press, 1992).

De Bono Conjugali, CSEL 41 (Vienna: Tempsky, 1900).

De Civitate Dei, CCSL 47–8 (Turnhout: Brepols, 1955).

De Dialectica, ed. Darrell Jackson (Dordrecht: Reidel, 1985).

De Libero Arbitrio, CCSL 29 (Turnhout: Brepols, 1970).

De Trinitate, CCSL 50 (Turnhout: Brepols, 1970).

Earlier Writings, trans. John H. S. Burleigh, Library of Christian Classics (Philadelphia: Westminster Press, 1953).

On the Free Choice of the Will, trans. T. Williams (Indianapolis: Hackett, 1993).

Soliloquies, text, trans., and comm. G. Watson (Warminster: Aris & Phillips, 1990).

Treatises on Marriage and Other Subjects, trans. Roy J. Deferrari (New York: Fathers of the Church, 1955).

The Trinity, trans. S. McKenna (Washington: CUA Press, 1963).

Brown, P., *The Body and Society* (New York: Columbia University Press, 1988).

—— *Augustine of Hippo: A Biography*, rev. edn. (London: Faber & Faber, 2000).

Dihle, A., *The Theory of the Will in Classical Antiquity* (Berkeley: University of California Press, 1982).

Jordan, Mark D., *The Ethics of Sex* (Oxford: Blackwell, 2002).

Kirwan, C., *Augustine* (London: Routledge, 1989).

MARKUS, R. A., 'Augustine', in A. H. Armstrong (ed.), *The Cambridge History of Later Greek and Early Medieval Philosophy* (Cambridge: Cambridge University Press, 1967).

MATTHEWS, G. B., *The Augustinian Tradition* (Berkeley: University of California Press, 1999).

MENN, STEPHEN, *Descartes and Augustine* (Cambridge: Cambridge University Press, 1998).

SORABJI, R., *Time, Creation and the Continuum* (London: Duckworth, 1983).

STUMP, E., and KRETZMANN, N., *The Cambridge Companion to Augustine* (Cambridge: Cambridge University Press, 2001).

WILLS, GARRY, *St Augustine* (London: Weidenfeld & Nicolson, 1999).

Boethius

Boethius: The Theological Tractates and The Consolation of Philosophy, text and trans. H. J. Stewart and E. K. Rand, rev. S. J. Tester, Loeb Classical Library (Cambridge, Mass.: Harvard University Press, 1973).

CHADWICK, H., *Boethius: The Consolations of Music, Logic, Theology & Philosophy* (Oxford: Clarendon Press, 1981).

MARENBON, J., *Boethius* (Oxford: Oxford University Press, 2003).

Late Greek Philosophy

PHILOPONUS, *Against Aristotle on the Eternity of the World*, trans. Christian Wildberg (London: Duckworth, 1987).

—— *On Aristotle on the Intellect*, trans. W. Charlton (London: Duckworth, 1991).

PROCLUS, *The Elements of Theology*, ed. and trans. E. R. Dodds (Oxford: Clarendon Press, 1992).

CHADWICK, H., *East and West: The Making of a Rift in the Church* (Oxford: Oxford University Press, 2003).

SORABJI, R. (ed.), *Philoponus and the Rejection of Aristotelian Science* (London: Duckworth, 1987).

Eriugena

De Praedestinatione Divina, CCCM 50 (Turnhout: Brepols, 1978).

Periphyseon (The Division of Nature), ed. E. Jeanneau, CCSL 161–5 (Turnhout: Brepols, 1996–2003).

Periphyseon (The Division of Nature), trans. I. P. Sheldon-Williams, rev. J. J. O'Meara (Dublin: Dublin Institute for Advanced Studies, 1968–95).

MORAN, D., *The Philosophy of John Scottus Eriugena* (Cambridge: Cambridge University Press, 1989).

O'MEARA, J. J., *Eriugena* (Oxford: Clarendon Press, 1988).

Islamic Philosophy

AVICENNA, *Metafisica*, trans. O. Lizzini (Milan: Bompiani, 2002).

AVICENNA LATINUS, *Liber de Anima*, ed. S. van Riet, 2 vols. (Louvain-la-Neuve: Institut Supérieur de Philosophie, 1977–83).

——*Liber de Philosophia Prima*, ed. S. van Riet, 3 vols. (Louvain-la-Neuve: Institut Supérieur de Philosophie, 1977–83).

CRAIG, WILLIAM LANE, *The Kalam Cosmological Argument* (London: Macmillan, 1979).

DAVIDSON, H. A., *Alfarabi, Avicenna and Averroes on Intellect* (New York: Oxford University Press, 1992).

ESPOSITO, J. L., *Islam: The Straight Path* (New York: Oxford University Press, 1991).

NASR, S. H., and LEAMAN, O., *History of Islamic Philosophy*, 2 vols. (London: Routledge, 1996).

PETERS, F. E., *Aristotle and the Arabs* (New York: New York University Press, 1968).

Anselm

Anselm of Canterbury:The Major Works, ed. B. Davies and G. R. Evans, World's Classics (Oxford: Oxford University Press, 1998).

Opera Omnia, ed. F. S. Schmitt, 6 vols. (Edinburgh: Thomas Nelson, 1946–61).

Proslogion, text with trans. M. J. Charlesworth (Oxford: Oxford University Press, 1965).

BARNES, JONATHAN, *The Ontological Argument* (London: Macmillan, 1975).

PLANTINGA, A., *The Nature of Necessity* (Oxford: Oxford University Press, 1974).

SOUTHERN, R. W., *St Anselm and his Biographer* (Cambridge: Cambridge University Press, 1963).

——*Anselm: A Portrait in a Landscape* (Cambridge: Cambridge University Press, 1990).

Averroes

Commentary on Plato's Republic, ed. E. Rosenthal (Cambridge: Cambridge University Press, 1956).

The Incoherence of the Incoherence, trans. and introd. S. van den Bergh, 2 vols. (London: Luzac, 1954).

Middle Commentaries on Aristotle's Categories and De Interpretatione, trans. C. Butterworth (Princeton: Princeton University Press, 1983).

On the Harmony of Religion and Philosophy, trans. and introd. G. Hourani (London: Luzac, 1961).

LEAMAN, O., *Averroes and his Philosophy* (Oxford: Clarendon Press, 1988).

Twelfth-Century Philosophy

DRONKE, P. (ed.), *A History of Twelfth Century Western Philosophy* (Cambridge: Cambridge University Press, 1988).

SOUTHERN, R. W., *Scholastic Humanism and the Unification of Europe* (Oxford: Blackwell, 2001).

Abelard

Dialectica, ed. L. M. de Rijk (Assen: van Gorcum, 1971).

Ethics (Scito te ipsum), ed. and trans. D. Luscombe (Oxford: Oxford University Press, 1971).

Logica, in *Peter Abelards philosophische Schriften*, Beitrage zur Geschichte der Philosophie des Mittelalters 15 (Munster: Aschendorff, 1919–31). [Contains *Logica Ingredientibus* and *Logica Nostrorum Petitioni*.]

MARENBON, J., *The Philosophy of Peter Abelard* (Cambridge: Cambridge University Press, 1997).

Maimonides

The Guide of the Perplexed, trans. S. Pines, 2 vols. (Chicago: Chicago University Press, 1963).

RUDAVSKY, T. (ed.), *Divine Omniscience and Omnipotence in Medieval Philosophy* (Dordrecht: Reidel, 1982).

Grosseteste and Albert

GROSSETESTE, ROBERT, *Hexaemeron*, ed. Richard Dales and Servus Gieben (London: British Academy, 1982).

Die philosophischen Werke des Robert Grosseteste, ed. L. Bauer, Beitrage zur Geschichte der Philosophie des Mittelalters 9 (Munster: Aschendorff, 1912).

McEvoy, JAMES, *The Philosophy of Robert Grosseteste* (Oxford: Oxford University Press, 1982).

WEISHEIPL, J. (ed.), *Albertus Magnus and the Sciences* (Toronto: Pontifical Institute of Medieval Studies, 1980).

Bonaventure

—— *The Journey of the Mind to God*, ed. S. Brown (Indianapolis: Hackett, 1993).
Opera Omnia, 10 vols. (Quarracchi: Collegium S. Bonaventurae, 1882–1902).

GILSON, E., *The Philosophy of St Bonaventure*, trans. I. Trethowan and F. J. Sheed (London: Sheed & Ward, 1965).

Thirteenth-Century Logic

PETER OF SPAIN, *Tractatus, called afterwards Summule Logicales*, ed. L. M. de Rijk (Assen: van Gorcum, 1972).

Aquinas

The Leonine edition (Rome, 1882–), which will include all of Aquinas' works, is incomplete and inconvenient to use. More convenient, and commonly derived from the Leonine text, are the Marietti editions of particular works, including the following:

In II Libros Perihermeneias Aristotelis Expositio, ed. R. M. Spiazzi (Turin: Marietti, 1966).
Quaestiones Disputatae I (De Veritate), ed. R. M. Spiazzi (Turin, 1955).
Quaestiones Disputatae II (De Potentia, De Malo), ed. R. Pession *et al.* (Turin, 1949).
Summa contra Gentiles, ed. C. Pera (Turin, 1961).
Summa contra Gentiles, trans. as *On the Truth of the Catholic Faith* by A. C. Pegis *et al.* (South Bend, Ind.: Notre Dame University Press, 1975).
Summa Theologiae, Blackfriars edn., 61 vols. (London: Eyre & Spottiswoode, 1964–80). [For English-language readers, this is the best edition, with Latin and English on facing pages.]

DAVIES, BRIAN, OP, *The Thought of Thomas Aquinas* (Oxford: Clarendon Press, 1992).
FINNIS, JOHN, *Aquinas: Moral, Political, and Legal Theory* (Oxford: Oxford University Press, 1998).
GEACH, PETER, 'Aquinas', in G. E. M. Anscombe and Peter Geach,*Three Philosophers* (Oxford: Blackwell, 1961).
KENNY, ANTHONY, *The Five Ways* (London: Routledge, 1969).
—— *The God of the Philosophers* (Oxford: Clarendon Press, 1979).
—— *Aquinas* (Oxford: Oxford University Press, 1980).
—— *Aquinas on Mind* (London: Routledge, 1993).

—— *Aquinas on Being* (Oxford: Oxford University Press, 2002).

—— (ed.), *Aquinas: A Collection of Critical Essays* (London: Macmillan, 1969).

KRETZMANN, NORMAN, *The Metaphysics of Theism* (Oxford: Clarendon Press, 1997).

—— *The Metaphysics of Creation* (Oxford: Clarendon Press, 1999).

LONERGAN, BERNARD, *Verbum: Word and Idea in Aquinas* (Notre Dame, Ind.: University of Notre Dame Press, 1967).

PASNAU, R., *Thomas Aquinas on Human Nature* (Cambridge: Cambridge University Press, 2001).

STUMP, ELEONORE, *Aquinas* (London: Routledge, 2003).

TORRELL, JEAN-PIERRE, *Saint Thomas Aquinas: The Person and his Work* (Washington: Catholic University of America Press, 1996).

WEISHEIPL, JAMES A., *Friar Thomas d'Aquino* (Oxford: Blackwell, 1974).

Duns Scotus

De Primo Principio, ed. and trans. F. Roche (St Bonaventure, NY: Franciscan Institute, 1945).

God and Creatures: The Quodlibetical Questions (Princeton: Princeton University Press, 1975).

Opera Omnia, ed. C. Balic *et al.* (Vatican City, 1950–), vols. i–iii: *Ordinatio* 1–2; vols. xvi–xx: *Lectura* 1–3.

Opus Oxoniense, ed. Luke Wadding, 12 vols. (Lyons: Durand, 1639).

Questions on the Metaphysics of Aristotle, trans. G. Etzkorn and A. Wolter, 2 vols. (St Bonaventure, NY: Franciscan Institute, 1997).

BOS, E. P. (ed.), *John Duns Scotus (1265/6–1308): Renewal of Philosophy* (Amsterdam: Rodopi, 1998).

BROADIE, A., *The Shadow of Scotus: Philosophy and Faith in Pre-Reformation Scotland* (Edinburgh: T. & T. Clark, 1995).

CROSS, RICHARD, *The Physics of Duns Scotus: The Scientific Context of a Theological Vision* (Oxford: Clarendon Press, 1998).

—— *Duns Scotus* (Oxford: Oxford University Press, 1999).

LANGSTON, DOUGLAS C., *God's Willing Knowledge: The Influence of Scotus' Analysis of Omniscience* (Philadelphia: University of Pennsylvania Press, 1986).

VOS JACZN, ANTONIE, *et al.*, *John Duns Scotus: Contingency and Freedom* (Dordrecht: Kluwer, 1994).

WILLIAMS, T. (ed.), *The Cambridge Companion to Duns Scotus* (Cambridge: Cambridge University Press, 2003).

WOLTER, ALLAN B., *The Philosophical Theology of John Duns Scotus*, ed. M. M. Adams (Ithaca, NY: Cornell University Press, 1990).

Ockham

Opera Philosophica et Theologica, ed. Gedeon Gál *et al.*, 17 vols. (St Bonaventure, NY: Franciscan Institute, 1985).

Opera Politica, ed. H. S. Offler *et al.*, 4 vols. (vol. i–iii Manchester: Manchester University Press, 1956–74; vol. iv Oxford: Oxford University Press, 1997).

Philosophical Writings, trans. P. Boehner (Indianapolis: Hackett, 1990).

Quodlibetal Questions, trans. A. J. Freddoso and Francis E. Kelly, 2 vols. (New Haven: Yale University Press, 1991).

Tractatus de Praedestinatione et de Praescientia Dei, trans. Norman Kretzmann and Marilyn Adams (Chicago: Appleton-Century-Crofts, 1969).

ADAMS, MARILYN MCCORD, *William Ockham*, 2 vols. (Notre Dame, Ind.: University of Notre Dame Press, 1987).

SPADE, P. V. (ed.), *The Cambridge Companion to Ockham* (Cambridge: Cambridge University Press, 1999).

Philosophy after Ockham

BURLEY, WALTER, *The Pure Art of Logic*, ed. Philotheus Boehner (St Bonaventure, NY: Franciscan Institute, 1955).

CAJETAN, THOMAS DE VIO, *Commentary on Being and Essence*, trans. L. H. Kendzierski and F. C. Wade (Milwaukee, Wis.: Marquette University Press, 1964).

KILVINGTON, RICHARD, *The Sophismata of Richard Kilvington*, introd., trans., and comm. Norman Kretzmann and Barbara Ensign Kretzmann (Cambridge: Cambridge University Press, 1990).

MARSILIUS OF PADUA, *The Defender of the Peace*, trans. A. Gewirth (Toronto: Pontifical Institute of Medieval Studies, 1980).

NICHOLAS OF CUSA, *Devotional Works*, ed. J. Doakes (Washington: Westminster Press, 1995).

CASSIRER, E., *et al.* (eds.), *The Renaissance Philosophy of Man* (Chicago: University of Chicago Press, 1959).

COURTENAY, WILLIAM J., *Schools and Scholars in Fourteenth Century England* (Princeton: Princeton University Press, 1987).

HUDSON, ANNE, and WILKS, MICHAEL, *From Ockham to Wyclif* (Oxford: Blackwell, 1987).

KENNY, ANTHONY, *Wyclif* (Oxford: Oxford University Press, 1985).

——(ed.), *Wyclif in his Times* (Oxford: Oxford University Press, 1986).

KRETZMANN, NORMAN (ed.), *Infinity and Continuity in Ancient and Medieval Thought* (Ithaca, NY: Cornell University Press, 1982).

ILLUSTRATIONS

ILLUSTRATIONS

INDEX

330